HOW THE SOUTH FINALLY WON

THE CIVIL WAR

Other books by Charles Potts

Loading Las Vegas	*1991*
The Dictatorship of the Environment	*1991*
A Rite to the Body	*1989*
Rocky Mountain Man	*1978*
Valga Krusa	*1977*
The Opium Must Go Thru	*1976*
Charlie Kiot	*1976*
The Golden Calf	*1975*
The Trancemigracion of Menzu	*1973*
Waiting in Blood	*1973*
Blue up the Nile	*1972*
The Litmus Papers	*1969*
Little Lord Shiva	*1969*
Burning Snake	*1967*
Blues From Thurston County	*1966*

HOW THE SOUTH FINALLY WON

THE CIVIL WAR

And Controls the Political Future of the
United States

CHARLES POTTS

津浪

TSUNAMI PRESS, INC.
WALLA WALLA, WASHINGTON

41516

Library of Congress Catalog Card Number: 94-61861

Potts, Charles.
How the South Finally Won the Civil War / Charles Potts
And Controls the Political Future of the United States

Jacket Design by Jeanne McMenemy of Calligraphica
Maps by Pat and Matt McKern of Word's Out
Typeset by Karen Yager of CompuTec

Includes Works Cited
Indexed

ISBN 0-9644440-0-3

Printed in the United States of America

First Edition

2 3 4 5 6 7 8 9 10

for

Scott Preston & Stephen Jacobsen

& their transformational impetus

Acknowledgments

The author and publisher gratefully acknowledge permission from the following publishers and authors to reprint excerpts from their work as herein recited:

Edward Dorn, *Recollections of Gran Apacheria*, by permission of the author.

Reprinted with the permission of Macmillan Publishing Company from *LONE STAR: A History of Texas and the Texans*, by T. R. Fehrenbach. Copyright © 1968, 1985 by T. R. Fehrenbach.

The Challenge to American Freedoms, Copyright © 1963 by University of Kentucky Press. Renewed 1991 by Donald O. Johnson. Used by permission of the publishers.

Carey McWilliams, *Southern California: An Island on the land*, a Peregrine Smith Book published by Gibbs Smith, Publisher, Layton, Utah.

Arthur M. Schlesinger, Jr., *The Coming to Power: Critical Presidential Elections* Copyright © 1971, reprinted with permission of the publisher, McGraw-Hill.

Excerpts from *The Cycles of American History* by Arthur M. Schlesinger, Jr. Copyright © 1986 by Arthur M. Schlesinger, Jr. Reprinted by permission of Houghton Mifflin Company. All rights reserved.

Weir, Robert M., *Colonial South Carolina*, pp. xiii-345. Millwood, New York: KTO Press, 1983. Reproduced with permission of The Kraus Organization Limited.

An initial version of the structure of *How the South Finally Won the Civil War* was published in the *North Coast Times Eagle*, Vol. 3 #3, in January 1992, edited by Michael Paul McCusker, in Astoria, Oregon.

Note: This format is in the precise wording stipulated by each of the individual acknowledgments.

Contents

List of Maps

Preface

How the South Finally Won the Civil War, and controls the political future of the United States, is the first book to make a fact based interpretation of how the southern domination of American politics prior to the Civil War was pieced back together afterwards into a resurgent southern domination that expresses most of the southern agenda that led up to the Civil War. It is a description of the structure of American civilization. It is a unified field theory of southern control of American political and military power. This post-Civil War southern victory did not happen overnight.

When President George Bush invaded Panama in 1989, few people realized he was recapitulating one of Confederate President Jefferson Davis' favorite ideas: the American empire should extend at least as far south as the Isthmus of Panama. George Bush re-married Jefferson Davis and Theodore Roosevelt in their southern dreams of a Caribbean empire during his invasion of Panama. After the blitzkrieg on Iraq to bring Kuwait back into the English speaking commercial and neo-colonial empire, Bush flew from Bermuda to Sumter, South Carolina, to welcome the airmen home and said, "No one doubts us anymore." The southern dominated United States is the functional remainder of the British Empire.

The Civil War was not a military victory for the South; it was a victory for militarism which makes its home in the South. All Ulysses S. Grant and William T. Sherman won were the decisive battles, the least interesting aspect of war. The War Between the States did not end · 1865. Just as Clausewitz described war as the continuation of diplomacy ɯ, ther means, peace is the continuation of war by subterfuge. The Civil War was fought over an agenda and the South never lost its un-reconstructed grip on its agenda. The rumble in the House of Representatives in 1995 originated in the South where politics are conducted with the intensity of war. In 1995 we also mark the 130th anniversary of Robert E. Lee's surrender to Grant at the courthouse in Appomattox. It is time to declare a Confederate victory.

All great ideas begin life as heresies. It is necessary to stimulate some reinterpretation of American historical patterns. History is a fable agreed upon, said Napoleon, and the only duty owed to it, according to Oscar Wilde, is to re-write it. If war is too important to be left in the hands of generals, why then leave history in the hands of historians?

How the South Finally Won the Civil War also briefly taps the roots of the English speaking culture and traces the development of the empire to World

11

War II when the U.S. took it over. History is hidden in a sea of facts, all data and no story. The salient facts are fished from the sea and shaped into a coherent story to make the meaning of English speaking history clear.

Historians don't concentrate on tableaus of such magnitude. It is left to creatures, such as Oswald Spengler, who defy the tidy taxonomies, to render the big picture. The big picture of the planet is spherical, as we learned from earthrise as seen from the Apollo landing on the moon. Many people in the United States suffer from the Ptolemaic view of history which imagines that the rest of the world revolves around them. Americans have had enormous sway over current events and in much of the 20th century, but the past isn't what it used to be. Time will rotate the North American portion of the sphere into perspective as its 15 percent of the green-blue blur of earth. While the English speaking empire may be presently working its will on the world, it is naive to imagine that it always will.

Envision American history as a series of overlays in color photography of a river moving ineluctably toward the sea. Think of it even as the Gulf Coast natives did, as *Misi Sipi*, or the Big River. This Big River is only one of many flowing into the ocean of historical time. Most of the significant tributaries of this Big River are farther upstream than the view of it from the embouchure permits. Too wide to see but dimly all the way across and looking inextricably mixed together, *How the South Finally Won the Civil War* is a record of the tributaries and how each contributes to the flow. When we are set free on the other side we will know both its surface and its depth. By taking the plunge we will be able to see the history of the English speaking people at a single glance and know where we have been as a people and where it might yet be possible to go.

In Tokyo, in Sumida Ku, a few blocks north of the grand new Edo and modern periods museum, there is a small, old two-story museum filled with artifacts from Tokyo's two modern disasters, the Kanto Earthquake of 1923 and the American fire-bombing of 1945. In the earthquake section is an approximately four-foot-cubed transparent plastic table. At half inch intervals from the top to the floor are separate plastic sheets with the depth location of the epicenters of recent earthquakes marked in red. The top panel is an outline map of Japan. From the top, it is possible to see the three-dimensional pattern all the way to the bottom, a view impossible to display on a flat surface.

The look into our Big River has been divided into five major tributaries to reveal the shape of American civilization, and each in turn is further subdivided into five tributary chapters. The foreground and background of the first major tributary presents the Civil War agendas for both sides and describes how war became the official state religion. It goes on to include the old world background of the English speaking peoples before and after the crucial pivot of Columbus. The first flow toward America is wrapped up with a discussion of the early British Empire, especially on Barbados and its successful transfer to Charleston, South Carolina, "in the Indies," as the first colonists chose to refer to it.

Tributary two commences with John C. Calhoun, the most influential American political philosopher and native son of South Carolina. How the South Carolina philosophy of John Calhoun was transplanted to take root in Texas follows. Who the land formerly belonged to joins the stream here. The Confederate Territory of Arizona is the missing link in the chain of southern power, personified by Senator Barry Goldwater. The ultimately successful Confederate drive for control of California began in Arizona. Prominent at the conclusion of the second tributary is Confederate President Jefferson Davis, political protégé of John C. Calhoun, for although the Confederate States of America were of short temporal duration, they were of nearly infinite political effect.

Beaten but unreconstructed, Jefferson Davis and Jubal Early, among others, put the Confederates on the comeback trail after the Civil War, which constitutes the beginning of the third tributary. The cattle drives out of Texas put the brand of the cowboy culture on the rest of the interior west, long a southern and Confederate goal. The Fraud of 1876 put Bourbon Democrats back in power in the South for victories for state rights and white supremacy. Theodore Roosevelt and his fellow imperialists revived the southern dream of a Caribbean empire and actualized it there, in Panama, and also in Hawaii and in the Philippines. California, admitted as a free state in 1850 with its power base in the quintessential union town of San Francisco, was gradually subducted by the machinations of power into a southern state as South Carolina and Texas found their military reflection radiating from Los Angeles, whose handful of residents (4,000+) were Confederate supporters in 1860. The Truman Doctrine (the Monroe Doctrine applied globally to containing communism) put the finishing touches on the literal Pentagon. The siege mentality of the South

Carolinians who had endeavored from their beginning in 1670 to recapitulate the English experience exactly, and of their spiritual kin the Texans from the Alamo, was confirmed as policy when the United States made a basket catch of the British Empire and became the world's foremost banana republic and an empire at (cold) perpetual war.

With the southern victory in place, contemporary history since World War II reveals the struggle all along to have been between the forces that conceived of the U.S. as a nation and the forces that successfully turned it into an empire. Empires are incompatible with democracy and as the Central Intelligence Agency (CIA) became President Dwight Eisenhower's secret army, he and other Texans such as Speaker of the House Sam Rayburn, the son of a Confederate cavalryman, and Lyndon Johnson, dominate the stagnant water of the fourth tributary. Jimmy Carter's administration was the single anomaly to the process of empire during this period. Ronald Reagan, who began his political life in the Democratic party of Harry Truman, revived the holy war of John Foster Dulles and gave the Truman Doctrine an enormous transfusion of imaginary money. The Texan Bush fell from the saddle with his Houston sidekick James S. Baker as the empire skidded toward terminal fiscal spasm.

The fifth and final tributary looks hard at the other consequences of Confederate victory. The movement of people within the U.S. toward the South and West since World War II has followed Department of Defense spending, the organizing principle of the empire. The corporate transnational plantation, which conceives of all labor as migrant and temporary, is the prevailing economic model. Half of Mexico wasn't enough in 1848; today it is being NAFTAed into the U.S. where it will one day be making policy for all of North America. The liberal nationalists, from William Jennings Bryan forward, were never able to articulate a winning strategy because they lack a convincing organizing principle. Ethnic and cultural diversity from two centuries of open door policy designed to attract an endless supply of cheap (slave) labor is helping to turn the empire into a police state.

Here then in a nutshell is the argument for *How the South Finally Won the Civil War*. The South finally won what they call the War Between the States because most of their favorite ideas are public policy in a United States dominated by the South. The cause was not lost, only temporarily misplaced. Washington was the father of our country but Jefferson Davis was the father of our empire. We have to teach ourselves to say the South won the Civil War.

Part I

Background and Foreground

"Everywhere the ceremony of innocence is drowned"

W. B. Yeats

1

What the Civil War Was Fought Over

Great ideas begin life as heresies and the core of ideas that form the heart of *How the South Finally Won the Civil War* is no exception. With such a provocative thesis, it is germane at the outset to establish the stakes, to state clearly what the War Between the States was being fought over. Wars may start with explicit agendas but the agendas can clarify over time and are modified by the vicissitudes of battle. Sometimes it is long after the smoke has dissipated and the gunfire has died down that it becomes clear who was fighting for what.

The story of the American Civil War has been told and retold many times. It is the central event in American civilization. As we look at the issues that divided the sections we begin to see what led them to battle. South Carolina did not merely secede from the union a few days before Christmas in 1860, the assembled delegates *"dissolved"* the union (Roland 1960, 1).

The status and interest issue of personal and regional independence, sometimes collectively referred to as "state rights," was felt most intensely in South Carolina where it had been simmering for a long time. The ambitions of South Carolina's chief aspirants for the Presidency of the United States, Charles Pinckney and John C. Calhoun, had been thwarted. Pinckney lost out to the early presidents from Virginia, Jefferson and Madison, while Calhoun's opportunities were fatally wounded when he resigned the vice presidency under Andrew Jackson over the 1832 issue of nullification, i.e. could South Carolinians "nullify," ignore or not pay, a federal tariff they understood as discriminating unfairly against their agrarian economy.

Clearly the Virginia Dynasty was superbly located both geographically and ideologically to provide the compromise leadership required by the early republic. Between the northeastern centers of power, Boston, New York and Philadelphia, and the southeastern centers such as Raleigh, Savannah and Charleston, leadership from the buffer state of Virginia was a logical choice. The 1828 election of Jackson from Tennessee, a native son of South Carolina, signified a shift in the center of power to the South and

West. Ever concerned with their economic independence and under the articulate leadership of John C. Calhoun, South Carolinians might have "dissolved" the union in 1832 over the issue of what they took to be unfair tariffs, but they were unable to get the requisite support from other southern states.

State rights, in this extreme reading where it means the right of a state to nullify or ignore any federal law that does injury to that state's interests, has long been put forward as the primary reason southern states seceded and the Civil War ensued. It is not wrong as a reason, but it is mistaken to attempt to understand it in isolation, for state rights as it had evolved as an issue by 1860 had acquired two other equally important, concentric and interdependent rings. The issues of slavery and control of the West had combined with state rights to become the primary nested combination of issues that divided the North from the South. Manifest Destiny became increasingly sectionalized, commencing with the Compromise of 1820 and then came to a boil over Texas, the Mexican War and control of California before ultimately resulting in the Civil War.

Many in the South have remained uneasy about admitting that the Civil War was caused by or fought over slavery, preferring to emphasize the state rights third of the triad. Gavin Wright, on the other hand, in *The Political Economy of the Cotton South,* states "that the Civil War was fundamentally caused by the economics of slavery" (1978, 4). Effective political control in the North and the South by 1860 had devolved two fundamentally and irreconcilably different ways of regarding slaves and slavery. Paralleling the advent of abolitionism, William Lloyd Garrison's newspaper, *The Liberator,* and the rise of the Republican party with its politics of emotion, the North had come to regard slaves as human beings whose right to "life, liberty, and the pursuit of happiness" was being denied. The prevailing view in the South regarded slaves not merely as property, but as capital, a most important form of property (Dowdey 1957, 316). In the pivotal state of Texas, for example, in 1860 "the assessed value of all slaves was $106,688,920 — 20 percent more than the assessed value of all cultivated lands" (Fehrenbach 1968, 307). It is a useless daydream of historical revisionists to imagine that the War Between the States was avoidable if only cooler heads had prevailed. While one side imagined it was liberating people, the other side saw it as destruction of capital. The slaveholding system not only recognized its slaves by assessment to be its most valuable asset, the labor they provided was considered to be part of the capital itself, devoid of independence. The Civil War was the inevitable result of the South's closely held need to protect its peculiar form of capitalism.

Some proof of the fact that slavery was one of the things being fought for can be found in the failure of the border states to join the Confederacy. Missouri, Kentucky, Maryland, and Delaware, all slaveholding states, but where slaveholding was less significant economically, did not follow the South into war, but chose, with some bullying, to remain in the Union. The well known example of the basically non-slaveholding section of Virginia leaving the Confederacy and being admitted to the Union as the free state of West Virginia is further proof. Finally, as Wright points out, "Almost all of the opposition to secession [from states that seceded] came from counties with very few slaves" (1978, 144). Slavery was an issue.

Prior to the political uproar over Texas, indeed right in the middle of the "Era of Good Feeling," the Missouri Compromise of 1820 was a good indication of growing sectional disputations over state rights, slavery, and control of the West. It was also directly if not exclusively responsible for attracting the attention of slaveholding Southerners beyond the national borders into Mexico, Texas, Cuba and the Caribbean, as it unintentionally provided for the sectionalization of Manifest Destiny. The Compromise of 1820 admitted Missouri as a slave state, even as it lopped the northern section of Massachusetts off and admitted it as the free state of Maine. This struggle for a balance of power, particularly in the Senate of the United States, would intensify as time went on. It is not a widely appreciated fact that in 1818, two years before the compromise, "Only the threat of congressional rejection deterred Illinois from attempting to enter the Union as a slave state" (Wright, 1978, 13).

Even southern slaveholders, happy to get two senators from Missouri on their side, were distressed that the compromise restricted their rights to take their slaves (their property and capital) wherever they wanted. It is important to keep in mind that the slaveholding class was a minority even in the South. William Seward, the erstwhile purchaser of Alaska from the Russians in 1867, who eventually became Lincoln's Secretary of State, pointed out that as of 1850 "The slaveholding class [350,000 people out of a national population of 20,000,000] has become the governing power in each of the slaveholding states and it practically chooses thirty of the sixty-two members of the Senate" (Beard and Beard 1925, 322). Seward went on to acknowledge that five of the members of the Supreme Court were called from slave states. This could help explain Chief Justice Taney and the Supreme Court's decision in the Dred Scott case of 1857 which declared the Missouri Compromise unconstitutional, precisely because it deprived slaveholders of their portable property rights.

The rights of slaveholders within slave states was not yet the issue. The issue was control of the West; would it be slave or free? The issue of recognition of the Republic of Texas, an independent slaveholding country on the Gulf Coast, was so sectionally charged that President Jackson withheld recognition until his final day in office. Eight years later, with most of the opposition coming from the North, whose rallying cry was that if we annex Texas, slavery will always be with us, the Senate failed a two-thirds vote to ratify a treaty annexing Texas to the Union. John C. Calhoun of South Carolina, acting briefly as President Tyler's Secretary of State, wrote a joint resolution that bypassed the Senate's exclusive reluctance, passed both houses of Congress by simple majority and annexed Texas to the Union on Tyler's final day in office.

The ensuing war with Mexico to establish American hegemony over Texas resulted in almost half of Mexico being ceded to the United States. The slaveholding South seemed to be on a roll. Bernard DeVoto chose to call 1846 *The Year of Decision*. Several authorities can be cited to demonstrate the belief that control of the West was at issue in the Civil War. Robert Leckie in his *The Wars of America* said, "Much of the dreadfully involved wrangle over Missouri was actually a struggle to control the Trans-Mississippi West" (1968, I:317). Margaret Coit, one of John C. Calhoun's biographers states "The Civil War itself has frequently been described as a struggle between the North and South for the dominance of the new West" (1950, 407).

By 1854 the Kansas-Nebraska Act had not only exposed sectional differences in the Democratic party, but had revealed the pecuniary interests of Senator Stephen Douglas of Illinois, who wanted Nebraska in the Union so he could get on with the building of a railroad to San Francisco. The South had also turned its attention to what Robert E. May (1973) described as *The Southern Dream of a Caribbean Empire*. This well written, thoroughly researched, and meticulously documented work makes clear that interest in acquiring Cuba, Nicaragua, Panama, Sonora, etc., for the purposes of expanding slavery, primarily originated in the South. At the same time it is necessary to note that there was some northern support for this incipient imperialism, just as "The Whiggish tendency to suppress sectionally disruptive issues also motivated the Whig-American attack on Tropical expansion" (1973, 201). Southern Whigs were not as expansionist oriented as Democrats in either section, but the southern Democrats were leading. There was minority sympathy for issues dear to each section on both sides, before, during, and after the Civil War.

The last two democratic presidents prior to the Civil War, Franklin Pierce of New Hampshire and James Buchanan of Pennsylvania, had profound southern support in their administrations. Buchanan was trying to annex Sonora and Chihuahua even in 1860 while Pierce's Secretary of War, Jefferson Davis, was widely acknowledged to be the most powerful member of his cabinet and administration. Burton Hendricks, in his *Statesmen of the Lost Cause,* says "They expected to take in a large part of what was left of poor Mexico; at times their ambition included all of Central America as far as Panama. Yucatan Davis particularly coveted, and, as Secretary of War in Pierce's cabinet, he was the directing schemer in plans for the annexation of Cuba" (1939, 47).

As astute an observer of the American scene as Alfred Kazin in his review of several Civil War books entitled "The Generals in the Labyrinth" could state: "Before the war, the South had dominated the American political scene. . . The South had fostered the Mexican War and had dominated the presidency even when the Northerners Pierce and Buchanan were in the White House. It dominated the Supreme Court and the Army," (1991, 63). Kazin also states that they were "fighting for slavery (and, of course, the domination of another race, without which many human beings cannot be happy)" (1991, 63).

The South controlled the presidency which controls through nominations, the federal judiciary and the Supreme Court. The President as Commander-in-Chief controls the military which before the Civil War was all Army. The presidency, the Supreme Court, and the Army was three-fourths of federal power, to say nothing of the fact that virtually half of the Senate was chosen by the slaveocracy.

It should be becoming clear by now that the nested triad of slavery, state rights, and control of the West, is cheek by jowl with another triad of white supremacy, an expansionist foreign policy, and control of the federal government. It was loss of control of the federal government in the 1860 election of Lincoln that precipitated South Carolina to "dissolve" the Union and other southern and slave holding states to follow its lead. While the Civil War was not fought ostensibly over control of the federal government, not having control lead directly to the secession and was a profound under-lying cause of the war. With their own Confederate government, Southern-ers no longer felt the need to control the federal government, nor were they momentarily concerned about acquiring more territory simply to control the balance of power in the US Senate, having formed their own Confeder-ate Senate. Their focus shifted instead to acquiring Arizona directly and recognition by the government of the British Empire.

Lincoln's Secretary of War Seward, more or less threatened war on England if they recognized the Confederacy, bluffing the British Empire out temporarily. "In *your* hands, my dissatisfied fellow countrymen, and not in *mine,*" as Lincoln so cunningly put it, "is the momentous issue of civil war" (Hofstadter 1958, 395).

The North was originally fighting for the simple issue of keeping the Union together. Midway through the war, with the Emancipation Procla-mation, the northern agenda enlarged to also include the emancipation of slaves. After the Battle of Gettysburg and particularly with Lincoln's re-election over McClellan, it became increasingly clear that the South and the Confederacy were not going to prevail in the decisive battles. The war from the southern vantage point became one of salvaging their dignity and honor.

Beringer, Hattaway, Jones, and Still, in their well argued and convinc-ing new book from the University of Georgia Press, *Why the South Lost the Civil War,* are prepared to make the case that ". . . in some respects the South did not lose the Civil War. Southerners eventually resolved the disso-nance between the world as it was and the world as they had wanted it to be by securing enough of their war aims — state rights, white supremacy, and honor — to permit them to claim their share of the victory" (1986, 440). This is a significant three legs up on the eventually complete southern victory. The North certainly won its share of a victory by keeping the Union together. Northern claims to have emancipated the slaves are significantly more problematic. Perhaps there was yet another reason for fighting the Civil War as Bruce Catton hints in *A Stillness at Appomattox,* when he says speaking of the terrible loss of life and inconsequential outcome of the Bloody

Angle at Spotsylvania: "There was no victory in all of this and there was no defeat. There was just fighting, as if that had become an end in itself" (1958, 144).

The Civil War had not only conferred on Lincoln more absolute power than any speaker of English had had since Oliver Cromwell (Schlesinger 1986, 279), it made the United States the foremost military power on earth. It also made the Confederacy the second most powerful military government on earth, with an almost complete fusion between the civilian and military aspects of government under President Jefferson Davis. As southerners groped about in the wreckage for their dignity and honor, they found in the tears of Robert E. Lee as he rode out of Appomattox, the saline solution even more powerful than blood that established the "Legend of the Lost Cause."

How the South Finally Won the Civil War continues to build on the three legs of victory claimed for the South by Beringer et al: state rights, honor, and white supremacy. It shows how the South finally won control of the West, the rights to an expansionist foreign policy, and with them eventually once again, control of the federal government. The cause was not lost, only temporarily misplaced. The South dignified its "loss" by glorifying its military history, making battlefields into religious shrines. The South was able to make war holy and turn it into the official state religion. Of 38 army museums open to the public, 27 or more than two-thirds of them, are located in the former slaveholding South (*Defense 91,* 53). The post-war establishment of the glorification of militarism that floats like a halo over the United States is held up by all six very strong legs of the ultimate southern and Confederate insect waltz to victory.

2

Holy War: How War Became the State Religion

War is a permanent human obligation, wrote the American psychologist and philosopher William James, ([1910] 1967, 664) in his widely reprinted essay "The Moral Equivalent of War." Despite the acumen he brought to the subject, no ready moral equivalent for war has ever presented itself. His essay is one basis for pleas left and right for national service of a nonmilitary nature, "to knock the childishness out of youth," as well as the home of such bastardized concoctions as the war on poverty and the war on drugs. It is as though if an issue can't be referred to as a war of some kind, it will attract no attention and die unripened on the vine. The failing political effort to persistently attach moral superiority to pedestrian policy decree by preceding it with the phrase "war on" should not distract us from the truth about the nature of war. It is *sui generis*.

"Reflective apologists for war at the present day all take it religiously," James said. "It is a sort of sacrament." Exactly what sort of sacrament is the fair question to be answered here. In 1994 to keep the faith, there was a three-week run-up to the 50th anniversary of D-Day and a two-week afterglow, making the celebration, with as many of the survivors of the original cast as could be assembled, take practically as long as the invasion itself. This paroxysm of religious bliss, taking over a month to celebrate Memorial Day, with cover stories and photo spreads in many magazines as well as almost total domination by D-Day in the pulpit on the church of TV news, threatened to make the celebration permanent.

Not only was there an uncoordinated effort to make the memory of the great war permanent, there were many piecemeal efforts to make it permanently false. *Time* Magazine's cover photo of General Eisenhower with the caption, "The Man Who Defeated Hitler" for example, distorts the facts that Hitler had three times as many divisions on his eastern front as the Allies eventually overran in Normandy. The United States suffered 250,000 casualties in WWII; The Russians 20 million. Had the United States suffered at the same order of magnitude as Russia, war in America would be substantially more difficult to romanticize. Stalin defeated Hitler, but in ` the Ptolemiac United States where the worship of the war religion is believed to revolve around an American center, inconvenient facts are miniaturized. The news magazines of course moved the religious ceremony right along to 10-page cover stories of the next war in Korea. In 1991 American flags were flying in profusion at the sacred ceremonies commemorating the 50th anniversary of the bombing of Pearl Harbor. The size of the celebrations in 1995 commemorating the defeat of Hitler and the atomic bombing of Japan as the knockout blows were delivered will be equal to the sacrament.

Looking through history for the roots of this pervasive sacrament and into how war became the state religion, we find Arthur Schlesinger Jr. characterizing some American political theology as follows: "The Calvinist mind pronounced America the redeemer nation — in the eighteenth century in Jonathan Edward's theology of Providence, in the nineteenth century in Josiah Strong's theology of expansion, in the twentieth century in Woodrow Wilson's gospel of world order and in John Foster Dulles' summons to a holy war against godless communism" (1986, 52). Three centuries of American political history have their compass read and almost boxed with religious nomenclature in this brief quote.

Nor is it an isolated occurrence in Schlesinger's *The Cycles of American History*. He quotes Wilson as wanting to "redeem" the world; sees Reagan as representing a mighty comeback of "messianism"; terms like *jihad*, crusade, infidel, freckle the text; he referred to Dulles as the "high priest" of the cold war; and noted Reagan's regression to the "holy war" of Dulles. This simply cannot all be coincidental. While Schlesinger himself prefers to believe that the United States is basically a secular society, his choice of terms to describe and report the different beliefs and operating systems of the politicians are accurate. The sinews of war in the United States are wrapped in churchy tones. Other than to lay all of this on the heavily trod doorstep of Calvin, some prominent Americans have made their donations.

"Traced to this source, the voice of a people, — uttered under the necessity of avoiding the greatest of calamities, through the organs of a government so constructed as to suppress the expression of all partial and selfish interests, and to give a full and faithful utterance to the sense of the whole community, in reference to its common welfare, — may, without impiety, be called *the voice of God*" according to the influential political philosopher John C. Calhoun, (1948, 39), whose treatise, *A Disquisition on*

Government, is rarely consulted but required reading. While secularists like Schlesinger and others in the quasi-enlightened late 20th century would be content to hear the simple voice of the people being described in Calhoun's essay, or at worst the "carnal larynx" of Theodore Roosevelt (Hofstadter 1965, 178), Calhoun, in fact the Godfather of the Neo-Confederate empire, thought he heard the voice of God. Historians trying to keep the record straight reduce human utterance to their rationalist bias. Military priests like Calhoun and Roosevelt on the other hand have men to lead into battle. And they are not apt to get them there by way of rational persuasion. In this type of appeal to higher authority to work the infidels into line, it is simple enough to make a metaphysical virtue of intellectual necessity, as Spengler puts it, and drag in God as the author (1926, 19).

There are exceptionally good reasons for militarists like Calhoun to hide in God's robes. The task of the peacemakers confronted by warmakers is described by James: "One cannot meet them effectively by mere counter-insistency on war's expensiveness and horror. The horror makes the thrill; and when the question is of getting the extremest and supremest out of human nature, talk of expense sounds ignominious. The weakness of so much merely negative criticism is evident — pacifism makes no converts from the military party. The military party denies neither the bestiality nor the horror, nor the expense; it only says that these things tell but half the story. It only says that war is *worth* them. . . that mankind cannot *afford* to adopt a peace-economy" (1967, 666).

What gives the military standpoint its superior position in all of these arguments is that a factual base for argument is not required. "Questions of fact are beside the point in theological disputation" (Chomsky 1973, 54). The rituals, the myths, the ideological controls, are all taken as articles of faith. They are beyond proof. War has been made holy to excuse itself from ever losing in its ritual defense of defense as the centerpiece of American policy.

The United States came into being as one upshot of the Revolutionary War and later fought the second half of the Revolutionary War as the War of 1812. Wars against the Indians, hopelessly romanticized by the movies, were grim genocidal business when they took place in the Colonies. The most costly in terms of per-capita deaths was the Yemassee War in South Carolina. Wars against Indians were still grim and genocidal as Americans marched their Manifest Destiny across North America. Little has changed up to the present day as the world witnessed the January 1st, 1994 (and still unresolved) rebellion of the armed highland Mayans in the Mexican empire state of Chiapas which may have reminded the oligarchies who negotiated NAFTA of the continued colonial nature of their exploitation.

It is no wonder that neither the Bush nor Clinton Administrations nor the Americans in general can come up with a coherent response to the "ethnic cleansing" taking place in the former Yugoslavia, since the United States is in fact a continental monument to ethnic cleansing. It is necessary to fight for what you get, especially if you are taking it away from someone else. While the Mexican War in the 1840s and the Spanish American War of the 1890s were such takings, it is the War Between the States or the Civil War that is the Eucharist in the United States.

Except for Gettysburg and Glorieta Pass, most of the significant battles of the Civil War were conducted in the South, on the turf of the Confederacy. Obviously the South did not win any of the decisive battles, the least interesting aspects of the Civil War, but the war itself was a victory for militarism as a solution to problems and it makes its American home in the South. Not only are most of the battlefields, which have since been turned into shrines, located in the South, but so too are most of the military bases and three-fourths of all the military museums. The lion's share of the military spending is disbursed there and the South is home to most of the military retirees.

The Civil War consolidated power and militarized it in Washington D.C. and especially in Richmond. The Confederate government, due to the nature of defense and Jefferson Davis' putative military genius, was a military government. War is likewise the organizing principle of the present United States government. The function of the military is to control the supply of metal and other commodities. The function of the economy is to raise money for the military (Adams 1967). The civilization has never been any more complicated than that. The complications are all added after the fact to create thickets for military expenditures to be squirreled away in. Americans are a people "whose specific character was born in the spiritual upheavals of 1775 and, above all, 1861-5" (Spengler 1928, 165).

Get used to thinking of the Civil War as a "spiritual upheaval." Beringer et al suggest in their introduction to *Why the South Lost the Civil War*, that explanations need to be sought in the emotional, spiritual, and mystical realms, and go on to claim that there is a "peculiarly southern military behavior" (1986, 20). The South was defeated but not crushed, humbled but not humiliated and "more united in defeat. . . Confederates seemed to forge a distinctiveness after the war that they had not had before or during it" (423). The peculiar spiritual character of Americans is specific to their southern military behavior. It will bear repeating that the distinctive Confederate forge took place after the war. William Jennings Bryan noticed it and "spoke softly of his pride in the South and predicted the coming of a great religious revival which would begin in the South and sweep across the nation" (Levine 1965, 340).

It is unlikely that Bryan was adumbrating the TV cracker barrel evangelists, nor did Bryan seem to notice that the imperialists he fought so diligently and so ineffectively for so many years, had adopted three-fourths of the pre-Confederate southern agenda. To be aware of the "baptized in blood" origins of the lost cause legend may not make people aware of how many Southerners defended slavery on biblical lines. The regression to a predatory economic impulse sought and continues to seek religious justification in the oldest extant source. Few people read the formal religious proclamations of Jefferson Davis. Nevertheless as Kazin points out, "What the cheerful Confederate [General Edward Porter Alexander] did not say was that the South in defeat recouped itself religiously. . . the creed became more sacred to itself than ever, a civic religion that lasted. . ." (1991, 65). Kazin caught the music right, even though he went on to say that the civic religion of the South's defeat, its lost cause baptized in blood, only lasted until 1920.

Writing of the tempest stirred up around then Democratic Governor Bill Clinton of Arkansas by the publication of a 20-year-old letter containing his principled objection to the Vietnam War, Robin Toner wrote in the *New York Times* of February 13, 1992: "The sentiments expressed in that letter are likely to stir old angers among many voters, particularly in the South, where military service is held in special esteem" (A12). Quite possibly the most significant aspect of Bill Clinton's victory will be that the American people elected someone who could tell the difference between a war that had to be fought (WWII) and a war that ought to have been avoided (Vietnam). With a secular view, all wars are not created equal. The ultimate survival of the American military civilization will depend on having leaders able to make those critical distinctions.

Far from petering out in 1920, the cause is alive and well and being a "civic religion," in little or no danger from the facts. The Vietnam War will function as a talisman for both sides forever, being as it was the place where the religious principle enunciated at the Alamo in the terse strategy of Buck Travis, "I'll neither surrender nor retreat," was finally ground to a halt. A military civilization with a single strategy is doomed. Half the males of Clinton's generation served the empire's military apparatus and half served the nation and their consciences in other ways. Recall that the Pledge of Allegiance is to the "nation" not to the empire. Contrary to the romanticized history of war, half the able-bodied men in the North and the South during the Civil War avoided military service in one manner or another, especially in response to the attempts at conscription which resulted in the Draft Riot in New York City where 119 people were killed. In addition to the propinquity of most of the significant Civil War battlefields being located in the South and handy for enshrinement, there are other things contributing to the essentially southern nature of the American military religion.

For one thing, "There is no hereditary leisure class of any consequence in the American community, except at (sic) the South" (Veblen [1899] 1931, 325). A leisure class has somewhat more time to devote to their devout enthusiasm for war. This martial spirit is predatory in nature and runs, as Veblen put it, in the direction of spiritual survival and reversion. This spiritual survival of a leisure class has a tendency to run to non-economic (that is to say, makes nobody any money or sense nor adds anything of truly durable value), employments: "Such are politics and ecclesiastical and military employments" (231). Only the leisure class has the time to kill on these fruitless reversionary behaviors. Everybody else is working for a living. The leisure class feasts on fruit plucked by other hands. The fundamentalist preachers, the gas-bag senators and representatives, and the generals, both active and retired, form the real trinity — the Father, the Son, and the Holy Ghost have been brushed aside — and make up the practical basis of that "old time religion" of politics, religion, and war, in one grand indissoluble southern knot.

Even in *Colonial South Carolina*, where the economics of leisure based on the exploitation of slave labor were getting their toe-hold, Weir could report that "The South Carolinians had given a good account of themselves, and they emerged from the encounter in high martial spirits" (1983,

82). The martial spirit is the one that needs to be tapped for political success. In the election of 1900, "McKinley was appealing to them while they were intoxicated by military triumph" (Glad 1968, 62). The military revival of the 1890s contained a huge helping of religious faith. "The gospel of American imperialism was preached at this time even more eloquently by the still younger Republican prophet, Albert Beveridge of Indiana" (Josephson 1940, 74). This propensity to use religious metaphor and nomenclature (gospel, preach and prophet) is a thin disguise for the predatory war it only partially conceals.

Religion, to be effective, requires condensed symbols of its expression of faith. The famous novelist Owen Wister, author of *The Virginian*, suggested that if Theodore Roosevelt were reduced to his chemical essence a "preacher militant" (Pringle 1955, 334) would be found. A fanatic flag waver would also be found, as he railed against those who would "haul" down the flag in the Philippines. Roosevelt's was a successful religious and emotional non-argument against people principled differently who felt Aguinaldo deserved a chance at the same kind of liberty the American Revolution had been fought for.

But it is the flag, "Old Glory," or alternatively "The first flag of the Confederacy Baptized in Glory at Bull Run" (Griffith 1933) as told in the text accompaniment to the movie, *The Birth of a Nation*, that is the ultimate symbol of military religion. Bruce Catton could speak of the "II Army Corps" as the most famous in the Union army: "It had stormed Bloody Lane at Antietam, it had taken 4,000 casualties at Fredericksburg without flinching, it had beaten back Pickett's charge at Gettysburg, and it had broken the Bloody Angle at Spotsylvania" (1958, 239). While the corps per se would not be expected to flinch, some of the 4,000 dying men undoubtedly twitched. This unblushing romance of war fulfills its religious purpose. Catton opens *A Stillness at Appomattox* with the report of a parade where all the regimental flags of II Army Corps were displayed. "The flags may have been worth seeing. It was the boast of this corps that although it had suffered nearly 19,000 battle casualties it had never yet lost a flag to the enemy" (1). Losing their opportunity to openly worship the flag of the Confederacy, the Southerners were able eventually to reattach their loyalty to the flag of the armies that temporarily vanquished them.

The idea of losing a flag as religious and military anathema did not begin in North America, but the tradition has been honed to a fine point there. Rosen reports "At one point in the Battle of Fort Moultrie the new state's blue and white flag was shot away" (1982, 53), but we are assured that it was promptly replaced during the first significant battle of the Revolutionary War in, where else, Charleston, South Carolina. Far from World War I in Europe, the United States Congress passed a sedition act that made it illegal, in a direct violation of the First Amendment to the Constitution, to utter "'disloyal, profane, scurrilous, or abusive language' about the federal government, the constitution, the armed forces, the uniform, or the flag" (Johnson 1963, 69). Not only shall the flag not be lost, it shall not be profaned either. In southern California during this period, the punishment was ridiculous for people who disobeyed this law, specifically the members of the IWW, the Wobblies, as "Prisoners were forced to kneel and kiss the flag" (McWilliams 1946, 288). Violations of the Bill of Rights are routine during wars in the United States.

There was something a little ominous in George Bush's persistent mis-recital of the Pledge of Allegiance to the flag during his 1988 election campaign. Bush would have been comfortable with the above mentioned sedition act, for he burned up what political capital he could get his hands on in a failing effort to pass an amendment to the Constitution to outlaw flag burning. The Citizens Flag Alliance, a coalition headed by the American Legion, has not stopped waving the Flag amendment idea.

During the Bush blitzkrieg of Iraq, under the headline "Raising Old Glory" on the front page of the Walla Walla *Union-Bulletin* for January 27, 1991, complete with an appropriate full color photograph, the text reads: "A Large American flag rises against a stained-glass backdrop at the Village Seventh-day Adventist Church in College Place [Washington] Saturday. The flag raising occurred near the end of the morning service, devoted in part to honoring service people in the Persian Gulf, as the men's chorus sang 'The Battle Hymn of the Republic'" (*UB* 1991, 1). Such a hair raising flag raising in a Christian prayer service cannot go unremarked upon.

Facing this irrefutable demonstration of the final alloying of war as the state religion symbolized by the flag to the tune of the North's marching song during the Civil War, further refracted through and smothered in the stained glass of Protestant Christianity, is an appropriate place to point out something pertinent about the war on Iraq. The war on Iraq was made in the South. When the votes in the Congress from the 11 Confederate states on the resolution to use force to enforce UN sanctions against Iraq are factored out of the totals, the resolution (a defacto declaration of war and support for the last 20 feet of Bush's hitherto undeclared war on Iraq) failed in both the House and the Senate *(Congressional Quarterly*, January 12, 1991), see chapter 21 for details. Several months earlier, the Associated Press delivered a photograph to its member papers that was published in the *UB* on Monday, October 29, 1990. There are six "Members of the U.S. Army's 1st Cavalry Division Support Command dressed in 19th century uniforms to present the colors during change of command ceremonies Sunday in the Saudi Arabian desert. The division is based at Fort Hood, Texas."

In the war as a romance department, there are four flags in this picture, the American flag, the Saudi flag, the Army flag, and the Division flag. The 19th century uniforms and desert backdrop hinting at the old Southwest, make this "Sunday ceremony" reminiscent of John Wayne-Audie Murphy-Ronald Reagan western cavalry-to-the-rescue movies, an overwhelmingly powerful set of religious icons. This is the cavalry to Calvary brigade.

War is our religious history. Political candidates do not deliver TV speeches without flags prominently displayed in either the foreground, side-ground, or background. The mandatory worship of the flag is their liturgy. George Bush wrapped his 1988 election victory in the American flag. In his mouth, the phrase "No More Vietnams" did not mean no more colonial wars, but rather that war should be short, sweet and savage. He declared a victory in Iraq and brought the troops home. The rising tide of testosterone lifted his popularity over 90 percent and made most public officials and news reporters so giddy with adrenaline and testosterone that making sense was beyond them for several months. Bush was washed out of office barely a year later in a post coital funk, a demonstration case of poor religious planning and bad timing.

Since Bush could not keep the Pledge of Allegiance straight, it will bear repeating and additional scrutiny. "I pledge allegiance, to the flag, of the United States of America, and to the republic, for which it stands, one nation, under God, indivisible, with liberty, and justice for all." Americans, most of whom attend the public school system, get so used to this recitation as the first order of business for each school day, that its transparent liturgical significance escapes them. It is the most important lesson, which is why it comes first.

The experiment in democracy that began the government of the United States provided in the First Amendment to the Constitution in the Bill of

Rights that "Congress shall make no law respecting an establishment of religion or prohibiting the free exercise thereof. . ." Over time, this came to be construed as a separation of church and state. Most Americans participate in the long contentious argument with the shorthand title of "prayer in school." Nevermind the Bill of Rights, a defenseless and routinely plundered catalog of ideals where the first order of business plows like a tank through the scattered phonemes of the First Amendment. The arguments over the right or need to pray in school serve to camouflage the real prayer, the Pledge of Allegiance, which has already taken place each day and is behind the students before the diversionary argument over prayer is even taken up.

Church, as ordinarily thought of in the Judeo-Christian tradition and the many other relatively minor orthodox religions, except for the concept of God, are meticulously separated from the activities of the state. This red herring activity serves to muffle any real discussions about fundamental beliefs. The ideals, belief systems, and behavior patterns of the "higher" religions, as they are called by Arnold Toynbee, only obtain on Saturday afternoons in comfortable surroundings. When push comes to shove, Buddhist, Moslem, and Christian soldiers will be as barbarian as they have to be. Meanwhile, the vicissitudes of life and deliberate choices have fused the military into the state as its own religion. Church and state, far from being separated, are a simultaneous and identical occasion in the United States, established by the Congress. The flag is the symbol of this religious fusion and the Pledge is the state prayer. Freedom of religion in the United States does not mean freedom from war.

There is one final step to take on the subject of this holy war and that is to find its ethnic basis which will be deeper than the southern dominated political geography of North America. When the English speaking colonists of North American numbered but a few thousand, England itself was awakening to power. "After 1688 the scope of British military involvement changed radically. . . Britain acquired a standing army and navy. . . a fiscal-military state, one dominated by the task of waging war" (Brewer 1989, 27). The closest model for the government of the United States, the British Empire, was dominated by the task of war. In his discussion of the fiscal basis of the British Empire, *The Sinews of Power*, Brewer goes on to quote the pithy dictum of Charles Tilly: "War made the state, and the state made war" (137). The feedforward loop in the shape of a Mobius strip with retired generals and admirals reciting the liturgy on TV as during the War on Iraq, stimulated some people to dub CNN as PNN or Pentagon Network News.

What exactly is the relationship between the Americans and their English progenitors? We get some hints from the oxymoronic titled *Imperial Democracy:* "The Reverend Josiah Strong, a Congregationalist minister. . . leader in the. . . American Evangelical Alliance, declared that America was taking from England the scepter for the Anglo-Saxon race. . . 'the Anglo-Saxon is divinely commissioned. . . [with] an instinct or genius for colonizing. . . peculiarly aggressive traits. . . will spread itself over the earth. . . down upon Mexico. . .'" (May 1961, 8). Here we meet up once again with Reverend Josiah Strong, already cited by Schlesinger as one of the perpetrators of the notion that Manifest Destiny was divinely inspired. Less theological heads had noted that the fierce competition for control of the West had sectionalized Manifest Destiny many years before the Civil War. Whether it be instinct or genius, divinely commissioned or humbly profane, the American acting out of the English Anglo-Saxon aggression is proof of the blood ties between them. The siege mentality endemic to the English, acquired in the more or less millennium of the 1100 years between Caesar's first invasion and the Battle of Hastings in 1066, is also basic to Colonial South Carolina, the Confederacy, and the United States since 1945.

It is always much simpler to project your aggressions outward, as a basic psychological observation, than to deal with them internally. The state sponsored projection of hostility in the form of war is the typical result. And to keep it decorous, nothing beats a colonial war waged far away against other races and cultures. Speaking of the Spanish American War, "The best informed writers had not credited the American navy with such enterprise and efficiency. Nor had anyone expected two hundred thousand men to be mobilized so quickly, old Confederates to take commands alongside former Union officers, Democrats and Republicans to enlist with matching zeal, or northern immigrants and southern Negroes to line up before recruiting booths" (May 1961, 220). Here we discover old Confederates and Union officers embracing for a chance to shoot someone else for a change. It is hard to miss the religious zeal. Make no mistake, Americans love war, they worship it, it is their reason to be. It is in fact so pervasive that even those such as Henry Wallace who would oppose it are co-opted by the nomenclature and metaphor. "We should everyone of us regard it as a holy duty, to join the fight for winning the peace" (MacDougall 1965, I:79).

If this love of war is attributable to the Anglo-Saxon nature of white Americans, spilling over even on to African Americans as in the war just cited, we have to get completely off the continent and into another culture to see it clearly. The real drama of history includes a multitude of cultures. Spengler says that ". . . to the Chinese all the music of the West without distinction is *march-music*. . . We ourselves have accent in our blood and therefore do not notice it" (1926, 228). He goes on to speak of "magnificent bishops of the old German empire who on horseback led their flocks into wild battle" (349). He speaks too of the necessity of a "mission," of how the power of the pulpit was replaced by the power of the press and how this "religion admitted no freedom of *attitude*" (419). English is a Germanic language and the Anglo-Saxon roots of American civilization are in the same soil as the roots of Germany and England.

In youthful culture one can see distinctions between *"politics and religion"* (1928, 121). In the more advanced-in-age condition of our civilization, such dichotomies are hopelessly fused. He refers to the Puritan "army of Cromwell and his Independents, iron, Bible-firm, psalm-singing as they rode into battle" (302). The United States has adopted holy war as its religion and excels, even in the Christian churches, at singing the psalms of war.

The current siege mentality set in with the bombing of Pearl Harbor. It was artificially extended with the Truman Doctrine. Maintaining the siege mentality (and the pipeline of money to the military South and the leisure class) in the absence of the Soviet Union or any other enemy of even remotely comparable scale is the theocritical challenge of the 1990s. Let us admit that the new trinity is meeting this challenge with the same siege mentality that infected Richmond during the Civil War. With a vitrolic fear and loathing of Washington, DC, even though it is their baby, the significance of the messianic drive to power of Southerners like Newt Gingrich is lost in the glazed eyes of the faithful as he delivers his vision of "salvation and redemption," as Lacayo reports in *Time* Magazine, to punctuated shouts of "Amen!" The use of the radio to rouse the rabble reminds the rational of the tail end of the Weimar Republic.

The freedom of attitude that is curtailed when Americans go to war, creates dissonance in people, the infidels of war, whose attendance at the religious ceremony contradicts their beliefs. Opposition to war ceases to be regarded as a free speech issue or even treason. It becomes blasphemy and heresy. For all its power, the religion of war has a central frailty that creates its constant defense. Democratic centralism, or the process of closing ranks *when attacked*, is absolutely essential for a nation to survive. When a nation is not attacked, but is in fact acting like an empire and embarking on imperial adventures to protect the advantages of the leisured few, to expect a closing of ranks violates the entire canon of democracy. To silence opposition to war, whether tactically, strategically, or politically, by forcing principled people with better ideas to keep their mouths shut, is to endorse rigidity and invite ultimate defeat. At that point the war religion most closely resembles witchcraft. The holy war of America's southern military symbolized by the flag has no moral equivalent. The freedoms for which the United States was founded are silenced at every critical juncture by the mute salute.

War is the permanent religion in the United States, symbolized by the flag and controlled by essentially southern mentality. Being religious activity, it is immune to assault from facts or logic. Peace lovers, such as Henry David Thoreau during the Mexican War, Andrew Carnegie, Grover Cleveland, and Mark Twain during the Spanish American War and the Aguinaldo Insurrections, Senators Frank Church and Wayne Morse at the beginning of the War on Vietnam, as well as Ron Kovic of Vietnam Veterans Against the War in his wheel chair vainly protesting the war on Iraq, simply don't have a prayer.

3

The Arc of Columbus: Old World Background

More than 500 years after Columbus landed on the islands of Hispaniola, it is worthwhile to keep at least three other things in mind. The "new" world had been discovered many times before, by Vikings and Norsemen under Eric the Red and his son Lief the Lucky, as well as innumerable times by Asiatic peoples coming over the dehydrated Bering Straits during glaciations and from the Pacific Islands to landfall on the western coasts of the Western Hemisphere. These prior discoveries didn't account for much with the basic Europeans as they were either unknown to them or had not yet been worked into a coherent system of thought.

The other two essential elements, although they may seem disparate, are crucial to comprehending the whole flow of events. This was the time of Copernicus (1473-1543) and the movement toward the more accurate solar centrific planetary system away from the classic earth centrific Ptolemaic. Old ideas die hard. Max Planck's fifth constant states that people who grow up believing one thing hardly ever change their minds and accept the truth of new discoveries, preferring to go to the grave with their misunderstanding intact. The next generation which comes of age familiar with the newer revealed wisdom accepts it as the truth. Fra Luca Pacioli, a contemporary of Columbus and Copernicus, invented double entry book-keeping in 1494. In other words, space came together simultaneously for the European system on the financial, geographical and astronomical planes.

This was no accident. Taken together with the other two, the Columbian rediscovery of the new world is the most significant event in cultural history since the deglaciation. Everything that has taken place in both the Western and Eastern hemisphere in the past 500 years is recent. Yet the English speaking people did not establish a permanent colony in North America until 1607 in Jamestown, Virginia, 114 years after Columbus. What took them so long and the relevant background to their late start before they finally completed the arc of Columbus and "at the turn of the [twentieth] century created a comprehensive fiction of Southern California as the promised land of a millenarian Anglo-Saxon racial odyssey" (Davis 1990, 20), is the focus of this phase of the discovery.

England appeared in the classical literature about 2,300 years ago. The Greek astronomer Pytheas, following prehistoric trade routes exploited by the Phoenicians and others, first circumnavigated the British Isles (Scullard 1979, 9). He found the land thick with inhabitants and already skilled at the working of tin. Known somewhat affectionately to the classical world as the tin islands, Great Britain spent more than 400 years as a distant and desultorily exploited colony of the Roman Empire. This was longer by far a period of historical time, it needs to be emphasized, than the current speakers of English have dominated and exploited North America.

One root of the American and English speaking past still flourishes in the military soil of Rome. Claude Pepper, the influential Congressman and former New Deal Senator from Florida, could charge during the beginning of the Truman Doctrine that this behavior would "Subject this nation to the serious accusations of aspiring to become the new Rome or the old Britain" (MacDougall 1965, I:134). The political philosopher John C. Calhoun, in his search for principles, found "the origin and character of the governments of Rome and Great Britain; the two most remarkable and perfect of their respective forms of constitutional governments" (1948, 91).

Even though he found them both remarkable and perfect, Calhoun felt the British government to be far superior, essentially for being able to hold its dominions under sway without "subverting its constitution" (105). This was a degree of perfection unattainable by the United States government, for in its pursuit of empire, its Constitution has been consistently subverted. Senator Daniel Webster of Massachusetts, one of John C. Calhoun's few peers, summed Calhoun up like this: "I think there is not one of us, when he last addressed us from his seat in the Senate, who did not feel that he might imagine that we saw before us a Senator of Rome" (Thomas 1968, 25). When Americans lean on Rome and the Roman Empire via England and the British Empire, it is a natural enough and sentimental choice of imperial cultural chains.

The Roman grip on England was loosened by its irretrievable decadence and what became successive waves of invasions by the Angles, the Saxons, the Vikings, the Jutes, and the Normans, themselves displaced Vikings from France who had previously colonized Normandy a few generations earlier. The British Isles were a pressure relief point for

European expansion during these darker ages. The depredations visited on the natives by the callous invaders make it simple to comprehend why the English have dug in so intently to repel subsequent invasions since the 1066 loss at the Battle of Hastings. During the contemporary era, Nazi Germany came close to invading. The ensuing peace and European economic cohesion threatens finally to make England a less standoffish and isolated parcel of the continent by use of the chunnel under the English Channel. The natural history of their island nature reinforces their chronic mental state of siege.

It was the Norman invasion and the subsequent fusion of language and culture between Norman French and native English that got the modern English ball rolling. Whether it was in the spread of doom at the end of the first Christian millennium "that the Faustian soul of this religion was born" (Spengler 1926, 167), or that "in the colonization-field of floundering Rome, on the other hand, the future Western Culture was ripening underground in the north-west" (1928, 42), England and the English were beginning to take shape.

The ongoing negotiations and strife in 13th century England, between various kings and the merchants who demanded that the King share power, resulted in the Magna Carta. The foundations of English speaking democracy were laid in this century, including the right to be represented when taxed. "In North America in the 1760s the powers of the colonial legislatures were opposed to the authority of parliament. Not only were duties evaded but the very legitimacy of colonial taxation was questioned" (Brewer 1989, 132). The English speaking colonists took their heritage seriously. They were recapitulating a principle, even by then some 400 years old, dear to the freedom in their hearts. These original taxing events in the economic foundation of freedom only took place, one place on earth. They didn't happen in Zimbabwe on the Zambezi, in Hunan on the Xiang, or in Rumania on the Danube. They took place on the Thames in England. English is the language of freedom.

Among the other baggage the Romans eventually dropped off in the British Isles, was the Christian religion in the form of the Roman Catholic Church. Not altogether trusting the priest class and the Popes, one of the driving forces behind Martin Luther's Reformation was the desire of the western European Christians to read the Bible in their own vernacular language. John Wycliffe's 14th century translation of the Bible into English —

people were put to death for making these translations as an example of how seriously the Catholic "Christians" who wanted it kept in Latin were able to take themselves — was a precursor for the later and more famous King James version done during the Elizabethan Renaissance. Luther, 1473-1543, is the fourth and equally brilliant star in the Columbian-Copernican-Paciolian constellation, an expansion of freedom on the theological plane, that transformed the world at the end of the 15th century. An important day in the life of the Catholic Dark Ages was drawn to a close.

Something funny and predictable happened when the people of northwestern Europe could read the Bible in their vernacular languages: they began to prefer the Old Testament. Those cultures where Romance languages related more directly to Latin became the vernaculars, Spain, France and Italy for instance, remained Catholic. The Germanic northwest became Protestant. Preferring the Old Testament, as anyone who can read is apt to do, the northern Europeans had the new model of the chosen people to follow without the patronizing misinterpretation of St. Paul. "The covenant of salvation, it seemed, had passed from the Jews [via the Reformation] to the American colonists" (Schlesinger 1986, 14). Schlesinger's *The Cycles of American History* tries, among other things, to sort out the different strains of American history into the experimental or destined paths. Taking the torch of the chosen people is another excellent way to relieve oneself of the responsibility and, with God as the author as we've already seen, let the destiny be manifest.

It was England's temporary destiny to be restless. According to the English poet George Herbert, restlessness was God's way of getting the people back. "During the past three centuries the spread of the English-speaking peoples over the world's waste spaces had been not only the most striking feature in the world's history, but also the event of all others most far-reaching in its effect and its importance" (Roosevelt 1899, 1). The booster spirit at the beginning of Theodore Roosevelt's light classic *The Winning of the West*, is a function of no perspective and difficult to miss. It stems from the English and the aggressive Anglo-Saxon past.

The waste spaces would not always be so tractable as they were in the mid-19th century and the decades of English hegemony, for less than a hundred years after Roosevelt's congratulatory edict, the English speakers would be once again up against the, this time peaceful, Japanese miracle (Kennedy 1987, 143 & 459). The Japanese had been there, on their share of the sphere of Earth in the way of the English speakers, since Perry had opened the door to the Tokugawa Shogunate's Japan. Opening Japan has the potential to be recorded as one of history's larger transformations. "This will give Japan what her ineluctable vocation as a state absolutely forces her to claim, the possession of the entire Pacific Ocean; and to oppose these deep designs we Americans have. . ." (James [1910] 1967, 664). The most recent great clash of American and Japanese designs in WWII ended with the atomic bomb.

Even in the time of Theodore Roosevelt the Japanese were perfecting "A challenge to the two great English-speaking peoples in the far east" (Perkins 1966, 60). Here is where the arc of Columbus completes the sphere and is threatened with sputtering out. For Japan, awakened by the social and economic cyclone unleashed by the speakers of English, is their most persistent rival. "Great Britain, however, is most suggestive, for the United Kingdom and the empire of Japan, both groups of islands lying on opposite sides of America, the one in the apparent path, the other in the wake, of the social cyclone, should be supplementary to each other" (Adams [1903] 1967, 189). The torch has been passed.

These very successful island empires, England on the European hand from which the English speaking American political experience springs, and Japan on the Asian hand where the American political experience bounces back befuddled, have other things in common as well. Each has continental rivals sufficient in size to do them in but lacking critical geographical and linguistic positioning to succeed. The Franco-German-Russian rivalry to the speakers of English has been kept in check. The English themselves neutralized Napoleon. The English and the Americans think they subdued the Germans although most of the credit goes to Russia, and the Russians were spent into bankruptcy by the profligate American Empire. China has been no match for Japan since the fall of the Qing Dynasty, during the industrial period, despite the successful Maoist revolution to relieve it of foreign domination. China is hobbled by its authoritarian political structure, rigid language and pervasively inflexible response to dynamic changes. Japanese linguistic flexibility, situational ethics, and process oriented research and development, make it a formidable rival. The two most highly irregular and hence oldest and most widely applied verbs in Japanese, *kuru* and *suru*, to come and to do, devolve into the fundamental question in *Nihongo*: what did you come here to do? North

America itself has been turned by history and the Panama Canal into a gigantic island. Its world position in the future depends on its staying on the trade route between Japan and Germany, between Asia and Europe, and not permitting itself to be bypassed into a Madagascarian future.

Choosing to lie about destiny is a more forgivable matter than failing to comprehend it clearly. History will have its way with people regardless of their degree of comprehension. It is far too easy in the space of a single lifetime like Theodore Roosevelt's, to operate completely on optimism and lose the perspective the millennial wide Germanic fatalism of Spengler can offer. The arc of Columbus really began to get its ultimate background bearings at the time of the most recent deglaciation when the speakers of proto Indo-European languages began to spread north and west out of Asia Minor.

This was no sudden sweep a la Genghis Khan, but "cumulative Celticity" (Renfrew 1989), a gradual movement from the mouth of one stream to another, from valley to valley, following the sun, until even the British Isles were peopled by Celts "mad for war" (Scullard 1979, 16). With no written record and short lifetimes, the only proof we have of their love for warmer weather was their worship of the sun. The celebration of the solstices at Stonehenge was an act of faith in the roundness of forces admired and as yet unknown. Their movement south and west in search of the sun, dominated by the elite and carrying their slaves across North America, was an equal expression of an act of religious and economic faith.

If the English speaking civilization is now up against the wall of the Japanese, it bears repeating that speakers of English were ultimately able to capitalize on Columbus's discovery and turn it into a worldwide command of most of the earth's surface. It was in this process that European and English speaking culture took on its planetary character. We can look into the heart of English speaking culture to find the force field of the English advance from a handful of English speakers in huts along the Thames on the plains of Kent. Shakespeare is the heart of English.

"Only thus can we understand Shakespeare's ceaseless change of scene as against the Classical unity of place" (Spengler 1926, 220). Not merely the constant shift of location, this jockeying for position in the struggle for freedom that English represents, but also the spread over time, the condensations of weeks, months, even years, into moments, rather than the classic static of a drama all taking place on the same day. A day of sameness in a classic drama of situation (like current TV sitcoms that broadcast and radiate the same unrelieved emotional static) when contrasted with an upheaval of character and incident pales by comparison. Destiny is incident grown enormous and multiplied. It is character acting upon the land without restraint. Only other characters can offer the restraints of their own competing personalities and interests. The English speaking peoples will eventually destroy themselves by an overweening attention to personal freedom and independence at the expense of the cohesive sustenance of larger group cooperation. The situation itself is fluid where centuries themselves can be compressed and condensed for maximal yield.

The English character seeking freedom, sought colonies in the new world to boost its revenue, admiring the work of Sir Francis Drake. The struggle for freedom from the King took the form in the 17th century of the Puritan Revolution. It was not merely as though "The victorious Puritans nevertheless exhibited considerable interest in the empire" (Weir 1983, 48), but that it was "Cromwell's *milieu* which called into life the British Colonial Empire" (Spengler 1926, 148). This is not just the heavy handed German ascribing to a milieu what is actually the work of energized individuals supported by the milieu they create. Spengler is on to structure hitherto ignored.

"The history of the Monophysites and their relation to Mohammed's *milieu* signify nothing whatever to the Islamic believer, but for *us* it is recognizably the story of English Puritanism in another setting" (1928, 47). Plunge into the soup of comparable milieus, the better to emancipate ourselves from the surface of history, "to thrust aside the artificial fences in which the methodology of Western sciences had padlocked it — before we can see that Pythagoras, Mohammed, and Cromwell embody one and the same movement in three Cultures" (303). Spengler is doing the cultural overstretch, an x-ray vision of the similar supporting structure. His unified command of information is made possible by being literate in more than one language and culture. Its depth is apparent when contrasted with the monocultural insights of Theodore Roosevelt.

"Pythagoras was not a philosopher. According to all statements of the Pre-Socratics, he was a saint, prophet and founder of a fanatically religious society that forced its truths upon the people around it by every political and military means" (303). That also sounds like an accurate description of the English speaking society and its political capture of North America. We have already had some exposure to the fanatical religious and military basis of modern American culture and the monophysitic or single nature of its creed. And though the details are not widely known nor well understood, English speakers have no trouble at all recognizing the fanaticism of Mohammed and even admiring, across the oceans and continents, the religious, political, and military spread of Islam from Medina to Tours in France, where the halt was called, and eastward on to the banks of the Ganges.

The challenge and struggle for the speakers of English will be to accept the essentially religious nature of their militant and political colonizing thrust across the planet. "This alone is sufficient to explain the intense vehemence with which the Arabian Culture, when released at length from artistic as from other fetters, flung itself upon all the lands that had inwardly belonged to it for centuries past. It is the sign of a soul that feels itself in a hurry, that notes in fear the first symptoms of old age before it has had youth" (Spengler 1926, 213).

There is double and triple significance being exposed here, for not only has the English advance been just such the righteous recklessness of a soul in a hurry driven by fear, its religious, military and political leaders all operated from the same cramped office. It is the office occupied by the wealthy leisured class that found its American expression in the South. The English too had seen the symptoms of its own old age in the terrible insights into its character rendered indelible in the poetic drama of Shakespeare, especially *King Lear*. In English, where the two most highly irregular verbs are to be and to have, the fundamental question is where are you and what have you got. Lear's question then is not "Shall I put my land in order?" but rather, where am "I" and how shall "I" divide it up? Shakespeare's best plays are all about power. They are historical dramas based on the lives of Roman emperors and English kings. They begin in fact and are warped into shape by the force of the poet into political fiction, the truth of which is deeper, outside and beyond the literal truth of what actually happened for it contains the dreaded meaning the actors as well as the characters, to say nothing of the audience, have been strenuously avoiding.

The further significance is that Spengler identifies the epochal "decline" of the West, that is to say the moment when it passed from culture to civilized barbarism, from city to megalopolis, from wonderful expansiveness to mere holding on and Caesarian administration, with the establishment of the British Empire's ultimate hegemony over the Franco culture of the Napoleons with Wellington's victory at Waterloo. In other words for the United States even as it escaped colonialism, it reached its apex in the work of the revolutionists, especially the Jeffersonian Bill of Rights, in the late 18th century. It will come as hard news to many Americans to realize that nearly all of their history as a nation, and more recently as the rest of the British or English speaking Empire, has been, contrary to their limitless capacity for delusion and self congratulation, the inevitable decline and reversion toward hollow English autocratic forms, which earlier had reached their fullest expression in South Carolina. Far from being an unlimited tending upwards, the political struggle in North America has been a holding action against the perpetual assault on the few rights assigned to some of the people at the founding and is only rarely characterized by timid attempts to expand those rights. The grand ascent was forever being thwarted by the autocratic shuffle sideways.

And thus like the Islamic cultures, forced to kneel, face Mecca and pray five times a day, the Americans must repeat on a daily basis, their religious rituals of hauling the flag up and down, pledging and saluting, throwing their money at phantoms in honor of the imaginary siege. The struggle for the soul of freedom in America as something new and fantastic was lost to the very European forces that rediscovered it. The arc of Columbus reunited the world into its European planetary image. The surviving progeny will be forever picking up the pieces.

4

The British Empire: Beyond Barbados

The English character was poised in the final quarter of the 16th century to make its mark on the known and unknown worlds. Despite erratic failures to establish colonies on the mid-Atlantic coasts of Virginia and North Carolina, Francis Drake had claimed California for England ". . . by the grace of God in the name of her majesty Queen Elizabeth. . ." on June 17, 1579 (Roche 1973, 151). Drake returned from his circumnavigation of the globe with his ship the *Golden Hind* laden with riches taken from the unarmed floating treasure chest, *Nuestra Senora de la Concepción*, off the Peruvian coast of South America. Popularly known as *Cacafuego* to the Spanish sailors, or "Shitfire" in English vernacular, the gold and silver had been taken from the Spanish who in their turn had ripped it off from the indigenous people of America. The queen and others would eventually receive a 4,000 percent return on their investment in this voyage (117), sufficient for Queen Elizabeth I to knight Sir Francis Drake. William Appleman Williams referred to Drake as a "cost-effective pirate" (1980, 18).

This was not Sir Francis Drake's first successful raid on Spanish assets in the new world. He had surprised a mule train loaded with silver on the Isthmus of Panama in 1572 (Adams 1967, 101), commencing a preoccupation with Panama by speakers of English that would get a boost from Jefferson Davis until ultimately Theodore Roosevelt announced that "I took the Isthmus," or in the summation of his vest pocket intellectual and house mouse friend Brooks Adams, "'. . . Roosevelt simply takes what he wants and denies having asked for it'" (Beringause 1955, 332). "Sir Francis Drake sacked and burned St. Augustine after raiding Spanish strongholds in the Caribbean" (Weir 1983, 7). Drake was almost literally all over the map at the end of the 16th century. "The likes of Drake and Hawkins may have harbored plans for English control of the oceans, but the crown lacked the necessary resources" (Brewer 1989, 11). Sir Francis Drake was doing all he could to teach the rest of the English how those resources were to be acquired.

A knight to the English and worthy of the sobriquet "Sir," Francis Drake was simply thought of as a pirate by the Spanish, a *bucanero*, a prototype of latter-day corporate raiders. The Spanish back got far enough up that they were determined to teach Drake and the English a lesson. They launched an invasion in 1588 across the narrow English Channel, which due to bad weather, poor planning and English dexterity, became known to history as the defeat of the Spanish Armada. It was a harbinger of bigger wars to come as economic and political contention between the speakers of Spanish and English would continue indefinitely in the new world.

It would be a while before the speakers of English could execute Drake's claim to California, or Nova Albion as he christened it, and Robert Millikan of Cal Tech in Irvine could say: "Southern California 'is today, as was England two hundred years ago, the westernmost outpost of Nordic civilization'" (Davis 1990, 56). Davis himself observed of Los Angeles, "Contemporary urban America is more like Victorian England than Walt Whitman's or La Guardia's New York" (227). Various parts of the United States would recapitulate selected aspects of England in the future, but England's future in the 17th century lay in expanding its colonial empire.

The 4,000 percent return on investment that the voyages of Sir Francis Drake represented were more than sufficient to light the fires of capitalistic acquisition in British eyes. "Tocqueville described the English ruling class as one which 'submitted that it might command,' which accepted constraints on its power in order to exercise that power more effectively" (Brewer 1989, 63). While private imperialism played a vital role in such entities as the Hudson's Bay Company and the East India Company, "It is worth remembering that the greatest naval buildups of the sixteenth and seventeenth centuries occurred under the most autocratic regimes — those of Henry VIII and Cromwell" (12). The autocratic state, in other words, developed a primary feedback loop between its military might and the economic activity whose tax burden made only a stab at providing the funds for the heightened military. Public deficit finance, or imaginary money, would provide the lion's share of the funds. Even though Churchill could later insist that the British Empire was spreading democracy, however unintentionally, it is also true as Brewer feels compelled to reiterate that "The heavy-handedness of British Rule increased the farther it extended beyond the metropolis" (XVIII-XIX).

The mixed reviews available for the English character exhibit some internal cohesiveness, leading one to believe that the truth must lie somewhere in the reconcilable contradictions. Brewer himself is English and Tocqueville's opinion from the Franco side is widely cited and available. Spengler could assert that there is no such thing as politically gifted people. "*Political talent in a people* is nothing but confidence in its leading" (1928, 442). While attempting to trivialize what gifts the English have, Spengler goes on to say: "The English as a people are just as unthinking, narrow, and unpractical in political matters as any other nation, but they possess — for all their liking for public debate — *a tradition of confidence.* The difference is simply that the Englishman is the object of a regimen of very old and successful habits, in which he acquiesces because experience has shown him their advantage. From an acquiescence that has the outward appearance of agreement, it is only one step to the conviction that this government depends upon his will, although paradoxically it is the government, for technical reasons of its own, [which] unceasingly hammers the notion into his head" (441). This seems to be a partial adumbration of the Chomskian concept of "manufactured consent."

But it may very well never have occurred to Spengler, whose notion of the English capacity to acquiesce chimes wonderfully with the Tocquevillian touch that they submit in order to command, that it is precisely the English capacity for public debate that imbues them with confidence. Confidence is created by the acceptance and support of peers. Public debate, or the exercise of free speech in the vernacular, a rare commodity in Germany and a very recent arrival in France (compared with its nearly 800-year tradition in England) has inherent capacities to leave peoples bereft of its benefits perpetually befuddled. They look for luck or other unsatisfactory mystical vehicles to carry the freight of their repeated defeats at the hands of the free speaking English. Unable to establish, maintain, or perpetuate free public debate in their own political languages, which would undoubtedly improve their political "talent," they misattribute English success. Free speech is crucial to political success, whether capitalist or socialist, not only at the level of creating the most useful policy, but especially with the workers on the line. Without the freedom to communicate fully without fear of retribution, management can never learn all the things they need to know about operations.

Gifted or not and however far from home they might be, the better to rowdy out the natives, "Regardless of the law, great powers will do as they wish to achieve the objectives of their ruling elites ('the national interest'), restrained only by cost or competing force" (Chomsky 1973, 24). This realpolitik expression of power is what enables an empire to consolidate its position and influence. England was the perfect incubator for a mercantile empire with talent for seafaring, expanding democracy at home and few compunctions about the use of power over other people, those not included in the racial, economic, or political elite.

Remembering our history of the Roman Empire and its effect as a temporarily successful model in the eyes of the British and Americans, consider: "But when, from about Hannibal's time, this world advanced into the state of unlimited plutocracy, the naturally limited mass of precious metals and materially valuable works of art in its sphere of control became hopelessly inadequate to cover needs, and a veritable craving set in for new bodies capable of being used as money. Then it was that men's eyes fell upon the slave, who was another sort of body, but a thing and not a person and capable, therefore, of being thought of as money" (Spengler 1928, 488).

The eyes fell upon the slave, as money, in the Old Testament, in the Roman Empire, in the British Empire, their English speaking North American colonies, and in the United States of America, where, protected by the Constitution, it had become the primary distinguishing feature between the North and the South by the time of the Civil War. A slave as a thing thought of as money rather than a human being in visible or invisible chains was the basis of southern wealth and a prime cause of the Civil War. "Once launched, the slave trade became immensely profitable and laid the foundation, in accumulated wealth, for the subsequent industrial revolution in England" (McWilliams 1951, 317). Although the slave trade may not have been equal in potential return to the Drakian standard of 4,000 percent, there was virtually an unlimited supply of bodies, particularly if those enslaved were natives of the Americas or Africa, or anybody other than white who could not speak English and activate an inchoate right to free speech.

The white supremacist and racist basis of the British Empire was centered on the English speaking peoples gift for greed in a predatory economy. They had themselves been prey to the Romans for 400 years and

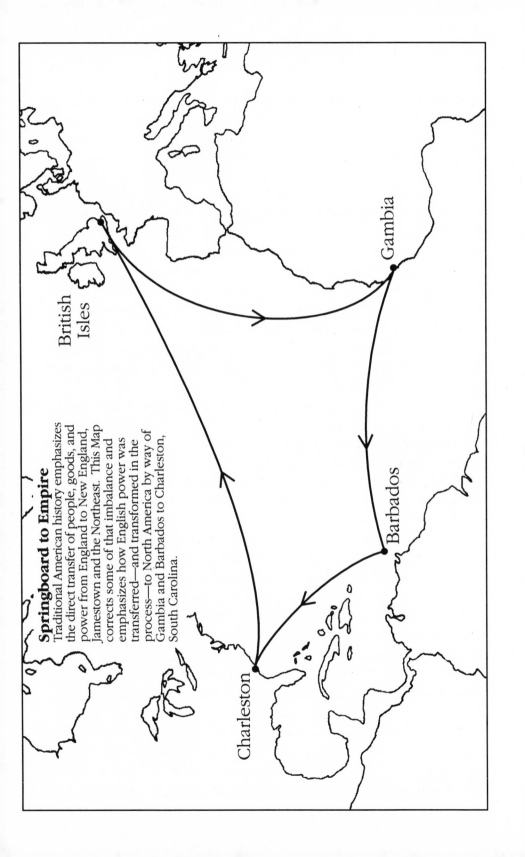

Springboard to Empire
Traditional American history emphasizes the direct transfer of people, goods, and power from England to New England, Jamestown and the Northeast. This Map corrects some of that imbalance and emphasizes how English power was transferred—and transformed in the process—to North America by way of Gambia and Barbados to Charleston, South Carolina.

British Isles

Gambia

Barbados

Charleston

to an assortment of looters and pillagers for another 600 until the Norman invasion of 1066. Once they had gotten on their feet, learned how to speak, (freely for instance), and acquired their sea legs in the form of Sir Francis Drake et al, only "cost or competing force" could be expected to restrain them.

"Not only did the traffic in slaves make for the accumulation of huge capital reserves but it greatly stimulated — it was the basis of — the famous triangular trade, commodities for slaves, slaves for sugar, and sugar for commodities, which largely made it possible for England to become the first great industrial power. The value of the slave-sugar traffic may be indicated by the fact that little Barbados, with 166 square miles of territory, was worth more to British Capitalism than New England, New York, and Pennsylvania combined" (McWilliams 1951, 318).

While the ripple effect through the English culture was entirely salubrious from their point of view as the negative drawbacks from the racist influence were intended to always be kept "off island" where the dirtier part of the work would be completed, the effect on Barbados was something else. Just as was later to occur in South Carolina, the Indians were, "decimated by novel disease, consumed by incessant labor, starved to make way for crop-destroying cattle and hogs of the Spanish — [so] the invaders turned increasingly to Africa for manpower" (Wood 1974, 5). Many of the islands of the Caribbean were made virtually free of natives by the extirpating power of the Spanish by 1627 and the time of the English establishment of their colony on Barbados. It was on Barbados that the American plantation economic system went through its incubation period, Barbados being the halfway house on the slave traffic island between Gambia and Charleston, South Carolina.

The predatory economy the Europeans palmed off on the Americas as the natives were extirpated and slaves from Africa imported, had a negative effect on poor people of their own race. "The European population declined substantially in absolute terms as economies of scale in the production of sugar allowed rich settlers to force poorer Europeans off the land" (8). While it might be expected that to move the economic generator to distant colonies would reduce economic exploitation of labor locally (in England), a predatory economy first and foremost makes room for the potential elite and the hereditary leisure class, even to the point of carving less well endowed members of their own race from a share of the economic pie. This process which Wood attributes to the need for economies of scale is still a force in the world economy as power and money continues to be consolidated in fewer and fewer hands.

There was also the developing predilection of the English, as reported of the Berkeley Hundred and Plantation Virginia of Jamestown, for private gain at public expense. "There was a tacit agreement, however, that no faction would expose the peculations of another as long as the private gain was made at the expense of the public domain" (Dowdey 1957, 110). Peculation, understood to be the deliberate misuse of public money, is an unhappy byproduct of the free speech process which also contains the right to keep your mouth shut and to tell only that part of the truth that is personally beneficial, not to mention outright lying. Inaccurate speech has been elevated by the prevailing gift of greed to the level of a fine art in the economic disintegration of the United States. Free speech is a right; accurate speech is a duty. Since speakers of English bow to the centrifugal force toward independence, they almost uniformly take their rights more seriously than they take their duties. The English speaking treasury will always be empty.

In time John Hay could speak wistfully of "the thousand ties of origin, language, and kindred pursuits binding America and Great Britain... 'There is a sanction like that of religion which binds us to a sort of partnership in the beneficent work of the world'" (Josephson 1940, 85-6). It is pertinent to notice that while Josephson was writing of the English-American ties circa 1900 when Victorian England began to notice her increasing dependence, he was publishing in 1940, just as English pleas for a second American rescue from the Germans were about to reach a successful pitch. That Hay found this relationship to have the sanctity of religion should not go unremarked on, considering that the joint work of the speakers of English is their economic holy war.

But in the mid-17th century there was no United States, no America of the sort Hay was admiring the English binding ties to, only the Atlantic coast of North America beckoning to the British. The phenomenal success of Barbados made them imagine they could transplant it to the mainland. Charles II was restored as King in 1661. British influence would lie in an expanding colonial empire which would provide it with increasing revenues. It would not become the financial center of western Europe for another two hundred years until the 1840s when British economic hegemony was secured (Kennedy 1987, 143).

To get there from here the Lord's Proprietors sought a charter from the restored King Charles II. "Theoretically the investment would be negligible and the profits would be quick" (Wood 1974, 13). The one time learning effect of the Drakian windfall will be difficult to shake. This angle of colonization to North America, following the trade winds of natural assistance rather than the direct Puritan hypocrisy of heading for Boston to establish religious freedom, has never received its proper emphasis. "In large measure, the permanent settlement which emerged at that date [1670] stemmed initially from the English colony of Barbados in the West Indies, unlike the other North American settlements which grew more directly from European sources" (6). The racial composition was also a recapitulation of that prevailing on the West Indian sugar plantations. Within two years, far more than half of the Blacks and nearly half of the whites in Charleston had come from Barbados.

Clearly then South Carolina and Charles Town were to have special relationships not only with the English but with the Caribbean Island of Barbados. South Carolina was going to be different. A deeper look will be taken at those special relationships and the South Carolina difference in chapter 5. The power of the British Empire, fueled by debt and slavery, would sail on into the 18th century, and finally get the upper hand over Napoleon in the 19th where its will was very often the law.

By the 20th century, its gnarled hands, still firmly ahold of the rudder if no longer in complete charge of the treasury, could engineer the carving of oil rich Kuwait out from under the remnants of the Ottoman Empire at the close of WWI. After George Bush and the Americans drove Iraq from Kuwait and tucked it back in to the English speaking Empire, Queen Elizabeth II went to Florida in May of 1991 to knight American field General Norman Schwarzkopf. The ultimate audit has not been conducted so it remains to be seen whether or not the return on the investment of the adventures of Sir Norman Schwarzkopf will equal the 4,000 percent standard return established in the English speaking empire by the adventures of Sir Francis Drake.

5

South Carolina in the Indies: Cultural Generator

The slave trade was so successful in Barbados, the overflow colony of South Carolina was established at Charles Town in 1670, just after the Restoration. William Appleman Williams characterized Shaftesbury's Charter of South Carolina as a "neo-feudal document" (1961, 56), designed to subvert the Spanish Empire. By 1720 there were twice as many African Americans in South Carolina as European Americans. The South Carolina difference was clear from the beginning and would remain apparent for centuries as John Gunther would later record in *Inside the U.S.A.*, South Carolina was "a case apart" (1947, 723). What exactly went into the mix that made the character of the South Carolinians so distinctive and so powerful is a fit subject for full-length books. Condensed to its crucial elements, it is presented here in its salient and essential forms.

When this character was fully formed and very influential by the time of the Civil War, Beringer et al have the following things to say of it. "In the East, on the other hand, South Carolina had as her most distinctive attributes her opposition to democracy. . . Even other Southerners some-times had a difficult time taking South Carolina seriously" (78-9). They went on to record opinions that it was a turbulent and mischief making little spot, too small to be a nation, and too large to be an insane asylum. This assessment by others sympathetic to the case of the South cannot be lightly dismissed, and it will be germane to bear in mind forever, South Carolina's "opposition to democracy."

"The first colonists thought of themselves, interestingly enough, not so much as inhabiting the southern tip of America [a role now usurped by Miami], but the northernmost tip of the West Indies — and West Indian influence is still very distinct in Charleston to this day" (Gunther 1947, 723). It was made clear early on that "No plantation. . . could be worked without a system of slave labor" (Dowdey 1957, 316). It cannot be over emphasized, since many authorities repeat it in one form or another, that "The South Carolina settlement had been little more than the dependent servant of an island master — in short, the colony of a colony" (Wood

1974, 34). The effect of this reliance for its cultural bearings on Barbados created a hermetic feedback loop. "Carolina's reliance upon Barbados for what slaves its white colonist could afford served to strengthen further the existing ties to the sugar island, and these bonds — in a circular fashion — helped predispose would-be planters in the mainland colony to black labor" (46). The most important leg of the three-way not quite isosceles triangular trade was firmly planted in Charles Town, (spelled all three ways, Charles Town, Charlestown, and eventually Charleston, as time and linguistic efficiency condensed it).

Even though Shakespeare's plays were performed in colonial Charles Town, Robert Rosen chose to emphasize, in his *A Short History of Charleston*, the classic nature of the case. "It is the tragic and ironic aspects of Charleston's history that give it such power. It resembles the classic Greek tragedy — " (1982, 6). He further characterized it as the fourth largest and most beautiful city in colonial America, with six times the trade of other American ports. He repeats what is no longer news that "Charles Town was an outpost of Barbados, a colony of a colony. . ." (14). Rosen also noted in somewhat religious terms that ". . . its unspoken mission was to build a miniature aristocratic London in the midst of a recreated English country-side inhabited by a landed gentry" (10). Here then was to be London in the new world, even though the Proprietors named it Charles Town after the restored King. It was the English speaking empire moving sideways recapitulating itself with the economic model of slavery.

"Thus, legend, chance, experience, and promotionalism came together, and for a moment at least it appeared that Carolina resembled our earthly birthplace" (Weir 1983, 34). These four elements of the illusion of paradise were woven into reality in South Carolina. The investors took their successful experience in Barbados, raised the expectations of like-minded speculators still in England, utilized the legend of renewal in "the fountain of youth" mythology, and put it all in place in the one area just far enough south to sustain the growing of rice and sugar. "South Carolina's governing class appeared to a European visitor as still thinking and acting 'precisely as do the nobility in other countries'" (Weir 1983, xiii), with whites enjoying the highest standard of living in North America.

Weir goes on to note that "If South Carolina had not become utopia, it was becoming distinctly more English" (102), and being provincial, "this elite patterned its behavior on English models in as many areas of life as possible" (130). The economic model is the one that matters the most. "South Carolinians became the most heavily committed to slavery of all North Americans" (170). It was in this Carolina in the West Indies that more African Americans entered North America through colonial Charles Town than any other slave marketplace.

It is necessary to move beyond historians however, to economists, sociologists and psychologists, to get the proper bearings on what slavery means and meant to South Carolinians. Ransom and Sutch, in *One Kind of Freedom*, state: "This was a firmly entrenched, universally held, and passionately defended belief in the inherent inferiority of the black race" (1977, 22). "White opposition to both education and landownership reflected a strong undercurrent of fear" (23). Fear and passion in the defense of notions of inferiority drive the men who feel those emotions to overrate their own abilities.

"During the predatory culture labour comes to be associated in men's habits of thought with weakness and subjection to a master. It is therefore a mark of inferiority, and therefore comes to be accounted unworthy of man in his best estate. By virtue of this tradition labour is felt to be debasing, and this tradition has never died out," wrote Thorstein Veblen in his 1899 classic *The Theory of the Leisure Class* (1931, 36). In the development of an elite aristocracy, Veblen goes on to say "At this stage wealth consists chiefly of slaves. . . Conspicuous abstention from labour therefore becomes the conventional mark of superior pecuniary achievement and the conventional index of reputability" (38). The hereditary leisure class in South Carolina became the leisure class by reinforcing the institution of slavery which relegated the labor to the blacks they both feared and hated. Veblen was also able to state in this same context that "Women and other slaves are highly valued. . ."(53). Feminists and other democratic sympathizers will find additional economic sense here and psychological sense in the frequently remarked upon, "The circumference of a pedestal was already beginning to circumscribe the sphere of white women in eighteenth century South Carolina" (Weir 1974, 231).

While summing up the information presented thus far, the picture of South Carolina begins to clarify. It was the colony of the English colony of Barbados, committed to slavery as they had inherited it from the English, opposed to democracy, and further committed to acting as much like aristocratic Englishmen as their circumstances would permit. Theodore

Roosevelt Jr. may be laughing up his sleeve when he says in his book *American Imperialism*, "In the Southeast they are pictured as the cream of the British aristocracy, which they certainly were not" (1970, 35).

It was likely a failure of talent rather than desire, for what they may have lacked in style, they made up in force. Veblen suggests that they recall for him the barbarian stages of industrial development (326) and their "Masterful aggression, and the correlative massiveness, together with a ruthlessly consistent sense of status, would still count among the most splendid traits of the class. These have remained in our traditions as the typical 'aristocratic virtues'" (236). Putting 'aristocratic virtues' in quotes must mean that although Veblen acknowledges it to be the case, he personally must have some doubts about its believability. Those doubts take the following form. "Except for the fear of offending that chauvinistic patriotism which is so characteristic a feature of the predatory culture. . . the case of the American colonies might be cited as an example of such a reversion on an unusually large scale" (197). Fear of giving offense to "chauvinistic patriotism," running at fever pitch in 1899 when Veblen first published *The Theory of the Leisure Class*, may have been tempering his view. The truth of their ruthless sense of status makes them simple to offend. It is taken as a religious affront to a belief system.

Although the character of the South Carolinians, as thus far revealed, may seem to some to be in need of an upgrading, the South Carolinians themselves held on to it, and have continued holding on to it, because it works. "South Carolina's gentry had come to possess a passionate devotion to the principle of personal independence" (Weir 1983, xiv). The yield to this behavior, although not quite Drakian in scope was significant as by 1771, nine of the ten richest (white) men in the colonies lived in or near Charles Town (214). During the late colonial period more South Carolinians than students from all the other colonies combined, studied in England (251). "English Standards governed the behavior of Carolinians. They were, others believed, 'more attached to the Mother Country' than residents of the northern colonies" (238).

The late colonial period, it needs to be kept in mind, was the period when the British Empire was gradually establishing hegemony over the French, soon to be led by Napoleon, never mind that the English public debt went up fifteen-fold between 1688 and the end of the American Revolution (Brewer 1989, 114). Debt increases government power, even as it saps its strength. "The propensity of early settlers to think of South Carolina as but a means to the end of returning 'home' to England in style contributed to the tendency to see land as just another commodity. . ." (Weir 1983, 230). We will meet up with more of this plantation mentality, which sees the land as something to use up rather than to live on, as the English speaking civilization sweeps west to California and beyond. Meanwhile, "though they still figuratively spoke of England as 'home,' they called South Carolina 'my country,' and out of their love for both proceeded to make the one as much like the other as they possibly could" (264).

During this period of the rise of South Carolina to be the jewel of the English colonies in America, by 1730 blacks outnumbered whites by two to one (123). This ratio held nearly up to the Revolutionary War when the population of South Carolina showed in 1775, 100,000 Blacks and 60,000 Whites (Klingberg 1975, 1). Barely one percent of the black population enjoyed free status (Wood 1974, 103). It is worth remembering that in 1704 "An Act for Raising and Enlisting such Slaves as shall be thought serviceable to this Province in Time of Alarms" (125) was passed and later revised in 1708. The Black role in the South Carolina military was significant until 1739 when it came to a screeching halt. "The Stono Rebellion was the largest slave revolt to occur anywhere on the mainland during the colonial period" (Weir 1983, 194). With most of the slaves there, it is only predictable that the largest slave revolt would occur in South Carolina. Even though whites tended to exaggerate the degree to which they were outnumbered in the colony and the entire colony was ordered under arms, "The *South Carolina Gazette* refrained from mentioning the Stono incident, which occurred within twenty miles of Charlestown" (Wood 1974, 298). This could have very well been the beginning of media manipulation of war and other unpleasant news in North America.

It was not the beginning of full scale war, yet it contributed to the creation of the idea that there is a "domestic enemy" that the aristocracy needs to be protected from. Hitherto the White South Carolinians had used the Blacks to help defend themselves against the Indians. "The Yemassee War of 1716 stands with King Phillip's War as one of the bloodiest and most costly of the colonial Indian wars. In proportion to the size of the populations involved, the loss of 400 whites in South Carolina represented a casualty rate almost twice that of Massachusetts in the earlier war" (Weir 1983, 85). Under siege from the elements, the Indians, and their own Black slaves, the South Carolinians took to protecting their projections of hostility by codifying their paranoia. This hysterical apprehensiveness about security, an occupational hazard in South Carolina, would later motivate many South Carolinians, including Andrew Jackson whose capture of Florida was intended to secure the perimeter.

The South Carolina colonial legislature was the first to adopt specific English statutes to make crimes against property capital offenses. Property here, it is worth recalling, means slaves primarily. They did not care for the lackadaisical way the British conducted the later war against the Cherokees (275). But by the time of the French and Indian War, as of 1757, "South Carolinians raised nearly five times as much in the annual revenue bill as had been customary in peacetime, and before the war was over, their tax per adult, white male was the highest of any colony" (288). Adult white males controlled virtually all of the assets North or South. In the South, where the assets were primarily slaves, they were especially eager to contribute to war. Immediately after that war, they became leaders in calling for the repeal of the Townshend Duties and other, from their point of view, unfairly legislated taxes on American colonists. They made March 18, 1766, the day the Stamp Act was repealed, a national holiday (299).

Note also that their assembly "did give its delegates to the Continental Congress power to commit South Carolinians to whatever the colonies jointly decided" (314). This could be a source for the belief that South Carolina had in fact joined a union, of the "more perfect union" kind that the Constitution established and which South Carolina later "dissolved" as it seceded. The initial goal of the South Carolinians "was acceptable terms of reconciliation with Britain, not independence" (327), for clearly they still considered themselves as English as the English. When push came to shoot however, "Though the ties of sentiment and economic interest helped to bind South Carolinians to the empire, other considerations prevailed" (331).

After the Revolutionary War, during which South Carolina lost more men than any other colony (Rosen 1982, 55), reinforcing its developing military tradition, the population tripled by 1788 while the re-establishment of pre-war commercial patterns put them deep in debt to their former enemies and friends, the English (Weir 1983, 337). Weir speaks also of their "extraordinarily volatile heritage" (345), their "tendency toward extremism" (344), and their "pervasive conservatism that retarded change" (341). This is not the description of a flexible group of cooperators.

"Historian George Rogers has observed, 'the same elite guided the destinies of the state from the Revolution to the Civil War'" (341). This was the same elite whose primary economic benefit and chief social problem came from "Slavery as the English adopted it" (Rosen 1982, 64) and bequeathed it to them.

As we approach the period between the Revolution and the Civil War, it is fair to ask why all this attention on South Carolina, at the relative expense of other southern colonies and states. First and foremost, it is its special relationship with England and the predominance of slavery within its borders that give it the look and feel of a leader. Farther toward the north, the Virginian reputation is toward gentility and leadership in ideas, rather than in war and economics, even though there also, English Clergy paralleled British military mistakes by refusing to accept differences caused by local conditions (Dowdey 1957, 176). The presidents of the Virginia Dynasty period kept the early republic together. *How the South Finally Won the Civil War* is partly the story of how it came apart. South of South Carolina, Georgia, itself unfounded as a bastion of convicts and hookers until 1733, 63 years and several generations *post* the founding of South Carolina, was later in exerting its leadership and in contrary directions. Florida was still under Spanish control until Andrew Jackson took it in 1819. The cultural impellers laid down in New England and the mid-Atlantic states, together with the effects of the Virginia Dynasty, are the received traditional American history. This challenge to the conventional wisdom, which treats South Carolina and the Confederacy as the minority aberration, is long overdue. The power of the deep South is widely and effectively diffused. South Carolina is the generator of southern, later Confederate, and ultimately national, leadership.

South Carolina was not the only gift from the West Indies to the United States. "[Alexander] Hamilton was bound by few of the emotional attachments and sectional prejudices that hampered the native-born American. An Anglo-French West Indian by birth and early training, he was able to survey American policy with the imperialistic outlook of an Englishman" (Bourgin 1989, 68). Henry Kissinger comes in the Hamiltonian model of a moderately effective arrogant foreigner with condescending views. Hamilton brought his imperialistic outlook to the discussions over the constitution and the fear that the chief executive would be too weak and succumb to Congress. "The Pinckney and Hamilton plans favored a single and powerful executive. . . . Pinckney gave the president a qualified legislative veto, and described in detail the executive's other powers, similar in content and form to those the president now enjoys" (55).

Charles Pinckney of South Carolina, the unsuccessful Federalist candidate for President in 1804 and 1808 during the heyday of the Virginian Dynasty of Jefferson and Madison, also gave the new Union and its Constitution the three-fifths formula for how slaves should be counted for purposes of allocating seats in the House of Representatives. Pinckney further delivered to the Constitution "The concept of the President as commander in chief" (59). Pinckney shared a belief in this concept of executive military power with John C. Calhoun, who in his *A Disquisition on Government* said: "From the nature of popular governments, the control of its powers is vested in the many; while military power, to be efficient, must be vested in a single individual" ([1850] 1948, 44). The President of the United States, whoever it might be, clearly owes his overweening military power, to this concept from South Carolina.

Overweening military power in the early 19th century belonged to the British who, unable to get used to the fact that they had lost the Revolutionary War, grew fond of impressing American sailors into their navy. "Nowhere was the public temper at higher pitch [1807] than in Abbeville, South Carolina" (Coit 1950, 46), Calhoun's home town. This and other English harassments would lead to the War of 1812. Charlestonians enthusiastically prepared for the War of 1812. The roll call of the young War Hawks of the Second American Revolution, on their way to Senator Henry Clay's house to get their marching orders, goes like this: "William Wyatt Bibb of Georgia, Peter Buell Porter of western New York, Langdon Cheves of South Carolina, Felix Grundy of Tennessee, George Poindexter of Natchez, Mississippi, William Lowndes of South Carolina, Samuel McKee of Kentucky, and John Caldwell Calhoun of South Carolina" (69). All from the slaveholding South save one New Yorker and *three* from South Carolina. The South has a predisposition to war.

"On November 29, 1811, the Foreign Relations Committee Report, largely although not entirely the work of Calhoun, sounded the first official note of war" (73). From the War of 1812 to the Compromise of 1850, the significant political history of South Carolina is also the story of the life, times, and ideas of John Caldwell Calhoun. He is so central to American history and the methodology of *How the South Finally Won the Civil War*, that the entire next chapter has been reserved for a more detailed presentation of the indelible influence of Calhoun. While we get on with some other significant and some more modern contributions of South Carolina to American political culture, we will leave Calhoun resting temporarily where he in fact is resting permanently, at or near the apex of this civilization. "The citizens of Charleston had appealed to his family that 'the remains of him we loved so well be permitted to repose among us,' there in the Westminster Abbey of the South" (516).

The United States and especially the South, as therein reported of the "Westminster Abbey," will never quite be free of England and things English. In the late antebellum period three-fourths of American cotton went to Great Britain and reflected 70 percent of their imports, according to Gavin Wright in *The Political Economy of the Cotton South* (1978, 91). Wright also reports that "Our characterization of the economics of slavery fits well with Immanuel Wallerstein's assertion that the function of slavery was to facilitate the flow of commerce in the capitalist world economy" (88). Since slavery provided an elastic supply of labor, it reinforced the perceived need of the South to acquire more territory for its indefinite expansion (55). These perceptions describe a virtually insatiable economic and ultimately political feedback loop.

The tremendous wealth of the slave holding class has been referred to before but it will bear repeating. "The average slaveowner was more than five times as wealthy as the average Northerner, more than ten times as wealthy as the average nonslaveholding Southern farmer" (33). Not only was slaveholder wealth growing rapidly, it represented the wherewithal in economic terms, of the power to take risks that could leave poorer folk destitute. "In a word, wealth was a basic defining characteristic of social class" (37). Beard and Beard (322) have already reminded us, via Seward, that 350,000 people in the slaveholding class controlled the political destiny of the South. The Civil War was a revolution of the rich, white slaveholding minority.

In John L. Thomas' edition of essays on Calhoun, Richard N. Current observes: "The central theme of Southern history has remained the same, but this theme is not what the older school of Southern historians said it was — the maintenance of white supremacy. It is the maintenance of the supremacy of *some* white men, and as a means to this end the fiction of a general white supremacy has been extremely useful" (1968, 152). The italics on *some* originated with Current. It requires no great leap of faith to acknowledge that sufficient proof has been presented that this supremacy of the white, wealthy slaveholding minority, a British Empire import from Barbados, had its American origination in South Carolina.

Also strongly propelled along by South Carolina was the need to extend their selective supremacy: "The following passage from the *Charleston* (S.C.) *Courier* avows it: 'Every battle fought in Mexico, and every dollar spent there, but insures the acquisition of territory which must widen the field of Southern enterprise and power in the future. And the final result will be to readjust the balance of power in the confederacy (sic), so as to give us control over the operations of government in all time to come'" (Hofstadter 1958, 344). This prophetic passage was published in 1847, quite before what most think of as the Confederacy came to be an operating concept, and while the war with Mexico to make Texas safe for slavery was in full swing.

Texas, firmly in the union as a result of the Mexican War, "was essentially no different from the South" (Fehrenbach 1968, 281), with 90 percent of its immigration coming from the old South (279). The long branch of the Texas reach goes clear back across the South. "The American planter was a recognizable reflection of his British cousin, in a completely rural atmosphere without the civilizing effect of London" (313). That feels like a fair characterization of rich Texans as uncivilized English aristocrats. The British can radiate the appearance of civility in London because the slaves that were making it the financial capitol of the world were far away in the colonies. This esthetic and economic distance was an advantage disallowed in South Carolina and Texas where the slaves were underfoot and on the literal doorstep. Many years before, Bonham, the weary lawyer and fellow South Carolinian of Buck Travis, delivered his own famous last words: "Buck Travis deserves to know the answer to his appeals" (211), before he rejoined him at the Alamo.

"Remember the Alamo" became the war cry of the Texans at the battle of San Jacinto. Sixty years later, "Remember the Maine" would become the battle cry on the floor of the United States Senate prior to the Spanish American War. "Some populists and agrarian Democrats had begun calling for war as soon as the *Maine* sank, among them Senator Marion Butler of South Carolina. . ." (May 1961, 145). If there is to be a war, "remember" is the operating verb here, South Carolinians will be leading Americans to it.

The Spanish American War had a predictable byproduct for South Carolina. "Tillman, a member of the naval committee, joined in the campaign, and by 1901 the most important economic decision in the modern history of Charleston was made. The Navy Yard came to Charleston" (Rosen 1982, 128). The military tends to put its money where its support is, and when the subject of the appropriateness of the yard going to Charleston came up, "Questioned, he [McKinley] stated that the federal patronage of South Carolina had been parceled out since ratification" (Glad 1968, 70).

Charleston was to become the leader of the preservation movement in the United States (Rosen 1982, 141), precisely because preservation is static and another word for reversion, to economic predation and barbarism. Once the naval yard came to Charleston, L. Mendel Rivers would not be far behind. He was the Congressman from the first Congressional District of South Carolina for 30 years and, due to the seniority system used to perfection by the South, became the chairman of the powerful House Armed Services Committee after World War II which continued funneling military money toward South Carolina.

Peace has always been a problem for people who make a righteous living making war and L. Mendel Rivers was no exception. He introduced a resolution to brand the free speeches of Henry Wallace a "Grave Disservice" (MacDougall 1965, 137) during the beginning of the Cold War. Wallace raised the issue of peace and was called a saboteur by Vandenberg and a crypto-communist by Churchill. "The most violent incident of the Progressive party campaign in 1948 was the stabbing to death, on May 7, of Robert W. New Jr., 28. He was a Charleston, S.C. port agent for the National Maritime Union, and Chairman of the local Wallace Committee" (407). Here we see some of that South Carolinian opposition to democracy that Beringer et al ascribed to it. Wallace got only 189 votes in all of South Carolina. "The Rev. Archie Ware, 66, voted on Aug. 10, in the Democratic primary at Calhoun Falls in Abbeville County. He was clubbed, stabbed, and left for dead" (737).

Left for dead at the end of the Civil War, South Carolina, the only state of the Confederacy that didn't send any unionists to fight for the north, was coming back into its own by World War II. John Nance Garner from Texas, Vice President to Roosevelt from 1933-1941, felt bitterly betrayed by Roosevelt's violation of the two term convention. Southern Democrats lined up with the big city bosses to knock Garner's replacement, the liberal Vice

President Henry Wallace, off the ticket in 1944. They settled on the unknown Truman, anointed as a compromise by Sam Rayburn of Texas, but their first preference was Senator James Byrnes of South Carolina.

Byrnes became Truman's Secretary of State. When he was questioned of the need to drop atomic bombs on the Japanese, Norman Cousins in his *The Pathology of Power* quotes Byrnes as follows: "'We wanted to get through the Japanese phase of the war before the Russians came in'" (1987, 42). Byrnes was already grooming a new enemy, necessary to maintain a military budget and the siege mentality.

In an interesting inversion on the British model of becoming more barbarous the farther they get from London, Americans frequently try to establish their ideal values far from home, while what goes on at home is far from the ideal. There was the Taxicab Riot in Greenville, South Carolina in 1947 (McWilliams 1951, 35). "Even before the Columbia riot, Isaac Woodard Jr., a Negro veteran, was removed from a bus in South Carolina and, in the course of a merciless beating, permanently blinded" (30). John Gunther also recites the sad story of the beating and blinding of Isaac Woodard, an honorably discharged veteran of World War II. There was a subsequent half-hour district court acquittal of the police officer, Lynwood E. Shull, who was accused of the crime. "This whole saga took place in the home state of former Secretary of State James F. Byrnes, during a year in which Mr. Byrnes was active in the extreme pleading for justice, democratic procedures, and fair play in regard to Bulgarian elections and the frontiers of Trieste" (1947, 686).

It is child's play to unmask hypocrites of empire in a global environment. "The starting point is to reconstruct the white supremacist genealogy of its essential infrastructure; the *homeowner's association*" (Davis 1990, 160). Davis was of course reconstructing infrastructure in southern California, the object of many desires including those of the South and the Confederacy. One influential southern Californian chose to reconstruct the infrastructure differently. "Welch, who was raised as a pious fundamentalist Baptist in North Carolina, chose to name his organization after a young fundamentalist Baptist preacher from Macon, Georgia, who was killed by the Chinese Communists" (Hofstadter 1965, 74). The John Birch Society grew out of southern religious fundamentalist preoccupations.

No one benefited more from this religious revival than Senator Barry Goldwater of Arizona, viz. "At a Republican leadership conference in

Charleston, South Carolina. . . strong preference for Goldwater" (Schlesinger 1971, 471). It was only an accident of geography that "Goldwater was nominated on the first ballot when the roll call reached South Carolina" (477), but it was fundamental geography that made the second plank of the Goldwater campaign platform "crime in the cities" (477). This was the beginning of the use of the code word for the "domestic enemy" problem that came ashore in South Carolina and won't go away. It is the critical racist basis of recent Republican success.

Goldwater's nominally unsuccessful campaign will be discussed in detail later. The critical question now is, "How did South Carolina become a bastion of Republican power politics?" We know it received its contemporary expression in Lee Atwater, late chairman of the Republican National Committee, who died of a brain tumor on March 29, 1991. With living and dying proof, it is not necessary to imagine someone so hateful that his own brain said that's enough. "This drawling son of South Carolina said, 'People in the South love someone who can kick somebody's ass. And the optimum defining-event situation is when somebody else throws the first punch. That's an American tradition; it's a southern tradition. That's why we like John Wayne so much'" (Germond and Witcover 1989, 126). Atwater recognized the importance of the South early in the Bush campaign and delivered all 37 delegates and 48 percent of the popular vote to Bush a week before super Tuesday in 1988 (151). On super Tuesday proper, Bush carried virtually the entire South, an amusing backfire on the Democratic plan to give the South its proper voice in American politics.

The proper southern voice in American politics is now Republican. Nothing so epitomizes the southern shift from Democrat to Republican as the career of Strom Thurmond of South Carolina. The then Democratic Governor Thurmond in 1947 tried to inveigle Eisenhower to become the Democratic standard bearer in 1948. Eisenhower demurred and took himself out of the race. Thurmond revolted, as South Carolinians are apt to do in their inimicable reversionary pattern when they don't get their own way. Thurmond's Dixiecrats or the State Rights party carried four states, Mississippi, Louisiana, Alabama, and South Carolina, and almost succeeded in throwing the election into the House of Representatives where Thurmond hoped a deal for Eisenhower could be cut.

Party affiliation is worth about one symbolic percent of the arguments in American power politics and by the Nixon era, Thurmond displayed some flexibility and switched allegiance to the Republicans. Only the name had changed; the politics remained reactionary. Nixon political commercials "had been provided by the Thurmond Speaks Committee of South Carolina" (McGinnis 1969, 124). Goldwater had carried the South and shown Thurmond the light so he helped Nixon, who got far more of the White vote in the South than did Eisenhower, still running in the 1950s on the as yet unpalatable Republican label.

As proof that nothing changes but the labels, NBC broadcast in the summer of 1991 on their "Expose" series, a report on labor conditions in Edgefield County, South Carolina. They showed footage of Senator Strom Thurmond riding on horseback in the Peach Day celebration parade. Edgefield County produces more peaches than the entire state of Georgia. NBC made allegations that the itinerant workers are controlled through the distribution of free crack cocaine. They showed a young black man who had just fled the fields and who said: "It is just like modern day slavery, except that you don't have a white man looking down on you. You have another black man looking down over your shoulder. It is like a black Klu Klux Klan" (NBC 1991). NBC also showed footage of Senator Thurmond hypocritically caviling about the evils of cocaine on the floor of the Senate. Senator Thurmond told NBC he didn't have the time to talk to them about conditions in Edgefield County.

The conditions for agricultural labor have changed little over the centuries since South Carolina's Barbadan beginnings. The slave and slave-like conditions are the basis of the wealth of the white aristocracy. The white aristocracy will part with its capital, slave or cash, only under penalty of superior force and death. From its English origination through its Barbadan incubation and on to its South Carolinian generation, the racist economic basis of the empire continues.

The language South Carolinians used to "dissolve" the union will bear repeating. ". . . the State of South Carolina has resumed her position among the nations of the world, as a separate and independent state, with full power to . . ." (Hofstadter 1958, 389). The case apart for South Carolina is truly immense and quick on the draw. "South Carolina put secession in motion a week after the election. The nursery of nullification was the sire of secession" (Fehrenbach 1968, 343).

South Carolina took the long reach out to become an independent nation, yet the Civil War put her back in the putative nation of the United

States. Her history and compelling ideas are the pituitary gland of the American political system. Quite simply, they control it. An Associated Press wire photo of George Bush and a cheering crowd on Monday, March 18, 1991, was taken at Shaw Airforce Base as he visited the namesake city of Ft. Sumter where the Civil War began. "Bush returned to the White House Sunday evening from Bermuda after stopping in Sumter, South Carolina, to attend his first homecoming for Desert Storm troops. He told a cheering crowd in Sumter that as a result of the war, 'No one doubts us any more.'"

Part II

Important Confederate People and Places

"Shine, Perishing Republic. . . heavily thickening to empire"

Robison Jeffers

6

John C. Calhoun: Godfather of the Confederate Empire

"He was the South incarnate," reports John C. Calhoun's biographer, Margaret L. Coit (1950, 517), and the truth of her assessment and others will be briefly ascertained and verified as Calhoun's character and indelible contribution to the Confederate Empire of North America are made too clear to miss. Born during the Revolutionary War in Abbeville, part of the upland country of South Carolina, in 1782 to a family of Scotch-Irish patriots, his talent took him through Yale and into the House of Representatives. Knowing how much he hated the British, Henry Clay of Kentucky was instrumental in Calhoun's appointment to the House Foreign Relations Committee, where he soon became the chairman.

The American love/hate relationship with the British was still in its hate phase, an afterglow of the passion for fighting stirred up in the United States by the recent Revolutionary War. That the fever pitch of anger over impressment reached its apex in Calhoun's home town of Abbeville has already been entered into the narrative, so too his leadership of the War Hawks and this second American Revolution from his position in the House. His unstinting nationalist support for President Madison during the War of 1812 (Thomas 1968, x) led directly to his eight-year tenure as Secretary of the War Department in the administration of James Monroe.

We will soon see in Calhoun's own writing how his philosophy of government was influenced in his early career by the West Indian Hamilton who "accepted the twin principles of class domination and exploitation as inevitable, and with them, the maxim that political power rests on the control of property" (Bourgin 1989, 69). The Constitution of the United States has frequently been described as an instrument for the control of property. This description was most certainly true prior to the adoption of the Bill of Rights, a contrarian document that attempts to set limits on what the government can do to the people. "J. Allen Smith regarded the replacement of the Articles [of Confederation] as a kind of capitalist conspiracy to establish the wealthy in control" (30). Conspiracy or not, Hamilton's aristocratic hand, guided by belief in class domination and exploitation based on property, way beyond his duel to the death with Aaron Burr, continued to guide the United States and John C. Calhoun.

"That government policy always benefited some and sometimes penalized others was obvious" (70) Bourgin goes on to report. The result being that Hamilton "therefore chose as his allies men of personality and fluid capital, whose relative position he correspondingly improved" (70). The romance of democracy is wrecked upon the shoals of realpolitik. What romance one might extricate from Hamilton and Calhoun is a love affair with the manipulation of money.

"The necessary result, then, of the unequal fiscal action of the government is, to divide the community into two great classes; one consisting of those who, in reality, pay the taxes, and of course, bear exclusively the burden of supporting the government; and the other, of those who are the recipients of their proceeds, through disbursements, and who are in fact, supported by the government; or in fewer words, to divide it into tax-payers and tax-consumers" (Calhoun [1850] 1948, 21). We are relieved to recognize the proprioception of Calhoun's summing up in fewer words the meticulous progress of his thought, even as, depending on which of the two great classes we might fall in, we might be outraged or bemused to find ourselves as either tax payers or tax consumers. Whatever use we might make of Calhoun's argument based on class, few writers can state the effects of governmental transfer of money any more clearly. The direct, contemporary transfer of income is but one obvious display of this principle.

Calhoun was practicing his philosophy long before he took the trouble to write it down for the edification of others. "After the War of 1812, when public sentiment seemed to be crystallizing in favor of federal participation in road and canal improvements, Calhoun's national bank bonus bill was vetoed by President Madison" (Bourgin 1989, 164). While we might see in this some measure of the thanks he got for supporting Madison so diligently during the war, it can also be seen as "the first presidential veto of an act of Congress exercised in defense of states' rights" (156). Since Calhoun was later to become *the* champion of state rights, we have to recognize in his wish to earmark bonuses and dividends from the bank's proceeds to internal improvements, an early division of the public into tax payers and consumers. The transparency of the scheme, as well as its modern tone, to create development by taxing the already developed, to redirect wealth toward the South and the West, is obvious and would in modified forms be both a bone of contention and an operating principle in the opening up of the West.

Calhoun was an ardent nationalist in these early days and the sincerity of his desire to connect the Atlantic seaboard with the interior is beyond question. He was "The most outstanding protagonist for internal improvements. . . [and] In the absence of an amendment, he emphasized the military advantages of roads and canals and particularly of military roads" (157). The recognizable similarity to the modern era's "National Highway Defense Act of 1951" will demonstrate the necessary military rationale behind the internal improvements that created the freeway system, the attendant and intended boon to the highway construction business, the oil and rubber business, and the manufacturers of automobiles. It was no boon to existing public mass transit, nor to the railroads who had received their largess long before, in the land grants, a form of national socialism. The "National Highway Defense Acts" were part of a conscious industrial policy that was intended to boost domestic consumerism of wasting assets and export the surplus production to colonies and other consumers. Thus does the government selectively cultivate and instill economic power in its friends, the tax consumers.

Even though "Calhoun emphasized the military usefulness of this program, he also comprehended that military power alone was too narrow a constitutional base on which to sustain such a broad program" (158). Unless of course, the ultimate if unstated goal, was to militarize the entire society. "He believed strongly that the Department of War should be made the official agency for the planning and executing of the great improvements program, and he even suggested that soldiers be employed (with an appropriate raise of pay) in aiding the construction of these projects" (158). It is to be expected that a Secretary of War in a developing bureaucracy would attempt to enlarge his power.

Calhoun's leadership was effective enough that he ran for vice president in 1824 on the democratic ticket with Andrew Jackson and wound up as vice president to the Federalist John Quincy Adams anyway, despite Jackson's loss of the presidency. By 1828 he had been elected vice president again, this time with Jackson as president. Philip Drucker has pointed out, in his essay discussing Calhoun's pluralism, that "An old saying has it that this country lives simultaneously in a world of Jeffersonian beliefs and in one of

Hamiltonian realities. Out of these two, Calhoun's concept of 'the rule of the concurrent majority' alone can make one viable whole" (Thomas 1968, 149).

The concurrent majority is a system of ideas that occurred to Calhoun as a result of the somewhat peaceful resolution of the balance of power problem in South Carolina. These ingenious compromises gave the coastal area around Charleston, with its wealthy plantation owners in the numerical minority, control of the state senate. The practical effect of the use of the concept of Concurrent Majority is that the rich will get their own way regardless of how few of them there are. The hills and uplands, where most of the voters lived, gained control of the house, although voting was still restricted to white males with property. It was an attempt to recognize that money and political power are not necessarily synonymous. "It was a device for securing justice for all minority economic groups within a population" (Coit 1950, 55). To believe this and follow Calhoun's line of thinking, it is necessary to believe that women and white men without money are part of somebody else's economic group, having no political or economic power of their own. Democracy must not be permitted to get out of hand. It is also necessary to keep in mind that African Americans were not thought of as an economic group in the population at this time; they were the capital of the coastal elite.

Calhoun was thinking of other minorities and he could confidently announce "Ours, sir, is the Government of a white race" (May 1973, 15). When asked by Webster what became of the principles upon which the republic was founded, Calhoun replied: "The principles you avow are just, but in the South, they are always understood as applying only to the white race" (Coit 1950, 292). Calhoun was frequently courageous in defense of the wealthy white minority.

The political marriage of convenience with Andrew Jackson, himself the personification of the shift of power to the South and West away from the Virginia Dynasty and the Adams family, ended with the Nullification Crisis of 1832. Calhoun resigned the vice presidency, the first ever to do so, and returned to the Senate from South Carolina. "Charleston had become an armed camp" (237) in 1832 as Coit reports it and South Carolina was provocatively close to exercising one of its famous walks when it doesn't get its own way. Jackson, shrewd in the use of power, addressed them in this manner: "Fellow-citizens of my native state" (238), thus foreshadowing the language of Lincoln's first inaugural and tactics in the next generation. Jackson, born in South Carolina, is yet another claim to fame of South Carolinian control of American government apparatus. He kept his dispute with Calhoun strictly in-house.

John Randolph of Virginia "knew that in Jackson's mind burned the obsession that Calhoun was the moving spirit of all disorder in the South and should be held accountable for whatever might occur there" (241). Jackson was not bluffing on his promise to use force to keep the union together and lacking support elsewhere in the South, South Carolina stayed in the Union temporarily. Calhoun's presidential ambitions in the Democratic party went by the wayside in his dispute with Jackson and tempered his hitherto ardent nationalism with a growing fondness for state rights as it stimulated his propensity to reversion. The most massive case of unrequited presidential fever in American history, Calhoun tilted more heavily toward the South and sectionalism as he became the peerless champion of the white slaveholding minority. Hofstadter sums him up very well, ". . . at heart he remained a Unionist as well as a Southerner. What he wanted was not for the South to leave the Union, but to dominate it" (Hofstadter 1959, 70).

That the United States ultimately got what Calhoun wanted for it is a theme of this chapter and of the entire book. In fact the United States had been getting what Calhoun wanted right along. Jefferson often daydreamed of the voluntary creation of an independent republic on the Pacific coast, due primarily to the distance, in which daydream he was echoed by Webster and even in the early expansionist plans of Thomas Hart Benton of Missouri. Not so Calhoun: "'Passion for aggrandizement was the law paramount of man in society, and that there was no example in history of the disruption of a nation from itself by voluntary separation'" (Schlesinger 1986, 150). Calhoun would go to his grave without knowing what a great example of this principle the Civil War would become.

Calhoun has the additional advantage, for an influential philosopher, of his relative obscurity. No one has yet successfully disputed the superior nature of Calhoun's head, nor the second rate nature of the politicians who occupied the presidency between the administrations of Jackson and Lincoln. He and his class will long "benefit from a natural tendency on the part of the privileged in any society to suppress — for themselves as well as others — knowledge and understanding of the nature of their privilege and its manifestations" (Chomsky 1973, 65). Calhoun would have understood

Neitzsche perfectly. "Neitzsche's 'slave-morale' is a phantom, *his master-morale is a reality*. . . Men of this sort do not broadcast their millions to dreamers, 'artists,' weaklings and 'down-and-outs' to satisfy a boundless benevolence; they employ them for those who like themselves count as material for the Future. They pursue a purpose with them. They make a centre of force for the existence of generations which outlives the single lives" (Spengler 1926, 350). And just as Bourgin observed of Hamilton that he chose men of personality and improved their relative position, so too did Calhoun. While Secretary of War he choose Jefferson Davis for the future and appointed him a cadet in the United States Military Academy (Thomas 1968, 23). Together, their purpose would far outlive their individual lives.

While Calhoun's personal career was on the downslope after 1832, the United States itself continued to expand. He took such an interest in the general southern position on the acquisition of   Texas, that he acted briefly as John Tyler's Secretary of State and composed the joint resolution that annexed Texas on Tyler's final day in office, even after the Senate, with northern opposition, had failed to muster the two-thirds vote necessary to ratify a treaty that would have annexed Texas in that more directly constitutional manner. Once Texas was into the union, he remained skeptical of Polk. "Here was a balancing act that offered little or no protection to the South. Even on slavery in Texas the new president was equivocal, to Calhoun's highly sensitive ear. 'Whatever is good or evil in the local institution for Texas will remain her own whether annexed to the United States or not,' Polk said" (Niven 1988, 290).

Calhoun was increasingly worried for the institution of slavery, even as he was among the first to promote it as a positive good. In Ralph Learner's astute opinion, "For Calhoun, not the least of slavery's salutary effects was its making the South the balance of the American political system" (Thomas 1968, 221). It reveals upon analysis that Calhoun's "concurrent majority" is in fact the mere tyranny of the minority in disguise. Louis Hartz wrote "For there are of course minorities within minorities — as Unionists like Hugh Swinton Legare did not fail to remind Calhoun of in South Carolina in 1832 — . . . and since Calhoun offers no reason why these should not be given a policy veto too, the idea of the 'concurrent majority' quickly unravels itself into separate individuals executing the law of nature for themselves" (Thomas 1968, 166-7). The concurrent majority's potential flirtation with anarchy stopped short at Calhoun's wall: as long as rich white men get their way, democracy will be secure.

The only substantive matter that Calhoun and Jefferson Davis ever disagreed on was the question which became known as "all of Mexico." Calhoun was frightened by southern sentiment for conquest and annexation of the entire country. "Mexico is for us the forbidden fruit; the penalty of eating it would be to subject our institutions to political death" (Hofstadter 1959, 85). The Garden of Eden religious metaphor will throw some light back through the "Holy War" and the American marriage of church and state. References to Calhoun's weak knees on the subject of Mexico abound. He found the support for it in Polk's cabinet disturbing (Niven 1988, 304-309), and Current reported he felt it would lead to dangerous social changes (Thomas 1968, 158).

It wasn't the first time Calhoun had been accused of treason. The first was during the Nullification Crisis. Calhoun was not easily intimidated. He opposed, almost literally with his dying breath, "the Taylor administration's proposal to bypass customary procedures and admit California as a free state" (Niven 1988, 340), during the heated debate over the Compromise of 1850. He purportedly felt that all the states acting together had conquered California. Many in the North had come to resent the earlier Compromise of 1820 because it didn't restrict slavery in the western territories altogether. As much as the South disliked the southern boundary of Missouri as the latitudinal bearing line marking the demarcation between slave territory and free, if it were extended to the Pacific coast, at least they would have southern California for slavery and the South.

Calhoun's class bias was compounded by his racism and it sometimes feels genetic, even when applied to the white race. "When the two come into conflict, liberty must, and ever ought, to yield to protection; as the existence of the race is of greater moment than its improvement. It follows, from what has been stated, that it is a great and dangerous error to suppose that all people are equally entitled to liberty" (Calhoun, [1850] 1948, 55). Calhoun would rather be alive than free, making him no philosophical buddy of Patrick Henry. Remember South Carolina's first goal was reconciliation with England. The unequal right to liberty is another of those impenetrable boundaries separating Americans by class as well as race. Here we see Calhoun coming down, not in the gregarious middle holding the Hamiltonian and Jeffersonian halves of the United States together, but squarely on the side of the aristocratic West Indian Hamilton, holding the rich white powerful class above all others. The score is 2-1 as the Jeffersonian principle of this democracy to stop the power of the few from riding on the labor of the many is now the minority position. The U.S. has been being tugged toward its ultimate destiny as an overripe banana republic all along, an enormous Barbados.

Regardless of the law, power will do as power can. Here is the basis of and the nature of the power of the elite. We need to discover more about its underlying psychological impellers. "The leisure class is the conservative class," according to Thorstein Veblen, and "The office of the leisure class in social evolution is to retard the movement and to conserve what is obsolescent" ([1899] 1931, 198). Nothing quite illustrates Calhoun's conservative nature and his efforts to retard movement as the Nullification Crisis of 1832. The issue here was tariffs, perhaps even abominable tariffs, which seemed to penalize the Southerners, who preferred to buy industrially produced items from England free of tax. The tariffs made the goods of the incipient industries of the North competitive in price with imported items. Why, asked Calhoun who felt that a state should be able to nullify or ignore any laws that did it economic harm, should the South subsidize the industrialization of the North?

In the great laws of capitalism, the only change that is permitted is larger profits. Any other change will be resisted and only acquiesced to if the long term profit holds promise of increase. "The demand for redistribution of wealth and power, if it passes beyond rhetoric, will not be tolerated by the privileged" (Chomsky 1973, xxviii). Calhoun and other conservatives can be counted on to retard any change that reduces profits or capital. Primary southern capital was slaves. Veblen goes on to characterize blond European types and trace their dominating influence as the master or leisure class to their "possessing the characteristics of predatory man in an exceptional degree" (225). Weir has already reminded us that this same elite guided the South and South Carolina from the Revolutionary War to the Civil War. They guide the United States still.

Predatory man has been dominant in the South for a long time. "This bias began among the early slaveowners themselves, who refused to acknowledge among the early runaways signs of rationality, emotion, and independence, which they hoped to both ignore and suppress" (Wood, 1974, 248). The transparent effect is to dehumanize their slavery capital. "The net result was a pattern of controls intended to define with increasing clarity and bluntness the social, economic, and even physical 'place' of the [B] black Carolinian" (271). It was Calhoun who put a conservative political philosophy underneath this pattern of controls that has served his political progeny well at keeping Blacks, wherever they might occur, in their "place."

Gavin Wright, in his *Political Economy of the Cotton South*, reminds us once again that "Across the South, slaveholders formed a class of great wealth with a distinctive unity of economic interest" (1978, 143). It has been shown already that Southern slaveholders were getting richer far faster than any other Americans. "What is the significance, then, of the growing divergence in wealth between slaveholders in the South and nonslaveholders everywhere?" (7). The accumulating divergence drove a wedge between the relatively poorer and more populous North, attempting to industrialize, and the richer slaveholding conservative South that cumulated in the Civil War.

Not the least of Lincoln's appeal to voters in the North was his resistance to permitting slavery to extend into the western territories, which gave free workers, White and Black, a chance at controlling the value of their own labor and effort. "Thus, slave labor, unlike free, was allocated according to marketplace principles of monetary profit, and we do not need to appeal to efficiency to explain the mutual affinity of cotton and slavery" (74). Slavery was inefficient and its introduction to the territories reduced the value of free labor. Control of the West, and the future value of labor, was at the enormous heart of the Civil War.

How well do some of Calhoun's ideas play in the West, in California? "The strategy of dominance used by colonial powers is the same as that used by the white majority in the United States in its relations with colored minorities" (McWilliams 1951, 338). McWilliams was speaking of California at mid-20th century. "The American race problem is simply a special version of the world colonial problem, which, in the last analysis, is a problem involving the exploitation of labor" (339). It appears as though Calhoun's class and racial dominance has traveled well and stood the test of time.

It will be recalled how the application of Calhoun's theory of the concurrent majority gave the power in the South Carolina Senate to the coastal area around Charleston and the white slaveholding class. "For at all times the farm groups, through their control of the [California] State Senate, have held a veto power on legislation" (McWilliams 1969, 268).

During the 1920s in California, the LaFollete Committee's investigations in California found "a conspiratorial pattern of malfeasance. . . outbursts of class violence and a constant undercurrent of class hostility" (McWilliams, 1946, 283).

So that was Calhoun's California in the 20s and 40s. What is it like in the 90s? Mike Davis in *City of Quartz*, Excavating the Future in Los Angeles, talks about permanent class warfare in California and suggests that the growth "required continuous transfers of savings from the rest of the country" (1990, 118). California is one of the big ratholes on the treadmill from tax payers to tax consumers. In California, they "have begun to wage war against the very immigrant labor upon which their master-race lifestyles depend" (208). Davis suggests that a Second Civil War began in the long hot summers of the 60s. "We live in 'fortress cities' brutally divided between 'fortified cells' of affluent society and 'places of terror' where the police battle the criminalized poor" (224). A great deal more of the uncanny resemblances of California to the South can be found in the chapter titled "How California Became a Southern State."

If slaveholders were once the wealthy master class, just how big is the "affluent society" presently? The Internal Revenue Service reports, in an Associated Press release of August 23, 1990: "Americans with assets of at least $500,000 make up only 1.6 percent of the population but own nearly 28.5 percent of the nation's personal wealth. The 3.3 million richest Americans had holdings in 1986 of $4.3 trillion, with a net worth of 3.8 trillion — almost enough to finance the entire federal budget for four years."

Arthur Schlesinger can let Thomas Jefferson remind us that "There is a natural aristocracy among men. The grounds of this are virtue and talents. . . there is also an artificial aristocracy founded on wealth and birth, without either virtue or talents; for with these it would belong to the first class" (1986, 429). The United States is led by an artificial aristocracy, free of virtue and limited in talent, definitely not of the first class. What, we are welcome to ask, does this have to do with John C. Calhoun?

Richard Hofstadter, a dean among American historians, chose to call his essay on the man and his work, "John C. Calhoun: the Marx of the Master Class" ([1948] 1959). Once upon a time the elevation of an economic theorist to the plane of comparison with Karl Marx, where few dare to aspire, was taken as a supreme compliment. Marxism, born of hard times, has fallen on even harder times. The master class on the other hand, superficially at least, is still doing quite well for itself. With the economic force field in reversed polarity, Marx could be characterized as the Calhoun of the poor and oppressed.

Hofstadter claims that Calhoun "had a remarkable sense for the direction of social evolution, but failed to measure its velocity" (88). Missing the velocity of social evolution is another way of saying that he did not know when the predictions he was making for the culture would come true, an occupational hazard of prophecy. A minority spokesman in a democracy, "It became his peculiar faculty, the faculty of a brilliant but highly abstract and isolated intellect, to see things that other men never dreamt of and to deny what was under his nose, to forecast with uncanny insight several major trends of the future and remain all but oblivious of the actualities of the present" (89-90). Calhoun does not seem so oblivious to present actualities as he does bound up in the internal contradictions of his positions and "caught in the classic agony of the brink-of-war philosopher" (Thomas 1968, 170) as Louis Hartz suggests.

What is more likely in Hofstadter's evaluation is that "The essence of Calhoun's mistake as a practical statesman was that he tried to achieve a static solution for a dynamic situation" ([1948] 1959, 89-90). This may have been a practical mistake and a tactical blunder but it paid handsome strategic rewards. Calhoun's uncanny insight for the future far outweighs what appeared to be mistakes to Hofstader or in the narrow confines of the 19th century. The substitution of static rigidity when dynamism is called for leads directly to the endemic predatory reversion to barbarism of the leisure and master class position. This is bedrock Calhoun and the current conservative reaction to any suggested dynamism.

Even though Hofstadter doesn't miss the important operative elements in Calhoun that "would cement an alliance between the agrarian South and West against the capitalistic East" (71), it makes more sense to recognize the difference between the "industrial" East and the agrarian South and West for the entire system was capitalistic. He correctly points to the equal importance of Calhoun's search for allies in the North when he quotes him as saying "'the interests of the *Gentlemen* of the North and of the South are identical'" (84). The italics on gentlemen are Calhoun's. Here we see the two major thrusts of Calhounism, to the geographical West as a place to expand slavery and to the class and business interests of the North, as a way to control labor of all kinds. "Northern business interests ought to join the

Southern aristocracy in keeping working people (white or black) in their place" (Rosen 1982, 91). The place of labor in this system doesn't get much respect. Richard N. Current, in the selection of essays edited by Thomas, could also chime in: "On behalf of the planter class he appealed again and again to fellow conservatives among the bankers and manufacturers of the North" (1968, 158).

There is no shortage of evidence that this classist and racist appeal was made and even that it succeeded. In his heart, Calhoun was a Unionist, Hofstadter has already reminded us. Calhoun wanted a Union dominated by the South. "Far in advance of the event, he forecast an alliance between Northern conservatives and Southern reactionaries, which became one of the most formidable aspects of American Politics" (Hofstadter [1948] 1959, 88). Hofstadter composed that evaluation sometime prior to 1948. Calhoun's forecast had been coming true all along, and it was right in the middle of the 1940s when it became not merely one of the most formidable aspects of American politics, but once again the controlling element.

John L. Thomas, in the introduction to the collection of essays *John C. Calhoun, A Profile*, characterized the essay he included by Jefferson Davis as "the account of an interested party restating Calhoun's premises with unqualified approval" (Thomas 1968, xvi). While that characterization is basically true, the hint of patronizing dismissal is no longer useful. A sober new look at Davis' opinion is long overdue. "They underrated the universality of his genius" (16), Davis reports, and they also missed the implications of Calhoun, "great as was his foresight, reaching toward the domain of prophecy" (24-5).

Prophets and geniuses aren't that easy to come by in American politics. Either alone is a cause for celebration. Both together are a revolution, in this case, the revolution of the master class. Drucker speaks, in this book of essays on how "Sectional and interest pluralism has molded all American political institutions. . . It is the explanation for the most distinctive features of the American political system" (136). Calhoun is the most articulate spokesman of sectional and interest politics. "He is considered both a representative of the American people and responsible to the national interest and a delegate of his constituents and responsible to their particular interests" (138). The difficulty in this Drucker restatement of the basic ideal of a senator or representative is that sectional and interest politics outweigh the national interest. The state, section, and particular interest, if it can marshall sufficient money, thrives; the nation and the national interest goes down the bankruptcy tube when Calhounism is forcefully applied.

"The major developments of American politics have been based on Calhoun's principle" (140). This may not always have been in the best overall interests of the United States. "It is, consequently, not that Calhoun was repudiated by the Civil War which is the key to the understanding of American politics but that he has become triumphant since" (140).

In the summation and resting of the case of John C. Calhoun, genius, prophet, foreteller of the controlling elements of American politics, triumphant since the Civil War, etc., his relationship with the city of Charleston cannot go unnoticed. ". . . realize that the city, with its gradual detachment from and final bankrupting of the country, is the determinative form to which the course and sense of higher history generally conforms. *World history is city history*" (Spengler 1928, 95). Calhoun hated Charleston and gave a haughty dismissal to its putative culture. Calhoun was a workaholic from the countryside and foresaw the work still ahead. South Carolina did not urbanize in the traditional sense. The early slavers lived in the city and visited their plantations. Calhoun's dismissal of what he correctly took to be their hedonism and decadence was an intuitional understanding that Charleston actually sprang into existence as the consolidated city-state that exploited the provinces, the end-state and end stasis of Spengler's civilization in decline. Charleston was born in the barbarism of slavery and turned immediately into civilization without ever having known culture.

Nevertheless, Calhoun successfully took its part as long as he didn't have to live there, in his great ongoing debate with the forces of democracy in America and as we have seen, even dead, Charlestonians wanted him to repose in their version of Westminster Abbey. "In the drawing rooms of Charleston. . . it was the portraits of Calhoun, no matter how damaged or crude, which hung in the place of honor. . . He had become a sort of great-grandfather to the entire state. . . In no other state, not even in Jefferson's Virginia, is there that strange bond between the dead and the living. They 'felt things' about Calhoun in South Carolina. They feel them still" (Coit 1950, 515). We too feel them still, across the length and breadth of the United States for the South could not have won the Civil War without him. There is some minor disputation over the Godfather of the Confederate Empire's exact final words, so we will leave it with Niven's version (1988, 343): "I am now completely comfortable."

7

Remember the Alamo!: First Texan

Cabeza de Vaca walked naked and barefoot across Texas in the 1530s, accompanied by two other Spaniards and a Moor. It is not likely in his eight-year sojourn that he would have ever reached Sante Fe except the Indians thought he was magic. This is the first of three chapters on the pivotal place of Texas in the history of North American political power. Shipwreck victims near present day Galveston, Cabeza de Vaca and his companions had been accompanying the expedition of Panfilo de Narvaez, "the last of the rich islanders to make a bid for power on the mainland" (Sauer 1971, 36). The Spaniards had been looking for ways to enlarge their Caribbean domain, some additional place to plunder, and the fountain of youth.

The march across Texas wouldn't get much easier any time soon. "While a dozen or more settlements were founded in Florida, largely as a protective flank for the silver of Mexico, the fate of these settlements was sealed when the British occupied Charleston in 1670" (McWilliams 1968, 26). The Spanish had plans, that went under with the defeat of the Spanish Armada, for a chain of fortifications up the Atlantic coast north of St. Augustine. Meanwhile their more successful "settlements in the borderland really consisted of a firmly rooted colony in New Mexico; an easily held and fairly prosperous chain of missions in coastal California; and a number of feebly garrisoned, and constantly imperiled settlements in Texas and Arizona" (26).

By the early 19th century, the struggle for dominion in the new world between the speakers of English and the speakers of Spanish had moved well onto the land from where Sir Francis Drake and others had begun it from the sea in Panama in 1572. For the entire time the Spanish maintained their "feeble" garrison at San Antonio de Bexar, they were not permitted to travel across west Texas to Sante Fe. The road from San Antonio to Sante Fe was *El Camino Real* via Durango, Mexico, then west and north to El Paso and up the Rio Grande (Webb 1931, 86), approximately 800 miles longer than a direct march. West Texas belonged initially to the Athabascan speaking Apache who were driven out of it by the even more tenacious Comanche.

In 1757 the Spanish had established a fortified mission at San Saba on what would have been the more direct route, only to have the Comanche promptly raze it. The Comanche, whose name *Komantcia* literally means in Uto-Aztecan "the people who love to fight," were native to the Uinta Basin but came to the headwaters of the Arkansas river and followed the supply of horses onto the Llano Estacado or Staked Plains of Texas. Compliments to the Comanche abound. "The Comanches became the greatest horse thieves of them all. . . . Utes and Wichitas and Apaches learned to ride; Comanches came to live on horseback" (Fehrenbach 1968, 31).

Once the initial glow from the plundering, raping and pillaging to which Spain had subjected Mexico — commencing with Cortez in 1531 — had begun to wear off, the Spanish began to loosen their grip. With the outrageously large returns on their investments tapering off to the mundane yield of colonial administration, Spain allowed the Mexicans to achieve independence. They inherited the feeble grip the dwindled Spanish empire had on San Antonio. Uncertain of the future there against the Indians, they granted Moses Austin the right to settle a colony of American immigrants in east Texas. Moses did not live to exercise the right but his son Stephen F. Austin colonized Texas in 1821.

Himself victimized by an early encounter with Comanche, Austin settled farther out of harms way and where the land was more like what he was used to. He was an able administrator and the Americans in Texas thrived, so much so that they began to encroach upon the Indians. From 1821 to 1836, the very success of Austin's colony — total population of 30,000 Americans then in Texas — began to make his Mexican benefactors nervous. The conflict of three cultures, indigenous Indians, Mexican, and American, led to the Texas War for Independence. "Thus it came about that the Texans were confronted by two foes to neither of whom they could surrender: *they had to fight*" (Webb 1931, 166).

With so many Americans in Texas or near Texas beginning to believe they had a claim to Texas, American Presidents in turn, Adams and Jackson, had offered to buy it, but their offers were spurned. General Antonio Lopez de Santa Ana, self-styled dictator of Mexico and putative "Napoleon of the West," attempted to impose dictatorial control over the Americans in Texas with a new constitution. On March 2, 1836, the Texans expelled the Mexican garrison at San Antonio and declared their independence.

What happened next, at "Pueblo de San Carlos del Alamo de Parras, Alamo for short" (Fehrenbach 1968, 72), is so well known, the rallying cry "Remember the Alamo!" is almost sufficient to recapitulate the entire story. The Americans moving west, and no less so those moving into Texas, were, as Fehrenbach suggests, "bound for the wilderness, on an Old Testament trek to build the new Jerusalem" (87). Whatever religious motivation the Texans may have had prior to the Battle at the Alamo, it was cubed and expanded exponentially by the result. "But at the Alamo history was altered. It is not easy to explain exactly why" (207).

The shoals under any attempt to explain why are where any historical boat will sink. The explanation is how, not why. "History may best be treated as a chapter of epistemology" (Spengler 1926, 119). We have already been treated to Lee Atwater's explanation of how Southerners like a good fight, especially if somebody else starts it. The religious beatification of the Battle at the Alamo, and by extension the other battles in the war for Texan independence and the subsequent Mexican War, lives in the vectors of the actual fighting where they intersect the words of Colonel William Travis' pithy personal strategy.

Buck Travis "had been trained at an academy in the state of his birth, South Carolina" (Fehrenbach 1968, 208). We know by now what it means to be from South Carolina and we see how that meaning carried westward to Texas, a fiercely independent streak that is happiest fighting. Ontogeny recapitulates phylogeny. Travis was killed at the Alamo along with 188 other basically southern gentlemen including Jim Bowie and Davy Crockett. Crockett was a former congressman from Tennessee who, fed up with the system, went west to liberate himself. It is important to recall that Travis addressed his message "To the people of Texas and all Americans in the world" (Leckie 1968, 321).

"I shall never surrender or retreat. . . I am determined to sustain myself as long as possible and die like a soldier who never forgets what is due to his own honor and that of his country — VICTORY OR DEATH" (321). In the new Jerusalem created in Texas and the United States, "I shall never surrender or retreat" has achieved the status of a Commandment. Fehrenbach claims that Travis' stand had won a "mystical title to the soil of Texas" (215). Two of the sources used here, to establish facts and buttress claims to meaning, Fehrenbach and especially Robert Leckie's two volume *The Wars of America*, were both published in 1968, at the height of the War in Vietnam.

War brings all former wars forward into the consciousness and reinforces the belief in the efficacy of war. Dead, people believe nothing, but war is beatified and made holy to the living by the loss of life and blood.

The slaughter of several hundred unarmed prisoners at Goliad intensi-fied the Texas fever for revenge. Revenge was sweet at San Jacinto as Houston, former governor of Tennessee and one of many protégés of President Andrew Jackson, demonstrated his grasp of military tactics and surprised the Mexican army during their siesta. Waiting for his turn to win, Houston had noticed that "The Texans were at perfect pitch" (229), and Fehrenbach reminds us that "For sixty terrible days Anglo-Texans had fought alone" (239).

Fehrenbach suggests that Jackson's private feelings were clear and that he wanted Texas. "The powers of the Presidency were not construed in the 1830's so as to allow him to engage the nation in war by executive action" (237), is offered as an explanation for his non-intervention. This was not the General Jackson who read the widest possible latitude into his capture of Florida a few years before. Either the office of the Presidency had mellowed him, or he was acutely sensitive to the feelings of northerners who would have howled their resistance.

Nevertheless, Houston "rode in front of his army to extend America, just as Wellington fought at Waterloo to 'preserve the England that produced such gentlemen as these'" (246). Here we see Fehrenbach attach the style and substance of Houston's victory over Santa Ana, the putative Napoleon of the West, to the victory of the British Empire over the *bona fide* Napoleon. With Texas independent under its own Lone Star Flag, the outlines of the tilt in power further toward the South and West, become clearer. "His national myths were more influenced by the Alamo and the burden of a century of a wild frontier than concepts conceived at Philadel-phia" (257). The Texas ID and its character "grew out of the terrible struggle for the land" (256). Less than 24 hours before he left office, President "Jackson capped his career in the White House by recognizing Texas" (251).

Recognition as an independent nation did not stop the hostilities with Mexico, who refused to accept defeat, much less to recognize the Rio Grande river as the boundary between Mexico and Texas. Neither did recognition stop the controversy in the United States about the extension of slavery and the possible annexation of Texas. For years both controversies simmered. The Whigs who replaced the old Republican party had opposed recognition and the extension of slavery. "All through the North the opposition to annexation was clear and strong" (Beard and Beard 1925, 280). Calhoun and the southern Democrats demanded the annexation of Texas. Northern opposition scuttled plans to annex Texas by Senate ratification of a treaty by a vote of 35 to 16 (Perkins 1966, 20). Failing that, it was finally annexed by joint resolution of Congress on President Tyler's last day in office, nine years after Texas had declared its independence. The struggle over Texas had become the focal point of the developing struggle over slavery between the sections and its extension into the western territories. It should be duly noted that the South won.

Or perhaps Texas won. In the economic history of the United states, "Worth noting is the fact that although Congress was timorous in all other matters, it was assertive as proprietor of the public lands in making long-range plans that looked forward to the ultimate settlement of these vast areas" (Bourgin 1989, 29). Bourgin was speaking of the period under the Articles of Confederation when the Northwest Ordinance and its attendant land survey system created a system still in use today that parceled the Ohio River Valley into sections and passed them out to deserving veterans of the Revolutionary War. Although California is known as the "Great Exception," Texas actually came into the union of the United States with several notable exceptions of its own. To begin with, they came in as a territory and reserved the right to divide at some hypothetical time in the problematical future into four additional states, the better to preserve the slaveholder's balance of power in the United States Senate. They were also able to palm off on the federal government, their entire "national" debt at the time of annexation with a Hamiltonian touch on a style of finance that would quickly become a Texan tradition. "Texas during the 1850s was financed publicly almost entirely by federal money" (Fehrenbach 1968, 278). Here we see the Texans writing themselves firmly down in the Calhoun system of class book-keeping in the "tax consumer" column. This in the teeth of the truth that Texans resented national interference, and finally "The state was permitted to retain title to all its public lands" (276). Not bad for a little country just learning how to exercise power.

The cliffhanger nature of both the recognition of Texas as a nation and its annexation to the United States, on the last days in office of Presidents Jackson and Tyler, parted the curtain on the future. Tyler was a slaveholding man and no friend of Whigs. He annexed Texas on March 3, 1845. "Next day, March 4, 1845, James K. Polk came into the White House. And Polk not only wanted Texas; he wanted California, too" (Leckie 1968, 322). In 1846, partially in response to growing clamors, particularly southern, that the Manifest Destiny of the nation required the acquisition of more territory, Polk ordered General Zachary Taylor to Texas. "The order to Taylor to occupy disputed territory was a provocative act; and Taylor's conduct was no less so" (Perkins 1966, 23). Many of the men later prominent during the Civil War fought with Taylor in the North of Mexico or General Scott in central Mexico, including Grant and Lee. Jefferson Davis distinguished himself in Northern Mexico at the Battle of Buena Vista.

The question of title to Oregon came up during this period also and it was settled by some tense diplomacy. Negotiating with other native speakers of English, Polk was able to take advantage of several hundred years of predictable opinions, postures and stances. Read Frederick Merk's *The Oregon Question* for his marvelous massage of the details.

As one result of the Mexican War, Mexico ceded to the U.S. the disputed portions of Texas, most of Arizona and New Mexico, the balance of Colorado, and all of the present states of Utah, Nevada, and California. Far from abating the controversy over slavery, instead the acquisition of this huge section of North America intensified it. We've already seen how Senator John C. Calhoun burned some political capital by relentlessly opposing those Southerners who wanted all of Mexico, the "forbidden fruit," who wanted the conquest to be complete, which in Calhoun's mind would make it terminal as well. Even with half of Oregon through diplomacy and half of Mexico by way of war, the religious appetite for expansion was unquenched.

"No wonder Southern statesmen saw, in the annexation of Texas and the conquest of Mexico, slavery and King Cotton triumphant — secure for all time against adverse legislation. Northern leaders were equally convinced that the Southern prophecy was true. Abolitionists and moderate opponents of slavery alike were in despair. Texas, they lamented, would "fasten slavery upon the country forevermore" (Beard and Beard 1925, 327). Here is another famous opinion with some more elements of genuine prophecy.

The more rational mind of Daniel Webster thought otherwise. Webster had always opposed the extensions of slavery and he opposed recognition of Texas and annexation of it, precisely because it held slavery (Webb 1931, 188). Webster burned some political capital of his own by opposing the Wilmot Proviso which would have banned slavery in all the lands ceded from Mexico on the grounds that slavery could not succeed there anyway, being prohibited by climate and geography and unsuitable for the production of cotton by slave labor. Webster alienated many supporters and helped the Senate to kill what he considered to be a provocative and superfluous law, which had passed the House, because he felt slavery was confined by nature.

Walter Prescott Webb goes to some pains in *The Great Plains* to reiterate and embellish Webster's political position with additional and more contemporary geographical and economical data. Webster and Webb are both wrong, mistaken not as to the nature of the Southwest starting at the Staked Plains or approximately the 98th Meridian, but mistaken as to the flexibility of the peculiar institution of slavery. Webb's own data (189) shows the growing of cotton through slavery to be largely confined to South Carolina as of 1791, two years before Eli Whitney patented the cotton gin. He correctly traces the spread of slavery and "King Cotton" to the West, where by 1849 it was bumping up on his idea of its limit.

Webb fails to take into account that cotton is not the only product successfully, if inefficiently (Wright), produced through slave labor. Recall that 9 out of 10 of the richest men in colonial North America circa 1775 were Charlestonians from South Carolina, prior to the large scale growing of cotton, whose fortunes are traceable to the slave labor production of indigo, cotton, and cattle. Slavery representing capital and dear to the hearts of the capitalist slaveowners can be and has been applied successfully to other crops, for example tobacco in Virginia and North Carolina and sugar on the island of Barbados. Presently more cotton is grown in California and Arizona than in the old cotton belt of the southeast. The Catholic Spaniards had enslaved the Indians in California long before the slaveholding Southerners could have located it on the map, much less made it part of their want list in the 1840s. The 98th degree of meridian is an imaginary boundary, confining neither cotton nor slavery.

The argument for the geographical death of slavery is one other face of the revisionist platform that the Civil War was an avoidable calamity. It wasn't. Referencing David Wilmot's speech in favor of his Proviso, DeVoto wrote "For twenty-six years the nation had refused to face the paradox at its core, the unresolved conflict at the base of its economy and its politics. If it had faced that conflict steadily during the preceding years, the death and destruction now ahead of it might have been modified or even averted"

(1943, 292). Not only does this educated chatter from a brilliant mind presuppose that political paradoxes can have rational solutions, it imagines the unimaginable, that capitalist slaveholders could be coaxed into relinquishing their capital. It will never be believed by anyone who has seen the fruits of his own enterprise put at risk by government policy. Political paradoxes aren't ironed out by historians and intellectuals in their spare time; they are resolved by war. Even before the Mexican War, "At some time between August and December, 1846, the Civil War had begun" (1943, 480), it was too late to stop.

The Mexican War itself was ". . . a presidential war of dominant Administration policy, carried out for strategic reasons against the wishes of a considerable body of public opinion" (Fehrenbach 1968, 268). The people who wished against it were basically the people of the North, the people farthest away from the scene of the spoils. Closer to the scene, Fehrenbach could delineate on a map (597), which parts of Texas were occupied by people from which southern states: Tennessee, Mississippi, Louisiana, Alabama, Missouri and Georgia. He would also say that Texans were the most European of Americans. "Its growth was merely the spread of a static empire. Texas was painfully making a new Virginia or Georgia" (318), or South Carolina.

The aggressive events of the late 1840s which gave the United States essentially its current continental boundaries reminded someone else of empire. "Mr. Lincoln was telling his countrymen that the achieved West had given the United States something that no people had ever had before, an internal, domestic empire, and he was telling them that Yesterday [the slaveholding South as the Confederacy] must not be permitted to Balkanize it" (DeVoto 1943, 480).

It was not the South's initial overriding intention to Balkanize the "empire," merely to dominate it. As the most European of Americans, in Fehrenbach's phrase, note also "'It was in Southwest Texas,' writes Dr. Edward Everett Davis, 'that fourteenth century feudalism met the southern plantation' and from this meeting came the large-scale cotton farming of Texas based on the use of migratory Mexican labor" (McWilliams 1968, 170). The Mexican system of peonage, essentially a Spanish feudal concoction, was as equally adept in the production of cotton as slavery.

The South dominated the United States in the 1850s, the heyday of the antebellum South, as it would not dominate it again until the 1950s. Texas was prominent in the southern domination. While Secretary of War Jefferson Davis and President Pierce maneuvered diplomatically to acquire Cuba, General Quitman of Mississippi was ready to invade. "A list of the general's Texas backers reads like a minor *Who's Who* of Texas politics in the 1850s" (May 1973, 49). The drive for more or all of Mexico was never derailed. "The number of American filibuster raids into Mexico in the 1850s is staggering" (147). In the effort to make a more important man out of Walker than he was (the man who set himself up as dictator of Nicaragua and legalized slavery there in 1854), his publicist Wheeler alleged that "Had he succeeded, he would have rivaled the fame of Houston" (97-8).

The fame of Houston waxed and waned during the decade of the cotton South, as he traded the governorship with Lamar. Houston opposed the secession of the South (he was drummed out of the corps for it) and dreamed of declaring war on Mexico (again!) as a way of reuniting the United States. Confederate Senator Williamson S. Oldham of Texas, who helped to lead Texas out of the Union over Houston's objections, would later express his opinion — after escaping to Mexico — that the Confederates lost because their spirit flagged, morale went down and they died of guilt and a failure of will (Beringer et al 1986, 32-4). At least Oldham demonstrated the tactical flexibility to violate the First Commandment of Texas and beat a prudent retreat.

While the Texans were still in the Confederacy and getting their licks in directly, James Reily, a prominent Confederate army official, wrote Postmaster General John Reagan in 1862 that Chihuahua sympathized with the Confederacy and "'. . . with Sonora and Chihuahua we gain Southern California, and by a railroad to Guaymas render our State of Texas the great highway of nations'" (May 1973, 254-5). Reily may have been daydreaming about sympathy from Chihuahua, but the shared agenda of the capture of California was more plausible. Even the ultimate plateau of Texas as the highway of nations itself would not forever be completely out of reach.

Houston, while still President of Texas before the question of annexation had been put to bed, was still planning strategically. DeVoto's summary of the gist of Houston's thought is worth quoting at length. "Well, in 1844, Sam Houston, then ending his second term as president of Texas, drew a map. It showed the domain his nation was eventually to occupy, the extent of its manifest destiny, if the movement for the annexation to the United States should fail. Houston's map has its merit as prophecy. If Texas could not be American, then Texas was eventually to include Oregon, New Mexico, and California — as defined above [54-40 or fight]. It was also to include the Mexican state of Chihuahua and thence westward to the Pacific. And it was to include Arkansas, Louisiana, Tennessee, Mississippi, Alabama, Georgia, Florida, the Carolinas, and Virginia. That is, the republic of Texas was to cover, besides some territory which is Mexican today, precisely the extent of the Far West and the Confederate States of America" (1943, 17-8). Houston was not guessing and he came close to conceptually corralling the eventual suzerainty of Texas political thought and control in the confines of North America. The fame of Houston will wax again.

Texas has a history. The six flags that have flown over Texas once represented the governments of Spain, France, Mexico, Texas, the United States, and the Confederate States of America. "Any nationalism in the Lone Star State was Texan nationalism, not southern or even American nationalism" (Beringer et al 1986, 78). Texas, settled essentially by Southerners, had notched the need for independence up another peg. The tail taught the dog how to wag.

Texas mythology was instilled and installed by the Alamo on cultural override of the "concepts conceived at Philadelphia" (Fehrenbach 1968, 257). The Texans began a divisional in American political life and the ramifications are yet to be completely manifested. DeVoto published in 1943. He could speak of a common texture of experience, how the habits and expectations of thought had already realized the empire (481). His contempt for the reversionary habits of the chattel slaveowners is genuine enough. He felt they were obsolete. "What was done at Montgomery was to file a last Bill of Review against reality and, when the nation dismissed it, to appeal from the dismissal to the final court" (282). For all his sage comprehension, DeVoto didn't quite live long enough (d 1955) to notice what was well underway during the last years of his life. The "final court" had not held its final session in 1943 when DeVoto maintained that the future had won and the past in the form of the Confederate South had been defeated.

The final session will never be held, only the proceedings of the last and most recent must be continually fed back into the loop. Only death is final and Confederate ideas die hard. The Texans are more interested in the bearings they received at the Alamo than the general vectors sprayed across the land from Philadelphia. The view of American history from Philadelphia is the conventional one, pious, slightly condescending, and half as

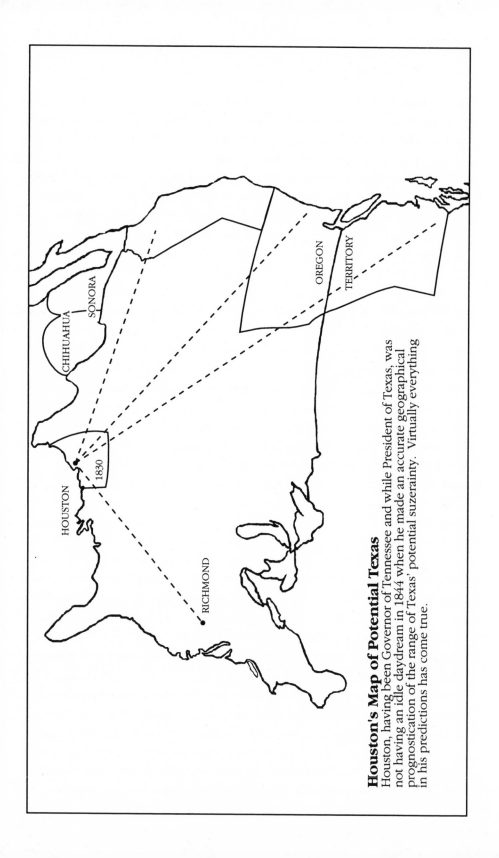

Houston's Map of Potential Texas

Houston, having been Governor of Tennessee and while President of Texas, was not having an idle daydream in 1844 when he made an accurate geographical prognostication of the range of Texas' potential suzerainty. Virtually everything in his predictions has come true.

articulate as DeVoto's. It contained, by the failure of a single vote on Jefferson's measure to abolish slavery everywhere, taken between the Articles and the Constitution, the flaw that would unravel it.

The conventional history comes out of Philadelphia asserting that Americans are all equal before the law. With a push from Boston and the New York bookkeepers, it rattled on to the Great Lakes and Chicago, Illinois, land of Lincoln, who kept the domestic empire, which by that time included San Francisco, together. It was during that astounding period between the end of the Revolutionary War, 1783, and the end of the Mexican War in 1848, a mere 65 years, when the speakers of English spanned the continent and came closest in their fundamentalist thirst for empire to emulating the forces of Islam under Mohammed. The English speaking colonies seem in retrospect to have been puttering around on the Atlantic seaboard for 150 years before they reached the critical mass which enabled them to make policy on the North American side of the Atlantic.

The Northern version of American history from New York to San Francisco, includes the South as supernumerary to its own aims. *How the South Finally Won the Civil War* is the presentation of a more viable southern model of American history, from Charleston to Los Angeles via Houston. This model asserts the primacy of the military control of power over the badly damaged idealism and the subservient and bankrupt economics of equality in the northern and conventional version.

We will see a great deal more of Texas as time goes on. "Roosevelt recalls with emotion those Texans of a 'barbaric age,' who raised the flag of the Lone Star State and precipitated a war of conquest with Mexico" (Josephson, 1940, 68-9). Things are never quite as simple as the Teddy Roosevelt version, but he plays a prominent role in the comeback of the Confederacy. "Thus the historical thinking of our latter-day Hamiltonians turned often with admiration to the earlier American pioneers who had overrun and conquered a whole vast continent" (69). In their haste to congratulate themselves, North or South, whether under the influence of the class politics of the Hamiltonians or not, Americans are prone to forget that the whole vast North American continent was inhabited when the first of their European and African ancestors arrived. This privileged ignorance of power retards their maturity. The Texas solution, like modern day Israelis according to Fehrenbach, or even like Old Testament Jews, was intended to be final. There are no Indian reservations in Texas.

8

100 Kuwaits: And the Rest is Real Estate

Naked aggression was not politically correct behavior for rogue Islamic fascists out of Baghdad such as Saddam Hussein. English speaking people conquering North America fought many of their most intense battles for title to the continent among themselves and against the speakers of French and Spanish. Although North America may have seemed to some to resemble an empty Garden of Eden ripe for plucking, it was in fact occupied by productive indigenous people. No history of the English speaking presence in North America can afford to do without at least a brief recitation of the history and treatment of the people who held title to the land at the beginning of the arc of Columbus. While sanctimonious, that is to say religious, American leaders such as President Bush can condemn naked aggression out of hand and punish it as they wish as long as their power holds out, it behooves them not to forget how their ancestors acquired the land which is the basis for that power. Only losers in the incessant struggle for power, such as Nazi Germany, are hauled before tribunals like the one assembled at Nuremberg to pass judgment upon complicit aggression and genocide.

The court of appeals for American war crimes at the moment is still in God's hands, the hands of the Great Spirit. Someday it will pass into the hands of people other than the speakers of English, where they can only hope that the righteousness of condemning others for what made them great, as they throw themselves upon the mercy of that distant court, will be treated charitably and not like the ungrateful hypocrisy that it is, of people powerful far in excess of their accumulated wisdom.

"All the accounts, Spanish, French, and English, agree that the eastern Indians lived well and at ease in a generous land which they used competently and without spoiling it" (Sauer 1971, 296). When Carl Ortwin Sauer, the founder of the Geography Department at the University of California at Berkeley says all the accounts agree, take his word for it, for he literally examined all the accounts. It was Sauer's life work to research and write a comprehensive geography of the state of the North American continent

101

based on the initial contact documents. His four volume *oeuvre* demonstrates a vital model of American scholarship and discipline, a seldom
consulted masterpiece.

Since all of the accounts on the Atlantic side agree as to the condition
and state of cultural and natural fusion, what about the Pacific Coast and
California? "The people of the Santa Barbara Channel in particular
impressed the Cabrillo party with the quality of their society as well as by
their good livelihood. They had abundant food from the sea and on land.
They were talented at working wood and stone. The visitors counted more
than fifty villages, some of them impressive in form and size. Life was not
only easy, it was spirited and good" (292-3). Perhaps it is no wonder that
the prongs of the European incursion recognized in this abundance their
imagined memories of paradise lost.

Samuel Eliot Morrison in *The European Discovery of America* repeats the
report of Barlowe who sailed with Raleigh on the cost of North Carolina:
"'We were entertained with all love and kindness and with as much bounty,
after their manner, as they could possibly devise. Wee found the people
most gentle, loving and faithfull, void of all guile and treason, and such as
lived after the manner of the golden age. The earth bringeth foorth all things
in aboundance, as in the first creation. . .'" (1971, 625). Everywhere, the
story is the same. The indigenes, to their peril, misunderstood the Europeans as spiritual beings, or magic as the aboriginal Texans treated Cabeza
de Vaca. "Peter Martyr, following Columbus, wrote in the same strain,
almost the exact words, [as Barlowe in North Carolina] about the peaceful
Arawak of the Bahamas. Here, as there, it may have been a golden age for
the invaders, but a tragic fate awaited the natives. Here, as there, the arrival
of Europeans set these kindly, hospitable people on their way to extinction"
(625-6).

Who were these peoples, these 100 Kuwaits, on their way to extinction?
The use of the word 100 is a handle. The actual count is closer to 300
individual tribes, groups, and cultural associations, speaking a dozen major
and unrelated languages, broken into dialects with numerous language
isolates, everywhere adapting themselves to the natural world as they found
it. An alphabetic list of all 300 would serve no structural purpose here but a
cultural area breakdown is in order. The schema of Eastern Woodlands,
Southeastern, Southwestern, Plains, Basin, Plateau, California, Northwest
Coast and Mackenzie areas is taken from Robert Lowie's *Indians of the Plains*.

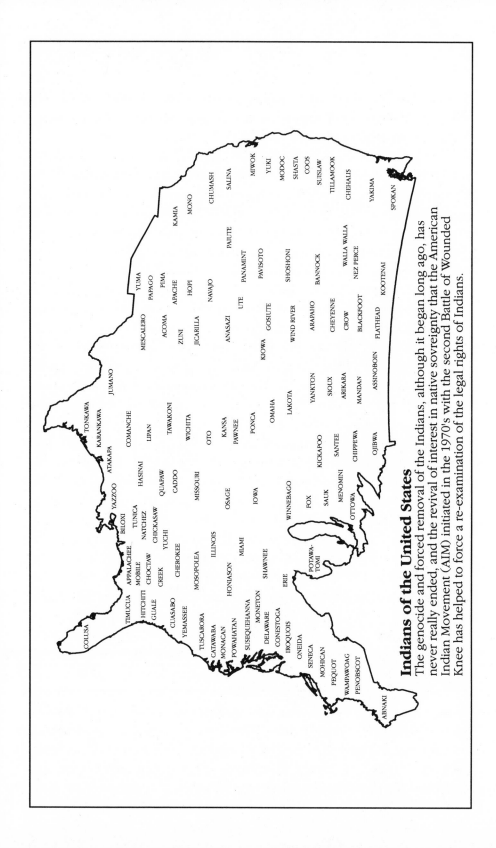

Indians of the United States

The genocide and forced removal of the Indians, although it began long ago, has never really ended, and the revival of interest in native sovreignty that the American Indian Movement (AIM) initiated in the 1970's with the second Battle of Wounded Knee has helped to force a re-examination of the legal rights of Indians.

In Lowie's personal provenance and area of expertise, the Plains, we find the following Indians listed with their declining population numbers as the European incursion intensified: Blackfoot, Piegan, Cheyenne, Arapaho, Gros Ventre, Plains Cree, Sarsi, Crow, Kiowa, Apache, Pawnee, Arikara, Wichita, Kiowa, Mandan, Hidatsa, Ponca, Dakota [Lakota], Assiniboin, Iowa, Oto, Oto-Missouri, Omaha, Osage, Kansa, Wind River Shoshone, Comanche, Ute, Kutenai, and Nez Perce ([1954] 1963, 12-13). Lowie goes on to tell us that the Pawnee actually contained four separate independent groups. Each of the cultural areas contained at least as many separate groups, tribes and nations. "Aboriginal United States was a land of ultrademocracy, every small group functioning for itself. The Indian was a lover of freedom. . ." (Wissler 1966, 129).

This love of freedom and proclivity for independent action would do them no good in their resistance to the Europeans. We note some of their tribal names became the names of famous cities or states in the current English speaking culture. The three major branches of the European incursion, French, Spanish, and English, treated the indigenes differently. The Spanish utilized the Roman model directly. "The immense debts of Roman politicians had for their ultimate security, not their equivalent in land, but the definite prospect of a province to be plundered of its movable assets" (Spengler 1928, 487). Movable assets as we will see later, included Indians for slavery as well as gold and silver. Spanish slaving had completely depopulated Barbados (Sauer 1966, 194) before the English turned it into a sugar plantation with African slaves. The Spanish military and ecclesiastical occupation of North America was centered on Tenochitlan, now the site of Mexico City. It brought soldiers and putatively celibate priests who produced Mestizos, garrisons and cathedrals, but few families and a feudal peonage coupled with contempt and confusion when confronted with land. In his conclusion to *Aztec Thought and Culture*, Miguel Leon-Portilla says: "Their culture of metaphors and numbers was overthrown by weapons of steel and fire" (1963, 182).

In the northernmost interior reaches of the Spanish empire in North America, in New Mexico, the Pueblo Indian Pope (pronounced popay, no relation to *the* Pope), organized the Pueblans and threw the Spanish out of New Mexico in 1588, the year of the defeat of the Spanish Armada. Pope made his rebellion stick for nearly 12 years, one of a few indigene military victories in the general narrative of defeat.

The French, far less racist than the English, and even more inclined than the Spanish to take native women as their wives, rather than merely produce children with them, have the best overall reputation for treating the indigenes like human beings. Even so, "The French observers were horrified, but could do nothing to stop the hostilities. By 1649 the deed was done. It is believed that more than ten thousand Huron were killed" (Wissler 1966, 131-2). The genocide of the Huron was not perpetrated by the French or at their behest. It was the work of the League of the Iroquois, who developed a passionate hatred for the Huron and "almost extermi-nated them" (Morrison 1971, 429). The Huron genocide is possibly the most gross example of Indian total war on one another where skirmishing was the more likely mode of conduct. It is recited here to underscore a point, that in war and competition for economic resources, human nature prevails; North America was not peopled entirely by a race of saints. Proof of the more friendly and mutually beneficial intercourse of the French with the Indians was available in mid-18th century. "The hardest fact of all had to be faced: the Indians by and large adhered to the French in the imperial war that broke out between England and France in 1754" (Prucha 1962, 11).

The British and their English colonists had been vying for Indian trade and support. How did they go wrong? "The Massachuset, whose popula-tion was estimated at 3000 in 1600, numbered only 500 by 1631 as a result of a terrible epidemic, possibly of small pox, and soon thereafter smallpox reduced them to a remnant population" (Oswalt 1973, 566). Pasteur's germ theory of disease was still 200 years from being formulated, let alone accepted by European civilization, much less the indigenes of 16th century North America. The Indians held the colonists responsible for the disease, and certainly they were the conveyors. There is evidence disease was some-times deliberately spread. King Phillips' War in Massachusetts set the tone in the northern colonies.

But "All the English colonies had an Indian problem. . . " (Prucha 1962, 5). The period of Indian adoration of Whites was over when they realized they were being displaced by speakers of English. English speaking colonists, unlike the French and Spanish, brought their wives and cattle and set up housekeeping in the new world. In *British Drums on the Southern Frontier*, the Military Colonization of Georgia, 1733-1749, Larry Ivers reports: "The South Carolinians had developed into a confident people, extremely warlike as a result of a decade of continuous and usually successful skirmishes with Spaniards and Indians" (1974, 5). We have already heard Weir's report (85) of the 400 white South Carolinian fatalities during the Yemassee War of 1716 in the context of the history of South Carolina.

The Indians, some of whom were gradually beginning to get the picture and who ". . . always lost in the end because incapable of preventing Europeans from being reinforced by sea" (Morrison 1971, 651), wound up on the wrong, losing side, in every major war. From East to West, six of the most revealing incidents in this perpetual war of displacement were King Phillip's War, Tecumseh and the Shawnees resistance at the Battle of Fallen Timbers, Black Hawk's War in Iowa, the Lakota resistance of Sitting Bull and Crazy Horse in the Battle of the Little Big Horn, the strategic retreat of Chief Joseph and the Nez Perce War, and the Fate of Captain Jack and the Modoc in California.

The more immediate concern of the Indians in the fateful transition between the English speaking colonies and the United States as an independent nation as a result of the Revolutionary War, was their organic alliance with the British. The Proclamation of 1763 which ended the French and Indian War restricted the American colonists from crossing over the Appalachian drainage ridge from the Atlantic Seaboard into the Ohio, Kentucky, and Tennessee River valleys. The Americans were beginning to feel they had a right to make policy of their own and this paper proclamation did not prevent Daniel Boone from entering Kentucky in 1769. So as the Indians fought alongside the French before, incurring the enmity of all English speakers, so now they fought with the British in their only realpolitik avenue of expression, incurring the enmity of the Americans.

The rush of Americans across the rest of Indian land in the historical time frame of a single life was to become known as Manifest Destiny. We have a sense of what the continent was like at the beginning of the arc of Columbus and the briefest outline of the treatment of the indigenes by three kinds of colonial powers. We turn now to their treatment at the hands of the Americans, victors in their Revolutionary War.

The first act under the Articles of Confederation was the land survey system known as the Northwest Ordinance, which provided for a system of land measurement and management and began distributing parcels of the Ohio River Valley to veterans of the Revolutionary War, veterans such as General George Washington, himself a surveyor, and soon to be the first

President of the United States. "The first and ultimate argument for dispossessing the Indians was religious" (Prucha 1962, 240). With God as the author and authority, anything is possible. The pervasive influence of the American religion of displacing Indians in God's name began right in the Massachusetts Bay Colony by the Puritan John Winthrop reciting *Genesis* to the effect that the marching orders are to increase and multiply, to replenish the earth and subdue it. The Old Testament nature of the American religion far outweighs any brotherly love extractable from the New Testament. Intellectual and legal reliance was placed on the arguments of Vattel, a famous Swiss jurist, who upheld the doctrine of the supremacy of the cultivator over the hunter (241). While it is certainly true that intensive agriculture can support a larger population, it is in turn true that industrial agriculture and industrialism generally can support an even larger population. Revisionists among us have suggested recently that agriculture may itself have been the original sin. Some of us will live to see whether or not the daisy chain from hunting and gathering man, to agricultural man, to industrial man, to electronic man, will in fact exhaust the capacity of the land and our ingenuity to force it to sustain us. The chain took a great leap forward with the American Revolution.

Although the American religion emulates the Jewish in its warlike qualities, Americans are not people of the Word, and barely go by the Book. Americans are the people of the picture. Hence the importance of image; whether it is favorable or derogatory will determine the nature of confrontations when cultures collide (Forbes 1964, 13). The early 19th century image of Indians held by Americans was largely derogatory. While for "Four hundred years, from 1513 until the beginning of the twentieth century, Europeans and Native Americans fought a relentless series of wars to determine the ownership of what is now the United States" (35), in particular the 19th century "struggle in the United States was. . . long and cruel and destructive" (35).

There are historians who separate the treatment of the Indians from the general thrust of Manifest Destiny. "A better-supported thesis is that Manifest Destiny and Imperialism were traps into which the nation was led in 1846 and in 1899, and from which it extricated itself as well as it could afterward" (Merk 1963, 261). This line of thinking reinforces the notion that Manifest Destiny only applies to wars for territorial aggrandizement against European and Spanish speaking peoples. Merk is a great micro-historian. His work on the Oregon issue is peerless. He permits himself, in the above quotation, a favorite generalization of Americans that the struggle with the Indians was a domestic issue rather than the imposition of policy on foreigners. "A truer expression of the national spirit was Mission. . . dedication to the enduring values of American Civilization" (261). We will see how this "Mission," yet more evidence of the religious nature of the American national life, and the enduring values of the civilization were applied to Indians.

"Calhoun realized that he had to face both ways simultaneously, leading Jackson and the westerners to believe that he was supporting their views by allowing the negotiations to proceed, and leading the Choctaws to believe that he was maintaining his policy of moderation" (DeRosier 1972, 55-6). Here we see one of the enduring values of the civilization, Calhoun's concurrent majority, at work while he was the Secretary of War in the Monroe administration, in the two-faced application of the principle of compromise by diplomatic subterfuge. The resulting Treaty of Doak's Stand and subsequent Treaty of Dancing Rabbit Creek would deprive the Choctaws of their land and leave them feeling betrayed. It was rationalized by Andrew Jackson as "'notwithstanding the opposition heretofore made to the treaty, they, at this time seem to be almost universally satisfied'" (68).

The Choctaws had multiple reasons to feel betrayed, not the least of which was the fact that they had fought alongside of Andrew Jackson and made significant contributions to his victory over the British at the Battle of New Orleans, which was actually fought two weeks after the war was over, due to the relative speed of 19th century communications. Jackson presented himself as a friend of the Choctaws then and would present himself as a friend of the Cherokees a few years later. Nevertheless, "all true Southerners would rejoice at the opening of this vast acreage of virgin soil to the cotton culture that was fast forcing the southern part of the United States into a unique mold" (68). There was no rejoicing, only weeping and wailing, among the Choctaw.

In a series of Supreme Court cases handled by the Chief Justice John Marshall, some tortuous decisions were handed down. To begin with Marshall had already decided that title to the land belonged to the discoverers in *Johnson and Graham's Lessee v McIntosh* in 1823 (Forbes 1964, 103), as opposed to the people who were in residence. With such a legal mandate, the Italians could push their claim to China based on the discoveries of

Marco Polo. In *Cherokee Nation v Georgia* and *Worcester v. Georgia*, he decided that Indians were dependent domestic nations, but also that they had distinct political rights and boundaries that were not to be violated by the state of Georgia. Jackson refused to enforce John Marshall's opinion (Prucha 1962, 244-5), a type of executive "nullification" of the judiciary. The Cherokee's joined the Choctaws among the betrayed and were placed on the "Trail of Tears." Jackson's selective refusal to cooperate and enforce Supreme Court decisions as the ultimate arbitration of law, as well as John Marshall's creative development of this personal tradition which has no basis in Constitutional fact, demonstrate the ad hoc nature of American use of power by men rather than by law.

The legal and illegal torture inflicted upon the Indians would see little rest. "In spite of the Supreme Court, in spite of solemn treaties, in spite of the Constitution, and in spite of a professed belief in the right of self-government for all peoples, the native groups east of the Mississippi were relentlessly driven westward and despoiled by avaricious whites" (Forbes 1964, 105). The Trail of Tears led the civilized tribes of the Southeast to Indian Territory, which was to be theirs in perpetuity. Perpetuity lasted for approximately 40 years before they were once again swindled out of most of their land. In 1889, Indian Territory became Oklahoma as it was opened to settlement by Whites. While Jackson is relatively famous for his participation in this series of frauds, less well known and frequently unremarked upon is the role of Thomas Jefferson.

Jefferson, the libertarian without equal, abandoned his utopian solutions and "ordered his lieutenants (especially Governor William Henry Harrison of Indiana Territory) to begin acquiring, as rapidly as possible, all Indian lands east of the Mississippi" (102). This harsh and ultimately definitive policy was a contributing cause to the War of 1812, by which time Jefferson could say, "'we shall be obliged to drive them with the beasts of the forest into the stony [Rocky] mountains'" (102). While it is possible to read into the policies and equivocations of Calhoun and Jackson, the consideration that the West was to be a haven for the Indians, "Jefferson's ideas implied a human cattle drive, as white settlers pushed Indians before them" (DeRosier 1972, 27).

Sectional politics played a role in Indian policy. "The Charleston, South Carolina, *Southern Patriot* editorialized that 'one of the reasons why certain people of the North are so strongly opposed to the Indian emigration. . . is that it will give the Southern and Southwestern States. . . an influence in the councils of the Nation which they do not now possess. . .'" (109). In addition to economic and political considerations, northern opposition also demonstrated more respect for the dictates of the Supreme Court as Marshall defined them and the operation of law under the Constitution.

All sections of the country had different economic interests in the acquisition of more land. The claim is made that the slave economy depended upon continued acquisition of fresh land, and that this expansionism was on an inevitable collision course with the desires of free white Northern settlers who had a "clear economic interest in excluding slavery from the territories" (Wright 1978, 137). Seen from a northern and eastern point of view, "in the free labor economy of the North, westward expansion threatened to hurt eastern business by driving up the wages of labor" (132). In any case, the expansion of slavery and the cotton plantation economy made possible by the removal of the civilized tribes west of the Mississippi demonstrated that "Federal policy to move all Indians from one vast area to another violates the very principles on which the United States was founded" (Oswalt 1973, 567).

One of the very principles on which the United States was founded was slavery. The Southerners were moving west and determined to take their slaves with them, where their future was just over the horizon. The argument for taking the continent for cultivators so that it could support a larger population was grounded in religious belief and rationalized as religious economics. Nowhere have the two faces of destiny, flip sides of a single coin, been played out anymore clearly than they have been in North America. It was the destiny of the Indians to be displaced; it was the Manifest Destiny of the English speaking Americans to displace them. And though slavery in America is frequently thought of as only applying to African Americans, Native Americans were also enslaved. It was a habit picked up from the Spanish.

"The 'discovery' of Florida by Ponce de Leon in 1513 was, in fact, an extension of slave hunting beyond the empty islands" (Sauer 1966, 160). The depth of the Spanish commitment to slavery is revealed in the observation that "It is significant that the first census in the New World was a statistic of native numbers as to age suited to labor" (vii). Slavery, an integral part of the Constitution of the United States, had a 300-year productive track record in North America, both of African Americans and Native

Americans, before it became an issue in the sectional drive and competition to control the West. "South Carolinians were *the* Indian slave traders of the North American continent" (Weir 1983, 26). Weir's is not an isolated assessment. "During the late seventeenth century, in fact, [South] Carolina was more active than any other English colony in the export of Indian Slaves" (Wood 1974, 39).

Wood is one of the few authorities to make use of the disclosures of Sauer and he can say the Indians "decimated by novel disease, consumed by incessant labor, starved to make way for crop-destroying cattle and hogs of the Spanish — the invaders turned increasingly to Africa for manpower" (5). The South Carolinians realized early that "Without good Indian relations 'you can never get in yo Negroes that run away'" (53). It became important after the Yemassee War for the slaveholding South Carolinians to keep the Indians and the Negroes separated (116), an early form of divide and keep conquering anybody other than white.

Indian slaving was not confined to South Carolina and the Spanish. It was prominent in the North as well. "New England had early taken the lead and throughout the colonial period held more Indians in slavery than any of the other colonies except South Carolina. . ." (Forbes 1964, 89). Forbes' work includes an entire chapter on "Red Slavery" and demonstrates its appearance in Arizona, California, and virtually everywhere there were Indians. *Indian Slave Trade in the Southwest* by L. R. Bailey gives a detailed account of conditions there. He recites a Utah legislative act referring to land "which really is Indian territory so far as the right of soil is involved" (1966, 209).

Indian rights were virtually to disappear in the 19th century including any claim to nativity. We have heard how John Marshall decided that land belongs to the discoverers and that the Indians represented "domestic nations" but the prize for legal linguistic oxymorons has to go to the decision of the Supreme Court on November 3, 1883 which decided that an American Indian is by birth an alien (Brown 1971, 391). Virtually everywhere else on earth, being born someplace automatically confers a claim to nativity if not citizenship.

What did these "aliens by birth" believe about themselves? In a chapter titled "The Mystery of the Indian Mind," Clark Wissler notes that when Indians pray they humble themselves. He contrasts this sincere humility with the formal humility of civilized man (1966, 305). The Indians realized they were at the mercy of nature; English speaking Americans have put nature at their mercy, so they think. Philip Drucker speaking of the distinctive flavor of Northwest Coast Indian religions notes they have "a set of beliefs revolving around the immortality of certain economically important species of animals, combined with a series of ritual practices to ensure the return of those creatures" (1963, 151). This fusion of cultural with natural history echoes Sauer's reports of it elsewhere. We have already observed the Indians sense of "ultrademocracy."

Indians were hard to confine with arbitrary rules, and Fehrenbach notes that the war parties of the Apache and Comanche went as far south as Jalisco (1968, 58). The Comanche seemed particularly contemptuous of European ideas, denying that they ever earmarked their horses. "Any Comanche could distinguish one horse from another by looks just as easily as he could tell one person from another" (Wallace and Hoebel 1952, 47). Clearly the Comanche believed in their horses. The Comanche were indifferent to Confederate attempts to regulate their behavior which asked them to support themselves and live in peace and quiet. "Nothing was asked of the Comanches except that they should no longer be Comanches" (304). In their despair after losing and being reservationized, the Comanche turned to *Ishatai* — Coyote Droppings in *Komantia* — the medicine man for spiritual guidance. It led to yet another defeat at the Battle of Adobe Walls (319-328).

In *Standing Bear v General George Crook*, Elmer S. Dundy a U.S. District Court Judge for Nebraska ruled on May 12, 1879 that "An Indian is a *person* within the meaning of the *habeas corpus* act" (Tibble 1972, 94) in one of the few instances of legal and human dignity extended toward native Americans. Few Indians were thought of as persons and the basic mode of operations against the Indians in any case was the policy of genocide and scorched earth.

"Kit Carson liked Indians. . . Famous as he was, the Rope Thrower never overcame his awe of the well-dressed, smooth-talking men at the top. . . Under Carleton's obsessive prodding, Kit Carson accelerated his scorched-earth program, and by autumn had destroyed most of the herds and grain between Fort Canby and Canyon de Chelly" (Brown 1971, 23-5). Carleton told Carson to tell the Navahos to "Go or we will destroy you." This kind of ultimatum delivered in the spirit of total war reveals a mean streak many Americans are uncomfortable confronting. "Before returning to Fort Canby,

Carson ordered complete destruction of Navaho properties within the canyon — including their fine peach orchards, more than five thousand trees. The Navahos could forgive the Rope Thrower for fighting them as a soldier, for making prisoners of them, even for destroying their food supplies, but the one act they never forgave him for was cutting down their beloved peach trees" (27). It is not difficult to understand how forgiveness could be asking for too much.

From the Navaho in the southwest to the Lakota in the North at the Massacre at Wounded Knee in 1890 where 300 of 350 Indians were killed and left in the snow (444), *Bury my Heart at Wounded Knee*, an Indian History of the American West, displays the savagery resorted to by the white Americans. "(He) was able to burn most of the Miami villages and destroy the Indian's corn just as the winter descended" (Fehrenbach 1968, 99). During the Civil War, Colonel John Chivington perpetrated the Massacre at Sand Creek (Bolton 1959, 208). Chivington had earlier ordered the slaughter of 500 captured Confederate horses and mules at the Battle of Glorieta Pass. During the congressional investigation that this slaughter of the innocents at Sand Creek inspired, his own men reported they had told him he would be committing murder but he was not moved by sympathy for Indians. Among the many mutilations, some soldiers cut "out the private parts of females and stretched them over the saddle-bows, and wore them over their hats while riding in the ranks. . ." (Forbes 1964, 47). There is a headpiece still worn in the American military called a "cunt cap."

The famous American mountain man, James P. Beckwourth, who was also Black or Mulatto, barely missed being pressed into service as a guide for Chivington as Carson had permitted himself to be used in the destruction of the Navaho. Beckwourth was for nearly 10 years known as Bloody Arm, a chief of the Crow Indians. The Crow had typically more friendly relations with the Whites because of his service. Although Beckwourth's memoirs are scorned by historians like Francis Parkman, who spent six weeks in Wyoming and wrote *The Oregon Trail* based on his experience, Beckwourth spent his entire adult life out west, discovering among other things the pass through the Sierras that bears his name (Bonner 1965). Beckwourth was as aware as anyone that the slaughter of the buffalo and their being brought to the edge of extinction was the result of an attempt to remove the Indian's source of livelihood and starve them to death, another form of scorched earth.

The story does not improve as it was played out farther west where in California "'survival of the Indians was in inverse ratio to the contact with the missions'" (DeMarco 1988, 6). The West was not to remain, in Theodore Roosevelt's famous description, "A game preserve for squalid savages" (Fehrenbach 1968, 446). The momentum of Manifest Destiny, sectionalized to the South and temporarily derailed by the Civil War, eventually reached all the way to Asia. Theodore Roosevelt Jr., in his book *American Imperialism,* says "When I left Puerto Rico I did so because I had been named governor-general of the Philippine Islands, a post it had always been my ambition to fill" (1970, 125). This suggests that perhaps the course of empire is nothing more than a jobs program, which is exactly how James S. Baker III of Texas, George Bush's Secretary of State, rationalized the war on Iraq to "liberate" Kuwait.

Displaced people suffer culture shock as reported of the still suffering Shoshoni-Bannock of Idaho in contemporary times (Forbes 1964, 170). Evidence for why they should feel that way can be adduced from the numbers. "In the Treaty of Fort Bridger in 1868, the Eastern Shoshonis gave up their rights to 44,672,000 acres of land lying in Colorado, Wyoming, Utah, and Idaho, to settle peacefully on their reservation of only 3,054,182 acres" (Trenholm and Carley 1964, 318). To have an estate reduced by that order of magnitude would depress anybody.

"A dangerous world demands military strength," opines Arthur Schlesinger Jr., "It does not demand the militarization of the national life" (1986, 162). The national life, as it pertains to Indians, was however militarized. Did the 19th century Americans exaggerate the danger, or did their exaggerated cure of displacing Indians exacerbate the danger to the point where genocide and scorched earth were acceptable responses? In a section called "Totalitarian America: The Unknown Land," Forbes says: "Almost completely unknown to most Americans, or of little interest to them, was the totalitarian state within a state that existed for over half a century — the Bureau of Indian Affairs and its empire of 'wards.' In the twentieth century many Americans have come to think of Nazi Germany and the Soviet Union of Stalin as prototypes of the all-embracing state, but Hitler and the Stalinists might well have been imitating the system of coercive culture change used earlier by the United States" (1964, 113). There is no brush wide enough to completely whitewash the history of white America's treatment of the Indians. "'The problem is that American machines are not equal to the task of killing communist soldiers except as part of a scorched-earth policy that destroys everything else as well'" (Chomsky 1973, 72). Nor is there a brush wide enough to prevent the American use of scorched earth policy elsewhere as illustrated by this soldier's opinion from Vietnam.

At the conclusion of the Apache Wars, "the soldiers began to close in toward the train, forcing the Apaches aboard the cars" (Faulk 1969, 163). Other people have been forced on trains, by the Nazis of course, but the special nature of the Apache demise caught the attention of the American poet Edward Dorn in his collection *Recollections of Gran Apacheria*. In "*La Maquina a* Houston" he declaims, "The first principle of warfare/where *All of Us* is the Army, and they are the people" (1974, np). The militarization of America is so complete that its first nature, even when it is not second nature, has been rendered invisible and goes generally unremarked upon. Nevertheless, the English speaking military occupation of North America was suddenly completed. The scorched earth will always be with us. The competition between the North and the South for control of the West took them to Arizona, one of the homes the Apache had been driven out of Texas to and a whistle stop on the thought train of Houston's map of potential Texas.

9

The Confederate Territory of Arizona

Confronted with a map of the Confederate Territory of Arizona, many people will be surprised to realize that it is not coterminous with the present state of Arizona. The Confederate Territory of Arizona actually consisted of those portions of the present states of Arizona and New Mexico south of latitude 34, with a western boundary at the Colorado River while the eastern boundary was shared with Texas. Currently, Arizona and New Mexico are divided East from West. The Confederacy chose to divide them North from South. There are significant political, economic and geographic reasons for the map taking this historical shape.

Most of the Southwest had been ceded by Mexico to the United States in the Treaty of Guadalupe Hidalgo that ended the Mexican War. The entire cession was divided into California and New Mexico, with California being admitted to the Union as a free state by the Compromise of 1850. There had been periodic but unsuccessful efforts in the U.S. Congress to render the entire remaining territory of New Mexico into smaller units more suitable to government management and development.

Most of the southern portion of Arizona and part of the southern portion of New Mexico were obtained from Mexico in an abrogation of Article Eleven of the Treaty of Guadalupe Hidalgo, known as the Gadsden Purchase. There were many compelling reasons for this purchase. Article Eleven delegated responsibility for enforcement of peace with the Indians in the area to the U.S. The Indians of course were filled with contempt for the concept of solid "international" boundaries, let alone the fluctuating one between Mexico and the United States. Their raids into Mexico increased Mexican demands for indemnification.

The structural difficulty with enforcing Article Eleven stemmed from the terms under which Texas had been admitted to the Union, retaining title to all its public lands. At the same time, the Indians became the "wards" or the responsibility of the national government. As has already been reported, there were and are no Indian reservations in Texas. As settlement advanced, Indians were displaced and compelled to plunder where they could to sustain themselves (Terrell 1972, 202). While the annexation scheme agreed to between Texas and the United States was the causative factor in Indian displacement, the Indians were made to carry the burden of blame in a not very cunning Anglo-Texan projection and misplacement of responsibility. Driven westward, the Apache coped with their situation and "In fact, one might say that the Apache actually occupied Confederate Arizona" (Trimble 1977, 163).

Beyond keeping the sporadic peace with the Mexicans and the Indians, American interest in Arizona was driven by the realization that the eastern portion of the presently United States needed to be connected across the political void to the West Coast or California by railroad. Since road building had devolved to be a function of the War Department under Secretary John C. Calhoun during the administration of James Monroe, so too did the question of the transcontinental railroad fall on the shoulders of Jefferson Davis, Secretary of War to President Franklin Pierce. According to Reigel's *History of the Western Railroads*, "The most important single survey was carried on under Secretary of War Davis, and the result submitted to Congress in 1855 in ten bulky volumes" (1964, 15-6).

While it might have been expected that Davis' recommendation would be for a southern route, it was also to be expected that northern senators such as Stephen Douglas of Illinois, who favored a route from Chicago to San Francisco, would object. The building of a transcontinental railroad would be held hostage to sectional contention until the immediate results of the Civil War were known. Douglas' pecuniary interest in the central route, (an extreme northern route, Minneapolis to the Northwest, had little support), did not lend his arguments moral or political suasion. As will be shown gradually by the political and economic development of the United States, Davis' recommendation of a southern route had the merits of economic, political, and geographical determinism, working in its favor. Davis had done his homework. "The significant part of [Davis'] report however, was the immense amount of information, which proved invaluable at a later time" (16). While Davis' opinion may have been biased in favor of the South, it was also predicated on compelling economic logic.

We need only to read the entire title of the work, *Reports of Explorations and Surveys, to Ascertain the Most Practicable and Economical Route for a Railroad from the Mississippi River to the Pacific Ocean*, to realize the width and depth of the work which actually takes up 12 volumes. What Davis was

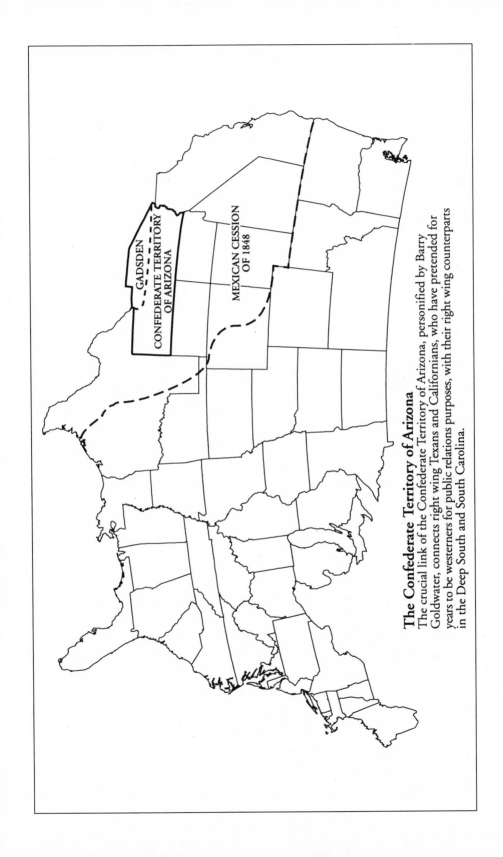

The Confederate Territory of Arizona
The crucial link of the Confederate Territory of Arizona, personified by Barry Goldwater, connects right wing Texans and Californians, who have pretended for years to be westerners for public relations purposes, with their right wing counterparts in the Deep South and South Carolina.

GADSDEN

CONFEDERATE TERRITORY
OF ARIZONA

MEXICAN CESSION
OF 1848

after in his own words is apparent in his instructions to Lieutenant John G. Parke for that portion of the report near the *Thirty-Second Parallel of North Latitude, Lying Between Dona Ana, on the Rio Grande, and Pimas Villages, on the Gila.* "The profile of the region traversed, showing the gradients which a road passing over it must encounter, is the information most wanted. It is therefore recommended that you take the barometric height at every point on the line to be surveyed which may be important in the elucidation of this subject" (1855, 4).

With the approval of the Mexican Government, they were surveying land still claimed by Mexico. When the barometer is read at every important point, the report to Congress showed the best transcontinental route to be south of the Gila River. To make his dream of a southern railroad route connecting the South to California acquire substance, Davis was the goad who pried the $10 million out of the United States Senate for the Gadsden Purchase. It delivered title to the land in southern Arizona upon which the Southern Pacific railroad bed lies to this very day.

The Gadsden Purchase was named after the ambassador to Mexico, James Gadsden, "a railroad man from South Carolina" (Trimble 1977, 121), and a scion of the famous Gadsden family of South Carolina. "Such a man was Christopher Gadsden, owner and builder of the Great Gadsden Wharf and an early champion of Charleston's mechanics" (Rosen 1982, 49). The Gadsden Purchase might very well have been much larger. When we consider that the U.S. only indemnified Mexico $15 million for the entire empire ceded as a result of the Mexican War, $10 million for the Gadsden parcel indicates two things. The price per square mile was going up astronomically and "The Northern Congress did not want a large territorial acquisition, fearing it would become populated by slaveholding Southerners" (Trimble 1977, 122).

These fears were entirely realistic as "The first Anglo-American settlers to arrive in Arizona were mostly from the states of the late Confederacy. Perhaps because of this circumstance, they lost little time in making Arizona a 'white buffer state' between the Spanish speaking people of New Mexico and those of Sonora" (McWilliams 1968, 83). James Buchanan, although from Pennsylvania, the last Democratic President of the United States when the South still controlled the federal government, had as little respect for the international border as did the Apache and wanted to establish forts on both sides of the border (Terrell 1972, 213), a thinly veiled ruse in his attempts to annex Sonora as late as 1860. Not only did white southern slaveholders quickly move to take physical possession of the area around Tucson, they brought some of that old time southern political panache with them. "The political imperatives inherited from the eighteenth century themselves produced a tendency toward extremism. . . Christopher Gadsden declared 'he would rather submit to the destruction of one half of the country than to give up the point in dispute'" (Weir 1983, 344). Extremism in defense of intellectual principles, native to South Carolina, is as old in Arizona as the presence of speakers of English.

The white speakers of English may have been introducing the slavery of African Americans to Arizona, but they were hardly introducing slavery. "In 1775 Father Thomas Eixarch purchased an Apache child in exchange for a horse and commented that along the frontier of Sonora it was common to barter for captives, although it was against Spanish law" (Forbes 1964, 92). Forbes also indicates that slavery by Hispano-Mexicans was actually tapering off in the eighteenth century and that some of "the captives became servants without liberty (although they were not property as were slaves in the southern United States)" (92).

This remarkable distinction between slaves as property (capital) and slaves as servants without liberty may have been without functional consequence to the slaves in question, even as it permitted the adoption of superior and groundless moral tones by some practitioners and is a crucial link in the economically hermetic relationship between slavery and peonage. The Civil War itself hardly put an end to such practices and Indian captives and children were for sale in Arizona in 1868, plus "peonage, the qualified slavery still prevalent in New Mexico, authorized by its laws, and encouraged and practiced by its people. . ." (96), was still extant.

Thus we see ontogeny recapitulating its political phylogeny of slavery and white supremacy in Arizona, just as it had in Texas, who got it from South Carolina, where it had been established by the British Empire from the overflow on the island colony of Barbados.

"The Confederate Congress passed an enabling act on January 18, 1862; and on February 14 of the same year, President Jefferson Davis proclaimed Arizona a territory of the Confederacy with Mesilla as the seat of government" (Arizona WPA 1940, 49-50). It is to be noted that this territory was not imposed on the area as "Most of the citizens in Tucson and Mesilla were southern sympathizers" (Terrell 1972, 224) and had formed the territory themselves. "On March 16, 1861, a Secessionist convention was [had been] held at Mesilla which declared Arizona to be a territory of the Confederate States" (Colton 1959, 198). Although Granville H. Oury was the first delegate to the Confederate Congress, he was replaced by M. H. Macwillie, attorney general for Colonel Baylor's military government, who served for the duration of the Civil War (202).

The entire area was filled with political and military confusion as Union soldiers and officers were deserting to take up arms for the Confederacy (224). The Texas Mounted Rifles, under the command of Colonel John Robert Baylor, marched into the territory and took control of Fort Bliss which had been abandoned by Union forces. Baylor announced the formation of a military government and appointed himself governor of the Confederate Territory of Arizona. He would later be confirmed in this position by President Davis, even though he labored under the delusion that Arizona was already safely in Confederate hands. He adopted a policy of extirpating Indians and selling the children into slavery, a policy endorsed by the residents of Tucson (224-6) but not by President Davis as it created diplomatic problems for the Confederacy as they appealed to England for recognition (Trimble 1977, 163). Except in the north, Arizona was settled mostly by Texans (Gunther 1947, 901), and that helps to explain the enlongated map of the Confederate Territory of Arizona.

During the Civil War, after the Union had reduced Confederate military influence in Arizona and New Mexico to wishful thinking, the U.S. Congress created the Federal Territory of Arizona in its approximate present shape although it included the Las Vegas area of present-day Nevada. It is worthwhile to notice the Union imagination dividing the territories east from west; in the Confederate imagination they were divided north from south. The Texans had made but few friends in the Sante Fe or northern area of New Mexico where the political power was during the period when they imagined that greater Texas included the entire drainage of the Rio Grande. The New Mexicans around Santa Fe did not care to be annexed to Texas. The Confederate Territory of Arizona, long, low and southern, revealed itself in realistic terms, in addition to its mineral wealth and railroading potential, to be a corridor to control of California. It is impossible to interpret the southern, Confederate and Texan thrust into Arizona any other way than as concrete evidence of the central position played by the issue of control of California and the West in the reasons why the Civil War was fought. The facts support this conclusion. In the East, President Davis would rationalize the war as a defensive one; in the West it was demonstrably aggressive and offensive.

The Civil War in the West, as it was nearly everywhere, was a family affair. The Union forces under Colonel Canby would ultimately defeat the Confederate forces led by his brother-in-law, former Union Major Henry H. Sibley of Texas. "In an audience with Confederate President Jefferson Davis, Sibley had presented a grandiose scheme of securing New Mexico, Arizona, and California for the Confederacy in one sweeping blow" (Terrell 1972, 226). Realize that the Territory of New Mexico at the beginning of the war encompassed everything between Texas and California. "With the possibilities of California's seceding from the Union, or at least the southern part of it, and of annexing some of the states of northern Mexico [a la Buchanan], it was of major importance for the Confederacy to acquire New Mexico" (Colton 1959, 3). We have seen realism operating in Confederate logic with the creation of the Confederate Territory of Arizona, not only from the crucial parts of New Mexico Territory, but from parts where the political sympathy was with them. But was there any realistic basis for dreaming about the secession of California, or even the southern part of it?

San Francisco, a city of 100,000 people and the center of power in California in 1860, had been peopled by free thinkers from all over the United States and the world in their crazy quest for gold and instant riches, the poor man's foot traffic on Sir Francis Drake's golden ladder of acquisition. There was little sympathy there for the Confederate slavocracy. Los Angeles on the other hand, was another matter entirely. Gordon DeMarco, in a section entitled "The Civil War — Los Angeles Chooses the Confederacy," makes the following observations. "In the presidential election of 1860 Los Angeles cast 356 votes for Abraham Lincoln. His opponents received 1700 votes. John Downey, a pro-secessionist Democrat was elected governor. It was said that the circle of Buchanan Democrats 'virtually controlled Los Angeles" (1988, 41). While Confederate sympathizers may have controlled Los Angeles, a quick look at the total number of votes relative to the population of San Francisco reveals their puny deliverable power. While the *Alta California* of San Francisco could charge that fully a third of Los Angelenos were "copperheads" or Confederate sympathizers in a Union State, DeMarco goes on to state that "It is not difficult to understand why some Californios 'supported' the Confederacy. It is perhaps difficult to understand why more didn't" (42). While the near term outcome of the Civil War dampened southern Californian enthusiasm for the Confederacy, "Nevertheless, Los Angeles was a Confederate stronghold in the early phase of the Civil War. . . [and] In 1865, U.S. soldiers had to be sent into Los Angeles to break up a crowd celebrating the assassination of President Lincoln" (43). Confederate support, mainly in southern California, was palpable but not yet large enough for the Confederates to capitalize on.

Regardless of the missing quotient of realism, "Confederate leaders planned to annex a corridor from the Rio Grande in Texas to the Pacific Coast of California" (Colton 1959, v). The Civil War and the initial military defeat of the Confederacy put this plan on hold for 60-80 years, "but since Confederate forces actually occupied most of New Mexico and Arizona at one time, the conflict in the Rocky Mountain West should be regarded as a significant campaign in the American Civil War" (vi). Because Colonel Chivington slaughtered all their horses during the Battle at Glorieta Pass, the Confederate Texans were forced to retreat on foot. By 1865, the Federal Territory of Arizona was almost two years old. But it must be remembered, "There were two Arizonas during the Civil War" (209).

If there were two Arizonas then, there must be only one now, finally admitted as a state to the Union at the relatively late date of 1912. What southern characteristics which it had during and before the Civil War does it retain? "Today more cotton is grown in California and Arizona than in the Five Cotton States put together" (Ransom and Sutch, 1977, 199). "With the first World War creating a sharp demand for long-staple cotton, the cotton kingdom jumped from west Texas to the Salt River Valley in Arizona" (McWilliams 1968, 173). On the subject of cotton at least, Arizona is more southern than the South.

Arizona retains a lot of the military character established by Colonel Baylor. When hearings were being held in Washington D.C. on the Dodd gun control bill, "three men drove 2,500 miles to Washington from Baghdad, Arizona, to testify against it" (Hofstadter 1965, 5). The Texan love of guns is alive and well in Arizona. When William Walker was "recommending a cofilibuster to Alexander Stephens [the soon to be vice president of the Confederacy] for an Arizona political appointment, he cited the man's 'unquestionable. . . devotion to Southern interests'" (May 1973, 112). Arizona political patronage is parceled out on such ideological lines. Theodore

Roosevelt was so good to his rough riders that he installed Benjamin Franklin Daniels, who had been in the Arizona Territorial Prison for a 'minor homicide,' as the warden of the very same prison (Pringle 1955, 139). In the American structure of jurisprudence and journalism, the only way a homicide can be considered minor is if it is carried out against some person who is other than white.

White racism is alive and well in Arizona, not always directed only at African Americans. Just after WWII, John Gunther observed that "Negroes are not conspicuous in the Southwest, though the war brought a good many to Arizona. They fall between two stools — in that they are not given as much economic opportunity as the North provides, nor are they treated quite like livestock as in the South" (Gunther 1947, 897). It is a treat not to be treated like livestock, the pleasures of which would be lost on whites. "When troops of the Confederacy under Captain Hunter seized Tucson during the Civil War, Ochoa was given the alternative of taking an oath of allegiance to the Confederacy or of leaving Tucson" (McWilliams 1968, 167). Estevan Ochoa, who would later be the first citizen of Tucson, fled, not caring to learn first hand what becoming a Confederate would mean.

"'The only difference between peonage and Negro slavery,' wrote Will H. Robinson, [in *The Story of Arizona*] 'was that a peon miner could not be sold from one master to another'" (145). Peonage thus supplanted slavery as the capitalistic labor supply of choice in the Southwest. On June 27, 1917, Mexicans were in the strikes at the Arizona copper mines and were subsequently boxcarred out to Columbus, New Mexico (197). It is to be noted that these strikes at the copper mines took place during the period of perfervid nationalism of WWI, barely five years after Arizona had been admitted to the Union. Civil rights and civil liberty violations during WWI are extensively documented in American history "On July 10 an armed posse rounded up sixty-seven strikers in Jerome and 'deported' them on cattle cars into California. Two days later another Sheriff's posse ousted over a thousand striking miners from their homes in Bisbee [Arizona], herded them onto cattle cars, and left them in the middle of the New Mexico desert near Columbus, where there was no food or water for any of the victims" (Johnson 1963, 89). First the Apache were put on box cars and railroaded out, then Mexicans and white striking miners. It is fair to suggest, based on the historical evidence, that anyone who is not both white and rich runs the risk of one day being railroaded out of Arizona.

This undeclared and illegal war against striking laborers, Mexican and white, should tell us much of what we need to know about the conditions of labor, organized and otherwise, in Arizona, birthplace of Caesar Chavez. The expression of Arizona's dominant political beliefs reached its apogee in the career of Republican Senator Barry Goldwater. "His beliefs came straight out of nineteenth-century laissez-faire doctrine" (Hofstadter 1965, 98). We can see how this doctrine is in fact more lazy than fair as Bourgin (1989) has pointed out the many workings of the federal government in the late 18th and early 19th centuries on behalf of projects, that in a strictly laissez-faire system, would have been undertaken by private capital.

"A political mirage for three generations of Arizonians, the Central Arizona Project is now a palpable mirage, as incongruous a spectacle as any on earth: a man-made river flowing uphill in a place of almost no rain" (Reisner 1986, 304). Well, water flows uphill in the west towards money. In a strict laissez-faire economy, no non-economic project like the CAP would ever get beyond the howling stage. Arizona is the most politically conservative state (312). However, "Barry Goldwater, scourge of welfare and champion of free enterprise, has been a lifelong supporter of the Central Arizona Project, which comes as close to socialism as anything this country has ever done" (11-12). Here we see Arizona signing on bigtime to the Texas principle of getting somebody else to pay for its projects, which also puts Arizona firmly in the tax consuming column of Calhoun's system of government by class.

This is an utterly organic classification for Goldwater, whom as we have observed found much of his bankable political support in South Carolina and the South. Goldwater's "extremism in defense of liberty is no vice" is as intellectually hollow as the earlier extremism of Christopher Gadsden. In *The Paranoid Style in American Politics*, Hofstadter characterizes political conservatism. "Goldwater thinks of conservatism as a system of eternal and unchanging ideas and ideals, whose claims upon us must be constantly asserted and honored in full" (1965, 94). Pass on the temptation to dwell at length on the Confucian and preter-fascist effort to avoid change which these ideas represent. Recall instead how Hofstadter described Calhoun's putative failure as one of trying to force a static solution onto a dynamic situation. Forcing static and unchanging ideas and ideals upon the dynamism of a constantly changing and diverging world is precisely what gives the conservative position, and the white leisure class it represents, its propelling reversion toward the ancient claims that barbarism makes upon us. Goldwater "remained forever a friend of the military" (Schlesinger 1971, 461).

Arizona is just such a place where reversionism to British Empire and Confederate military ideals of racist exploitation dominate. In spite of the efforts of Carleton and Kit Carson to starve the Navahos out with their scorched earth policy, the rebuilt Navaho Nation exists in northern Arizona. While there are many other Indians and at least half or quarter breeds alive in Arizona, the Navaho is by far the largest extant group in the entire United States. Some of it is attributable to the matriarchal and matrilocal structure of the Navaho culture. Some of it is also due to the fact that the Navaho, an Athabascan speaking people from much farther north who refer to themselves as *Dine* or the people, moved into the Southwest within the time frame of their own historical memory, displacing the *Anasazi*, or the old people. Unlike some other Indians who imagined they had always been where the European types found them, the Navaho know better. They also know that since they displaced the *Anasazi* and were displaced themselves, so too the white Arizonans who hold political power now are hardly immune to displacement or indispensable in God's eyes.

With an Indian "empire" in its own backyard, the people still exploited for Uranium and coal, Arizona models the British Empire, right down to the reconstruction of London Bridge at Lake Havasu City. It received its white political and military bearings from Confederate railroad men from South Carolina and the Texas Mounted Rifles under Colonel Baylor. By latitude, geography, crop production and political inclination, Arizona is the link that lies in the pathway of the Confederate Empire's expansion to California. Its political affiliation with the states of the old Confederacy was demonstrated in the Confederate election of 1964 — and in every election since — when Goldwater carried it and five states of the deep South. It was declared by its minority white citizens to be a Confederate Territory in March of 1861. Arizona was a Confederate Territory then; it is Confederate territory now.

10

Jefferson Davis: The Father of the Confederate Empire

Lieutenant Jefferson Davis resigned from the United States Army in 1835 in order to marry the first love of his life, Sarah Knox Taylor. Sarah was the daughter of then Colonel Zachary Taylor who did not want his daughter married to a career Army man with an uncertain future. Sarah had insisted she would marry Jefferson with or without her father's consent and that someday he would recognize Jefferson's value. Zachariah Taylor had lost two daughters and very nearly his wife and Sarah to bouts of the bilious fever in 1829 in Louisiana. After the wedding, Jefferson and Sarah went south on the Mississippi River to live on his brother Joseph's plantation called Hurricane, 30 miles south of Vicksburg.

Plunging into plantation work, both Jefferson and Sarah contracted malaria and Sarah died. Deprived of his bride of less than 90 days, he was deathly ill himself. Recovering from his personal bout with malaria, the 27-year old Jefferson Davis visited Havana, Cuba, where he was accused of spying as he sketched some army barracks. He impulsively booked a passage to New York and went on to Washington D.C., where he met among others, a young representative from New Hampshire named Franklin Pierce. Jefferson returned to Mississippi to put down the roots of a massive depression. "For the next seven years Jefferson Davis remained a recluse on Davis Bend" (Strode 1955, 93-109).

If Jefferson Davis seemed a stoic statue as history passed him down to us before Hudson Strode's humanizing biography, the formative experience of losing the two greatest loves of his life, sacrificing one to gain the other, goes a long way towards explaining the denial in his formal posture of pain. Depression was not uncommon on the southwestern frontier. Captain Meriwether Lewis, the famous explorer, had succumbed to it. Neither was there any treatment for Jefferson Davis beyond his family's love.

Jefferson Davis, like many male children of his generation, North and South, black and white, was named after President Thomas Jefferson. Born in Kentucky, he went back there on horseback to Catholic school at age seven, passing by the Hermitage and receiving his first tutelage from the even then awesome "Old" Hickory Andrew Jackson, who was still in his forties and fresh from his victory at the Battle of New Orleans (13). The hermetic web of personal contacts that seams American military history together is typified by the career of Jefferson Davis. His own report of Secretary of War Calhoun's appointment of him as a cadet to the United States Military Academy at West Point has already been cited (Thomas 1968, 23). Davis' models and sponsors were the dominant military, intellectual and political figures of the age.

The subject matter in those days at West Point included *On the Constitution*, a law textbook by Judge Rawle of Pennsylvania, "who upheld the doctrine of the constitutionality of secession" (Strode 1955, 44). Davis personally studied the subject using Kent's *Commentaries* (45), as the Rawle book had been discontinued. Ideas are not as discontinuous as books, though cited in their pages. Their shelf life is as long as the belief system that registers them. Calhoun and Davis never ceased believing in the constitutionality of secession. Among Davis' peers passing through West Point in the 1820s, many of whom cared little for formal religion having found one that works, were Albert Sidney Johnston and Robert E. Lee. Lee would later say, as the shambles of the Civil War were settling on his head and the national or Union cemetery had been placed in his pasture at Arlington like another totally unnecessary thorn through his heart, that "the biggest mistake of my life was to take a military education" (Burns 1990, PBS:VI).

Jefferson Davis' continuing military education would take him after graduation to Wisconsin and Iowa. Although Davis had been born in Kentucky, he had lived for a few years at a time in Tennessee, Louisiana, and Mississippi, before going to New York and West Point. He had been all over the land he loved, a moving about that demonstrates how modern the 19th century really was as even then ambitious young people were frequently on the move. The movement of the ambitious toward the West forced the Black Hawk War with the Sauk and Fox Indians. Black Hawk, the defeated Indian chief, was escorted to Jefferson Barracks "in a steam boat, under the charge of a young war chief [Lieut. Jefferson Davis], who treated us all with much kindness. . . The people crowded to the boat to see us; but the war chief would not permit them to enter the apartment where we were — knowing, from what his own feelings would have been, if he had been placed in a similar situation, that we did not wish to have a gaping crowd around us" (Hawk 1971, 140).

Unelaborated prophecies abound in the life of Jefferson Davis, from his naming to Zachary Taylor's unease at his wedding to Sarah to the sensitive assessment of Black Hawk as a prisoner of war. All Americans are prisoners of war of one kind or another. Captain Abraham Lincoln of the Illinois Mounted Volunteers was in the Black Hawk War, as was Taylor, Scott, Twiggs, Anderson, Johnston and future politicians too numerous to cite (16), all looking for a badge of medal, the touch of honor, the ticket to political office, that only killing Indians in the 19th century could bestow and deliver. Anderson would defend Fort Sumter; Twiggs, Johnston, and Davis would fight for the Confederacy.

After seven years of army life, enough he thought to pay the government back for his West Point education, Davis grew bored with the futureless fight with the Indians and the army's pettiness. His but barely requited love for Sarah Knox Taylor directed his attention toward her, to whom he had become secretly engaged, over her obstinate father's wishes. Before her death, Jefferson Davis displayed flexibility of character. "'One of the most humorous, witty, and captivating gentlemen whom I had ever met, I did not think he showed to me any signs of such sober abilities, as these wiser heads had so cordially accorded him'" (Strode 1955, 85). Davis was widely regarded as "one of the brightest and most promising officers in the whole army," where he undoubtedly kept his wit and humor in check.

Jefferson Davis was pried out of his Hurricane depression and seclusion with a seat in Congress. Pending war with Mexico, he re-enlisted in the army and marched with his former father-in-law to Texas. Colonel Jefferson Davis was a hero of the Battle of Buena Vista. Commanding the Mississippi Rifles, "two regiments of volunteers formed a V with the open end to the enemy. Into those yawning jaws came the lancers, at first at a trot, and then slowing to a walk, and the storm of fire that came from each side of the V of Buena Vista annihilated the head of the enemy column and broke the tail in a dozen pieces" (Leckie 1968, I:352).

Jefferson Davis' famous V formation is a risky tactic as the superior cross fire power can easily lead to soldiers being mowed down by friendly fire. But the future belongs to risk takers and wounded in the foot with a boot-full of blood, he refused to leave the field (Strode 1955, 182). Taylor cited Davis for "coolness and gallantry" (184) and came to realize that his daughter had been a better judge of men than he. Davis went to the Senate and Taylor went to the White House as a Whig. They parted intellectual and political company on the subject of extension of slavery.

The row over admission of California to the Union as a free state, culminating in the Compromise of 1850, was as intense and divisive as the issue of slavery itself. Zachary Taylor, who had been born in Virginia and transported at the tender age of eight weeks in saddle bags to Kentucky, would not live to sign it. "He became ill with acute gastroenteritis, from which he might have recovered had not his doctors sprung to his side to stuff him full of calomel, opium, ipecac and quinine, after which they bled and blistered him until, on July 9, 1850, the Angel of Death came to his rescue" (Leckie 1968, 384). A healthy man could be killed with that combination of medical interventions. Small wonder then that the iatrogenic death of President Zachary Taylor should have stimulated the exhumation of his remains during the summer of 1991 for the purpose of additional autopsy to determine whether or not his enemies had had him poisoned.

The atmosphere had been permanently poisoned by the time President Millard Fillmore signed the Compromise of 1850 into law. The times had also taken the life of the lion of South Carolina, John C. Calhoun. Southern politicians, led by Robert Barnwell Rhett of South Carolina and William Yancey of Alabama, met at Nashville, Tennessee, to discuss the possibility of immediate secession. It never happened but Rhett and Yancey would be back. Davis spoke of his "'superstitious reverence for the Union'" (Strode 1955, 230), another of those long forecasting prophecies, not only for the Union, but the Union as Davis eventually imagined it after its deconstruction in the Civil War and then its eventual domination again by an unreconstructed South.

His visit to Cuba as a young man trying to recover from his grief at the loss of Sarah, made a permanent impression upon him. Even before the California question, Cuban patriots under the command of General Lopez "Sought Jefferson Davis as their commander to liberate Cuba" (211). Davis recommend Robert E. Lee instead. "The soldier and the Senator had a long talk, and they must have recalled the Latin American overtures to Sidney Johnston when they were at West Point together" (212). Lee declined. This particular Cuban revolution fizzled. "General Lopez was garroted, while several young Southerners of prominent families were executed against a wall" (212).

In the strong southern flavor of *The Evolution of American Foreign Policy*, Dexter Perkins writes, "There was a hunger for Cuba in the eighteen-fifties, especially on the part of the South. . ." (1966, 25). Jefferson Davis left the Senate to become Franklin Pierce's Secretary of War, where he was widely regarded as the most influential person in the Pierce cabinet and administration. The Democratic victory had rescued foreign policy from its Whiggish drift.

When thinking of the wealthy, white slaveowning Southerners and their distinctive economic interests, particularly the insistence on the expansion of slave territory, it is vital to keep Edward Phifer's description of them in perspective. "What must be understood is that the slaveholder was not at heart an investor; he was a speculator. . . his primary interest was in appreciation" (Wright 1978, 142). This distinction between investing and speculating as reported in *The Political Economy of the Cotton South*, is crucial for understanding the 1850s, the antebellum South and the cotton-slave economy's most superficially prosperous hour. "As the cotton economy spread. . . Her planters, working exhausted land, and hard pressed to compete with the fresh soil of the interior. . ." (Hofstadter 1959, 71), sought to speculate elsewhere from their base in the cotton candle they were burning at both ends. Investors seek income and profits; speculators, remember Sir Francis Drake, favor high risk transactions hoping for unusually large profits.

The search for unusually large profits directed the attention of the pro-slavery expansionist South in two directions. They had already regained control of the federal policy apparatus. They looked West and for a way to connect the South to California by railroad. They ran into Senator Stephen Douglas of Illinois who "had extensive personal real estate investments which would benefit from the [central route or northern] railroad" (Wright 1978, 155). Davis and Pierce were opposed by Southerners who felt that it would be unconstitutional for the government to undertake the construction. Recognizing that he was getting nowhere, he abandoned the attempt with "statesmanlike wisdom and temperance" (Davis [W.C.] 1991, 270), even though the preponderance of facts and information was on his side. The real lost cause is in attempting to change minds that are already made up with religious bias through a skillful presentation of the facts. Facts are not persuasive in religious disputation. Jefferson Davis's 12 volume "Railroad

Survey" of the potential routes, to use the short title, in his capacity as Secretary of War, is famous for its thoroughness.

He brought this same thoroughness to the effort to modify the U.S. Army for service in the deserts and on the great plains. His experiences in Texas had demonstrated how ill equipped it was. His passion both for the military and for thoroughness is one reason why, after the Civil War, the first place to begin the resurrection of his reputation was the United States War Department, where he was acknowledged to be the most effective Secretary of War of all prior to the Civil War. While William C. Davis, in his new biography, *Jefferson Davis, The Man and His Hour*, chooses to treat that "hour" of his life lightly, he does state that he "had run a cabinet department that accounted for fully one-third of the government's administrative duties and budget so well, that few questioned his capacity for the presidency" (280). Jefferson Davis was serious presidential timber in 1860, even though seriously handicapped by the rife sectionalism.

While he was frequently ridiculed for introducing camels from the Levant into the Southwest, it was a perfectly logical (and productive for as long as he was managing it) experiment, for he knew that successful armies had been supplied logistically on camel back for millennia on deserts greater than the Great American one. Before the Mercedes Benz, it was fundamental Islamic transportation. If there is comic relief to be found with camels in the deserts of Nevada, perhaps it should be sought in the "political opposition from the mule market in St. Louis" (Trimble 1977, 124). The sterile mule as a draft burden animal of choice, the equine equivalency of a static solution to a dynamic situation, was bred to perfection by General Ashley in the nearby Ozark Mountains.

Jefferson Davis and the southern expansionists also looked further south to what Robert E. May chose to call *The Southern Dream of a Caribbean Empire*. "Jefferson Davis expressed such reasoning when he supported a congressional bill to acquire Cuba on the basis that it would 'increase the number of slave-holding constituencies'" (May, 1973, 11). We've already seen General Lopez finding the garrote in his search for Southern support for a liberated Cuba (27). But what is not so apparent is that "Virtually every year up to the Civil War, American adventurers would formulate schemes to invade, or would actually invade, some part of the Caribbean region" (29).

While the region wide support for the general imperative to acquire a Caribbean empire is readily apparent, the agreement on strategic initiatives broke down at the tactical level. General Quitman of Mississippi, a Jefferson Davis rival for power and influence, wanted to hustle up some guns and take Cuba by force, with the generous aid of Texans. Pierce and Davis, attempting to acquire Cuba by diplomatic means, that is to say without firing a shot, felt it necessary to rein him in, even as they distanced themselves from the Ostend Manifesto, which was a piece of free-lance foreign policy generated in Europe which threatened Spain with military action if she refused to relinquish Cuba (46-70). Diplomatic stances require people to adopt ticklish positions and Davis tried to pin the failure to acquire the island on a lack of congressional cooperation (65) even while "Davis [feeling] it imperative to make such a reassurance is indicative of the strong feeling for Cuba in the South" (73). While John Quincy Adams, one of the few northerners who attempted to acquire Cuba, could rely on some unwritten laws of political physics which to him at least indicated that because of its proximity, Cuba should fall like Newton's apple in the direction of American gravity, it was not to be. Differences over Cuba would create distress in "the North-South coalition holding the national Democratic party together" (75).

Disagreement over tactics would eventually doom the Walker episode in Nicaragua to a fizzled fate also, even as "The New York *Evening Post* termed his achievements part of the 'irresistible law of modern colonization'" (78). Walker, this wild and crazy guy, had earlier captured La Paz, declared a republic of Lower California, and pretended to annex Sonora (84). When Walker had control of Nicaragua, he legalized slavery and though "Davis favored the Walker regime, Pierce had already taken a stand against filibustering" (96). Walker's slaveocracy in Nicaragua would receive diplomatic recognition temporarily because "Pierce, in addition, calculated that recognition of Walker would pressure the British government into accepting the American interpretation of the Clayton-Bulwer Treaty" (101). Not only do we see modern (Reaganite) colonization taking place in these machinations, we see the modern fallout, diplomatic and political, that accompanies it. Everybody is constantly grinding their own axe, as the Clayton-Bulwer treaty called for joint American-Anglo development and exploitation of an Isthmusian canal through Panama. Walker would pose as a champion of slavery, for political purposes and in the U.S. House of

Representatives, "A vote revealed that William Walker's campaign to become a symbol of slave expansionism had succeeded" (120). This "nineteenth century version of the banquet circuit" (120) would lead the New York *Times* to accuse Walker of "'laying the basis' for a 'Southern Slave Empire'" (133).

These were heady days in the antebellum South; even if they were largely unsuccessful in acquiring more territory, the activities reveal the depth of feeling. Sometimes the politicians were hemmed in by a strict reading of their own laws. "Davis, for instance, asserted that the United States Navy could only enforce the neutrality laws within American territorial waters" (119). This kind of legal circumspection on the part of Davis was not part of the enabling repertoire of Andrew Jackson when he went after Florida. Nor would it be a part of Theodore Roosevelt's thrust toward empire. But here we see the South, tied up in knots by "The Whiggish tendency to suppress sectionally disruptive issues [which] also motivated the Whig-American attack on tropical expansion" (201).

President Pierce would fail to be renominated, but James Buchanan, another Democrat, this time from Pennsylvania, would be elected president. Not the least of Buchanan's claims to support were his efforts on acquiring Cuba, which he would reify by urging the Congress to assume control of Chihuahua and Sonora, as late as 1860. Meanwhile, the Kansas-Nebraska Act of 1854 had made all territory open to slavery and the Dred Scott Decision of 1857 declared the Compromise of 1820 unconstitutional. This compromise had originally put a lid on the legal squabble between the sections over the extension of slavery and had been legislatively responsible for directing the attention of southern slaveholding speculators outside the national boundaries of the United States. "In summation, the secessionist call for a tropical confederacy was the culmination of the sectionalization of manifest destiny before the Civil War" (243).

Jefferson Davis, the most prominent southern leader during this period, had inherited John C. Calhoun's mantle in the Senate to which he returned upon the election of Buchanan. His administration as President of the Confederacy can be seen as the logical extension of the Buchanan Administration without the Whig, now Republican, and northern opposition. Davis believed the slaves were being supervised by a superior race. Lincoln seemed to join him in this opinion of white superiority. On August 14, 1862, prior to the Emancipation Proclamation, Lincoln addressed some free black men of the North: ". . . not a single man of your race is made the equal of a single man of ours. Go where you are treated the best, and the ban is still upon you. . ." (Lincoln 1953, V:372). One of the places where African Americans were not going to be treated the best was Illinois, Land of Lincoln, where in November 1863, "a majority of 100,000 voted for a new article in the Illinois Constitution prohibiting any Negro, free or slave, from immigrating into the state" (Strode 1959, 312).

We see in the 1850s what Jefferson Davis and the expansionist Southerners were fighting for: control of the federal government, control of the West, and control of a southern and larger empire outside the official borders. These issues divided the nation along sectional lines. South Carolina dissolved the Union and Jefferson Davis was the assembled representatives of the slaveholding South's choice on the first secret ballot at Montgomery to be President of the Confederate States of America.

The Constitution of the Confederate States of America as rewritten to reflect what they felt the United States Constitution really meant, included a passage outlawing slave trade and the importation of slaves from the United States. This plausibly humanitarian gesture was in fact an effort to shore up the value of capital by restricting the supply. In continued southern emulation of the British Empire, the Confederate Constitution was based on the British budget system, offered the president a line item veto and required a balanced budget. These last two items would later stimulate the otherwise moribund political imagination of the Neo-Confederate Ronald Reagan and his latter-day conservative cronies, apparently in perpetuity. The single six-year term for the president became a favorite "reform" idea of yet another Neo-Confederate, Lyndon Johnson, whose disastrous policies prevented him from seeking re-election, and who then sought some loftier terrain to strike a noble pose on, after delivering the copper quarters.

All competent authorities are in agreement on the subject of southern domination of the United States government prior to the Civil War, including Alexander Hamilton Stephens of Georgia, who was elected Vice President of the Confederacy at Montgomery. He had been reluctant to secede because he felt the South had always controlled the government, especially in its important moves. We've heard from William Seward on how this southern control was basically designed by the minority slaveholding class. Alfred Kazin could assert without fear of contradiction that "Before the war, the South had dominated the American political scene. . . [including] the Supreme Court and the Army" (1991, 63).

Walter Prescott Webb, the great Texas historian, repeats the news that in the East the South was well prepared and exhibited unusual skill. "They were accustomed to leadership, to political domination, to victory in the halls of Congress and in the field of presidential elections. They had a talent for success in these things" (1931, 192). Webb goes on to remind us of the southern victory in Texas, the victory on the Compromise of 1850, the victory of the Kansas-Nebraska Act, the Dred Scott decision in their favor interpreting the Constitution as they did, and the southern victory in the elections of 1852 and 1856. A final southern victory had all the trappings of inevitability.

Such was the situation in 1861 that it was the Union that was fighting for survival. The South had done nicely within it and imagined they could do even better without it. The ultimate contest for history and politics is the control of the future and the interpretation of the past however, not the past itself. And control of the future meant control of the West. "The South might win all the battles in the East; but unless it could win in the West also it was sure to lose the contest, for it was there that the final decision would be made" (193). The "final" decision in the West would be a long time coming in.

The more immediate decision in the far West resulted in the Union forces under Canby wresting control of Arizona and New Mexico from the Confederacy. But not before the zealotry of the Texan Colonel Baylor had thrown up some obstacles for Jefferson Davis. "President Davis was not pleased when he learned of the order [to kill Apaches wholesale]. . . Selling the idea of slavery, the 'peculiar institution,' to Europeans was difficult enough without this added complication" (Trimble 1977, 163). On the eastern front, diplomatic recognition was felt to be crucial to the Confederate cause. It will not do to pass without comment on the irony of European sensitivity to slavery, especially among the English, who had recently given it up after developing it to a high economic art form and sequestering it in South Carolina where it still flourished.

In fact the Europeans, at least the upper classes, did have more in common with the Confederacy. Speaking of the English, "In fact, the innermost sentiments of the governing classes and the aristocracy, as well as those of European Royalty, were hostile to the United States" (Hendricks

1939, 136). The more egalitarian northern part of the United States had a more complex and democratic series of role models than the direct emulation of the English aristocrats which characterized South Carolina, who were only too happy in turn, to spread aristocratic notions westward. John Quincy Adam's son Charles, Lincoln's ambassador to the Court of St. James (and father of Brooks Adams, the peripatetic geo-politician), noticed how the United States was hated and feared in Europe. "The press, like the upper classes, was predominantly and often eloquently pro-Southern" (Strode 1959, 163).

However much European aristocratic, royal and media sentiment may have favored a southern victory, whose Constitution made tariffs illegal and called for free trade, a harbinger of GATT, diplomatic recognition was eschewed. It was eschewed in Mexico also. Perhaps ambassador Pickett, who had once said "Southward the star of empire takes its way" was not the right man to send on that diplomatic mission. Senor Mota thought he would have a difficult time convincing the Mexicans that the Confederacy was their natural ally, since Jefferson Davis had publicly coveted Mexico all his political life. Pickett's gambit was the intriguing notion that there really isn't any difference between slavery and peonage. While this raised Mexican umbrage even as it reduced the talking points as to which system is the most humane or efficient at the exploitation of labor, it wasn't convincing.

The similarities and differences between slavery and peonage are worth book-length treatment. Reduced to their essentials, they both represent class, race, and cultural exploitation of people deemed to be inferior. Peonage is ultimately less expensive than capital because peons are expendable and not provided for during slack time when they are not producing directly. The capitalist commitment to slavery provided quarters, was on-going (Jefferson Davis had provided a dentist and day care for his slaves [Strode 1955, 119]), and not salable as a concept to the Mexicans. The Aztecs, Toltecs, and other powerful pre-Columbian Mexican civilizations had practiced slavery, but mid-19th century Mexicans correctly located the source of the pressure they were feeling in the slaveholding South.

Critics of Jefferson Davis' two volume history, *The Rise and Fall of the Confederate Government*, often lament that it is mostly military history when they would prefer more political insights. It is a military history because the Confederacy was a military government. Jefferson Davis, correctly or incorrectly, considered himself to be a military genius. He had demonstrated valor and leadership in the heat of the Battle of Buena Vista. He had demonstrated a capacity for administrative genius as Secretary of War. He harbored a desire in fact to be the field commander of the Confederate troops. The history of the South, of Jefferson Davis, and of the Confederacy is one in which the military aspects dominate even when they don't completely rub out the more taciturn political elements.

"When one examines Confederate history to determine the reasons for Confederate defeat, one studies both military and civilian decision making, for they amount to the same thing. . . This close connection between the civil and the military was not true in the North, at least not to the same degree. . ." (Beringer et al 1986, 25). While we are looking here for reasons for victory not defeat, this opinion from an entire school of historians about the inseparability of the military and the civilian is a shared aspect of the shared search for the truth. They go on to say ". . . never lose sight of the tight interrelationship of military and civilian decision making. . . and Confederate will was the point at which the two came together " (27).

Was Jefferson Davis a great leader? He was elected if not popularly, at least by a quorum of his exact peers. Thomas R. R. Cobb, brother of Howell Cobb of Georgia, a Davis rival for Confederate leadership, expressed the pithy opinion that Davis was "not great in any sense of the word" (Hendricks 1939). Cobb would also say that the power of will has made him all that he is. This is the same will, the Confederate will of Jefferson Davis, that binds them and their military history together. Cobb, one of the only witnesses to the secret meetings in Montgomery as reported by Burton Hendricks in *The Statesmen of the Lost Cause*, would regrettably be killed in the battle of Fredericksburg.

This fusion of the military and the civilian is still strong in contemporary American life. For instance, while it might be argued that President Truman's dismissal of MacArthur was an assertion of "The principle of the supremacy of the civil over the military authority," it could also be argued that it was Truman "following the counsel of his military advisors," and as such was just one military decision of two military choices, even if made by the rube from Independence, who as the commander-in-chief is considered to be a non-military individual for public relations purposes.

In John Blassingame's study of *The Slave Community*, he at one point contrasts military life with life on the plantation. "Scholarly studies of the army show that it is a close, highly stratified, authoritarian, neo-feudal, paternalistic institution providing all the biological and psychological needs of its members except sex and family life" (1972, 218). He did not find the military at all like life on plantations, for which it would be a poor model for "the plantation was irrationally organized and understaffed with bureaucrats and guards. . . could not survive if it systematically tortured, starved, or exterminated its inmates. . ." (218). What slavery and the Army have in common is their neo-feudal origination and their demonstrable reversions to barbarism.

Midway between the Civil War era and contemporary times, Theodore Roosevelt, who was to do his share to fuse the military with the civilian aspects of American life, "dwelt on his devotion to the South and quite forgot that he had once branded Jefferson Davis a traitor comparable only to Benedict Arnold" (Pringle 1955, 7). Davis, still alive for the insult, attempted in vain to rebuke Roosevelt. Another of the curious family aspects of American and Civil War history is the fact that Theodore Roosevelt had two maternal uncles from Georgia serving in the Confederate navy. "Captain James D. Bullock, an officer of the old navy, of high ability as a seaman, and of an integrity which stood the test under which a less stern character might have given way, was our naval agent in Liverpool" (Davis 1958, II:248). James Dunwoody Bullock has also been described as the Secret Service of the Confederate States in Europe.

The haunting question of the value of Jefferson Davis' leadership is often diffused by comparisons to the military genius of Robert E. Lee, the darling of both sides in contemporary times. "Lee could have lost most of his battles but won the war, Nolan writes; instead he won most of his battles and lost the war" (McPherson 1991, 10). No reputation is safe in the continual re-examination of history from differently enlightened perspectives. McPherson reviewing Nolan's revisionist history of Lee reports "that the very qualities his admirers praise are those that ensured Confederate defeat: 'devotion to the offensive, daring, combativeness, audacity, eagerness to attack, taking the initiative'" (10). Even Lee's leadership is not universally applauded.

If Lee took command in 1862 and staved off the military defeat for three more years, it was Davis who appointed him in timely fashion. Lee surrendered; Davis fled. "Davis and others, who shared his views [J. William Jones, Jubal A. Early], excessively proud of the Confederacy and their roles in it, fell into the class proudly labeled 'unreconstructed.' It was such individuals who established and ran the historical societies, veterans' organizations, and cemetery associations. Like Davis, they reduced their postdecision dissonance by claiming that the South should have won, even if it did not" (Beringer et al 1986, 407). Bruce Catton's *Reflections on The Civil War* repeats this theme. "He stuck by his guns and, to the day of his death, maintained that all that he and his fellow citizens had tried to do was right and proper" (1981, 152).

The rightness of what they were doing failed initially on some peripherals: reluctance of four slaveholding border states, Missouri, Kentucky, Maryland, and Delaware, to join them; superior leadership by Canby in the West; their failure to ship the 1861 cotton crop. For a system placing a high value on state rights, the necessity of consolidating power in a central command was devastating. Governors Zebulon B. Vance of North Carolina and Joe E. Brown of Georgia resisted the centralizing of power to the point of treason. Even at that they may have been less trouble for Davis and the Confederacy than outright re-Unionists like Holden in North Carolina.

This consolidation of power in the central government took place in the North as well. "And the rise of New York to the position of world-city during the Civil War of 1861-5 may perhaps prove to have been the most pregnant event of the nineteenth century" (Spengler 1928, 99). Pregnant or not, New York City was the site of the anti-draft riot in 1863 that killed 119 people and wounded another 300, the most deadly civil disturbance in American history. It reflected something Davis himself felt. "Unalienable rights are unknown to this war-begotten theory of the Constitution" (Davis 1958, II: 763). Both the Confederacy and the Union in their drafts and conscription attempts ran headon into American independence and the constitutional right to refuse involuntary servitude, such as in the coal mining country of Pottsville, Pennsylvania (Zbick 1992, 25).

Davis is the best source of his own unreconstructed attitude when he says of the right of secession: "I recognize that the war showed it to be impracticable, but this did not prove it to be wrong. . ." (764). People confuse leadership with eloquence in the misbegotten notion that a poor idea well stated will get you into less trouble than a good idea garbled. Before the Civil War, Davis could speak to a packed house in Faneuil Hall in Boston. He created the second most powerful military government in the 19th century out of thin air and will. The issue is not his leadership; the issue was the choice of direction.

Leadership is doing the right thing. Management is doing things right. The initial southern failure in the Civil War was a failure of management, not of leadership. This is demonstrated conclusively in Davis' inability to delegate consistently, revealing confusion regarding the distinctions between management and leadership. When Americans say, formerly in jest, presently in dead earnestness, that Germany and Japan won World War II, they are not merely referring to the results of history independent of the actual fighting, but to something more profound at the bedrock of culture that guides history. The Japanese were fighting for an empire dominating Asia and they eventually got it, albeit commercial rather than the poor military model they had picked up from the speakers of English. Germany wanted to dominate Europe and now it does. These are the victories of culture driven belief systems. Battles, the least interesting aspect of war, are won and lost by generals. Wars are won by ideas that never rest.

Jubal Early, Jefferson Davis and other unreconstructoids proselytized the South with their agenda; they didn't live long enough to recognize their ultimate victory. "It may seem to require amazing mental agility to conclude that the Confederacy had won victory. . . The south had indeed preserved its view of the Constitution, white supremacy, and honor. . . If the war was lost over slavery and independence, the peace was waged — and won — for state rights, white supremacy, and honor" (Beringer et al, 1986 417). The only mental agility required to recognize the ultimate south-ern victory is an open mind with a wide enough lens. When professional historians examine the factual evidence and come to conclusions of partial victory, the more complete victory hitherto obscured by the shadows of history and northern prejudice will be recognized in time. Charles De Gaulle of France once opined that success in politics was simply discovering the inevitable and then supporting it.

Jefferson Davis spent 720 days imprisoned at Fort Monroe, five of them in leg irons. William C. Davis, no relation, in *Jefferson Davis, The Man and His Hour*, states "His was the uncompromising spirit of Andrew Jackson, of John C. Calhoun, of the heroes of the Alamo, of men who never gave up no matter the odds. Then too, he was their martyr, crucified in the shackles and dungeon of Fort Monroe in atonement for all of them" (1991, 705). The allusion to MacBeth in the subtitle, wishing to limit the Jefferson Davis impact to an "hour" of strutting and fretting upon the stage to be heard from no more, takes us in exactly the wrong direction. It imagines his radiating influence is stopped by the walls of his Richmond tomb and represents a failure to correlate the more ancient 19th century facts with their more modern 20th century implications. W.C. Davis puts much prophetic religious nomenclature in place, crucified in shackles, atonement, the spirit of his political ancestry in Jackson, Calhoun, and most of all the Alamo, but the martyr's journey hardly ends there; it was just getting underway. Jefferson Davis was traveling in the inevitable direction.

When General Robert E. Lee, one of the few Confederates not to personally pin the "loss" on Jefferson Davis, surrendered his sword to General Ulysses S. Grant and rode back through his men crying, the fixating moment of the ultimate southern victory fell with the tears from his eyes. The Legend of the Lost Cause would be driven underground, into the fertile soil of the Confederate will, personified by Jefferson Davis, where in due time it would ripen and surface triumphant. "Davis never gave up his belief in the desirability of acquiring Cuba. He thought it would be well if the United States owned all the land from the Canadian border to the Isthmus of Panama, and he was convinced that United States citizenship would prove a progressive benefit to the peoples of Mexico and Central America" (Strode 1955, 299). The Civil War is over and the passage through the Confederate comeback milestones begins. George Washington is the father of the country, the United States. Abraham Lincoln "freed" the slaves and kept the Union together for eventual re-domination by the South. Jefferson Davis is the father of the Confederate Empire of North America.

Part III

Confederate Comeback Milestones

"We started up the trail, October 23rd"

The Chisholm Trail

Second Texan: The Chisholm Trail North

One of the longest branches of the Confederate comeback trail began in Texas. It was covered with cattle and headed north. It was the Chisholm Trail which ran from Austin, the capitol of Texas, to Abilene, the quintessential cowtown created at the railhead by Joseph G. McCoy. We have already seen how the Texans Baylor and Sibley were quick to lead the Confederates west into Arizona and New Mexico. "Arizona was settled, except in the north [Mormons and Navahos], mostly by Texans, and Texas influence shows itself in the trends toward industrial farming and cattle as a big industry" (Gunther 1947, 901). As we follow the spread of Texas north and into the rest of the West, it will be useful to keep in mind Sam Houston's map of potential Texas.

The Texas cattle kingdom began in south Texas between the Nueces River and the Rio Grande, precisely that piece of real estate, title to which was disputed between Mexico and Texas, where the Mexican War began. Texas beef was significant to the Confederate troops before the Union cut off the supply at the Mississippi River. Sporadic and inconsequential efforts to drive cattle to markets north and east to develop a business prior to the Civil War had convinced a few people that the venture could be made sound.

Raising and marketing cattle as a business, even as a ranching business, began elsewhere. "The cattle industry in California, however, had reached its zenith and had begun to decline at about the time that Texas became the cattle nursery of the nation" (McWilliams 1968, 152). The trade in hides between California and Boston, where Richard Dana worked along the California coast in the 1830s, originated on the large Spanish style rancherias. McWilliams writes also of the "semi-feudal" (155) nature and organization of these ranches. "In the lower Rio Grande Valley a way of life developed that was quite similar to that which had prevailed in early California. Here was to be found the same patriarchal setup in which a few large Mexican landowners lived an idle and lordly existence based on a system of peonage. . . The peon was always in debt" (85). The Spanish origins of ranching, the cattle business, known as "kingdom" in Texas (kingdom itself is a feudal word), are well known.

Less well known and equally pertinent was the development of the cattle market. Young Daniel Drew was flush with money he had received for taking someone else's place in November of 1814 during the War of 1812. With the war over in a few weeks, he used the money to buy cattle, salted their forage and sold them at a great profit, on the cost of the salt and water at least, to Heinrich Astor, brother of John Jacob Astor (Drew 1969, 42-54). This was the origination of the Wall Street term, "watered stock," an early form of junk bond on the hoof.

Drew points out that Astor had developed the habit of leaving the actual market at the southern end of Manhattan Island and going north to meet the drovers, the better to select out the prime beef ahead of the other butchers. This process of going out to look over stock and buy it before it got to the market stretched the cattle trail the length of Manhattan Island, and then off into the hinterland of New York, all the way to Chicago and on into the center of Kansas during Drew's lifetime. The closer you can get to the source, the better deal you can make. It was the market in Chicago that McCoy was to hook the Texas cattle to at Abilene.

Daniel Drew, who in his own words taught Jay Gould and Jim Fiske everything they knew, was a prime stock manipulator and helped to create Wall Street and the stock market in their primary 19th century form. It turned him into a lover of war as "I felt that the Boys in Blue, sometimes tramping all night through fever swamps and across mountains, or lying in the camp hospitals sick and wounded and dying, earned all the monthly pay they got. Because they were beating the waters so to speak, and we in Wall Street were getting the fish. . . When Richmond was finally taken, I for one was sorry to have the War come to an end. . ." (frontflap). Thus is made understandable the notion of the pregnant growth of New York City during, and as a result of profits to be made from, the Civil War.

It is fitting that the mercantile spread of the English speaking empire should have been centered in the Empire State, (later even in the Empire State Building), in a new city named after an old (York) in England, which had in fact been taken from the Dutch when it was originally known as New Amsterdam. Made pregnant by the Civil War, New York delivered the goods during the robber baron capitalist Republican heyday in the war's aftermath. Daniel Drew was there at its creation, speaking of how a drover

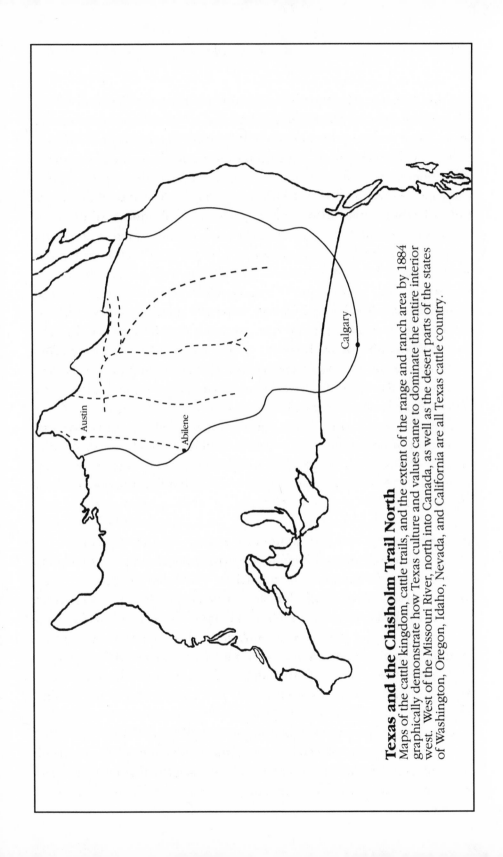

Texas and the Chisholm Trail North
Maps of the cattle kingdom, cattle trails, and the extent of the range and ranch area by 1884 graphically demonstrate how Texas culture and values came to dominate the entire interior west. West of the Missouri River, north into Canada, as well as the desert parts of the states of Washington, Oregon, Idaho, Nevada, and California are all Texas cattle country.

likes his critters because they mean money. On the other hand he was wistfully charmed by the attitude of his helpers. "Cattle boys get real fond of their critters . . [and] often get to like them out of real affection" (48). For the love of cows and cattle, some people are willing to do all of the work.

While three widespread roots of the cattle market, business, and kingdom are hereby traced to the divergent geographies of California, New York and Texas, cattle actually came on board earlier in South Carolina. Cattle had been useful for feeding immigrants in Barbados and with like use in mind, they were brought to South Carolina. "The cowboy who ranged the woods alone is as much the archetype of the black Carolinian in this era as Yeamans was of the exploitative planter" (Weir 1983, 174). We now have three variations on people who do the work in the cattle business. We have peons on the old Spanish and Mexican rancherias in Texas and California, we have Daniel Drew's "cattle boys" in New York, and we have Black slave cowboys in South Carolina. Black slaves from Gambia, where the care and feeding of cattle predates its practice in England, were much favored by the South Carolinian plantation owners.

We know who does the work; where does the word that presently describes the worker originate? The research of Peter Wood is worth quoting at length. "Might not the continued predominance of 'cowboy' over alternative terms such as 'cattleman' represent a strange holdover re-flective of early and persistent black involvement in the American cattle trade? This most American of words was already applied during the colo-nial period to men stationed at cowpens with herding responsibilities. Gray, *Agriculture*, I, 147. During the Revolution the word was used with a de-rogatory connotation (cf. 'house-boy') to describe American Tories who made organized raids on the cattle of Whig farmers [rustlers?]. Marshall W. Fishwick, 'The Cowboy: America's Contribution to the World's Mythol-ogy,' *Western Folklore*, XI (1952), 78. As late as 1865 young Negroes with livestock responsibilities were still being designated as 'cow boys' (two words) in the plantation records of the Southeast. U.B. Phillips and J.D. Glunt, eds., *Florida Plantation Records* (St. Louis, 1927), pp. 566, 568, 570" (Wood 1974, 31).

It is a source of wonder in American ingenuity, Yankee and Texas know-how, that they could take two highly insulting terms alone, for it still can be fighting words to call somebody a cow, jam them together and mount the result on horseback to create a romantic hero, cowboy, when it is still an insult as a two-word phrase "cow boy." It is significant that some of this American contribution to world mythology comes from plantation records from Florida, the state that still raises the most beef in the United States. Western domination of the cattle business was and is a mirage. "But, with all this, we must not ignore the fact that, after all, the West (even including Texas) did not produce many cattle" (Webb 1931, 226). Webb cites statistics to claim 34 percent in 1880 for all the West including the Dakotas and California. This could be the origination of the insult "all hat and no cattle."

The Civil War left the South devastated, broke and poor and there was a need for "the music made by real money rattling in the pocket" (217). "Ending the South's dependence upon the single crop, cotton, was seen as an indispensable step in securing a prosperous future for the region" (Ransom and Sutch 1977, 150). One solution was the cattle business in Texas. It is not easy to overstate the role of Texas in the South, the Confederacy, and in the United States. We need to remember that between 1821 with Stephen Austin's first foray into Texas and the close of the Civil War in 1865, only 44 fast years elapsed. The 19th century had already acquired the speed and momentum typically associated with the 20th. During those 44 years, Texas, which had been nominally French, passed through Spain's feeble fingers to Mexico, to Independence, into the United States, out of the United States into the Confederacy, and back into the United States, all in the span of less than a single lifetime. Loyalty in such a political tempest becomes like Robert E. Lee's for northern Virginia, intensely personal and local. "Any nationalism in the Lone Star State was Texan nationalism, not southern or even American nationalism" (Beringer et al, 1986, 78). The 60 terrible days when they fought alone, especially including the 10 days of death and victory at the Alamo, forged a national character.

After the Civil War, the Texans put this character to work in the cattle business. Cattle were worth $4 per head in Texas and $40 per head in the north. The practical question was how to connect the $4 cow with the $40 market (Webb 1931, 216). Here we see the daydream of the speculator who discounts overhead in the rush to realize the American Dream of the fantastic profits once racked up by Sir Francis Drake. The appealing three-word American imperative of "get rich quick" will die a hard death. Yet a few actually make it. The legendary W.T. Waggoner Estate in northern Texas, "an empire built from a ranch two-thirds the size of Rhode Island, appears to be crumbling under the weight of a squabble between the founder's third and fourth generation descendants. . . . Ranch history stretches back to pre-Civil War Texas. . . In 1870 legend says, father and son drove a herd of Longhorn cattle to stockyards in Kansas and rode back to Texas with $55,000 in their saddlebags" (AP *UB* 4-22-91).

The creation of the cattle kingdom in Texas after the Civil War went through five steps: from origination in the Nueces country, to Texas ownership on horseback, the disorganized drives to the north, the permanent depot at Abilene, and the deliberate spillover as it flowed to the rest of the west (Webb, 1931, 224). "Within a period of ten years it had spread over western Texas, Oklahoma, Kansas, Nebraska, North and South Dakota, Montana, Wyoming, Nevada, Utah, Colorado, and New Mexico; that is, over all or a part of twelve states" (207). All of these 12 states are included in Houston's map of potential Texas and the cattle kingdom branded them all with that peculiar Texas conservative political nationalism. South Idaho is left off Webb's list, though it is as Texan (and Missourian) as it is Mormon. In David Stoecklein's photographs of *The Idaho Cowboy*, in a picture of a bunkhouse titled "Cowboy Condo" from the Winecup Ranch on the Idaho-Nevada border, hangs the stars and bars of the Confederate flag (1991, 94). "They exploded not a business, but a new way of life, across the entire North American West. They made a culture. . . from Brownsville to Calgary" (Fehrenbach 1968, 554).

This cultural "explosion," not a bad military metaphor as Fehrenbach also refers to the culture as being "shot" across the American west and even into the Canadian part of Houston's map, carried some reversionary tendencies in those saddlebags. "The great majority of all Texans were then, and for decades remained, Southern Farmers. But out beyond the 98th Meridian the Plains sun burned through the fogs and lifted the burdens of Southern history. . . across twelve Western states, cowmen were essentially the same" (559). During this period, the Texans reformed their constitution. "The constitution of 1876 was in spirit and letter an instrument of the older, agrarian South" (436). Origins are difficult to shed. "The Texans who crossed the Sabine were still Southerners. . . The men who moved across the 100th meridian, and from there to Wyoming, were Western Americans" (566). Prior to 1968, when Fehrenbach published his history of Texas, the term Southerner lacked the cache and the political punch of Westerner. While there is no reason to bog down in the quicksand of semantics, in the approximately one human lifetime they had to operate in, the Southerners who crossed the Sabine into Texas were in some cases the very same people who moved on into the West and carried the values of the South with them. Ninety percent of the Texans then were from the South and 90 percent of Texas is still in the South. Texans get more political mileage from the convenience of referring to themselves as Westerners. Regardless of the nomenclature, their origins are on the public record.

"The United States was far from a unitary nation. . . For some years however, Texas and its Southern Allies maintained an acceptable stabilization and compromise" (633). Here we see in Fehrenbach's astute separation of Texas from its "Southern Allies," the differentiation in the southern recovery that is now traveling in both directions. As the Texas cattle kingdom put its political brand on the rest of the West by going north, the rest of the South looked to Texas for leadership and another chance. "Thousands upon thousands of Southern poor whites, seeing the hopeless landscape around them, determined to move to Texas" (603). Among these immigrants to Texas in 1877 was five-year-old Sam Rayburn whose father was a Confederate cavalryman from Tennessee. If Texas was going to lead the South, as it certainly does, let alone the United States, its leadership would prove to be more useful, absent any change in values, pitched from the West rather than the South. Thus the other huge line of force on Houston's map of potential Texas is run back across the rest of the Confederate South.

"The Texan's thirst for empires was guileless and natural" (641). We could quibble over the lack of guile, but the naturalness is basic. The Texas thirst for empire is the same thirst that stirred the Puritans in 17th century England to create an empire in Barbados and South Carolina, which in its natural turn, left the keys to the estate in Texas hands. In Texas and elsewhere in the South of course, thanks to Jefferson Davis and the other unreconstructed Southerners, it had become "something of an honor to have been a Confederate. . . [and] it was next to impossible to be elected to anything, unless the candidate had worn the gray" (439).

The Texas thirst for empire was satisfied temporarily in its political domination of the rest of the west, an old southern and Confederate goal. The United States "Had not yet begun its vigorous foreign policy of imperial expansion" (Webb 1931, 501) but it would be with us directly. "The collapse of 1885 converted ranching from an adventure into a business" (240), that is also to say from speculation into investment, and the blizzards in Montana and Wyoming in the late 1880s took whatever profit might have been left there and froze it to death.

The oil and energy business would in turn keep the Texas style churning icons and profits once again clear through Montana and Wyoming into Calgary, Alberta. Even the portions of these states not dominated by the cattle business, such as the Cascade portions of Washington and Oregon, follow another facet of the Texas model. Bonneville Power Administration, hydro-electric development on the Columbia River, and the nuclear reservation at Hanford were all designed to tilt the federal treasury in the state of Washington's direction, a Calhoun style tax-consuming region. To the present day, Colorado is a poor man's Texas. Neil Bush, the son of President Bush, migrated there and milked the system. "Son Neil, recruited in the mid-1980s to be a director of Denver's high-flying Silverado Savings and Loan, was reprimanded by federal authorities after Silverado failed, requiring a $1-Billion bailout" (Phillips 1994, 100). As portions of the Congress try to rein in unnecessary subsidies, such as passing a law in 1991 to raise by 340 percent, the federal grazing fees on public land in the West to their market value in private sector pastures, the icon trotted out on horseback and TV to object, was the about to be ruined Colorado rancher literally named Sam Houston.

The Texas style spread easily to California with ". . . the breezy manners and the swagger of a Texas 'cattle king.' These are the men who have luxurious homes in San Francisco and Berkeley as well as gracious mansions in the valley towns. . . they have no precise counterpart in American life, with the possible exception of the rich Texas cattle and oil barons" (McWilliams 1949, 169). Anyone looking for opulence in the city based on extractive policies in the countryside, will recognize the reflection of the luxury and wealth of the slaveowners residing in Charleston (or their New England summer homes), where this kind of capitalism got its American start.

"Roosevelt thought and talked the Texans' language; he was West-seeing and imperial; only his Republicanism and his Eastern origin kept him from becoming a major hero in the state" (Fehrenbach 1968, 642). The natural magnet of empire picks up a Republican, the complete effect of whose career will become part of the discussion shortly. Frederick Jackson Turner's *Frontier Thesis* supposedly closed the books on the American frontier in 1890, about the time Theodore Roosevelt was out ranching on the northern plains, chafing at the bit to invade somebody. Available land for poor white Southerners in Texas and elsewhere was scarce by 1890, and Oklahoma, formerly Indian Territory, was opened up for settlement. The Republicans under Benjamin Harrison, hoping to consolidate conservative gains in the U.S. Senate, quickly admitted six states from the "empty quarter" to the Union in these years: Idaho, Washington, Wyoming, Montana, North and South Dakota. It was not enough to rescue Harrison's Presidency from the resurgent Grover Cleveland in 1892, where among other things Cleveland would resist demands to annex Hawaii. His Secretary of State on the other hand, Richard Olney, ". . . received a letter from a Texas congressman encouraging him to 'go ahead,' on the grounds that the Venezuela issue was a 'winner' in every section of the country" (Hofstadter 1965, 154). Here we see demonstrated that wonderful Texas ability to generalize feelings about what would be good for Texas to the entire nation. Roger Q. Mills, Democratic Senator from Texas in the U.S. Senate, on March 24, 1986 said: "The Monroe Doctrine is as old as humanity. God was the author of the Monroe Doctrine" (May 1961, 32). We laugh at our own peril in the face of people, Islamic, Hebraic or otherwise, who make God the author of their doctrines.

Leapfrogging temporarily the great age of Imperialism we find "The Southern-born President's [Wilson] speeches aroused deep, nostalgic pulls in the American Middle-class breast. . . The strong Texan flavor of Wilson's Administration has sometimes been overlooked" (642). Not anymore. "Texas was ahead of the nation as a whole in belligerency in 1917. . . Since 1900 Texas had increasingly fused back with the nation in foreign policy, especially when foreign policy was basically imperial" (643). Texas fused back in with the ultimate intention of leading. Ten percent of all combat casualties in WWI, 5,000 men, were from Texas. Wilson had called for "incomparably the greatest navy in the world" (Levine 1965, 57), the greatest navy after the British Navy model. While Fehrenbach would maintain that there is no evidence that Texans liked war, he could also report that "A cotton farmer from Farmersville named Audie Murphy gained more combat awards in World War II than any other man in the U.S. Army" (1968, 654). The awards resulted from his killing a few hundred Germans.

The Texas flirtation with Republicans and Imperialists was so strong that Hoover carried Texas by 26,000 votes in 1928 (650). From there it was but a short step to, "As both *Fortune* and Gallup Polls showed, Texans were the most belligerent people in the United States toward Germany and

Japan. Texan interventionism far outran even that of the South" (653). The bonds of thought that bind Texas to the South and South Carolina were further revealed in the news about Strom Thurmond in 1948. "The Dixiecrat candidate carried one county, Houston's Harris, the biggest metropolitan area in the state. No one ever discovered exactly what this signified" (658).

It signified the beginning of the contemporary urban South's wholesale desertion of the Democratic party, hinted at in Hoover's 1928 victory in Texas, and the establishment of their loyalty to conservative Republicans. Southern political bearings remained essentially conservative, even as it took until the mid-term elections of 1994 for a majority of the congressional, state, and local seats in the South to be held by Republicans. The people of Houston, the economic capitol of Texas, just saw this party switch — a little more racist and further to the right — coming first and voted for Hoover and Thurmond in turn.

From not being able to be elected to anything unless a candidate had worn the gray in the Reconstruction years, Thurmond, a Neo-Confederate nearly without peer, was wearing the panache of the gray in 1948. By the end of WWII, Houston's map of potential Texas was all but complete. Thurmond bolted the Democratic party in a snit because he couldn't get Eisenhower to be the Democratic candidate. Four years later, "The 'Democrats for Eisenhower' raised more money for the Republican candidate in Texas than the Republican organization itself. . . Eisenhower the first Texas-born President, carried the state by 100,000 votes" (659). From Eisenhower forward, "In several of the larger states — Texas and Florida most obviously — the Republicans had been growing generally more competitive with every election" (Germond 1989, 153). Thurmond would molt into his true colors in the 1960s and join the Nixon Republican party.

Eisenhower, who ran as a New Yorker having served a term as president of Columbia University, completes the Confederate circle of the Chisholm Trail. Texas had finally and effectively annexed New York — Daniel Drew's New York of stock manipulation and speculation grown huge on the fruit of war. Eisenhower was born in Dennison, Texas, on October 14, 1890. Dennison is on the cattle trail that once led from Texas to Sedalia, Missouri. Eisenhower was raised in Abilene, the prairie dog town of a dozen log huts that McCoy turned into the depot of exchange for the cattle kingdom (Webb 1931, 220-1), so his identity is sometimes assigned to the lower Midwest when it is politically convenient.

"Who can say that Abilene was less significant than Appomattox?" (222) Webb asks rhetorically as he describes the importance of its being the connection between northern commerce and southern produce. Webb goes on to lament "Though the civilization of the cattle kingdom was as complete within itself as was that of the Old South, it was not independent, but subject to the general conditions of the nation" (238). The industrial revolution that temporarily boxed the Confederate compass would also fence the cattle kingdom in, but a Texas boy from Abilene would one day lead the nation and the empire.

The West was a test of America's depth perception. Imagining as in the East that settlement and influence followed the lines of latitude (Phillips 1969, 41-2) will get you nowhere in the West, except for Cascadian Washington and Oregon where politics somewhat resemble those in New England and the Great Lakes region of the upper Midwest. This pattern peters out at the Mississippi and Missouri Rivers where the Texas northbound cowboy pattern takes over. The political character, style and intent of the interior West moves on longitudinal North-South lines and was made in Texas. With the political impact of 28 Senators, (when Idaho and Arizona are included), the majority of whom vote consistently as if they were southern conservatives whether Republicans or Democrats, control of the United States Senate is virtually guaranteed when the 20 from the rest of the Confederacy are added. Even so, Texas can one day cash in another of the other powerful chips that its annexation made possible — eight additional southern Senators from Texas — when and if it chooses to divide into five separate states.

Abilene is where the North and the South got back into economic bed together. It is the midpoint of the X-Y axis of American history. The southern impellers welling up out of Texas with the cattle kingdom, fanned out from there in the other directions to an ultimate Texas and southern leadership of the entire country. By the time of the Eisenhower epoch, the United States was once again dominated by the South. One of the consistent southern goals, before, during and after the Civil War, control of the West, was delivered by Texans on horseback following the Chisholm Trail.

12

State Rights: The Southern Resurrection

State rights in the South prior to the Civil War were understood at the theoretical level as making the states the superior policy making body over the federal government and at the practical level of enforcing white supremacy and domination over the African American slaves, freemen and Native Americans. While one immediate outcome of the Civil War was an attempt to reverse this understanding of both theory and practice, and it was Jefferson Davis' and the South's oft stated reason to be fighting, the actual picture that emerges is not so clear cut. Over time, white Southerners were able to reassert their cherished opinions to regain white supremacy, their honor and state rights.

It is well understood that the slaveholders considered their slaves to be their private property and capital. The Magna Carta, 13th century document espousing rights in English says: "Neither we, nor any other, will take the wood of any man for castles, or for anything else which we are doing, except by the permission of him to whom the wood belongs" (Swindler 1965, 306). While manumission or the volunteer freeing of slaves occurred in small measure prior to the Civil War, by the time of the Emancipation Proclamation in 1863, and certainly feared earlier with the election of Lincoln, the mandated freeing of slaves was understood in the South as the taking of capital without "permission." The bloody resistance to this process that the American people have come to know and love as the battles of the Civil War is well known. Far less well known is the stiff and intermittent resistance it ran into immediately after.

"Mississippi in 1865 made it illegal for freedmen to rent or lease farmland, and provided for them to work under labor contracts which they could not break under penalty of prison" (Zinn 1980, 194). Since the majority of freed men were poorly disposed to travel, being broke, illiterate and Black, they wound up working on the same plantations where they had been slaves. The long reach of the Emancipation Proclamation was unenforceable. Nineteen of twenty-four Northern states didn't allow blacks the right to vote in 1865 (204) anyway. The reversion to the plantation system was swift and, given southern logic, inevitable. "The elementary economic logic of slavery in a setting of land abundance has been outlined many times: if land is available to all comers, and if cultivation may be practiced at any scale without major loss of efficiency, then there will be no way for an entrepreneur to achieve a large absolute profit except with unfree labor" (Wright 1978, 11). Unfree labor in Wright's phrase meant slavery; it could also mean unfree labor as mandated by statute in Mississippi, promising prison for breaking a contract.

With lack of experience on both sides, labor and management, slaveholders and former slaves, Ransom and Sutch's *One Kind of Freedom, The Economic Consequences of Emancipation*, suggests "It was only natural that they attempt to recreate the plantation regime as nearly as possible" (1977, 56). "They" leave little doubt as to the minuscule amount of freedom proffered to former slaves. "Yet, while the overseer's name had been changed to indicate the new order, his duties remained virtually the same" (57). So too did the duties of the former slaves and they were to remain the same for a long time indeed. The Civil War had also removed whatever cash the plantation owners might have had, so there was no money to replace stock or destroyed equipment, let alone to pay wages to former slaves. Their solution, partly outlined above, included "of necessity a crop-sharing labor system with the displaced and starving Negroes. By this grim expedient for survival, the paternalism of the plantation was extended into the present" (Dowdy 1957, 316). Share-cropping, with the former slaves perpetually in debt to the merchants and the "company store," kept the South in a vicious cycle of poverty.

The immediate loss of the Civil War altered the character of white Southerners, especially the slaveholding ruling class who were used to getting their own way, but also the other whites who now faced the spectre of equality with Blacks. "More united in defeat and the subsequent Reconstruction than in their brief independence, Confederates seemed to forge a distinctiveness after the war that they had not had before or during it" (Beringer et al 1986, 423). They went into the war representing the fierce independence typified by South Carolina and other individual states and came out of the war with a brief and bitter four-year dose of nationalism. Defeat had to be rationalized some useful way. "Toward the end of the war, and after it, some Southerners came to feel that the lost cause did not signify that God had abandoned His chosen people. Rather they owed defeat and the changes that accompanied it to a merited punishment and a greater destiny, which they should not resist but welcome" (102).

Inasmuch as the belief in slavery was absolutely fundamental, so fundamental that they fought a religious war for it, it would be expected that they began to search in the ruins for the clues to their further religious destiny. Since their chief distinguishing feature beyond their independent streak was their treatment of African Americans prior to the Civil War, it remained their chief distinguishing feature after it. "Having fought a war for slavery, they surrendered it unwillingly to Confederate policy and later willingly (though not graciously) to Union policy, for they were coming to the conclusion that they would be able to control black labor just as well without the peculiar institution as with it" (399). This "conclusion" about their capacity to control black labor and its ramifications will resurface from time to time in the narrative, as the capacity to control labor is a basic theme of the Calhoun vision of American politics.

With or without slavery, how is black labor to be controlled? In *Colonial South Carolina*, Robert Weir refers to the tradition of "beating up of quarters," apparently a young man's pastime, where every white man was a guardian of law and order. In this tradition "Lay one of the tangled roots of vigilantism and nineteenth century lynching" (1983, 195). Terror, in plain English, was and is a device for controlling labor. While legal controls were abundant, such as those put almost immediately into place in Mississippi, extra legal controls were just as swiftly employed. "The first battle in the political contest for white supremacy was won outside the halls of legislatures and the courts of law. It was waged, in the main, by secret organizations, among which the Ku Klux Klan and the White Camelia were the most prominent. . . The whole South was called 'the Empire' and was ruled by a 'Grand Wizard'" (Beard and Beard 1925, 382). It would not be long before "White Supremacy [was] sealed by New State Constitutions" (385). The symbol of the Scottish Cross, chosen and employed by the Ku Klux Klan and displayed in David Wark Griffith's movie *The Birth of a Nation*, based on Thomas Dixon's novel *The Clansmen*, has a haunting, white-sheeted beauty and terror. Exactly what nation and what kind of nation was being given birth to in this process?

Nations are put together and operated, unless they wish to go under, by classes of people representing the community values. "Lawyer, clergyman, doctor, and — a tradition that never saw birth in the North — soldier were the genteel occupations: at the base of all these, around which they revolved, was the landed slave estate" (Fehrenbach 1968, 310). A dozen similar citations could be made, pointing out what has become so familiar it seems obvious, that soldiering and the military were not traditions in the North, and yet the consequences of it are rarely explored. Of all these "non-economic" occupations as described by Veblen and reiterated by Fehrenbach, it is the tradition of the soldier, inseparable from its political and ecclesiastical support, that is basic to the South.

Although Fehrenbach's description was of pre-Civil War Texas, the passing of the war only changed the description in the following particulars. When Texans faced the task of re-writing their constitution in 1876, the details were agreed upon by "John H. Reagan (ex-Postmaster General of the Confederacy), and a bevy of generals who had worn the gray. . . more than twenty had held high rank in the C.S.A." (434). We have to remember that Texas and the other states writing new constitutions were walking on a plank straight out of the colonial South Carolina Commons which asserted that they were "subordinate to no power on earth" (Weir 1983, 298). The insubordinate nature of South Carolina surfaces repeatedly. Even among southern moderates, such as James S. Hammond, who wrote to the poet William Gilmore Simms just prior to the War Between the States in 1859, southern superiority is flaunted. "The South is and will be henceforth nearly united and we can always divide the North and govern it essentially" (Craven 1957, 412).

As we have seen so far in this discussion, the South was nearly united after the Civil War on some rather hard news. It clung in defeat to its traditions, the military and the exploitation of labor. "The wave of reversion seems to have received its initial impulse in the psychologically disintegrating effects of the Civil War. Habituation to war entails a body of predatory habits of thought, whereby clannishness in some measure replaces the sense of solidarity, and a sense of invidious distinction supplants the impulse to equitable, everyday serviceability. As an outcome of the cumulative action of these factors, the generation which follows a season of war is apt to witness a rehabilitation of the element of status both in its social life and in its scheme of devout observances and other symbolic or ceremonial forms" (Veblen 1931, 373). We have seen that "clannishness" definitely followed the season of war in the South. The post war South also saw, at the level of higher education in the universities, the development of fraternities, which

"Are an expression of that heritage of clannishness which is so large a feature in the temperament of the predatory barbarian" (379).

The entire nation, North, South, and West, suffered the "psychologically disintegrating effects" of the Civil War. The effects on the North were no less barbarous than in the South, for there occurred "the recrudescences of outlawry and the spectacular quasi-predatory careers of fraud run by certain 'captains of industry'" (373). Daniel Drew's career of fraud, already cited in its role in the growth of New York City as the world city, as well as its barbarous use of the hapless soldiers doing the actual fighting, was both typical as well as an example that many others followed. The tremendous scope of the behavior of the robber barons is beyond the purview of *How the South Finally Won the Civil War*, however much it dovetails with it. New Yorkers are famous for taking people aside and telling them how important, central and powerful New York City is in the American scheme of things, but the truth is that Wall Street, the financial engine of the empire, whose annexation by southern military machinations was completed at the beginning of the Cold War, and whose current domination by electronic transnational stock manipulation, has been subservient to Neo-Confederate political control ever since.

The re-union of fraud and recrudescence North and South occurred in 1876. "Dr. Eckenrode's answer to the question of who won the Civil War provides a biased but illuminating answer to the related question of who profited by the Bargain of 1876: 'All that had been accomplished was the exchange of one set of masters for another. The industrialists, far more cruel and relentless than the planters had ever been, now ruled the country and ruled it like hereditary lords.' The real meaning of the Bargain of 1876 was revealed the following year when the railroad workers precipitated the first acute labor crisis in American history" (McWilliams 1951, 266). It should be apparent to even a casual observer that the reversion to a predatory economy, North and South, was stimulated by the psychological disintegration of the Civil War, and the resultant exploitation of labor was keeping pace. What exactly was the nature of the so-called "bargain" of 1876.

The Democratic party, under Samuel J. Tilden, who received more than a quarter million more votes than the Republican candidate Rutherford B. Hayes and yet "lost" the election, described it in Section 8 of its 1880 party platform: "The great fraud of 1876-77, by which, upon a false count of the electoral votes of two states, the candidate defeated at the polls was declared

to be President, and for the first time in American history, the will of the
people was set aside under a threat of military violence, struck a deadly
blow at our system of government. The Democratic party, to preserve the
country from the horrors of a civil war, submitted for the time in firm and
patriotic faith that the people would punish this crime in 1880. This issue
precedes and dwarfs every other" (Johnson and Porter 1973, 56). Since the
national Democratic party was the party being defrauded, this term will be
used in subsequent discussion.

As this hat trick after the election of 1876 developed, "the electoral vote
actually stood at 184 for Tilden and 165 for Hayes, with twenty votes in
dispute, Florida's 4, Louisiana's 8, South Carolina's 7, and one of Oregon's
3, where the Democrats claimed a Republican elector was disqualified. Tilden
needed 1 vote for victory; Hayes needed 20" (Schlesinger 1971, 194). Sidney
Pomerantz' essay on this election showed one result of the deal. "The
ex-Confederate, Senator David M. Key, who became Postmaster General,
and was entrusted with the disposal of vast patronage, hopefully to wean
away enough conservative white Democrats to build a new Republican party
in the South" (215), demonstrates the forward look of the Republicans
toward the South. On February 26, "Southern Democrats meet secretly
with Hayes's Republican representatives and conclude the Compromise of
1877, in which Southern Democrats agree to support Republicans in
exchange for withdrawal of federal troops from the South and ending of
Reconstruction" (Brown 1971, 315). The electoral commission put together
to solve this dispute then awarded all 20 votes to Hayes with the entire vote
totals of some parishes in Louisiana thrown out. This was the modern
beginning of conservative Republican cooperation with conservative southern Democrats, who were given control of their state houses in a victory for
state rights. This conservative cooperation across, party, state, and sectional
lines, is the major force in American political power, the threat and use of
force and fraud.

The way this power broke in two directions in 1877 reveals the major
fault lines in American politics. Eric Foner in *Reconstruction, America's
Unfinished Revolution 1863 * 1877*, claims that "Among other things, 1877
marked a decisive retreat from the idea, born during the Civil War, of a
powerful national state protecting the fundamental rights of American
citizens" (1988, 582). As the culture retreated from protecting the rights of
American people, it advanced with weapons to protect the rights of

property. "Nor did the Federal Government prove reluctant to intervene with force to protect the rights of property. Within three months of the end of Reconstruction, the Hayes administration confronted one of the bitterest explosions of class warfare in American History — The Great Strike of 1877" (583). The retreat from the protection of human rights to advance the protection of property rights describes the fundamental division of American politics as a class war and clarifies the position of the ruling conservative coalition, to whom "life, liberty, and the pursuit of property," is the operating principle.

It is a matter of public record that President Hayes toyed with the idea of provoking a war with Mexico, always a popular favorite, "to divert attention from the shady deal by which he had robbed Tilden of the presidency" (McWilliams 1968, 109). The immediate ramifications of the fraud of 1876, however, were primarily domestic. The withdrawal of federal troops gave Democrats re-control of South Carolina, Louisiana, and Florida, precisely the states where the vote totals were alleged to be in dispute (McWilliams 1951, 265). The reversion of northern Republicans is where the real prize for political pusillanimity belongs. "The Republicans, however, could see that a new class opposition might arise; hence they were disposed to strike a bargain with the planter dynasty. Instead of resolving the Emancipation dilemma, they seized upon it as a means by which the appearance of democracy could be used to frustrate the democratic process. . . Reconstruction was a prolonged race riot" (262). The "appearance" of democracy, amongst a people like the Americans with whom pictures are sacred, will always be accorded more importance than actual democracy, especially when it is being dispensed by the ruling conservative coalition.

The Supreme Court of the United States, judges of which during this period were almost exclusively appointed by Republicans, provided the judicial corollary to the Fraud of 1876. "In the Cruikshank case (1876), the Civil Rights cases (1883), the Harris case (1889), and *Plessy v. Ferguson* (1896), the Supreme Court nullified the Civil War amendments so far as Negroes were concerned and placed the Bill of Rights outside the protection of the 14th Amendment. . . These decisions made it possible for the South to legislate the Negroes' subordinate status; that is, to enforce this status by law" (267). Klingberg quoting Ralph H. Gabriel from his *The Course of American Democratic Thought* reveals that "The withdrawal of the northern armies by President Hayes and the decision of the United States

Supreme Court of 1883 virtually nullifying the Civil Rights Act of 1875 ended northern intervention on a large scale in the race relationships between white men and the Negro. With the tacit consent of the North, the Southern states assumed control of their own internal affairs as had been the ardent demand of John C. Calhoun, before 1850" (1975, 4). It is remarkable what persistence in the vectors of a belief system can accomplish. It was precisely this persistence that permits the strong belief in the South that "If the war was lost over slavery and independence, the peace was waged — and won — for state rights, white supremacy, and honor" (Beringer et al 1986, 417). There is insufficient factual evidence to contradict this conclusion. It is only a matter of time and familiarity before the North believes it also.

Having achieved what they wanted in state rights, white supremacy, and honor domestically, it was also only a matter of time before the South began to reassert itself internationally in foreign policy. Hayes, who would never have been President without the help of Southern Democrats, tried to invoke the Monroe Doctrine in March of 1880 to keep European interests in Panama at bay (Liss 1967, 15). The Republicans would lead the march overseas with help from southern Democrats. The Republican platform of 1896 states: "The Hawaiian Islands should be controlled by the United States and no foreign power should be permitted to interfere with them" (Beard and Beard 1925, 485). Native speakers of doubletalk, Republicans didn't think of themselves as foreign to Hawaii in 1896. Democratic President Grover Cleveland had resisted the developing impulse to absorb Hawaii. "Henry Cabot Lodge, favored annexation. . . Hawaii stood like 'a Gibraltar in the pathway of American commerce'" (May 1961, 18). Here we see the reversion to type and barbarism finding British Empire metaphors to rationalize its aggression. The Republicans, officially at least, once had human rights, the abolition of slavery, uppermost in mind. While their departure from the old official line might have been predicted, aggression was business as usual and no big thing for Southerners.

"It was slightly less of a departure for the senior Democrat on the Foreign Relations Committee. John Tyler Morgan of Alabama was nearly seventy, old enough to have been an elector in 1860 and to have cast his vote proudly for the proslavery ticket of Breckinridge and Lane, been a brigadier general in the Confederate army, and his state's senator ever since the compromises of 1876; old enough too, perhaps to have vivid memories of pre-Civil War southern expansionism" (19). Here we begin to see the ducks lining up in rows: an elderly southern senator with a sinecure on his seat since the fraud of 1876, a proslavery elector and Confederate general, reviving the daydream of southern expansion by actively participating in the annexation of Hawaii with its coolie-driven pineapple plantations.

"Hawaii was also the laboratory in which the formula for American Expansionism, — the outward expression of our domestic racial imperialism — was first worked out. Nations that practice imperialism must also practice racism" (McWilliams 1951, 171). The cheek by jowl juxtaposition of domestic with international racism and imperialism as practiced by Americans is one of the chief distinguishing features of their civilization. The fraud of 1876 "cleared the way for the future annexation of the islands, for if Negroes could be constitutionally disenfranchised in South Carolina, ways and means would be found to cope with the native Hawaiian majority in the islands" (175). The fraud didn't stop with the annexation either for "The Civil War amendments to the Constitution, which had been used as the bait to induce the Hawaiians to ratify the treaty, proved to be of as little protection to the Hawaiians as to the American Negroes" (175).

Claus Spreckles, who started the sugar business in California, had opposed the annexation of Hawaii where he was deeply involved in the sugar plantations because he bought the inducing lines about protection for worker rights and was afraid that annexation would result in restrictions on his coolie labor. "Coolie labor was, and is, the backbone of the plantation system" (McWilliams 1969, 82). He didn't have that much to fear. Once again we see slavery and plantation agriculture far to the west of the 98th Meridian. The abrogation of rights was not restricted to slaves, former slaves, and coolies, however. By 1920 in California, "The National Labor Board. . . found that Constitutional rights had been openly disregarded. . . free speech and assembly. . . excessive bail. . . and that a Federal Court injunction had been flouted" (225). When it comes to the exploitation of farm labor, developed to the level of the economic art of slavery in the pre-Confederate South, states and white owners have all the rights, in the South, in California, and in Hawaii.

Former Confederate generals such as Morgan of Alabama, were not restricted to service in the United States Senate. "The first governor general of the Philippine Islands was Luke E. Wright. He was a veteran of the Civil War, having served in the Confederate Army. He belonged to the

Democratic party. I mention this latter because he was appointed by a Republican President — namely, my father — which indicated clearly our original policy, which was to divorce partisan politics completely from our colonial administration" (Roosevelt 1970, 151). This appointment does clearly demonstrate the bipartisan nature of *American Imperialism*, Roosevelt's choice for the title to his book.

While Roosevelt thought of it as a partisan divorce, it was in fact evidence of the bipartisan marriage of Republican imperialists and Confederate Democrats and the chummy interior lines of thought they shared creating the empire. This is not to imply that Republican and Confederate cooperation was immediate and complete. "Although the Solid South, for obvious reasons, was going to support Bryan, there was a notoriously strong imperialist sentiment in this section" (Glad 1968, 85). Among the sources Glad bases his opinion on are the correspondence between Theodore Roosevelt and his Confederate uncle Bulloch. James K. Jones, the senator from Arkansas, received a letter from his campaign manager. "'In my own county, men who have voted the Democratic ticket all their lives, voted Republican this time, openly boasted of it and gave as the reason, that they did not want any more 5 cent cotton'" (83). The ordinary people also were sending a message, restore, if and when you can please, the profits to the growing of cotton.

While the major thrust of American imperialism under Roosevelt deserves and will receive a chapter all its own, we pass over it here lightly, broadly establishing its Confederate nature, in order to follow the leads nurtured by the Fraud of 1876 into the present. For while Cleveland's Secretary of State Olney could say in 1895 that "'Today the United States is practically sovereign on this continent and its fiat is law on the subject to which it confines its interposition'" (Hofstadter 1959, 134), it was based upon a lot of "free" and mutually beneficial protection from the British Navy. Once the South got a hand into the Republican party, it was not about to fold it. "The well-worn suggestion that representation from the Southern states was disproportionate was then made again" (Pringle 1957, 394), at the 1912 Republican convention.

We've already seen how crazy the Texans were for WWI, so crazy that 10 percent of the casualties came from their soil. "Most Charlestonians supported the war, which brought an increase in jobs for the Navy Yard and spurred the growth of North Charleston" (Rosen 1982, 130). War is always popular in the South because each time one is fought it gives the Southern military-religious-political three handed grip a greater hold on the United States and drives it further in the centripetal direction of reversion. "Academic freedom still rested upon the shaky foundation of local prejudice and whim" (Levine 1965, 354). The whims referred to in this discussion of the "monkey trial" are the whims of state righters who believe the Bill of Rights applies only when they want it to apply.

The cooperation between Southern Democrats and Republicans was not lost on Daniel J. Tobin of the Teamsters. "'Any student is aware that a coalition of Southern Democrats and Republicans work hand in hand'" (MacDougall 1965, I:45). Nor should students be unaware that Glen Taylor, the Progressive party candidate for Vice President in 1948 and senator from Idaho, had led a "Successful fight to refuse a seat to Theodore G. Bilbo, just re-elected senator from Mississippi after a campaign in which Negro voters had been terrorized to stay away from the polls" (143). Terror, it will be remembered, is an old and effective American political tactic. Senator Eastland of Mississippi was the Senate's leading red-baiter. Five days after Truman revealed his civil rights program, "The Southern Governor's Conference met at Wakulla Springs, Florida. They denounced his proposals and appointed a committee to go to the white house to demand concessions on the 'white supremacy' issue. Governor Strom Thurmond of South Carolina recommended a 40 day cooling off period" (385). Thurmond deserves to be more famous than he is for ratifying the continued treatment of farm labor in the peach orchards of Edgefield County, South Carolina.

Thurmond's contemporary, the Democrat Jimmy Carter of Georgia, "failed to capture a majority of the white vote in the South" (Germond 1989, 37), which can only mean that it went to the Republicans, as early as 1976. The foundation of the Republican victories in the South was first clearly laid in the Fraud of 1876. While some people might wish that elections were issue based, the consultant Treleaven who elected Bush to Congress from Houston in 1966, noticed that his client was aware that more people vote for irrational, emotional reasons than professional politicians suspect (McGinnis 1969, 38-40). Republican appeal to irrational emotions is about all that is left of the Republican party of Fremont and Lincoln from 1856-1860.

The relationship between war and emotions is critical in elections, as Kevin Phillips, a former Republican political professional who referred to parts of the South as the "Yahoo Belt" (127), knows. He told the Nixon people in 1968 "This has a decidedly dovish impact as a result of the visible content and it does not seem suitable for use in the South and Southwest" (90). Dovishness does not sell well in the South. On the other hand, don't get brutal. "A picture of a wounded soldier was a reminder that the people who fight wars get hurt. . . So bury the dead in silence before you blow North Carolina" (90). The Republicans have come a long way on the astute advice of Phillips and others, although Phillips seems to be deserting them as he bashes the rich in *Boiling Point* thusly: ". . .Until late 1990, when the rich became a target again, the top 1 percent of Americans of the 1980s had reassumed the place they held in the 1880s and 1920s in a restored conservative fiscal theology" (1993, 114). Phillips' discussion of the "theological" characteristics of the basically Republican heydays of the 1880s, 1920s, and 1980s does not include the heyday of the antebellum South of the 1850s, although that period in the South shares seven major parts of the 10 characteristics he assigns to the conservative heydays (35) and is definitely related phenomena as is the fact that 10 of the richest white men in the American colonies in 1771 were Charlestonians. Regardless of the warped nature of speculative economies, the safest patriotic picture is still the flag flapping in the breeze, harmless, commendatory, romantic, and everybody knows what the visual nominalization stands for — whatever they think it stands for.

As we look back through the fog that lifted the burdens of southern history off the plains of Texas and the plantations of the South and deposited them on all American shoulders, look back from the perspective of the CIA. "As for the agency's long-range forecasts, they have always been written ultimately with one thing in mind: assuring a continued and prominent foreign-policy-making role for the unelected government at Langley, [Virginia]" (Hitchens 1991, 64). The unelected government at Langley is only one version of the new power of the South. Another is located in the natural environment. From a state by state report card on the nation's environment from Durham, North Carolina, and the Institute for Southern Studies, in 1990: "This detailed rating of states' environmental health, including the natural ecosystem, built environment, and human health, concludes that the Southeast is worse off and less protected by state environmental policies than other areas of the country" (ZPG 1991, 2). This is just one more unhappy manifestation of state rights, including the property right to ignore the natural world, made possible initially by the Fraud of 1876.

We can look back from another perspective. "The Neo-conservatism of the 1980s is a replay of the New Conservatism of the 1950s, which was itself a replay of the New Era philosophy of the 1920s" (Schlesinger 1986, 38). Since Schlesinger does spend some time discussing the Klingberg foreign policy microcycles, it only takes an iterative imagination to extend this conservatism to the rampant Republican imperialists of the 1890s and back of that a succinct 30 earlier, the Confederate conservatism of the 1860s. Hip and pitiful liberal magazines in the United States, such as *The New Republic* and *Harper's* have taken to abbreviating Neo-conservative to Neo-Con. We can keep the Neo-Con but understand it for what it really represents: Neo-Confederate.

The Neo-Confederate perspective is one that will warm the cockles of John C. Calhoun's heart, as Hofstadter was kind enough to remind us that what Calhoun really wanted was "not for the South to leave the Union, but to dominate it" (1959, 70). This was the greater religious destiny Southerners learned to read into their initial defeat. They would once again revive the skill to divide the North and rule it essentially. "The promise of freedom and equality that accompanied emancipation remains as yet unfulfilled despite the lapse of more than a century" (Ransom and Sutch 1977, 199). The Fraud of 1876 was the linchpin that gave the South two big legs of the ultimate Confederate victory for state rights and white supremacy. It also, contained the seeds of the renewed Southern expansionism. "In the sphere of politics, the period witnessed the recovery of white supremacy in the South. . . Alaska. . . Samoa. . . the Hawaiian Islands. . . Cuba. . . Puerto Rico. . . the Philippines. American influence in the Pacific and the Orient was so enlarged as to be a factor of great weight in world affairs. . . foreign and 'imperial' policies were united with domestic issues to make up the warp and woof of politics. In the direction of affairs, the Republicans took the leadership, for they held the presidency during all the years, except eight, between 1865 and 1900" (Beard and Beard 1925, 505). In the career of the quintessential Republican Theodore Roosevelt, the complete Confederate victory was getting closer all the time.

13

Alone in Cuba: Theodore Roosevelt's Empire

Theodore Roosevelt was born carrying the gene for imperialism. He had two maternal uncles who were prominent in the Confederate Navy. His mother was from Georgia. "The blood brotherhood between history and coincidence has rarely been better demonstrated than by the fact that one of her ancestors took part in an ill-fated attempt to colonize the Isthmus of Darien, just east of Panama. . . William Patterson. . . late in the seventeenth century. . . Command of the Isthmus, he knew, would guarantee for all time the commercial supremacy of Great Britain" (Pringle 1955, 6).

The commercial supremacy of Great Britain was not in doubt in 1890, the year the great frontier closed on land and a half dozen states from the empty quarter were admitted to the union. It was also the year of the publication of Alfred Thayer Mahan's *The Influence of Sea Power on Civilization*. Since this book extolled the role of the navy in the British rise to prominence, it was received as gospel in England. Theodore Roosevelt, himself the author of *The Naval War of 1812*, would give Mahan his first enthusiastic review in the *Atlantic Monthly* (McCullough 1977, 251). Roosevelt's enthusiasm for England, the navy, and the empire never wavered. Chapter 13 details Roosevelt's contribution to the Confederate Empire of North America.

History is as much a pulse as it is a cycle. The notion that American foreign policy was essentially conservative immediately after the Civil War depends on drinking the bathwater of the dotted lines the Manifest Destined Americans drew around the "Indians" which enabled them to make believe the wars against the Indians were domestic rather than foreign. With California and Oregon in the Union, everything between the oceans was ipso facto "domestic." "But with the eighteen-nineties a new generation had grown to manhood, a generation to whom the bitter bloodshed of the Civil War was only a glorious memory" (Perkins 1966, 40), emphasize "glorious." Having consolidated their position in the west with victories against the Indians everywhere except at the Battle of the Little Big Horn, American hungry eyes once again discovered Cuba. Cuba had been the darling of many Southerners with expansionist eyes, including those of Robert E. Lee and Jefferson Davis.

The tenacity of Jefferson Davis and his leadership of the unreconstructed Confederates had already paid off in the South's victories in the realm of state rights and white supremacy. The southern dream of a Caribbean empire was desperately seeking fruition. "In a sense the southern dream of a tropical slave empire survived even after the Confederate defeat" (May 1973, 255). Not all politicians were equally persuaded by their glorious memories of the Civil War or the gospel of the English navy. President McKinley was "Several times commended for gallantry during the Civil War, [and] he had come out as a major at the age of twenty-two" (May 1961, 113). Veterans at least have a chance to learn something first hand about war and "McKinley viewed with anguish the unrelenting needs of what he referred to as the 'empire business.'" (Wilson 1970, 162).

Theodore Roosevelt was too young to have been a veteran of the Civil War. He was a teenager in love with the glory of growing strong and focused on his memories of the future. Cleveland, who preceded McKinley and resisted the pressure to annex Hawaii, received an anonymous letter on March 23, 1896, detailing the sentiment of the South. "The South dearly loves a fighter, & if you will now show yourself strong and courageous in the defense of Cuba, you will have a solid South at your call. . . Strengthen the Army and Navy of this country & in this way give employment to the thousands of idle men who need it" (68). The possibility that the aggrandizement towards empire is a jobs program has surfaced before. Cleveland would resist the temptations of Cuba, in office and out.

For all his interest in a Caribbean empire, Jefferson Davis was a paragon of rectitude in the application of force outside "American territorial waters" (May 1973, 119). He was one of the few conservatives, as Schlesinger claims for all of them (1986, 47), who actually was committed to the rule of law. It was "Not until the summer of 1898, when the war with Spain produced once more a union of hearts, did Congress relent and abolish the last of the disabilities imposed on the Confederates" (Beard and Beard 1925, 384). And why not, after all the power in the country was united once again on a white supremacist, aggressive, imperialist adventure.

How did Roosevelt and the imperialists overcome the Cleveland and McKinley inertia at the top? For one thing, "In 1898 our people had read the word 'war' in letters three inches high for three months in every newspaper. The pliant politician McKinley was swept away by their eagerness, and our squalid war with Spain became a necessity" (James 1967, 662). William James' partisanship shows in his choice of adjectives, pliant and squalid, but was he exaggerating? The United States was becoming a modern country, subject to the vicissitudes of the media. "A perusal of the metropolitan newspapers for 1898 and 1899 and of the literary, military, commercial, and religious press of those years reveals that editors and feature writers never tired of describing the glories of empire. . . [there was] an overpowering public demand for colonial expansion. . ." (Glad 1968, 58). James lived through it; Glad went back and looked at it. Their conclusions, while not identical, suggest they were reviewing the same phenomena. It should be noted that Glad presupposes the printed word is reflecting the public demand, rather than creating it.

Richard Hofstadter believes that the dynamic elements were Theodore Roosevelt, Senator Henry Cabot Lodge, and the Adams brothers, Brooks and Henry. ". . . if the matter had been left either to public clamor or to business interests, there would have been no American entrance into the Philippines in 1898" (1965, 163). The notion of a public clamor or demand has been denied by Hofstadter, who points us to other instigators. "Whoever produced the American empire," so says Arthur Schlesinger Jr., "it was not a broad populace electrified by the imperial idea" (1986, 152). While he fingers the same individuals as Hofstadter, all following Admiral Mahan, he maintains that they "Represented an atavistic revival of an obsolete warrior class. Their fin de siecle imperialism was a flash in the pan" (152). The atavistic nature of this enterprise, that is to say its reversionary tendency to barbarism, is difficult to refute or ignore. Far from making the warrior class obsolete, however, it made them contemporary. American imperialism, under several disguises, has weathered the passage of time well. And it was brought then and is presently maintained by "Sensation-mongering sheets like William Randolph Hearst's and Joseph Pulitzer's. . ." (May 1961, 71). Yellow journalism, encouraged by Roosevelt et al, needled the people into it.

The tendency to empire had been planted with the seeds of the republic in Madison's turning inside out the idea that a republic, in order to be successful, had to be small. "Madison and his supporters had made their revolution: the logic and the instrument of empire had become the foundation of American society. . ." (Williams 1980, 47). The 1890s version of this logic stemmed from the frontier thesis of history and "Having defined everything good in terms of surplus property, the problem became one of developing techniques for securing more good things from a succession of new frontiers" (Williams 1961, 374). The burden of this emphasis on property acquisition is unequally shared in the empire. The anti-intellectual consequences of the frontier thesis simply offered surplus property as a substitute for thought. Americans will pay dearly for their hatred of ideas.

They think their history demonstrates unique principles, that it is above Santayana's dictum that those who refuse to learn from history are condemned to repeat it. The Spanish American war was a demonstration of the power of the press in its new religious role of popularizing the conviction that adjusts all minds and religiously quarantines opposing attitudes. The American religion of war got a big boost from Roosevelt. What he thought of his opposition in William Jennings Bryan is indicative. "'He goes down with the cause and must abide with it in the history of infamy. He had less provocation than Benedict Arnold, less intellectual force than Aaron Burr, less manliness and courage than Jefferson Davis. He was the rival of them all in deliberate wickedness and treason to the Republic'" (Pringle 1955, 113). There is little tolerance for any freedom of attitude in this bombast, where the first refuge of the military religion is to accuse those with differing opinions of treason. Some of the choices were ". . . ranging from a permanent occupation of the Philippines to an immediate and cowardly surrender to Aguinaldo. Bryan certainly did not advocate the latter of these alternatives; but this was the interpretation forced upon him by the opposition, notably Roosevelt, who stormed about the country decrying the dastardly attempt to haul down the flag" (Glad 1968, 84). We know the religious ceremony is reaching a climax whenever the flag is unfurled.

Roosevelt's archaic belief that leaders should be feudal knights, left ". . . a relevant model for later leaders" (Williams 1961, 370). Pringle, his rather sympathetic biographer, lampoons him for telegraphing Brooks Brothers for the military uniform of a dandy (128), says that "Any indictment that brands Roosevelt a jingo and an imperialist is supported by ample evidence" (116), and reports that while the "Rough Riders" were training in San Antonio, ". . . he begged Lodge not to permit consideration of peace overtures until Puerto Rico had been taken, Cuba liberated, and the Philippine Islands seized" (131). Let there be no peace, at least not until Teddy himself had had a chance to do some real fighting. There are consequences to labeling somebody a weakling and having them fixate on the adolescent capacity to overcome it aggressively. Reformed wimps become the biggest bullies.

Negative opinion on Roosevelt is supported by unsympathetic writers as well, viz. the "Shrill, volatile Acting Secretary of the navy, Theodore Roosevelt" (Wilson 1970, 236). Roosevelt wrote a biography of Thomas Hart Benton, described as "amateurish and hastily written," to extol Benton, who "possessed in the author's eyes the virtue of having sounded forth, perhaps earlier and more powerfully than all others, the call to 'Manifest Destiny'" (Josephson 1940, 68-9). In this same work he castigated Thomas Jefferson for being a "timid, shifty doctrinaire." "Doctrinaire" was Roosevelt's idea of a dirty word and a profound political insult, one he used with relish to describe Woodrow Wilson. In addition, Henry Cabot Lodge, fellow traveling imperialist, who was the biographer of Hamilton, "always spoke of Jefferson as the villain, as Beveridge did later in the monumental Life of John Marshall" (68). There is no room in this religion of military expansion even for Thomas Jefferson, much less William Jennings Bryan. And the reason is not far to seek.

"The Americans, he wrote, sprang fully into national life, became a distinct nation, only at the moment when they began their work of conquest" (70). For the people who believe this, the reversion to barbarism is complete and finished. It has already been pointed out that Roosevelt would be a hero in Texas if he wasn't draped under the label Republican (Fehrenbach 1968, 642). Richard Hofstadter is at his sarcastic best dismissing Roosevelt as Philistine and superficial, the darling of those "who had never walked behind a plow" (1959, 230). He was in short, "the master therapist of the middle classes" (231). The thinness of the personality that led the American reversions to barbarism is precisely thin at the moment of reversion, when Roosevelt imagined the national character took shape. Roosevelt was the one man most responsible for our entry into the Philippines.

Hofstadter's opinion didn't improve with age and additional information either. He laughs at Roosevelt's contemporaries who thought they heard the voice of God where "we can discern the carnal larynx of Theodore Roosevelt" (1965, 178). He further noticed the existence of the religious impulse in the military victories. "The quick victories won by American arms strengthened the psychological position of the imperialists. . . success, as in a Calvinist scheme, is taken as an outward sign of an inward state of grace" (175).

Thomas Jefferson wasn't around to object to this state of grace on principle, but there were plenty of others who objected. The Anti-Imperialist movement that grew up around opposition to the Spanish American War was based chiefly on abstract political principles, namely the idea that government derives its just powers, not from superior force of arms, but from the informed consent of the governed, hence to impose American will on other people would be to do irreparable damage to the principles upon which the republic was founded (Harrington 1935, 212). Mark Twain, William Dean Howells, William James, Charles Eliot Norton, Andrew Carnegie, William Potts, Grover Cleveland, William Jennings Bryan, to name just a few of the leaders of this 750,000 member movement, were ridiculously ineffectual in the face of Roosevelt and the yellow journalists. "The people were stirred by the thought of distant possessions, of an experience second to none, a 'world power' on whose territories the sun would never set" (230). The adumbration of the English is apparent in this passage. Boston and some Bostonians, an original source of currently discredited ideas about American and human liberty, would keep the organization going until its ultimate demise in the 1920s.

The successes of this group were chiefly literary and Finley Peter Dunne is the author of the sarcasm that Roosevelt should name his book of war reminiscences "Alone in Cuba" (Harrington 1937, 664). The little that was published by the opponents of imperialism is credited to the "difficulty of placing anti-imperialist productions" (667), an immediate and unhappy byproduct of democratic centralism, the selective power of the press. How is it possible to rationalize Bryan and all those with him on this issue as traitors, except with the most reversionary blinders. "Rather, it is pure imperial ideology, beyond the reach of evidence or debate" (Chomsky 1973, 63). Chomsky was describing the religious faith in the anti-Communist crusade of the war on Vietnam. The Spanish American War was the source both of American imperial ideology and the democratic centralism that accompanies it. The "inevitable limitations on democracy under a highly centralized, militarized state capitalist system of the contemporary

American variety" (289) were being put in place by men who publicly vilified Jefferson.

Having stirred the country up with jingoistic choices, the imperialists fall back on fate. "'We have no choice as to whether or not we shall play a great part in the world, that has been determined for us by fate'" (McCullough 1977, 380), so says a character in Joseph Conrad's novel *Nostromo*. "'We shall run the world's business whether the world likes it or not.'" But this "Preclusive imperialism, here and elsewhere, was the motive" (Schlesinger 1986, 143), meaning if we don't take it somebody else will. "The private powers of the economy want free paths for their acquisition of great resources. No legislation must stand in their way. They want to make the laws themselves, in their interests, and to that end they made use of the tool they have made for themselves, democracy, the subsidized party" (Spengler 1926, 506). Roosevelt has been called a little Caesar before, by George Will and others. It comes with the territory of military reversion and as well as being the moment when America's national destiny begins. It is also the moment when America's unique offering of liberty through self determination perishes.

It was not an accident and "It is worth remembering that the greatest naval buildups of the sixteenth and seventeenth centuries occurred under the most autocratic regimes—those of Henry VIII and Cromwell" (Brewer 1989, 12). Caesars and autocrats belong together. "In Germany as elsewhere, imperialism and navalism went hand in hand" (May 1961, 187). They were first nature with Theodore Roosevelt, nephew of Confederate admirals and admirer of Admiral Mahan. "To be sure the imperial drive is often masked in defensive terms" (Chomsky 1973, 49), and Roosevelt lacked the guile to be anything but true to his type. "'I feel even more strongly on the question of our attitude towards the outside world, with all that it implies, from seacoast defense and a first-class navy to a properly vigorous foreign policy'" (Hofstadter 1959, 217). From defense to offense is typically no more complicated a maneuver, once you have a fleet at sea, than turning it around. And in one of those rare moments, when insight would flash upon Roosevelt, he could prophecize that he hoped he wasn't "'personally realizing all of Brooks Adams' gloomiest anticipations of our gold-ridden, capitalist-bestridden, usurer-mastered future'" (220), but of course he was all of that and more.

The opposition, led first by Grover Cleveland in his split shift in the White House, and then by William Jennings Bryan, who was to be turned away three times from the doors of power, certainly saw Roosevelt and the imperialists that way. "At last, true to Brooks Adams's prediction, capitol resorted to the equivalent of force. Not long before election, the Republicans pulled their last trick out of the bag. Bulletins were posted in factories, rumors started, and speeches made. Workmen realized the implication of their employer's threats to close shop if Bryan should win" (Beringause 1955, 152). See ". . . Bryan's nomination as the protest of the American People against monopoly, the first great struggle of the masses of our country against the privileged classes" (Wilson 1970, 219). Bryan's famous Cross of Gold speech can be read as a protest of the tax payer objecting to the tax consumers, in the terms of Calhoun's master class. Bryan would be beaten in 1896 by McKinley, upon whose eventually assassinated coattails, Roosevelt, the youngest and most immature man to ever be President of the United States, would glide into the White House. "McKinley was receiving and welcoming acceptance as hallmark for the haves and those supporting the establishment as such. . . The common understanding that the G.O.P. candidate was again drawing labor votes via employers who got the word to their hired help to vote Republican or else" (227), R.I.P., democracy.

Character assassination, even with such a broad, rigid, and inviting target, is only useful for the illumination it provides for the actual deeds. The U.S.S. *Maine* blew up in Cuba in 1898, killing the crew of 260. The cause was never established (231). All American history regarding Cuba, including Davis and Lee's midcentury preoccupation, was rushed by the explosion back into consciousness as the imperialists made "Remember the Maine!" as famous as Remember the Alamo! Theodore Roosevelt was at this time an assistant to the Secretary of the Navy.

"On the Sunday before 'War Monday' (April 25), Dewey, aboard his flagship *Olympia*, led out his squadron, and on official orders from the Acting Secretary of the Navy, headed for undisclosed points within Spain's Philippines colony" (237). Secretary of the Navy Long had left his office for a day, right after the *Maine* explosion, and "The preparations for this move had been secretly ordered well in advance of the war, on February 25, 1898, by the high-handed Assistant Secretary of the Navy, Roosevelt, on a day when his superior Mr. Long had left him in temporary charge as Acting Secretary. . . Thus the armed force of the United States hurled her into the race for imperial colonies in the tumultuous Orient" (Josephson 1940, 84). It is useful to recall that Andrew Jackson as President didn't feel like the Constitution gave him the authority to commit troops to assist the Texans revolting in Mexico. The narrow reading of the commander in chief section of the Constitution suggests that it applies in defensive situations. In contemporary times, the president himself has to defend his behavior when he commits troops halfway around the world. The model for this outrageous behavior did not come from the president, nor the secretary of war, nor even the secretary of the Navy, but from an impetuous assistant. "This cable, sent by Roosevelt while Long was resting at his home, made possible the naval victory at Manila Bay" (Pringle 1955, 125). The role of free lance commander in chief was not sufficient for Roosevelt and he resigned to train his Rough Riders in Texas for his personal assault on Cuba and San Juan Hill, General Quitman revisited. Theodore Roosevelt was not exactly alone in Cuba. "Still another gamecock was on board the convoy which arrived on June 22, Major General Joseph Wheeler, whose last deeds of valor had been as an officer in the Confederate Army. His old nostrils quivered as he smelled gunpowder again. He rushed into the fighting before Santiago shouting, 'The Yankees are running! Dammit! I mean the Spaniards!'" (132). There's nothing quite the equal of a good short war to tone up American militarists. "Secretary Long, probably glad to be rid of him, later wrote in his diary 'his going into the army led straight to the Presidency'" (127).

American history is replete with examples of military careers leading straight to the presidency, starting with Washington, the general of the American Revolution. The presidents of the Virginia Dynasty were all veterans of the Revolutionary War. General Jackson's military resume is well known, likewise General Grant. The military, being the basis of the belief system, is the controlling factor in American politics.

The putative victory at Manila Bay would prove to be hollow, even for Roosevelt, its chief instigator (Hofstadter 1965, 165). It would take him a while to come to this conclusion. The American victory over the Spanish was a farce; the American victory over Aguinaldo in the Philippines was a tragedy. Senator Hoar of Massachusetts had this to say to his colleagues on the subject of the Aguinaldo Insurrection: "'There is not one of these gentlemen who will rise in his place and affirm that if he were a Filipino he would do exactly as the Filipinos are doing; that he would not despise them if they were to do otherwise. So much at least they owe of respect to the dead and buried history — the dead and buried history so far as they can slay and bury it — of their country'" (Beard and Beard 1925, 498). The vote in the U.S. Senate on a Resolution sponsored by Senator Bacon from Georgia (the least Confederate of all Southern states) to free the Philippines early was a 29-29 tie. The tie vote was broken by the then Vice President Roosevelt as it had become a party issue and the Republicans wanted to keep the Philippines (Hofstadter 1965, 171). In reviewing Filipino and Puerto Rican troops brought to Washington for his inaugural as president, ". . . the President called out that they hardly looked to be the victims of imperialism as his critics had charged. 'See the slaves rejoicing in their shackles!' he cried" (Pringle 1955, 256). The unintended irony of soldiers dressed in uniforms provided by their conquerors being referred to as slaves rejoicing was undoubtedly lost on Roosevelt. But even the most empty mind can change if there is room. By 1907, Roosevelt had acquired the requisite perspective to look upon his work askance and notice that ". . . the Philippines were the Achilles' Heel of our strategic position and should be given 'nearly complete independence' at the 'earliest possible moment'" (Hofstadter 1965, 187).

Richard Hofstadter, in *The Paranoid Style in American Politics,* is certainly aware of the qualifying nature of the adjectives. Nearly complete independence, as well as being an oxymoron, is just that type of hanging on overbite that gives American foreign policy its neurotic circus quality. The Democratic Party Platform of 1908 addressed the subject of the Philippines in this manner: "We condemn the experiment in imperialism as an inexcusable blunder which has involved us in enormous expense, brought weakness instead of strength, and laid our nation open to the charge of abandoning a fundamental doctrine of self government" (Johnson 1973, 150). As William James pointed out, the peace party makes few recruits with this line of thinking.

It has been noticed by everybody interested in imposing their power on others in Southeast Asia, the Spanish, the English, the Japanese, and the Americans, to name a few recent imperialists, that while there could be a Philippines independent of the United States, there could never be an independent Philippines. It is a strategic position not large enough to defend itself from imperialists. The American attempt to impose first genocide and then democracy on the Philippines resulted in the satrapy of

General Ferdinand Marcos. This grotesque fraud (even his widow would like to be president, complicit as she was in their looting of the people's treasury — close to the Drakian standard of 4,000 percent) was patronized by the United States for decades. Fortunately for the Filipino independence movement, Mount Pinatubo buried Clark Air Force base under several feet of ash and the American Navy withdrew from Subic Bay. It took a volcano and a little help from natural history to make the imperialists in the United States realize how far away and irrelevant, except as an entropic energy drain, the Philippine Islands really are.

Even though it could and has been said that Theodore Roosevelt's career as an imperialist began with his out of hand orders to Admiral Dewey to take Manila and the Philippines, it didn't end there. Having annexed Hawaii in 1898, by resorting to the expedient of a joint resolution to get around the Senate two-thirds majority requirement a la Texas (Perkins 1966, 150), the Spanish American War also added Puerto Rico and Guam. "General Anderson accepted still another volunteer member of the new American Empire" (Wilson 1970, 250-1). It is not entirely clear who was volunteering whom and for what.

The real object of Roosevelt's usufruct was the Isthmus of Panama, some real estate that had been on his family's want list for centuries, and a big plank in the southern and Confederate agenda since the 1850s had witnessed the sectionalization of Manifest Destiny. "'No single great material work which remains to be undertaken on this continent is of such consequence to the American People" (McCullough 1977, 249), so said the by now President Roosevelt in his first message to Congress. The voyage of the *Oregon*, from California through the Straits of Magellan to the Caribbean war against the Spanish, had given the imperialists a vivid demonstration of the military need for a canal. While the canal is frequently rationalized as being for commercial purposes, it is always to be understood that the commercial purposes for which it is used provide the taxing stream that funds the military. The power is only implied cosmetically to the commercial sector like pancake makeup on a whore. "Travelers in the Canal Zone derive the impression that they are in the midst of a gigantic military installation, and by the same token the Panamanians have felt that an important segment of their territory is occupied by the forces of the United States" (Liss 1967, 24). Both of these reported impressions accurately reflect the situation.

Panama, as students of geography are aware, was once part of the supposedly sovereign nation of Colombia. Its role in American military history is tightly bound up with that of Nicaragua, another place in Central America narrow enough to support American fantasies about a trans-oceanic canal. The vote to fund a canal in Nicaragua failed by five votes, largely on the strength of a postage stamp displaying a volcano. In the retrospective provided by Mount Pinatubo in the Philippines, perhaps the stamp was not misused after all by opponents of the Nicaraguan route. That still left the Isthmus of Panama in Colombian hands and on Roosevelt's front burner when "He was spared the necessity [of grabbing it] by a timely revolution. On November 3, 1903, Panama renounced its allegiance to Colombia and three days later the United States recognized its independence. This amazing incident. . ." (Beard and Beard 1925, 509), would hardly be the last amazing incident and "revolution" to dovetail so nicely with American imperial policy.

The relative speed of the diplomatic recognition indicates the level of fervor. So too does Roosevelt's own observation that "'If they had not revolted, I should have recommended Congress to take possession of the Isthmus by force of arms'" (McCullough 1977, 382). Years later Elihu Root would suggest to him that he had been accused of seduction and then proved that he was guilty of rape (383). For Roosevelt was restless for acclaim and would say "Accordingly I took the Isthmus, started the canal and left Congress not to debate the canal, but to debate me — " (384). This bit of bombast was delivered in the Greek Theatre at the University of California at Berkeley in 1911, not a modern stage, where an imperialist and his opinions would be hooted down by the 1960s. While still president and without Congressional funding "On his own authority, he ordered the ships to sail out of Hampton Roads, [Virginia] and circle the earth by way of the Straits of Magellan, San Francisco, Australia, the Philippines, China, Japan, and the Suez Canal. . ." (Beard and Beard 1925, 515). This was an early demonstration of how the funding power of the Congress is perpetually in tow to the commanding in chief power of the president. The Congress, stranded in his wake, could not very well leave the Navy stranded halfway around the world.

Roosevelt left the presidency in the hands of William Howard Taft. Taft had been the Governor of the Philippines as well as Roosevelt's Secretary of War, where among other duties, he supervised the construction of the Panama

Canal. Taft would be a one-term president due to Roosevelt's unsatisfiable impetuosity which led him to the Bull Moose third party charge in 1912 and, blind as he was, delivered the presidency to Woodrow Wilson. He would become apoplectic later at Wilson and Wilson's Secretary of State Bryan for the monetary damages paid to Colombia for the loss of Panama and the Canal Zone because he felt that "'The payment can only be justified upon the ground that this nation played the part of a thief. . .'" (Pringle 1955, 234). Roosevelt was beginning to get the idea.

The idea of control of Panama and the Canal, brought to fruition by Roosevelt, had been a southern American obsession, at least since Secretary of State Henry Clay of Kentucky in Monroe's cabinet in 1823. President Van Buren ordered a survey conducted there in 1839. A treaty for the construction of the Canal was signed with the Republic of New Granada in 1846. Jefferson Davis never abandoned his interest in it. It is amusing to realize that Roosevelt, who accused Davis of treason, would embody the final ironic actualization of one of Davis' favorite ideas and policies. The Clayton Bulwer treaty with the English provided for a joint development. The English were careful watchers of the Roosevelt epoch in American Imperialism.

"England had a stake in American victory, he [H.W. Wilson] contended, partly because the other races would measure Anglo-Saxon fighting qualities by America's performance against Latin Spain" (May 1961, 222). In *Imperial Democracy*, a great book and an oxymoron in motion, the power of the press had been underestimated. "The best informed writers had not credited the American navy with such enterprise and efficiency. Nor had anyone expected two hundred thousand men to be mobilized so quickly, old Confederates to take commands alongside former Union officers, Democrats and Republicans to enlist with matching zeal, or northern immigrants and southern Negroes to line up before recruiting booths" (220). The love of war, deepened and broadened in the American psyche by the Civil War, returned in an instant. The English were not disappointed by the performance of the Americans and their attitude was summed up by "Joseph Chamberlain, the distinguished liberal statesman. . . the next duty of Englishmen 'is to establish and maintain bonds of permanent unity with our kinsmen across the Atlantic. . . The Stars and Stripes and the Union Jack should wave together over an Anglo-Saxon alliance'" (Beard and Beard 1925, 496).

This episode took place during the Victorian period in England, when the British Empire had passed its peak and was beginning to loom down the funnel of decline. "The editor of the latter [the *National Review*] remarked that America might be of use to Britain in the great Anglo-German struggle that he so often prophesied" (May 1961, 221). This opinion must have been buttressed "When the famous British warship designer Sir William White made a tour of the United States in 1904. . . he was shaken to discover fourteen battleships and thirteen armored cruisers being built simultaneously in American yards (although, curiously, the U.S. merchant marine remained small)" (Kennedy 1987, 243). It should not be lost on us that "In general, this group of imperialists was inspired by the navalist theories of Mahan and by the practical example of what they on occasion called Mother England" (Hofstadter 1965, 164). Ontogeny continues to recapitulate phylogeny, as America under the Rooseveltian imperialists returned to the example of the British Empire and their roots in South Carolina (where many of the ships that were shaking Sir William White were under construction in Charleston) and where as colonists "They were. . .'more attached to the Mother Country' than residents of the north-ern colonies" (Weir 1983, 238). The permanent American unity with England, especially the empire, was merrily on its way.

The Democrats objected to being co-opted into the British Empire against their principles "'As we are not willing to surrender our civilization or to convert the Republic into an empire. . .'" (Beard and Beard 1925, 503). This was the minority position however. Roosevelt was leading the procession. "He was not an imperialist, he insisted. It was inconceivable to him that Americans could ever be viewed as imperialistic. In all the United States he had never met an imperialist, he once said before an audience in Utah. He was personally offended by the charge. Expansion was different; it was growth, it was progress, it was in the American grain" (McCullough 1977, 255). Unfortunately for Theodore Roosevelt's image in history, one of the visages carved into Mt. Rushmore in South Dakota, he passes the duck test for imperialists. He walks like an imperialist. He talks ("speak softly and carry a big stick") like an imperialist. He may refer to himself and his behavior any way he cares to. Roosevelt was the epitome of an American imperialist.

It was not entirely coincidental that the English longing for American assistance in their economic struggle with Germany, would bear fruit almost exactly at the moment the Panama Canal was completed. "For by ironic, tragic coincidence the long effort at Panama and Europe's long reign of peace drew to a close at precisely the same time. It was as if two powerful and related but vastly different impulses having swung in huge arcs in the forty some years since Sedan, had converged with eerie precision in August 1914. The storm that had been gathering over Europe since June broke on August 3, the same day the *Cristobal* made the first ocean-to-ocean transit" (McCullough 1977, 609). History is designed by the blind who call the shots. Its pattern refused to reveal itself to, and was mercilessly refracted through the warped lenses of, Theodore Roosevelt.

The American imperialists had not merely attracted the European attention of the English, their racial and linguistic allies, but also the attention of the imperialistic strain in the French, their traditional allies on the subject of liberty and freedom from subjugation by London. "In France, the veteran breaker of cabinets, Georges Clemenceau, stood ready to rally forces on any issue and his *Justice* was one of the few French papers to side with America on the Cuba issue" (May 1961, 194). Clemenceau, the multi-lingual (fork tongued) author of World War II, thought this of Theodore Roosevelt: "His name was the 'one which sums up the beauty of American intervention. . .'" (Perkins 1977, 418). The "beauty" of American intervention in World War I and World War II was lost on Congresswoman Jeanette Rankin of Montana, the only congressperson to vote against American entry into both wars to save the British Empire, but it was not lost on Franklin Roosevelt. "Franklin Roosevelt had learned geopolitics from his cousin Theodore and from Admiral Mahan long before he learned idealism from Woodrow Wilson" (Schlesinger 1986, 203). Not only had FDR learned geopolitics earlier and preferred it to idealism, he was a scion of the family of New Yorkers who carry the imperialist gene.

In the middle of the Civil War, with the rise of New York on the ill-concealed profits of war, we see the American expression of Spenglarian doom, for the arcs that McCullough saw in 40 year sweeps are merely minor blips on the sweep of 400 year arcs, where urban areas dominate the land. New York was the home base of the robber barons from the end of the Civil War up to the Spanish American, until even its laws drove them to incorporate in nearby New Jersey. Spengler's monumental work, comparing among other things, the decline of the Mediterranean civilization with the decline of the western European civilization relates them on the one hand to the mathematics of Pythagoras and on the other Descartes. "Both, expanding in all beauty, reached their maturity one hundred years later; and both, after flourishing for three centuries, completed the structure of their ideas at the same moment as the Cultures to which they respectively belonged passed over into the phase of megalopolitan Civilization" (1926, 90). The significance of Spengler's identification of this pattern is very nearly lost on the increasingly illiterate United States. But for the handful of readers who can comprehend, in the electronic dark ages of the 1990s, America's own Victorian watershed, "Imperialism is Civilization unadulterated. In this phenomenal form the destiny of the West is now irrevocably set. . . The expansive tendency is a doom. . . It is not a matter of choice. . . the indwelling tendency of *every* Civilization that has fully ripened" (36-7). So as Roosevelt imagined that our culture only began with our conquests (which actually began in the 16th and 17th centuries), it was in fact placed beyond culture and into the civilization of a new Caesarism with his virtually unconscious reiteration of the pattern.

America had a culture only briefly in the late 18th century in the idealistic work of the Revolution and the Bill of Rights. The best parts of the Jeffersonian impulse were continually being dragged to the right by the reversionary effects of southern capitalism, slavery, and the militarization of the country that the Civil War imposed. By the time of Theodore Roosevelt and World War I, which he was so anxious to get in to it is embarrassing, the reversion had taken yet another giant Confederate step backwards toward barbarism. The popularity of war in Texas and the South has already been remarked upon and is not a matter of serious dispute. Texas put its brand on the rest of the West immediately after the Civil War and through the work of the tireless unreconstructionists like Jefferson Davis and Jubal Early, white supremacy and state rights were added to the growing format of a Confederate victory. Honor was established, and then maintained in their iron will, by the gracious surrender of Lee at Appomattox. Roosevelt gave them back their dream of a Caribbean empire and filled it with actual colonies. President George Bush's invasion of Panama in December of 1989, to put it firmly back into the empire from its wobbling orbit, was yet another and only the most recent recapitulation of Jefferson Davis' favorite foreign policy ideal.

The remaining bone of contention was control of California. The value of this real estate had been recognized, coveted, and claimed by the

Spanish, their Mexican successors and assigns, the indigenes who lived there before them for eons in relative peace, and by the United States who admitted California as a free state in 1850. The gold rush cut short the immediate Confederate demand and desire for California. Theodore Roosevelt, who was never too sure of where he was, speaking in southern California in 1905 could say: "When I am in California, I am not in the West. I am West of the West" (McWilliams 1946, 313). Perhaps California is a province apart or on its way to becoming the "most dynamic Asian" country as *Billion* magazine from Hong Kong described it. In the next chapter we will take up the discussion of how California became a southern state, helped along in this regard by General Otis, who was born in Marrietta, Ohio, a Civil War Veteran, and who was breveted a general in the Spanish American War.

14

How California Became a Southern State

With Jefferson Davis and the South out of the way as obstacles to the construction of a transcontinental railroad, the golden spike was driven into the Union Pacific tie near Promontory Point north of Great Salt Lake in 1867. San Francisco now had steel rails connecting it all the way to New York. One year later, with the overthrow of the Tokugawa Shogunate and the Meiji Restoration in Japan, the actualization of Commodore Perry's 1853 attempt (with one-fourth of the U.S Navy) to lay shipping lines and the ocean going rails right into Tokyo Bay was realized. It marked the first parameters of what would became a perpetual American attempt to open the Japanese market. San Francisco, the quintessential union town and economic capital of the free state of California, seemed destined to remain that way, the westernmost outpost of the American dream of "liberty, equality, and justice for all." What took place in the next 80 years would alter that destiny as the power in California was shifted south to Los Angeles. Chapter 14 is a narrative and analysis of the salient details of how California became a southern state.

Southerners like Jefferson Davis, rather straightforward in their thinking, had noticed that if the Missouri Compromise line of 1820, even though they didn't agree with what they considered to be unconstitutional restrictions on slavery north of that latitude, were to be extended to the Pacific Ocean, everything south of Monterey would be southern slave territory. Under the chapter subtitle, "Southern Plans for Union with the West," Charles and Mary Beard report an easily documented thesis: "It was long the design of Southern statesmen like Calhoun to hold the West and the South together in one political party" (1925, 307). That California was the object of the southern intentions can be seen clearly in Calhoun's objection to "the Taylor administration's proposal to bypass customary procedures and admit California as a free state" (Niven 1988, 340). We have seen how the Confederate efforts to maintain their established beachhead in Arizona Territory had as their ultimate motive the forging of a corridor to control of

191

southern California, where even though the population was minuscule, the Confederacy had significant support (DeMarco 1988, 41-3).

The Compromise of 1850 had admitted California to the Union as a free state, creating the "great exception" as it never passed through a territorial phase. It had passed through many other phases however, before becoming part of the United States and several of them are significant. The struggle for control of California can be understood as the struggle for control of the latitude, the land, and the labor.

From the nearly paradisical existence of the channel Indians as reported by Sauer (1971), they passed into the hands of the Spanish. "Where the Spanish found adaptable Indians, they always worked to incorporate them into the state as third- or fourth-class citizens to form a laboring class" (Fehrenbach 1968, 65). The Spanish Franciscans who built the chain of missions in California found plenty of adaptable Indians. "The weakness of the Spanish-Mexican settlements in California consisted in their dependence on cheap Indian slave labor" (McWilliams 1946, 47). This Catholic system created on the coast of the great exception may not have been all that exceptional. "In many respects, the social structure of Spanish California resembled that of the Deep South: the gente de razon were the plantation-owners; the Indians were the slaves; and the Mexicans were the California equivalent of 'poor white trash'. . . At the base of the pyramid were the Indians, upon whose unpaid labor the entire economy was based" (McWilliams 1968, 90). Slavery was a basic economic institution in California, just as it was on the Atlantic Coast of the South, where "For Calhoun, not the least of slavery's salutary effects was its making the South the balance of the American political system" (Thomas 1968, 221).

Competent authorities, disregarding Catholic obfuscation, are in agreement that "the forced labor system of the original Franciscan missions was tantamount to slavery" (Davis 1990, 330). The unpaid labor at the base of the American economy South and West is worth tracking. "Some called their condition on the ranchos peonage. Others, like the colorful Horace Bell, Chronicler of Los Angeles during its first decades of Yankee rule, called it 'slavery.' . . In his book, *The Cattle on a Thousand Hills,* Robert Glass Cleland compared the rancho in economic and social terms with the medieval English manor" (DeMarco 1988, 15). Cattle and hides were a thriving business in California, the market in Boston opened in 1822, when, at about the same moment, Austin first settled in Texas.

Carey McWilliams, whose work is basic to understanding California, has been described as "the Walter Prescott Webb of California, if not its Fernand Barudel. In his oeuvre, in other words, debunkery transcended itself to establish a commanding regional interpretation" (Davis 1990, 35). The special kinship between California and the South was readily apparent to him. "Farm labor is California's 'peculiar institution' in much the same sense that chattel slavery was the South's peculiar institution." (McWilliams 1949, 150). The conclusion was shared by the San Francisco Morning Chronicle: "'In many respects, it is even worse than old-time slavery'" (151). Lincoln, among others, felt that slavery was having a deleterious effect on the owners as well, and the effect was transposed to California. "Hence they are driven to defend the system and its consequences much as slave-owners were driven to defend chattel slavery" (160). The system and its consequences, with its intent to keep or drive the labor in the economic direction of subsistence, is still with us today.

"It is a story of nearly seventy years' exploitation of minority racial and other groups by a powerful clique of landowners whose power is based upon an anachronistic system of landownership dating from the creation, during Spanish rule, of feudalistic patterns of ownership and control" (McWilliams 1969, 7). The many references to medieval and feudal patterns in American agriculture should make us realize that the experiment in democracy being conducted in the United States was not shared in large scale crop production, where the models heavily favored European imports. "Through the instrumentality of the Mexican land grants the colonial character. . . was carried over " (12). The ownership of the land in South Carolina had been granted to the Lord's Proprietors. "The plantation system had been established. . . In many respects, California had developed a colonial economy" (88). And the scale of operations and its effects were and are not limited to North America. "By the use of a number of illuminating pictures, he [Claus Spreckles Jr.] had clearly demonstrated that precisely the same labor, that is, cheap coolie labor, was being used in the sugar-beet industry in California as was used in the Philippine Islands and in Hawaii" (85). In other words the exploitation of labor other than white was not only acceptable but de rigueur in overseas colonies as well as domestic ones. The predictable results are summed up by Davis Morgan of the University of California: "This large class of uneducated, underpaid, under-housed, and under-fed labor has made it possible for farmers to sell their crops for less than actual cost of production" (174). The consequences of domestic colonization present an enormous unresolved contradiction in the American polity.

Even though Catholics in California thrived on slavery before the Americans, it was the salubrious union of fourteenth century feudalism with the southern plantation in Texas that created the modern cotton plantation (McWilliams 1968, 170). We've seen cotton leapfrog the 98th Meridian into Arizona and from there "In 1910 the first cotton was planted in the Imperial Valley of California" (174). Treatment of the workers leapfrogged with the product. "In a speech in 1927, Simon J. Lubin had said that California growers were treating the Mexicans like peons, corralling them in barbed-wire stockades on the ranches" (190). It was Jefferson Davis, we can recall, who sent his ambassador Pickett to Mexico seeking diplomatic recognition with the observation that there was really no difference between peonage and slavery. "Dr. Stuart Jamieson points out that Mexicans had become dissatisfied with their 'distinct status as a lower caste, which they held because of their poverty, color, and cultural attributes. Their position. . . in many ways came to parallel that of Negroes in the Southern States. . .'" (194). Whatever different nuances of intent between slavery and peonage can be elucidated, the effect on capitalism is the same: cost of labor at the lowest possible rate. The patterns of Mexican employment in California agriculture are large scale and utilize employment by groups rather than as individuals. The intent is clear, "To keep Mexicans earmarked for exclusive employment in a few large-scale industries in the lowest brackets of employment" (215).

McWilliams' long experience in California agriculture, he was for years the state director of immigrant housing, his documented use of expert testimony in addition to his own, as well as the howls of protest that greeted the publication of his award winning *Brothers Under the Skin,* all reinforce the fact that he is an authority who has to be taken seriously. That his compassion seems to place him on the side of the vast laboring majority might also be explained by the difficulty of drumming up much sympathy for the California land-owning class, outside of that class itself. They are in many ways a recapitulation of the intense minority capitalists of the slaveholding South during the antebellum mirage of the 1850s with two crucial new twists: they are industrialized and incorporated. How they got to be this way is illuminating.

The booster impulse in American history is at least as old as the success-ful English slave traders, plantation owners, and speculators who had done well by themselves in Barbados, lifting the anticipations of fellow specula-tors with tales of the profits to be made in South Carolina. Once the boosterism was on shore, and control of the policy lifted from London by the Revolutionary War, California was "The culminating speculation, in fact, of the generations of boosters and promoters who had subdivided and sold the West from the Cumberland Gap to the Pacific" (Davis 1990, 25). It should not go unnoticed that during the transfer of additional medieval and southern plantation norms to California between 1848 and 1920, San Francisco was still the predominate center of power. The boosterism had to be turned up a notch in Southern California and it was cranked up by people "Who at the turn of the century created a comprehensive fiction of Southern California as the promised land of a millenarian Anglo-Saxon racial odyssey" (20).

The foundation for this racial odyssey was laid during the Mexican War. "The connivers, Mexican and American, had rushed through huge grants on the eve of American occupation" (McWilliams 1969, 13). The colossal scale of this land grab was epitomized by Henry Miller, a German immigrant who received the help of the railroads. "It was not long before Miller and Lux owned an empire in California as large as the Kingdom of Belgium" (32). Miller was among the most rapacious, but he was hardly alone. "In 1870, 1/500 of the population of California owned one half or more of the available agricultural lands of the state" (23). The Southern Pacific Railroad, a special case and combination of railroad, corporation, and plantation, owned 2,598,775 acres in Southern California alone (17). A 57,000 acre "farm" in Colusa County was ninety miles wide (51). The result of this "Land monopolization and the availability of cheap labor" (103), was the predictable plantation system.

We have seen that the English "short-timers" in South Carolina devel-oped the habit of thinking of land as just another commodity (Weir 1983, 230). It is not just another commodity, it is the basis for wealth and power, for as the statement of purpose of the National Association of Realtors begins, "Underneath all is the land, . . ." The gold *under* the land was the commodity that quickly tripped California temporarily out of southern hands. The gold *of* the land was to make huge sections of California largely indistinguishable from the South. "Chevron owned 37,793 acres in the immediate vicinity, in addition to 42,000 acres scattered elsewhere in the valley. In second place, with 35,897 acres, was the Tejon Ranch, one of the great land empires of California — 272,516 acres all told. The principal stockholders of the Tejon Ranch are members of the Chandler family, which owns the Los Angeles Times — the strongest voice for water development in California for the last eighty years. . . In last place with 16,528 acres — a plot of land that is still considerably larger than Manhattan Island — was the Southern Pacific Railroad, the largest private landowner in California" (Reisner 1986, 384-6). Reisner also mentions the other oil companies, Getty, Shell, and Tenneco, in the plantation business in this section of the San Joaquin Valley where two-thirds of the land was owned by eight corporations. These huge plantations are not to be confused, except perhaps in the case of the Tejon Ranch, with the "family" farm. "The Hotchkiss ranch near Los Banos may be taken as a fairly typical California cotton 'plantation' or factory" (McWilliams 1969, 195), complete with Negroes from Louisiana and a corporation store. With all this wealth in the "Industrial feudalism in California agriculture," it is astounding to learn that "Hulett C. Merritt, member of one of the families that has figured prominently among the large landed industrial interests of California. . . [was] convicted in Federal courts, April 2, 1919, for hoarding food supplies" (183).

With plantation agriculture on such an enormous scale based on the exploitation of labor and coupled with the petrochemical industrialization of agriculture, could labor problems be far behind? In spite of the delay caused by the Civil War and the subsequent Reconstruction, "In 1881, the Southern Pacific opened a new line by way of El Paso to New Orleans; and in 1885, the Atchison, Topeka, and Santa Fe line was completed to Los Angeles" (60-1). The railroad finally connecting California to the South, an old dream of Jefferson Davis, would increase the stakes of the developing competition between northern California and the South centered on Los Angeles. The agriculture was feudal and southern throughout the state. The shift in control from the North to the South would hinge on control of the supply of labor.

During the Civil War itself, it has been noted how the South sought and failed a connection to southern California, which was not without its realistic basis for "The northern half leaned toward the Union while the agrarian southern half favored the South" (Trimble 1977, 161). This leaning toward the South was established by vote as "In the presidential election of 1860 Los Angeles cast 356 votes for Abraham Lincoln. His opponents received 1700 votes" (DeMarco 1988, 41). These statistics are recited under the chapter subheading "The Civil War — Los Angeles Chooses the Confederacy." Los Angeles was to remain a "Confederate stronghold in the early phase of the Civil War" (43).

It is useful to keep in mind that half of the original 44 settlers of the Nuestra Puebla de la Reina de Los Angeles carried African blood with only two white Spaniards and one Chinese among the Indians, Mestizos, and Mulattos (8). The four legs of the Los Angeles cultural and racial rectangle (McWilliams 1946, 315) were a melting pot ready to boil. "The previous year [1853] California had more murders than the rest of the states combined and Los Angeles had more than occurred elsewhere in California" (McWilliams 1968, 131). There was approximately one murder per day in a population of 4,000, or very nearly 10 percent of the population. If life seems violent in LA now, the truth is, things have calmed down considerably from its frontier days. To match the early homicide rate would require hundreds of thousands of murders.

The Los Angeles population of 4,400 in 1860 compares poorly to San Francisco's 156,802 (DeMarco 1988, 40). As the curtain was drawn on the stage of competition between the two cities, the resources were hardly equal, with San Francisco sporting 35 times the population. "Los Angeles, meanwhile, remained a torpid, suppurating, stunted little slum" (Reisner 1987, 54). San Francisco, on the other hand: "In finance it was the rival of New York, in culture the rival of Boston; in spirit it had no competitor" (54).

Richard Henry Dana Jr., a Harvard law student on leave from his studies and working in the hide trade on the California coast in the 1830s, remarked on how distasteful it was to stop at San Pedro — the port for LA — with its tarpits and insects. Dana predicted that the Bay area was where the capitol would be with its lovely mission district, but his future shock, when he returned 20 years later, is worth reiterating. "In 1835 there was one board shanty. In 1836, one adobe house on the same spot. . . then came the *auri sacra fames*, the flocking together of many of the worst spirits of Christendom; a sudden birth of a city of canvas and boards, entirely destroyed by fire five times in eighteen months. . . and as often rebuilt. . . one hundred thousand inhabitants. . . the most quiet and well-governed city of its size in the United States" (1937, 392-3). That was after he had gotten used to it. Initially the postscript, "Twenty-Four Years After" to his handsome literary and geographical classic *Two Years Before the Mast*, reported "The past was real. The present, all about me, was unreal, unnatural, repellant" (388). Dana was astounded also at the number of people he met on his second visit to California who had read his book. It was once required reading and with the addition of the postscript reveals what Paul Theroux referred to as a Chinese conundrum: the more attractive a place is the more people who will be attracted to it, thus reducing the initial attractiveness.

We are aware of the "Requirements for an abundance of cheap, skilled, mobile, and temporary labor" (McWilliams 1969, 65) for plantation agriculture, emphasis on temporary, for in California it disappears completely off the farm when the particular task is completed. "Its mammoth farm factories have been built by cheap Oriental and peon labor, imported for a particular purpose and discarded as soon as that purpose has been achieved. For over half a century this sordid business of race exploitation has been going on. . . " (134). The overall summation of what is now referred to as "agribusiness" is revealing. "California agriculture is monopolistic in character; it is highly organized; it utilizes familiar price-fixing schemes; it is corporately owned; management and ownership are sharply differentiated; it is enormously profitable to the large owners" (266). Four out of five of these characteristics, minus incorporation designed to evade the law and conceal the ownership, were also characteristic of cotton plantations in the antebellum South, which also were monopolistic, highly organized, with differentiation between management and ownership, and above all, highly profitable.

The profits were and are protected in the following manner, "For at all times the farm groups, through their control of the State Senate, have held a veto power on legislation" (268). We will recall the conclusion Calhoun came to of his concurrent majority which gave control of the South Carolina senate to the slaveholding plantation owners of Charleston. Translated into English, Calhoun's "concurrent majority" principle means, the rich shall have their own way, no matter how few of them there are. McWilliams suggests that these California corporations are not owned by farmers at all. "The large shipper-growers 'farm by phone' from headquarters in San Francisco or Los Angeles" (1949, 157). The owners live in the city, much as they did in Charleston. And like South Carolina, there is a

". . . tendency on the part of the people to think of California as a province apart, sovereign in its own right, a self-contained empire" (364).

But people other than farmers live in the cities of San Francisco and Los Angeles, since it is not possible to operate a self-contained empire on the production of food and agricultural products alone. One of the migrants to Southern California was "General Otis (he was breveted Major-General for 'meritorious conduct in action at Calocan' during the campaign in the Philippines)" (McWilliams 1946, 275). Included among the adjectives used to describe General Otis are disgraceful, depraved, corrupt, crooked, and putrescent. He organized the community in defense of the open shop, and by the decision of this one man "Los Angeles became immersed in a half century of bloodshed, violence, hatred, class war, oppression, injustice and a destruction of civil liberties which was to turn it into the low spot of American culture and democracy" (275). General Otis, who "fought rebels at Antietam, Spaniards in the Philippines and unions wherever he found them, especially at his newspaper. . . [where] he kept 50 rifles in a store-room and shotguns in the newsroom in case of trouble with trade union-ists" (Cox 1992, 2B), would recognize the 1992 version of the scene he helped create where the Siamese twin problems of the recession and union organizers had the LA *Times* at bay.

In the beginning of the turn of power toward LA, "Otis and his colleagues were quick to realize that the only chance to establish Los Angeles as an industrial center was to undercut the high wage structure of San Francisco, long a strongly unionized town. . ." (McWilliams 1946, 276). San Francisco was one of the few places in the United States where a general strike was ever even contemplated, much less successful. Wages in LA were from 20-40 percent lower than in San Francisco. "It was precisely this margin that enabled Los Angeles to grow as an industrial center. Thus the maintenance of a cheap labor pool became an indispensable cog in the curious economics of the region" (277). Capitalists had learned something basic from the experience with slavery: the lower the cost of labor the higher the rate of profit.

Fittingly enough, the showdown was to come in the cotton fields of southern California. "The Tagus strike had particular significance. . . owned by the Merritt family [and] was regarded as the citadel of reaction. . . Vigilante groups were formed at Lodi, under the command of Colonel Walter Garrison, the Fuhrer of the California farmers. . . the culmination of the wave of strikes came in October in the cotton fields" (McWilliams 1969, 219). This was not a small strike; the workers were mounting a challenge at the basis of the reversionary economy. "18,000 workers joined the strike. . . the strike embraced the entire San Joaquin Valley, with the union attempting to picket, by patrols, a string of cotton plantations extending down the valley for 114 miles" (220). As is typical of serious strikes, attempts were made to break it with scab labor. "Additional Mexicans had been recruited, and advertisements had been placed by the cotton-gin companies for Negroes in the South. The strike, the largest of its kind in American history, lasted for twenty-four days" (223-4).

One of the consequences of using military metaphors in what is otherwise domestic activity can be seen in the application. "The first militarist of space in Los Angeles was General Otis of the Times" (Davis 1990, 228). It is not accidental but the working out of belief systems, "As in Otis's fortress Times building, this is the archisemiotics of class war" (231). The class war in California was led by General Otis and the Chandler family who were typical of power in Los Angeles and successful enough in their booster efforts that sometime around the end of WWI, Los Angeles became the most populous city in California. "Political power in Southern California remains organized by great constellations of private capital, which, as elsewhere, act as the permanent government in local affairs" (102). If a military metaphor is employed, people in the other class, that is to say those without capital, are considered to be enemies because they have goals or values that are opposed to those of the capitalists. "Permanent class warfare also reinforced bourgeois political discipline. . . Smashed the labor movement in Los Angeles with the aim of giving the Otis-organized Merchants and Manufacturers Association a competitive advantage over their regional rivals in union citadel San Francisco" (113).

Meanwhile, in union citadel San Francisco, the decision was made to join the strikes. "On July 19, 1934, the unions in San Francisco called a general strike. Not a wheel moved in San Francisco. When the general strike was broken, by the intervention of the National Guard, a statewide reign of terror was unleashed by the authorities" (McWilliams 1969 226-7). The power in California had been moved from the Union town of San Francisco to the recently and soon to be increasingly militarized seat of southern sympathy in Los Angeles. "Sympathetic to the cause of the Confederacy, Los Angeles was for years a 'bad town' for Negroes"

(McWilliams 1946, 324). One of the consequences of the boosters working out Jefferson Davis' economic geography "To make LA the primary rail center of the Southwest" (Davis 1990, 110), was that the use of the National Guard to break a strike had precedents in the railroad strike earlier when two companies of the first regiment of the United States Infantry had broken the railway strike (McWilliams 1946, 278).

The comments of Mr. Shelgrim in Frank Norris' *The Octopus*, relative to whose in charge, are instructive. "'Try to believe this — to begin with — that railroads build themselves. Where there is a demand sooner or later there will be a supply'" (Norris 1935, 285). Capitalists are famous for falling back on the bedsprings of "supply and demand" to excuse their actual behavior, which is to stimulate an artificial demand and then to fill it up with government money from which they take the profits. "'Control the Road! Can I stop it? I can go into bankruptcy if you like. But otherwise if I run my road, as a business proposition, I can do nothing. I can not control it. It is a force born out of certain conditions, and I — no man — can stop it or control it.'" (286). Determinism is the choice of fatalists whose options are self-occluded.

Resistance to turning California into a southern state was as ineffectual as the Anti-Imperialist League's resistance to the war against Aguinaldo in the Philippines. "Then came the End Poverty in California (EPIC) movement led by Upton Sinclair" (MacDougall 1965, 190). Literature is a hopeless tool applied to correcting the excesses of money and power. John Steinbeck's *The Grapes of Wrath* turned the pain of poverty into the abstract suffering of journalism and is quite possibly the worst famous book still in print.

But the switch in the levers of power to southern California had to benefit somebody, such as Edward Doheny, of Mexican oil and Teapot Dome fame, the richest Catholic in Los Angeles (Davis 1990, 331). No discussion of the switch in power to the South would be complete without mentioning the movies. D. W. Griffith's *The Birth of a Nation*, based on the novel *The Clansmen*, was correctly accused of being racist, and of bringing the movies permanently to Los Angeles (DeMarco 1988, 111). Its reversionary dip into the southern racist past also reflected the fact that "the Ku Klux Klan [was] (then waxing in power throughout Southern California)" (Davis 1990, 116). Three fiery crosses blazed on the hills on June 10, 1935 (McWilliams 1969, 240), as the "Industrial Association of San Francisco and the Associated Farmers, the two groups functioning now as a single unit" (261), continued consolidating power over agriculture. The movies were the perfect tool for the mythological boosterism of the people of the picture.

There are two other elements in this picture of southern control of southern California and the most basic one is water. Just as Charleston was protected from Sherman's March by the swamps which surrounded it, so also does natural history finally dictate to California. "More than any other thing, the Pacific High has written the social and economic history of California" (Reisner 1986, 345). Even though it is said in the West that water flows uphill towards money (13), the money has to come from somewhere. The growth of LA "Required continuous transfers of savings from the rest of the country" (Davis 1990, 118). In California, as in Texas, they were following a dream financed by other people's money, and "More than anyplace else, California seems determined to prove that the Second Law of Thermodynamics is a lie" (Reisner 1986, 369).

The Second Law of Thermodynamics has nothing to prove, but "What Congress has chosen to do, in effect, is purify water at a cost exceeding $300 an acre-foot so that upriver irrigators can continue to grow surplus crops with federally subsidized water that costs them $3.50 an acre-foot" (482). The House of Misrepresentatives will never be able to adequately explain this subsidy and yet "In California most farmers pay $5 to $10 an acre-foot, while city-dwellers pay up to $250 for the same amount. Those who use the least pay the most, and those who use the most pay the least" (Wood 1990, 4). If the actual cost of food, including labor and water, was factored into the price, the price would go up and the consumer's diet would improve. Meanwhile, "This means that 70 percent of the profit on what is supposed to be some of the richest farmland in the world comes solely through taxpayer subsidization — not crop production. . . Illegal subsidies enrich big farmers, whose excess production depresses crop prices nationwide and whose waste of cheap water creates an environmental calamity that could cost billions to solve" (Reisner 1986, 502). *The Cadillac Desert*, among many other things, makes perfectly clear how the Calhoun principle of the actions of government divide the people into two great classes, the taxpayers everywhere in the case of water in California, and the tax consumers, the wealthy individuals and corporations this system, eventually to be overmatched by the second law of thermodynamics, is designed to benefit.

The second and remaining element in the southern control of southern California is just as basic as water, although it won't be found on the periodic table. It is the military that General Otis and associated boosters brought to Southern California. Again from fairly humble beginnings, the First International Air Meet took place in 1910 at Dominguez Field (DeMarco 1988, 94-5). But "By 1945, aircraft contracts passed $7 billion. World War II literally catapulted Los Angeles out of the Depression" (144), even as it catapulted it permanently into the western bastion of the Confederate empire. "The war in the Pacific arrived in time to bring the region its real industrial revolution. . . First, the inter-regional capital flows that had been the source of Southern California's prosperity were now institutionalized in national defense appropriations that shifted tax resources from the rest of the country to irrigate the Los Angeles area's aircraft plants and military bases" (Davis 1990, 120). Anything can appear to thrive when irrigated with sufficient taxpayer money. "The militarization of the Los Angeles economy conferred the largest single quotient of economic power upon enclaved air craft corporations. . ." (121).

California is the world's largest disorganized military base, including Vandenberg Air Force base, named for the senator from Michigan who was the father of NATO. The traffic on the "Cadillac Desert" is predominantly military. "The high Mojave for the last fifty years has been preeminently the Pentagon's playground. . . 'the most important military airspace in the world' — ninety thousand military training sorties are still flown every year" (4). Neither was this the out of control accident that determinists would have us believe. "Similarly, since the 1940s, the Southern California aerospace industry and its satellite think-tanks have assembled the earth's largest single concentration of PhD scientists and engineers" (17). Who brought all these scientists to Southern California? "Cal Tech, together with the Department of Defense, substantially invented Southern California's postwar science-based economy" (55). The inventor of Cal Tech was Robert Millikan, who said "Southern California 'is today, as was England two hundred years ago, the westernmost outpost of Nordic civilization'" (56). England, the mother of the Confederate Empire, makes a timely reversionary appearance.

The patterns are evident in the smaller towns as well. Who worked in these plants when they weren't providing the music but "An extraordinary spectrum of Jazz, blues and R&B [men], dominated by musicians from the Southwest circuit of Texas, Oklahoma, Kansas and Louisiana (the region that had sent the most Black migrants to work in the West Coast's war plants)" (64). A little east of Los Angeles, "Whites from the South compose the majority of the population of Fontana" (397). It was where "The brutal murder (and its subsequent official cover-up) of O'Day Short, his wife and two small children, indelibly stamped Fontana — at least in the eyes of Black Californians — as being violently below the Mason-Dixon Line" (399). The spread of the industrial economy put agriculture in Fontana out of business but before it did, "Fontana Farms, meanwhile, had expanded to a full-time workforce of five hundred Mexican and Japanese laborers — comparable to the largest cotton plantation in the Mississippi Delta" (382). Fontana was the home of Kaiser Steel during WWII, but "The first symptom that all was really not so well in Fontana redux was the sharp increase in white supremacist agitation and racial violence after the layoffs at the mill" (424). When the periodic recessions and depressions of the reversionary economy strike, "Inside the cafe the counter is occupied by an apparition of Lee's Army after Appomattox: lean, bearded, hollow-eyed and taciturn" (430).

Apparitions and literal visions of the South predominate in southern California, and the essential infrastructure of the white supremacist geneal-ogy (160), (the supremacy of some white men) is found in housing. "At the same time, acting as private Jim Crow legislation, deed restrictions were also building a 'white wall' around the Black community of Central Avenue" (161). Segregated housing is not confined to southern California.

Even northern California came to resemble the South as reactionary Republican politicians like Governor Goodwin Knight and Senator Will-iam F. Knowland, parcelled the rich highland section of Oakland, known as Piedmont, away from the rest of the city. It is an enclave of 10,000 rich white reactionaries surrounded by hundreds of thousands of increasingly poor and desperate African Americans, Mexican Americans, and what was once known as "poor white trash." It recapitulates conditions in Colonial South Carolina, which has its own Piedmont. It accomplished economi-cally what the Jim Crow laws in South Carolina and elsewhere attempted to accomplish legislatively. Piedmont is surrounded by Oakland, California, and resembles a white homeland, just as Soweto was a homeland for blacks. Apartheid in South Africa was modeled on the Jim Crow laws, and like the case of Piedmont, California, is a living demonstration of the futility of having a racist English speaking empire in the backyard.

How the racist English speaking empire in California translates into politics will give us the final clue before recapitulation. As Barry Goldwater of Arizona was formulating his southern strategy for the 1964 election, his three-man advisory committee was headed by "the reactionary former Senate Majority Leader, William F. Knowland of California" (Schlesinger 1971, 471), one of the prime architects of the Piedmont predicament. That Goldwater should have won 51.4% (473) of the Republican vote in the 1964 primary shows not only how close the outcome was and how thin the balance of power, but how powerful a winner take all strategy can be. Previous prominent California Republicans included Earl Warren, a former governor and for years the Chief Justice of the U.S. Supreme Court.

Goldwater's victory in Republican California was literally the revival of conservative Republican politics there. Southern California has given the United States three conservative Republican Presidents: Hoover, the first Republican to carry Texas; Nixon; and Ronald Reagan. That Hoover was able to carry Texas, even by 26,000 votes, is an indication of how much the Republicans had changed since their first nominee from California, John C. Fremont in 1856. Clinton was the first man since Coolidge to be elected President of the United States without carrying Texas. Although Goldwater failed in his southern strategy to unite the South, partly due to his running against another Southerner, he carried five of the states of the Confederacy and was particularly popular in South Carolina.

South Carolina has since become "a New Hampshire below the Mason-Dixon line. . . launching Ronald Reagan in 1980 and George Bush in 1988 to sweeping super Tuesday victories across the region" (Cook 1991, 28). South Carolina's primacy in Republican presidential politics is the legacy of the late native son, Lee Atwater, and was made possible in large measure by its mirror image in southern California. Just as Charleston was "more linguistically diversified than any other spot in the mainland colonies" (Wood 1974, 169) as a result of African slave importation from many places, "The bookkeeper at the Hotchkiss Ranch [in California] had to be a trained linguist" (McWilliams 1969, 118), for the same reasons. The plantation economic system opened its exploitive doors on both coasts. More than 100 languages are currently spoken in Los Angeles.

What in particular makes California a southern state? California is exactly in the latitude of the South, below the Mason-Dixon line, even if on the West Coast. The comparable climate, similar division of land into huge plantations, and the exploitation of labor, as in slavery, are southern hallmarks. Connecting southern California by railroad to the South increased the cultural exchange and provided vivid proof that Jefferson Davis' Railroad Survey indicating a southern route would carry more people and move more freight at less cost was accurate and realistic. The romantic escapism of the movie business made *Gone With the Wind*, a paean to southern foolishness released in 1939 just in time to warm up Depression-weary Americans for World War II, the most popular movie of all. The white racist basis of politics in Oakland, San Francisco, and Los Angeles originated in the South, designed by John C. Calhoun. The powerful effect of the militarization of the economy of southern California provided the capstone that tilted California power from the once union citadel of San Francisco to Los Angeles, now becoming widely regarded as the capitol of the third world. Los Angeles was the primary beneficiary of the siege of the Cold War which recapitulated Confederate conditions. The arc of power radiating from the pentagon in Virginia that sweeps through South Carolina on its way across Texas and Arizona has Los Angeles as its last continental expression. Jefferson Davis and John Calhoun are perhaps truly comfortable at last. Most of what they wanted for the South, in and out of the United States, including the control of California, finally came to pass. California is a southern state.

15

The Truman Doctrine: The Prism of Empire

Henry Wallace was FDR's heir but Harry Truman was his successor. The events under FDR's umbrella leadership of the trifurcated Democratic party that led to the occupation of the White House by a politician from Missouri, a slaveholding southern but not a Confederate state, are worth reconsidering. Their significance increases with the gradual adoption of English policy that led to the Truman Doctrine. As one commentator modestly put it, "at stake was the entire course of world history" (Walton 1976, 16).

The broad outlines of the course of world history since the Spanish American War are familiar. The enthusiasm for war and the predatory temperament it reinforces among the members of the hereditary leisure class (Veblen 1931, 247), stimulated those members until they were finally able to maneuver the United States into the position of defending the British Empire in its two cycle war against Germany. American support for Britain against Germany was broadly hinted at as a reason for English interest in the outcome of the Spanish American War. Speaking of the first phase of that cycle, Dexter Perkins, in his *The Evolution of American Foreign Policy*, suggests that "To some Americans the British courtship has always seemed too clever and too self-interested to be admirable; but why should not Great Britain have sought American friendship?" (1966, 65). Friendship was not quite all that they were seeking, and over the principled and well thought out policy of neutrality developed by Wilson's Secretary of State William Jennings Bryan, "It is not strange, therefore, that the administration witnessed the British violations of international law with considerable complacency, and gave to the protests it felt compelled to make a somewhat *pro forma* character" (67). They are us, would be one way of racially and culturally putting it, or we are becoming them.

Just how closely they are us is more apparent now since "We have come a long way from the very straightforward bulletin prepared in 1922 by the Office of Naval Intelligence on 'The U.S. Navy as an Industrial Asset'" (Magdoff 1969, 175). The contemporary American Navy is more apt to

disguise its intentions, such as reflagging Kuwaiti oil tankers, but its activities are just as transparent. The domestic consequences of following
England into battle in World War I demonstrate the propensity and capacity of belligerents to adopt one another's tactics. "William E. Borah of Idaho
was one of the few Senators to view censorship with alarm: 'It is not necessary to Prussianize ourselves in order to destroy Prussianism in Europe'"
(Johnson 1963, 56). Nevertheless, even as jailed European critics of the war
were released soon after the Armistice, many Americans in jail for speaking
out where free speech is supposed to be protected, had to wait for liberation
until the administration of Calvin Coolidge, many years later.

The intolerance didn't cease once WWI was over however. "This great
Red Scare of 1919 was in many ways simply a continuation of the war
hysteria with its intolerance of pacifist, radicals, and even a few prowar
radical organizations like the Non-Partisan League" (120). While the
emphasis was shifting from pacifists to alien revolutionists — remember it
is practical psychology to project hostilities rather than deal with them — a
great many "aliens" were located within the United States. Led by J. Edgar
Hoover and directed by A. Mitchell Palmer, the Attorney General of the
United States, "Late in the afternoon on Friday, January 2, the raids began.
Close to 5,000 persons were arrested in the first two days, and possibly
another 1,000 in the weeks that followed. Federal agents stormed into
every Communist (and many a non-Communist) meeting house in the
nation and arrested everyone, citizens and aliens, Communists and non-
Communists, drove them off to the nearest federal building and then tore
the meeting houses apart" (141). The "Prussianization" of the United States
was well underway with the identification of Communists as enemy
number one.

World War I sapped some more of the British Empire's strength. It had
been ebbing since the turn of the century. Henry Luce, whom Joseph
Kennedy Senior would identify as the most powerful man in America, as he
sat down to enjoy a victory dinner celebrating the election to the presidency
of John Kennedy in 1960, editorialized in *Life* magazine a year before Pearl
Harbor. "His editorial was a plea for the USA to 'take over' and to run the
world as successor to John Bull" (MacDougall 1965, 33). The power of the
press and the media in the English speaking world is always underestimated.
The effect of that power is sometimes obvious and sometimes subtle. It was
apparent to many "that after 1938 FDR had lost political control of the

Democratic party to the Dixiecrats, who with the Northern Republicans were a majority in Congress" (880), as the ruling coalition reappears. While it was also apparent that "the Congressional system of seniority in determining committee chairmanships has always overwhelmingly favored the South" (387), it is frequently overlooked that the southern faction of the Democratic party had power beyond their numbers because they were the balance. They could throw their weight around within the Democratic party or without it by aligning with the conservative Republicans.

Partly to achieve equal time with his 1940 Republican opponent Wendell Willkie, who as might be expected, was an announced supporter of assistance to the democracies, FDR gave 50 over-age destroyers to Great Britain and "Received in return the right to construct naval and air bases on the soil of various British colonies, stretching all the way from Cape Breton to Trinidad" (Perkins 1966, 89). By establishing the American backflow over the receding British Empire to Trinidad, a mere 200 mile sail from the Barbadian point of origin, the two-way traffic in the English speaking empire was picking up speed.

The Atlantic Charter, another marriage of convenience between the ideal and the practical consummated by Roosevelt and Churchill, demonstrated again the mutual "Interests and objectives of the great English-speaking peoples" (90). The connubial metaphor is apropos for Perkins goes on to say "With Britain, in the years from 1941 to 1945, there was maintained an alliance of unusual intimacy" (97). If the United States was being married in public to the British Empire, it acquired its other major alliance surreptitiously with Russia, as "[FDR] made one of the very few secret deals in the history of the United States" (101), at least up to that pre-CIA point.

If there was contentment at the heart of the US and British alliance, cemented into action by the attack on Pearl Harbor, not the co-prosperity sphere's most lucid moment, there was little contentment in the factionalized Democratic party. John Nance Garner, a millionaire from Uvalde, Texas, who had once said "'Farming is not a profitable industry and in order to make money you have to have cheap labor'" (McWilliams 1968, 178), was vice president to FDR from 1933-1941. He was carrying the colors of the southern faction of the Democratic party. The Republican Herbert Hoover had broken the Democratic lock on the "solid" South in 1928 by his 26,000 vote victory in Texas. Political power from the South emanates from Texas and it had become important for the Democratic party to stop taking the South for granted.

John Nance Garner had several reasons to believe he would be the Democratic nominee in 1940, not the least of which was his power base and the two-term tradition. Although Roosevelt had lost control of the Congressional Democrats, he was able to override the two-term limitation by appealing to the other two major factions of the Democratic party, the labor leaders and the big city bosses. In partial exchange for the continued support of labor, Henry Wallace of Iowa and a distinguished member of FDR's New Deal cabinet, in Bruce Catton's opinion, "'He may very well have been the most efficient Cabinet member in the Roosevelt Administration'" (Walton 1976, 4), received the nomination for vice president. John Nance Garner was doubly miffed and the southern faction of the Democratic party, soon to be led by Governor Strom Thurmond of South Carolina, went away very unhappy. A law of politics ascribed to Senator Everett McKinley Dirksen of Illinois goes something like this: get elected; get re-elected; don't get mad — get even. Wallace's elevation "angered the Southerners and the big city bosses. As we shall see, they got their innings four years later" (8).

The marriage of convenience and interests between the British Empire and the United States, and indeed their two phased war against Germany, was the geopolitical expression of ". . . the deep loneliness, and that ancient German impulse towards the South which has been the ruin of our best, from the Saxon emperors to Holderlin and Neitzsche" (Spengler 1926, 335). The lonely 400 year impulse toward the South, which had washed the English up on the island of Barbados, had run out of places to express itself except in fratricide. The fratricide of the Civil War, the fratricide of World Wars I and II, and the fratricide among the factions of the Democratic party all dovetailed into the grand question: what on earth will we do when the war is over?

Jumping the gun even before the war was over, the first item on the southern agenda, where fratricide is a public obligation, was to get rid of Wallace. Vice President Wallace started out with the support of the delegates at the 1944 convention and "So irresistible were they that the will of the delegates had to be overwhelmed by intrigue, manipulation and main force on the part of the interests that could not tolerate the idea of Wallace as President of the United States" (MacDougall 1965, 10). Wallace's real strength — he was a brilliant thinker and administrator but an inept politician — was with the labor faction. Roosevelt, a tired old man who would be dead in a few months, was complicit not only in the lukewarm support he passed out with double messages but also in having sent Wallace on a fact finding mission to Siberia and China six weeks prior to the convention (Walton 1976, 16).

The serious opposition centered its support on two Southerners, a typically brilliant southern "heads we win, tails you lose" strategy. Their first choice was Senator James F. Byrnes of South Carolina, but he was as might be well imagined, opposed strongly by organized labor, the CIO, and the Negro faction of the party (MacDougall 1965, 16). Senator Truman of Missouri was adroitly proposed by Congressman Sam Rayburn of Texas (19), who would later be Speaker of the House of Representatives when the Texans finally took over. The awful compromises of politics boiled the choice down to Truman, as Philip Drucker explains: "Truman was 'eligible rather than Wallace, Brynes or Douglas precisely because he was unknown. . . in short because he had no one trait strong enough to offend anybody anywhere'" (Thomas 1968, 139).

In the inevitable political fallout from this decision, Byrnes was to become Truman's Secretary of State and Wallace would remain as Secretary of Commerce, a holdover from FDR, who had sacked Jesse (referred to by FDR as Jesus H.) Jones from Houston, Texas, from that position. Jones brought the bacon back to Texas during the war and depression in the form of the Houston ship canal. Five southern democratic senators would oppose Wallace as Commerce Secretary until he finally resigned in disputes over foreign policy: "Byrd of Virginia; McCarran of Nevada; McKellar and Stewart of Tennessee; and O'Daniel of Texas" (MacDougall 1965, 14).

Wallace objected to policies as they developed. "Approximately 80 per cent of Truman's proposed budget for fiscal 1947 was to pay for wars: past, present and future; no reduction would be possible without a cut in military appropriations" (71). "Our navy is determined to get Saudi Arabian Oil" (169). Wallace would be the Progressive party's candidate for president in 1948 having said: "I am not leaving the Democratic party. It left me. Wall Street and the military have taken over" (311). It is not an accident nor a great oversimplification for Wallace, a man supported by labor who returned the support, to notice that the primary capitalist and economic center of New York and Wall Street had in fact cut the deal with the southern controlled military to include him out. The northern Republicans and Democrats, who controlled the financial engine of the United States, had been chosen as allies by militarists from the South, the informal Calhoun party.

The magnitude of this mistake and reversionary decision can be seen in its timing. "The year 1945 was a crucial one in the history of this country and of the world" (29), even though the crucial decision was actually made in 1944. "And therefore Time either finds no place in this system at all, or is made its victim" (Spengler 1926, 125). Was time the victim or were Americans victimized by time? Time after all is only the medium of exchange human political activity takes place in, as the Rabbi John Oliver Simon of Berkeley once put it in *The Grass Prophet Review*, "Politics is men distorted by time" (1968, 3).

Truman quickly chose to distort time. "An example being California, where the favoritism shown conservative millionaire oilman Edwin W. Pauley" (MacDougall 1965, 24), who had had a hand with Rayburn in proposing him for vice president, was typical, as was "the appointment of FDR-hating former Sen. Bennett Clark of Missouri" (24). Jobs were made available for the "Missouri Gang," old buddies of Captain Truman from Battery D, 129th Field Artillery AEF (American Expeditionary Force) from World War I. Lest we think the militarization of the American government was a fantasy of Wallace partisans, the following is quoted from the *Army and Navy Bulletin*, January 18, 1947: "'Today the army has virtual control of foreign affairs, commencing on the home front with General Marshall'" (26). Their own opinion of their power is not an isolated one. David Lawrence of the then *United States News*, March 21, 1947: "'Never before have the army and navy been so powerfully placed in governmental controls. And never before has the United States adopted so stern a foreign policy'" (27).

The stern foreign policy was matched by a stern domestic policy. "However, when the coal miners struck on May 21, 1946, the President seized the coal mines, and four days later he appeared before a joint session of Congress to make perhaps the most violently anti-labor speech that any President of the United States ever made. . . . Labor leaders were aghast and used. . . the appellation 'slave labor bill,' to characterize Truman's proposals" (42), shades of the Great Strike of 1877. The Prussianizing went too far for the United Auto Workers Executive Board and was, "the climax of a series of surrenders by the Truman administration to the demands of reactionary industrialists to make peacetime strikes illegal and impose a fascist system of involuntary servitude upon American workers, including millions of veterans of the nation's victories against fascism" (43). Even though the UAW would attempt to strengthen its position by imputing its negative effect on veterans, the source of the policy decisions, foreign and domestic, was clear to Senator Claude Pepper of Florida who held little hope for near term improvement when he groused "'With conservative Democrats and reactionary Republicans making our foreign policy as they are today'" (97).

Henry Wallace was less charitable in his assessment. "We now have a clearly defined policy for the Near East, but it is a policy for war, not peace. We have accepted the bankrupt and bankrupting British policies in Greece and Turkey. . . It is Hoover's thinking that guides our foreign policy" (199). While Arthur Schlesinger maintains that "Still one can divide the classical theories of imperialism into four broad categories: apologias; economic interpretations; sociological interpretations; and geopolitical interpretations" (1986, 119), a case could be made that American imperialism post World War II has at least one foot in every category and is in fact the summation of all four, namely theological. It is done because it is believed. "The great instrument of imperialism, Schumpeter added, was the institutionalization of the warrior mentality in the 'war machine,' the professional military caste. . . Created by wars that required it, the machine now created the wars it required" (126). While Schlesinger adds the warrior mentality of the professional military caste into the equation with one hand, he seems to withdraw it with another, when he states that "The revisionist tactic of substituting biography for evidence is not persuasive" (201). It is not the biographies per se of Truman from Missouri in the old slaveholding South, nor of the military reactionaries like James Byrnes of South Carolina that he surrounded himself with that is in question. The fatal flaw in Schlesinger is his inability to recognize that no amount of facts, however complete and judiciously organized, can be given the power of persuasion to alter the religious belief in the superiority of the military solution. Beliefs are held; people are not persuaded out of them with facts.

Schlesinger attempts to debunk the open door or economic interpretation of American imperialism. His evidence seems to include: "Why, for example, should Roosevelt and Truman, both engaged in bitter struggles with the business community at home and both persuaded of the folly and greed of business leaders, have allowed those same business leaders to dictate their policies abroad?" (201). While it is true that business leaders, in their effort to reduce expenses and enhance profits, will try to avoid contributing to the tax stream that bankrolls the military, and that their only wish for the government is for it to get off its back in Reaganese, it is for the ultimate benefit of the military that business thrives. When the military-business coalition's policies dovetail so nicely as they did after World War II, it is good politics to pretend somebody else is leading. Schlesinger is aware that "the military are not the agents of the capitalists" (154) but he doesn't face the facts that the force in the equation is going the other way: capitalism is the agent of the military.

While Schlesinger asserts that Truman did not reverse FDR's policy and that the bomb was not dropped to intimidate Stalin (189), he refers to no evidence. "Elliot Roosevelt quotes his father: 'I think I speak as America's President when I say that America won't help England in this war simply so that she will be able to continue to run roughshod over colonial peoples'" (MacDougall 1965, 34). Is it likely that Roosevelt himself was planning to run roughshod over colonial peoples? Robert R. Young, the chairman of the board of the Chesapeake & Ohio Railroad said: "We are kidding ourselves if we believe the atomic bomb was dropped on Japan. . . No, the atom bomb was dropped not militarily but diplomatically upon Russia" (25). It is not likely the evidence would be found in a memo to Stalin. Early in *The Making of the Atomic Bomb*, Richard Rhodes points out that Roosevelt assembled a committee of advisors of which "Every man owed his authority to the President" (Rhodes 1986, 378). This committee of atomic advisors included Vice President Wallace, Secretary of War Stimson, Army Chief of Staff George Marshall, Ambassador Bush and Conant. The commander in chief wanted to keep the atomic secrets close to his chest. It is significant that Stimson, Wallace and Kennan were the only three eventually silenced voices for a sphere of influence approach to foreign policy under Truman. The Universalist approach carried the day.

If the bomb was not dropped to intimidate Russia, are we to believe that it was necessary to bring a speedy halt to the war with Japan? Norman Cousins, in *The Pathology of Power*, doesn't agree, "As Eisenhower's memoirs emphasized, that neither the bomb nor an invasion was necessary to defeat Japan" (1987, 33). The supreme allied commander in Europe's opinion was ignored, as was the advice of other military men. "There is little question that Japan could, in due course, have been brought to her knees without the use of the new weapon. . . But to say this is by no means to say that the decision taken in August 1945 was not an intelligible, and a defensible, position" (Perkins 1966, 106). The defense of this position, articulated by Churchill, reveals it to be supra-military or religious. "'The historic fact remains that the decision whether or not to use the atomic bomb to compel the surrender of Japan was never even an issue. There was unanimous, automatic and unquestioned agreement around our table; nor did I ever hear the slightest suggestion that we should do otherwise'" (107). The unanimous, automatic and euphoric use of the bomb accelerated the end of the war and "The euphoria of the Second World War began the imperial process" (Schlesinger 1986, 160). Let us look through the euphoria into the Truman policies.

Was the Cold War necessary or was it simply the war that the militarists required? The endemic religious background of the United States stimulates the Universalist tendency in American politicians to the degree that Woodrow Wilson had said "We have come to redeem the world" (54), whether the world was prepared for redemption on American terms or not. "There was in 1940 a very real monster to destroy and after 1945 another very real monster to contain" (54). This assessment leaves aside an important argument to be taken up later, namely why ally with Stalin to destroy Hitler when the best position might have been to let the two "monsters" destroy themselves and sell arms to both sides.

While not losing sight of Stalin's personal problems, keep in mind that the Russian devastation in WWII included 20-25 million people killed, versus approximately one-quarter of a million American lives lost. Russia "Was never in those first postwar years a military threat to the West requiring a militaristic policy by the United States. So grievous were Russia's wartime wounds, so powerful was the United States, that such a threat simply did not exist" (Walton 1976, 39). The threat existed in the shape of war itself, for without a plausible enemy, what use is the military. "It should not have taken Harriman to convince Truman that the Russians would not fight. After the terrible beating they had taken from the Nazis — perhaps the most terrible in the history of war — they were in no position to fight" (46). While the Russians were in no position to fight, they permitted the Nazi destruction of what would have been their resistance to taking over Poland, necessary, in their hyper security conscious thinking, to prevent a reprise of the German slaughter. Peace and continued alliance with Russia as well as "Russian hope foundered on three events which the Kremlin could well have interpreted respectively as deliberate sabotage (the loan request), blackmail (lend-lease cancellation) and pro-Germanism (reparations)" (Schlesinger 1986, 186).

Whatever the Russian interpretation, the Truman and American interpretation was to begin hallucinating Communists everywhere. From being allied with the Russian Communists in Europe and with the Chinese Communists in the war against Japan, their status as public enemy number one, from the tail end of WWI was revived. There were no other suitable candidates. "Clearly the Truman administration wanted the Wallace movement to be colored Red, and indeed, it took surreptitious steps to achieve that end" (Walton 1976, 231). All efforts toward peace were vilified. "What did lead to disaster was the psychology, the psychosis even, that Truman and his administration brought to these matters" (42).

The anti-Communist psychosis caught on quickly, even as what would eventually be called the Truman Doctrine, was enforced in Hollywood, home of the image makers of the people of the picture. "And the great playwright Bertolt Brecht was driven from America in 1947 by the pre-McCarthyite political witchhunters much in the same manner he was forced to leave Nazi Germany the decade before" (DeMarco 1988, 143). It should not be surprising that the visual hallucination of Communists should center on the movies, the home of celluloid hallucinations, and in May of 1947, HUAC (the House Un-American Activities Committee) came to Hollywood to investigate subversive and Communist influences in the motion picture industry (157). While this may appear ludicrous in the 1990s, it was in deadly earnest. Speaking of the contemporary movie *True Lies* as a "first-rate tool of empire," Stuart Klawans also reported in *The Nation* that "Having long been both tool and symbol of the American Empire, moving images are now becoming its substance as well" (249). This has become possible partly because "The United States is by far the most visually organized country in the history of the world" (McLuhan 1968, 133). Regrettably, the manipulative possibilities inherent in these conditions have only begun to be exploited. In the HUAC infested late 1940s, "Glen Taylor was the principal speaker at a 'Free the Movies' rally in New York's Manhattan Center" (MacDougall 1965, 309). Senator Taylor was Wallace's Progressive party running mate.

The anti-Communist crusade dominated the United States for decades. Goldwater took it to its most feverish pitch and saw it not so much as a burden but as an elixir, "The great imperative of our existence" (Hofstadter 1965, 126). Goldwater would drag the Republicans so far to the right that even his chief rival, Nelson Rockefeller's statement for the Republican party platform's first item was: "1. The growing vigor and aggressiveness of communism demands new and profound effort and action in all areas of American Life" (White 1988, 388). The area of action they were thinking of in the mid-60s was Vietnam of course, where "Never has there been the slightest deviation from the principle that a noncommunist regime must be imposed regardless of popular sentiment" (Chomsky 1973, 28).

Anti-communism was a disaster in Hollywood and Vietnam, likely due to the truth in the artless remarks of General Patton. "Perhaps, the most perfect, because most naive, expression of this belief remains the late General Patton's remark that the Nazis were, after all, not so very different from Republicans or Democrats" (Thomas 1968, 141). Or perhaps this remark as reported by Philip Drucker is more proof of Clemenceau's observation that war is too important to be left to generals. They might, after all, screw up, and not be able to distinguish between the sides. One American general who knew where he was getting help from and who did not screw up was Vinegar Joe Stilwell in China. The Communists in China, Mao Zedong, Chou Enlai, and Chu Teh, provided the most effort in the allied war there against Japan (Tuchman 1971, 477-8).

Their reward for this service was to be drop kicked back into the middle of the 19th century, where their struggle for Chinese independence from foreign domination originated. "Was it not as early as 1844 that the American commissioner, Caleb Cushing, taking advantage of the British Opium War on China, negotiated with the Celestial Empire a successful commercial treaty? Did he not then exultantly exclaim: 'The laws of the Union follow its citizens and its banner protects them even within the domain of the Chinese Empire?'" (Beard and Beard 1925, 477). The American empire, following the British lead even that long ago, was too rigid to change in 1945 and the Chinese Communists were vilified also. "This was the first in a rising crescendo of attacks on loyal, intelligent Foreign Service officers who outraged American supporters of Chiang by their accurate, hard-hitting reports about the corrupt and incompetent Nationalist government. . . [they] were harassed out of service. . . by anti-Communist hysteria" (Walton 1976, 66). Militant anti-communism, practiced as a religion remember, has no place in its pantheon for facts.

The disregard of facts in the pursuit of ideological and religious goals is deliberate and indicates a strange element in Truman's decision making. "Of the stock of dead forms that he had in front of him, he really saw only the few that he wanted to see, and he saw them as he wanted them — namely, in line with his own intention and not with the intention of the original creator. . . the inner force of a Being is never so clearly evidenced as it is in this *art of deliberate misunderstanding*." (Spengler 1928, 58). The result of this art of deliberate misunderstanding is known as the Truman Doctrine, the cornerstone of American foreign policy in the middle of the 20th century until the self-inflicted collapse of communism in the Soviet Union 45 years later.

The Truman Doctrine was the cornerstone of American imperialism and the stepping stone was the faltering British Empire. "Since the end of the war Greece had been under British occupation. . . The British found the occupation a heavy burden. . . Would the United States step into the breach?" (Perkins 1966, 110). It is precisely at this point that the United States made the basket catch and became the rest of the British Empire. As has been made apparent throughout the text, the actual shift of power was a gradual one and only appeared to happen overnight. One result of the Revolutionary War was policy generation on the American side of the Atlantic. Since the end of the War of 1812, disputations with the British were ironed out through negotiation. The English speaking peoples found a way to make every political and economic disagreement mutually beneficial. The similarity in aims was reinforced after the end of WWI with a naval conference in Washington in 1921. This conference "gave the United States parity with Great Britain (which, for some mysterious reason, had become a point of sentimental importance with large elements of American opinion), and it fixed Japan in a position of permanent inferiority" (61). The adolescent lust and thrust of Theodore Roosevelt and the imperialists who had created the U.S. Navy was the basis for the sentiment for parity. The psychological reversion to barbarism is no longer mysterious.

Japan participated in this conference and "Demanded that the United States abdicate its physical power in the Orient. . . American opinion would not have understood the failure of the conference" (61). This was an early example of the United States finding it easy to extract what it needs from

Great Britain and being baffled by the ability of the Japanese to outnegotiate speakers of English.

Sir Winston Churchill came to Fulton, Missouri, after World War II and delivered the famous "Iron Curtain" speech. "Mr. Truman invited Mr. Churchill, then vacationing in Florida, to speak at Westminster College as a personal favor to Major General Harry Vaughn, an alumnus of this small school which almost nobody else had ever heard of" (MacDougall 1965, 30). The speech referred to the "'fraternal association of the English-speaking peoples'" which meant in practical terms "'joint use of all naval and air force bases in the possession of either country all over the world which would perhaps double the mobility of the American navy and air force'" (30). For another short while at least, not everybody was taken in by this invitation to participate in the empire. Congressmen Adolph J. Sabath of Illinois, speaking in the *Congressional Record* of March 13, 1946 said: "'It is gratifying to all honest-to-God Americans that American newspapers were not misled by the shrewd efforts of Britain's Winston Churchill in his Fulton speech to inveigle America into saving England's tottering empire, as we have saved her national existence twice already. . . Presumably he hopes to avoid that liquidation with our help'" (30). Churchill had said upon being selected Prime Minister that he hadn't been elected to oversee the liquidation of her majesty's empire.

The vote to keep Greece in the English speaking empire and save the right-wing colonels there was 287-107 in the House and 67-23 in the Senate. Since both houses had Republican majorities, the vote was a demonstration of the power of the conservative Republican and Bourbon Democrat coalition. The Universalist application of the Truman Doctrine led Henry Wallace to condemn it: "I say that Truman with his present advisors and his present willingness to cooperate with Wall Street and Republican reactionaries inevitably will continue to implement the Truman Doctrine of arming every reactionary government which is willing to fight Russia" (233). While the risks of such policy might have been apparent to politicians with more brains and experience, in the case of the United States "The military shield becomes a blank check. The patron ends up the prisoner of the client. What an empire!" (Schlesinger 1986, 161). The coalition that ratified the Truman Doctrine was to keep the forces of controversy at bay for 20 years. "The Fulbright hearings were a constitutional confrontation of the first order, long, long overdue. They ended more than a generation of assumed executive branch omniscience in foreign policy, and congressional acquiescence to that omniscience" (Halberstam 1979, 492). And even the Fulbright-Johnson confrontation was between two powerful southern politicians.

Truman delivered the speech setting up the vote on the Truman Doctrine on March 12, 1947. It was accompanied shortly thereafter by "Executive Order 9835, calling for the first loyalty investigation of Federal employees" (MacDougall 1965, 130). The suspicions didn't end there. "A climate had developed by 1948 in which criticism, dissent from official assumption, or even the discussion of alternative policies was not only deemed heretical but un-American and traitorous" (xi). We have seen before how the dissent from the military position is referred to as heresy. If you imagine you are under siege, democratic centralism is the only permitted response. "In recent years, however, a strange new notion has gained ground. It is the idea that the government has options with respect to truth. A possible beginning date for this departure is 1947 with an act setting up the Central Intelligence Agency" (Cousins, 1987, 206). While we will see much more of the CIA, "The damage the CIA has done to American democracy is most evident, I think, when we look to Congress. The Senate and House have been routinely deceived by the agency and by foreign governments assisted by the agency — this is the dark heart of Iran-Contra" (Hitchens 1991, 61). It is not accurate to refer to a government that believes it has options with respect to the truth as a democracy, for the truth is that "American political institutions are simply inadequate for the democratic control or direction of foreign policy" (MacDougall 1965, xii).

The United States passed through the prism and turned into the rest of the British Empire with the Truman Doctrine. Cultural history is a subtext of natural history where process is irreversible. Once passed through, a state cannot be re-established. It becomes history at the point of passage, subject to interpretation and immune to change. Since the process is irreversible, it makes little practical difference that "Henry Wallace was essentially right and Harry Truman was essentially and tragically wrong" (Walton 1976, 355). This news will have its greatest value for future democracies tempted toward empire.

Nevertheless, sense has to be made of the situation. "Half a century after the neo-federalists, two world wars had created a great military establishment, and the Cold War made it permanent. . . A hard precipitating factor. . . has been the emergence of a new class of professional warriors" (Schlesinger 1986, 153). Schlesinger accurately asserts that "A dangerous world demands military strength. It does not demand the militarization of the national life" (162), but that is precisely what happened. It was pressure from the South, with its military traditions, that demanded the militarization of national life. In addition to the creation of the CIA, the National Security Council in NSC-68, further strapped the military into the seat of power. "The armed services, anxious to retain roles and budgets acquired during the war, sought justification by uncovering a new enemy" (205).

The new enemy of Communists and communism was to be contained no matter what the cost. It is significant to notice that Schlesinger suggests and then corrects himself unconvincingly that "In time British persuasion — or rather the persuasion of events — prevailed, and the United States took command of the democratic camp in the Cold War" (215). The British persuasion and their perpetual concerns with the balance of power was the overriding factor that bought into and reinforced the American military intentions. "The irreducible factor accounting for American involvement in the Cold War was undoubtedly the venerable Jeffersonian concern about the balance of power" (202). And that was a venerable attempt to burnish the ridiculous American behavior into respectability by associating it with Jefferson. He is only one political fixture on the balance of power poles stretching back to the beginning of the English speaking drive for hegemony over the lion's share of the world's goods and services in the form of empire, but hardly the irreducible factor. The Jeffersonian "marriage" to the British Navy was a defensive impulse. His concerns pale in the face of those of Hamilton, Jackson, Calhoun, Jefferson Davis, Theodore Roosevelt, and Truman, for "After all those years, the South was reintegrated as part of the empire" (Williams 1980, 184).

The early economic phase of the Cold War was the Marshall Plan which lasted from 1948 to 1952. This rebuilding of the European allies sans Russia to provide a bulwark against the Communists had the intended effect of keeping the American economy stimulated in the absence of overt war. Curiously enough, it demonstrates a major principle of total war, that good enemies are indispensable and more essential than good allies, as Japan, Germany, and Italy were rehabilitated and China and Russia boxed out as Communist enemies. It also demonstrates the mutually reinforcing interior lines of control between the military and the benefits of Wall Street capitalism. "That the role of the military inevitably has been much enhanced, that military considerations play a central role in our budget, accounting for 50 per cent of federal expenditures, and that the balance between civil and military power is not what it once was. So far we have avoided the danger of military control of policy, in the sweeping sense. . ." (Perkins 1966, 148). Not really. The only sweeping sense in which the danger of military control of policy was avoided was in the superficial application of the appearance of democracy to the bipartisan coalition making foreign policy. Far too much of the sweeping has taken place under the rug.

The previous moment in American history when the balance between military and civil power had been so tightly meshed together was under the leadership of Jefferson Davis in the Confederate States of America. The civil and military aspects of the Confederate government were literally fused together, as they have been in the United States since the adoption of the Truman Doctrine. Control of this policy by the coalition was predicted by John C. Calhoun. "Far in advance of the event, he forecast an alliance between Northern conservatives and Southern reactionaries, which has become one of the most formidable aspects of American politics" (Hofstadter 1959, 88). It is not merely one of the most formidable aspects, it is the controlling aspect. Richard N. Current, publishing an essay entitled "John C. Calhoun, Philosopher of Reaction" in 1943 said: "Now, if ever, is the time for right-wing Republicans to join with Bourbon Democrats in the sort of reactionary alliance that Calhoun envisaged. . . the real objects of their attack will be the social controls which liberals will seek to maintain in the interests of world peace. . ." (Thomas 1968, 163).

This reactionary alliance and its domination of the Confederate Empire of North America since the late 1940s is the fifth big link in the Confederate comeback victory chain. The first appearance of this alliance in the Fraud of 1876 returned the power of state rights and white supremacy to the unreconstructed South. The restless energy of the Texans, soon to acquire complete control of the government, spread southern norms and culture throughout the rest of the interior West, with the self-serving help of a "British financial invasion" (Rifkin 1992, 89-90). Theodore Roosevelt and the imperialists captured large sections of the Caribbean for the empire. With the direct assistance of archreactionaries like General Otis and the Chandler family of the LA *Times*, southern California was nurtured from a small enclave of Confederate sympathizers into a racist, red-baiting, open-shop southern state practicing plantation agriculture, with a military economy fueled by federal spending.

Virtually everything the Confederates were fighting for, short of outright slavery, has come to pass including a perpetual war, which keeps them reminded that they are always on the defense in a continuous state of siege, as they were during the Civil War. The very War Department's name was changed in the late 1940s to the Department of Defense, both to clean up its image and to reinforce the endless nature of its arrangements. The perpetual state of war as a consequence of becoming the rest of the British Empire nudges back into place one of the Colonial South Carolina desires from the pre-Revolutionary War days: "The goal, clearly, was acceptable terms of reconciliation with Britain, not independence" (Weir 1983, 377). South Carolina is not independent of either Britain or the North, but it is the permanent American home of the emotional leadership of the Confederate Empire of North America.

If the South got nearly everything it wanted as a result of the Civil War, subterfuge and historical forces that led up to and were unleashed by the war, the North's share of the victory seems ultimately counterproductive. Lincoln kept the Union together for eventual southern domination. The do-gooder aspects of the early Republicans who were going to free the slaves in the South has its modern counterpart in the do-gooder aspects of the southern dominated United States, which went on record as attempting to free everybody from the dangers of communism. The North's initial military victory implies that no political entity will ever get out of the Union peacefully. Since the Union has now been globalized under Southern control, neither states nor nations that might feel they are being kept in the Union by force will be allowed to leave the empire peacefully.

Just as the South is the balance of power in the United States and hence dominates it, the United States as the rest of the British Empire is the balance of power in the world and dominates it. Neither of these minority advantages will endure forever. The English balance of power model has overridden the experiment in democracy launched in 1776. Southerners felt power slip through their fingers in 1860 and it took them an uneven 85 years to get it back. From the late 1940s on however, the story of American history is largely the story of Southern consolidation of power and the consequences of having turned into the Confederate Empire of North America.

Part IV

Confederate Empire on the Modern Stage

"Texas, the South, the United States, in that order"

Jack Seward

16

The Fabulous Fifties: Made in Texas

Comprehending American history after 1947 is made much simpler if the realization is kept in mind that it is no longer the history of a country; it is the history of an empire, largely designed in Texas. "The spectacle of the United States rushing out into the world-arena, to confront Russia and China there, was stranger still" (Toynbee 1966, 41). Toynbee felt like this was a reversal of the isolation that had come to be associated with the United States but in fact it was one result of the Allies delivering a "knockout blow," in his terms, to the rival Fascists, which left the United States to set up a universal state. "The creation of a universal state checks the headlong decline of a disintegrating civilization" (Toynbee 1972, 256), and "Universal states are, let us remind ourselves, essentially negative institutions" (267).

The difficulties of operating an empire democratically were sufficiently insurmountable that the executive choice was made to keep the empire together at the expense of many of the country's previously democratic elements. "Acting *ad hoc* in the absence of any clearly enunciated policy vis-à-vis Asiatic Communism, consulting neither Congress nor the people but using the enormous accrued powers of the presidency as though he were any absolute monarch, he [Truman] had put America into what was, in point of casualties, her third largest war" (Leckie 1968, II:335). This attribution of absolute monarchy did not emanate from some peacenik or "military fairy" in Sir Norman Schwarzkopf's memorable phrase, but from a military historian and former Marine. Neither is Leckie's an isolated opinion. "Harry Truman committed American forces to the war [Korean] on his own authority. . . Congress surrendered the war-making power to the executive and has never reclaimed it since" (Schlesinger 1986, 280). These citations do not describe the behavior of a democratic country. They describes the behavior of an ideological and autocratic empire and "What happens to democracy when decisions made by a leader leave the citizenry with no effective choice?" (Williams 1961, 463).

Schlesinger believes that "The perennial threat to the constitutional balance. . . comes in the field of foreign policy" (277), exactly that part of the policy field that an empire demands. This was indeed a perennial threat to the constitutional balance and division of power in the American democracy as originally constituted. We'd seen the congressional power usurped before by Theodore Roosevelt, who objected to the point of distraction that anyone should think he or America was imperialistic. "Mr. Truman would say, 'We are not at war,' and to speak of the 'war' in any executive department was to incur the presidential wrath. Always it was the Korean 'Conflict,' a euphemism probably coined to fob off the fiction that the United States was directing a 'police action' at the behest of the United Nations. The reverse, of course, was true. . ." (Leckie 1968, II:335). War and imperialism frequently require euphemisms for their successful conduct and to disguise their real intentions. Leckie's clarity leaves him, however, as he goes on to attribute the hidden cause of Mr. Truman's War to mistakes Roosevelt permitted to occur at Yalta and concludes by describing Truman's decision as among the "noblest and most efficacious in the annals of American arms" (II:335).

The actual source of the error was Truman's incapacity to listen effectively, part of his art of "deliberate misunderstanding," to the experts on China in favor of the jingoism of the China lobby. If Mao Zedong would have had anybody but Stalin to turn to for help, there would have been no need or framework for close cooperation between the Russians and the Chinese in the Korean or Vietnam Wars. Truman's floundering the United States into an empire with the Universalist agenda of containing communism was the most influential series of unnecessary events in the 20th century. "Manifest Destiny, in the twentieth century, vanished," according to Frederick Merk, and "Not only did it die; it stayed dead through two world wars" (1963, 265). Truman, and the southern drivers in his militarized government, undoubtedly felt like Manifest Destiny had been dead long enough. When they rushed at the invitation of the defunct British Empire to fill the breach for the right-wing colonels in Greece, Harlow Shapely, the Harvard Astronomer said: "'If you mean oil, why say Greece?'" (MacDougall 1965, 129). "And the wielders of this power, if they are to remain in the saddle, must use every effort to make sure that these sources of supply are always available on the most favorable terms" (Magdoff 1969, 195).

It will be recalled that Truman emerged from obscurity to the vice presidency at the suggestion of Sam Rayburn, the Speaker of the House of

Representatives from Houston, Texas, and the son of a Confederate cavalryman. Theodore White referred to Rayburn as the "sachem of the American Congress" (1988, 43). This term of Algonquian origination, meaning supreme chief, in reference to leaders of the Iroquois Confederation is not misapplied. For two decades, "Sam Rayburn held power in Washington. Presidents came and went — Roosevelt, Truman, Eisenhower, Kennedy — but whoever was President, Sam Rayburn was Speaker; he held the post he had dreamed of as a boy for almost seventeen of the twenty-one years after 1940, more than any other man in American history. Over his branch of government his power was immense, so great that it spilled over into the government as a whole" (Caro 1982, 759). Rayburn had much power to spill, not only over the branch of government where he held official position, but over the Democratic party and Texas leadership of the South. The sputtering presidency of Harry Truman, as Texas and the South dragged him to the right, especially the fact that he was in office at all, is attributable to the power of Sam Rayburn.

This is one of the things T. R. Fehrenbach had in mind when he said, referring all the way back to the Confederate Texans that "They could not get Texas out of the Union, but they could and did get a lot out of the Union for it" (1968, 439). It will be remembered that the tradition of Texans milking the national cow began with their most favorable annexation. "Texans, in office and out, had a long habit of accepting any Yankee dollar they could get. . . One study showed that this, over a period of thirty years beginning in the 1930s, topped the national average by 27 percent" (652). These are the opinions and conclusions, not of an adversary, but of a Texas patriot. "If there was a single trend in the entire period following World War II, it was that Texas, despite drought and oil gluts, grew increasingly more prosperous" (659).

Even in the empire beginning to be dominated by Texas, domestically at least, there was still the matter of the 1948 election. Harry Truman, as many masters of the straddle eventually discover, wasn't particularly popular with anybody. "While other labor leaders were still toying with the idea of trying to force Eisenhower on the Democrats. . ." (MacDougall 1965, 179), "'It is interesting to note,' Wallace said, 'that the Eisenhower boom is coming from the South'" (474). Governor Strom Thurmond of South Carolina did all he could to get Eisenhower to carry the Democratic banner. Sam Rayburn excoriated Henry Wallace on the Marshall Plan (475), to keep the Democratic party from even looking toward the left. And Elliot Roosevelt, FDR's son, said: "The Democrats have the opportunity. Eisenhower should be their candidate" (180). Henry Wallace himself was of the opinion that "Gen. Dwight D. Eisenhower could be elected President on either major party ticket" (239).

Henry Wallace resigned as Secretary of Commerce and formed what became known as the Progressive party. He had found himself increasingly *persona non grata* in the Democratic party and was vilified by Congressman Richard Nixon of California as a "Fellow Traveler," a red-baiting style that would become second nature to Nixon. Wallace had denounced the Mundt-Nixon House bill on subversive activity (368). Wallace's Progressive party running mate, Senator Glen Taylor of Idaho said: "'All this red scare is designed solely for the purpose of preventing criticism of this bipartisan foreign policy, the real purpose of which is to keep generals employed and pass out juicy plums for a continuing armament program to the vested interests of America" (342). There is more truth than poetry in those observations. Senator Taylor had led the fight against the Selective Service Act. *"The story of the Progressive party of 1948 is one of an unsuccessful attempt to impress the electorate with the prime importance of foreign affairs as they related to world peace"* (330). MacDougall chose to emphasize his conclusion with italics.

Wallace received a Texas reception in Austin. University students had a sound truck playing *The Internationale* as they displayed the Hammer and Sickle. Catholic War Veterans and others tried to prevent him from speaking at all. "His greatest thrill on the present trip was the temporary breakdown of racial segregation that occurred during his visit to Austin, Texas " (161). Wallace and Taylor would attempt to hold integrated rallies throughout the South. Senator Taylor was jailed in Birmingham by police commissioner Bull Conner, who was exercising the state right to tell people which door of a church they could enter.

The Republican Dewey imagined that he had the election in the bag. The Democrats, where Senator Olin D. Johnston of South Carolina had "revealed his intention of personally nominating Eisenhower" (473), were in deep disarray, chiefly because Eisenhower demurred. Unwilling to stick with Truman, their political Frankenstein, the Dixiecrats, led by Governor Strom Thurmond of South Carolina, took one of their famous walks. Governor Dan Moody of Texas was another leader of this southern secession from the Democratic party, but "The most vociferous Dixiecrat, in attempting to obtain the floor and announce the defection of 13 out of Alabama's 26 delegates, was Eugene "Bull" Conner, Birmingham's Police Commissioner" (477).

More than two serious candidates for president in the United States is an indicator of an interesting election, such as 1860, 1912, 1948, and 1992. It is also the indicator of failed leadership. The Dixiecrat strategy was to collect enough votes to throw the election into the House of Representatives, where, surprise, Sam Rayburn could once again engineer a president, and the appeal to Eisenhower would be revived. Thurmond of South Carolina carried four states, Alabama, Louisiana, Mississippi, and South Carolina, but not enough to throw the election to the House. Wallace got nearly as many popular votes as Thurmond, but they were spread all over the country except for a token handful in the still segregated South. Truman, as everyone knows, muddled to victory. A switch of less than 30,000 votes in Illinois, California and Ohio, would have given the presidency to Dewey. A switch of 12,500 votes in California and Ohio would have put the election into the House of Representatives, where Truman would have led, but Thurmond's 39 votes would have been the balance of power from the hard line Neo-Confederate South.

Minority victories bring minority rule. Truman started the Korean War as a fallback position to errors previously committed. Never far enough to the right for the militarists, his firing of MacArthur led Republicans to demand his impeachment. MacArthur himself, as befits a military empire, "was given the equivalent of a Roman triumph from coast to coast" (Leckie 1968, II:384). Nothing about the Korean War had anything to do with American "national" interests or security. It was the security of the empire that was at stake. Questions of empire boil down to power. "Power remains the decisive motive — balances of power, disparities of power, vacuums of power, illusions of power" (Schlesinger 1986, 127). American colonial wars, of which Korea was one, are exercises in search of psychological security through the use of political power. This unflattering portrait of the American military empire culture is replete with their unnecessary insecurity.

The goal of industrial and financier controlled policy, according to Walter LaFeber, was to result in "'the creation of an informal American empire in which the United States, after a brief colonial fling, used its economic might to secure hegemony without the embarrassment of traditional colonialism'"

(Schlesinger 1986, 130). This so-called neo-colonialism, much as Strabo recommended it to the Caesars, went on simultaneously with the more traditional colonial and military embarrassments such as Korea. The economic results of this use of power were similar to those in the British Empire 200 years ago. "What the Industrial Revolution in Britain did (in very crude macroeconomic terms) was to so increase productivity on a sustained basis that the consequent expansion both in national wealth and in the population's purchasing power constantly outweighed the rise in numbers" (Kennedy 1987, 146). Neo-colonialism, especially the extraction of oil, was the basis for the famous American standard of living. "In the underdeveloped regions almost three times as much money was taken out as was put in" (Magdoff 1969, 198). And Calhoun, whose ideas we have seen at the fulcrum of power in the tax consuming paradise of Texas, said: "Nor could it prevent the plunderers from using the enormous wealth, which they extorted from the impoverished and ruined provinces, to corrupt and debase the people" (Calhoun 1931, 97). Calhoun was describing the effects on the Roman Empire, but it could just as easily fit the car and gassing of America's suburbs. The debtor model forced upon the world economy by the belligerent Americans after WWII condemned the American people to consumerism. The solution to the problem of who would pay for all this empire, extracted from the increasing level of activity and demonstrated as war, was "to convert the short-term liability into a long-term funded debt" (Brewer 1989, 116). Thus the rich are enabled to go on getting richer.

The Pentagon generated history of war in the recent United States, to minimize their own subversion and aggression, frequently casts "the United States as a victim merely responding to situations created by others" (Chomsky 1973, 103). While "It might be argued that a healthy democracy would impede imperial planners. . ." (58), they proceeded with their articles of faith by clothing them in secrecy. General Eisenhower, the darling of the Dixiecrats in the Democratic party, took out the Taft and Warren wings of the Republican party, and became the first president of the United States born in Texas. He was raised in Abilene, northern terminus of the Chisholm Trail. This new heft on the haunting question from Texas historian Walter Prescott Webb regarding the relative significance of Abilene and Appomattox weighs in clearly. Eisenhower was the picture perfect superintendent of the Truman Doctrine which had globalized the Monroe Doctrine and reintegrated the South into the empire. With another southern general leading the United States from the White House, the Civil War was over and the South had finally won.

Eisenhower brought the Korean War to a halt. And "Instead of sending regular forces into combat abroad, Eisenhower silently turned the CIA into the secret army of the executive branch. . . in August 1953, the CIA over-threw Mossadegh and restored the Shah [of Iran]" (Schlesinger 1986, 395). The CIA and its companion, the National Security Council, had been created from the perceived necessity to operate an empire. While "The earliest forms of organized government depended for their foundation upon the discovery of writing" (Brewer 1989, 221), the rise of the British Empire saw a corresponding increase in the growth of spying. The British had trade in mind, the Americans trade plus anti-Communist ideology.

It is easy to agree with Schlesinger that "Eisenhower released a danger-ous virus in American society and life" (398), when we consider that among the governments either overthrown or corrupted by his CIA included Egypt, Laos, Cuba, Zaire, and Indonesia. Closer to home and back in the southern dream of the Caribbean empire, "In the private-interest 1950s, the Eisenhower CIA threw out a radical government in Guatemala at the behest of the United Fruit Company" (147). Just as in the early British Empire, "Some of the richer traders [qua lobbies]. . . were cozily intimate with the departments of state, others were kept out in the cold" (Brewer 1989, 248). The selective hand of government rewards its supporters. Even during WWI "The indefatigable Hale (closely associated with the Carnegie interests) was also the chief catalyst in organizing the National Research Council in 1917 to support Woodrow Wilson's war mobilization. The NRC was the scientific-military-industrial complex in embryo" (Davis 1990, 55).

Secrecy and silence seemed to go hand in hand in the Texas 1950s, where Eisenhower was president, Rayburn was the Speaker of the House, and Lyndon Johnson was the majority leader in the Senate. Virtually noth-ing of political consequence occurred that wasn't first agreed to by these three Texans. The domestic passivity of Eisenhower who did not speak out on McCarthyism or the Brown V. Board of Education decision desegregat-ing the schools (Schlesinger 1986, 390), both of which would have offended the South, would become a Republican and imperial tradition. "He had not particularly liked the Supreme Court decision and he seemed in no rush to force Southerners to comply with a law he disliked" (Halberstam 1979, 310). "From June 1955 to June 1960, Eisenhower officials refused information to congress forty-four times — more times in five years than in the first hundred years of the republic" (391). So much for the former democratic Congressional power of oversight and the spread of the belief that government has options with the truth. Henry Wallace had "accused the HUAC of using the 'technique of political gangsterism and tyranny' in its attempt to gain passage of the Mundt-Nixon bill, 'as the first step toward a reactionary police state.' This seems, at first glance, like rather extreme language, but the committee was guilty of extreme practices and the FBI and the CIA were guilty over a period of years of police-state methods — *agents provocateurs*, anonymous letters, attempts to disgrace those whose politics offended them, manipulation of evidence, intimidation, and so on" (Walton 1976, 242). Christopher Hitchens, in a contemporary evaluation of the CIA on the domestic front, suggests "I am going to leave aside the overseas memorials — the graveyards filled by the noisy Americans in and around Saigon; the torture chambers constructed and used in Iran by SAVAK; the jail cell that held Nelson Mandela, whose arrest the CIA played a part in; the statues of dictators propped up by the agency — that mark the CIA's collusion with the most degraded elements in Third World Politics" (1991, 60).

Third World memorials to Eisenhower's CIA include fascist dictators left and right, General Chaing Kai Shek on Formosa and General Franco in Spain, as well as Marshall Tito in southern (Yugo) Slavia. Sam Houston's latter-day Texans had taken power and in the act of applying his universal principle of Texas power all across the West and back through the states of the original southern Confederacy, they annexed New York as well, which was the politically prescient power base Eisenhower ran from. Just as it would later prove to be politically convenient for George Bush to style himself a Texan, in 1952 it was politically sage for Eisenhower to run as a New Yorker. Texas annexes New York. And having annexed New York, the city world trade funneled through in the 1950s and 60s, they continued to make communism the universal scapegoat for their own imperial designs.

The Texas appetite for empire was not satiated by the acquisition of major parts of the Caribbean empire that had long been a southern dream, nor of the destabilized remnants of the Spanish and British Empires, including everywhere English was spoken, nor by their NATO alliance in non-Communist Europe, nor by their continued economic occupation of Japan. The Texans developed a yen for the rest of the French empire in

Indo-China as well. They braced themselves to watch the French lose at Dien Bein Phu and then "More significantly, before the ink was dry on the Geneva Agreements of 1954, the National Security Council set forth an explicit program to undermine the agreements and undertake the use of force in violation of law" (Chomsky 1973, 22). Clearly, Eisenhower and the Texans were disposed to follow the laws of the United States, much less those of international bodies, only when they personally approved of them. The NSC directive 5429/2 of August 20, 1954, "is a clear and explicit violation of the law" (101). These inseminating moves to deny the Geneva mandated plebiscite to the Vietnamese people for fear Ho Chi Minh would have won the election and defeated the Catholic collaborators would lead to the pregnancy of continuous American involvement in the internal affairs of Vietnam until the disastrous abortion of the evacuation of Saigon in 1975.

The feigned passivity of Eisenhower, which seemed ingenious at the time, actually permitted him, while promoting the United States as the victim of Communist aggression, to promote himself as the victim of military and scientific forces. He could say "Yet, in holding scientific research and discovery in respect, as we should, we must also be alert to the equal and opposite danger that public policy could itself become the captive of a scientific-technological elite" (Cousins 1987, 73). While he may have been fingering a real danger in this excerpt from his farewell address, what had he done about it when power was his to burn. "A related concern to him was the growing institutionalization of militarism in America" (107). An odd concern, considering that the former general used the Army staffing model for his own executive operations. "Yet the atomic plants continued to spew them out almost as though the act of manufacture was a manifestation of our manhood" (102). Eisenhower was right to be concerned about the production of nuclear weapons.

This president, who was concerned about the force reductions under Truman, would elevate to priesthood, John Foster Dulles, who would lead the rhetorical holy war against godless communism as his Secretary of State, while still manifesting concerns about the growing militarization of the United States. "Yet he weakly allowed the build-up to proceed" (Schlesinger 1986, 403), from 70 targets to thousands. The "weakly" is what doesn't fit here, as the Atomic Energy Commission had recently relinquished control of the atomic weapons to the Department of Defense. Although Eisenhower could say in apparent exasperation "Why don't we go completely crazy and plan on a force of 10,000" (404), he probably thought he was kidding. In fact, "There were approximately 1,000 nuclear warheads when Eisenhower entered the White house, 18,000 when he left" (404).

None of this could have gone on without his approval, so the feigned reluctance for public consumption feels like part of the masterful dissembling of a leader getting what he wants, whether consciously or unconsciously, while permitting the illusion of being manipulated by forces outside his control. "We still like Ike" was what was said for his re-election campaign in 1956. And it is probably what would be said about him still, so effective was he at keeping the bad news offshore with the secret army of the CIA. Eisenhower is exactly the fulcrum between the present and the Civil War. As a youth in Kansas, Eisenhower did not read about the Civil War as he did other wars because it was still news. Veterans of both sides lived in Abilene and in the 1890s the Civil War was not yet history, much as Vietnam is still news for the men on both sides of the struggle in the 1990s. But by 1915 after graduating from West Point, Eisenhower could rhapsodize on military valor from Cemetery Ridge at Gettysburg where he would one day retire to his farm to fade away (Eisenhower 1967, 44). From that vantage point, Eisenhower could hallucinate the entire Battle of Gettysburg and preside over the Pentagon in Arlington in Lee's beloved Virginia, next door to Arlington National Cemetery, a fitting monument to the futility of military education.

Eisenhower towed the junior Senator from southern California, Richard Nixon, into the vice presidency. Nixon, a seasoned red-baiter, had defeated Helen Gahagan Douglas for a seat in the Senate. Douglas had co-sponsored the Douglas-Mahon Bill that created the AEC (Atomic Energy Commission), which for a while at least had civilians controlling atomic weapons. The pink pamphlet of the Nixon campaign accused her of voting "the Communist line." "Nixon was hand-picked by Kyle Palmer, the political correspondent and the real political boss of the Los Angeles *Times*" (Davis 1990, 160). We are familiar with the role of the LA *Times* in the effective southernization of California. It was right here where "The old guard, led by Kyle Palmer and Norman Chandler [the editor], engineered the rise of Richard Nixon from Congress to vice-presidency" (123). When Nixon ultimately resigned in 1974, there were "only a tiny handful of Deep

South senators and congressmen supporting him" (Halberstam 1979, 702), reluctant to give up one of their own.

But in 1960 Nixon was the Republican candidate for president opposed by John Kennedy for the Democrats. "It was hard to find space between the candidates on the issues. Schlesinger finally had to publish a pamphlet titled 'Kennedy or Nixon — Does It Make Any Difference?'" (Collier and Horowitz 1984, 247). Even though Kennedy from Massachusetts had won the nomination, the power of Texas and the South was very much apparent in the person of Lyndon B. Johnson as the vice presidential candidate. Since Hoover in 1928, no one had been elected who hadn't carried Texas, not so much because of its electoral clout, which is significant but hardly overwhelming, as because of its radiating cultural influence which means if you are winning in Texas, you are winning in two-thirds of the country. Kennedy's speech in Houston on the subject of his Catholicism and the separation of church and state is indicative. "'We can win or lose the election right there in Houston on Monday Night,' said Sorenson to a friend during the Los Angeles weekend" (White 1988, 260). The speech was a success and "The next day he barnstormed to growing crowds under the patronage of Lyndon B. Johnson and Sam Rayburn." (262).

And so Kennedy won by the whisker of less than one vote per precinct and ultimately it didn't make much difference. The people are fed a steady diet of confusion between the state and the establishment, and nowhere is it more misleading than in the notion that we can change things by electing different people. "But we are in reality changing the wrong people. . ." (Williams 1980, 11). "There would never be any debate over the Kennedy decision to expand the minimal Eisenhower commitment there [Vietnam]. It was a presidential time, it was the height of the Cold War, there were Communists over there, and so he just did it" (Halberstam 1979, 449). The Eisenhower commitment, though minimal in terms of manpower and advisors, was rockhard in intention to neither surrender or retreat, as per Buck Travis at the Alamo. Kennedy was boxed in with Southerners. In the quest for a Secretary of State, Henry Luce, the most influential media man in America had his innings. "Fulbright was unacceptable; later he [Luce] took credit for the selection of Dean Rusk" (352), from Georgia. Does it surprise anybody that the choice narrowed down to two Southerners, or that General Maxwell Taylor was all over Kennedy's policy. "Again Taylor was in charge" (Collier and Horowitz 1984, 291).

Kennedy inherited the Eisenhower position in Vietnam and worsened it. He inherited the NSC and CIA plans to invade Cuba and modified them only to the extent that it failed. "His first appointments, to the dismay of O'Donnell and other aides, were to reconfirm J. Edgar Hoover as FBI director and Allen Dulles [brother of the late high priest of anti-communism] at the CIA" (253), thus insuring the continuity of the secret army, the government and the police state. "Like every Democratic President since Roosevelt after 1938, he [JFK] inherited a House controlled by a conservative coalition made up of Republicans and Southern Democrats" (Schlesinger 1986, 409). Here is the Calhoun concurrent majority in full swing. After the failure at the Bay of Pigs, the South "was a land apart in its hatred for the administration" (Collier and Horowitz 1984, 301). The southern obsession with Cuba is a basic Confederate reflex.

Kennedy was an almost indistinguishable part of the institutional presidency of anti-communism inaugurated with Truman in 1948. His bias toward imperialism is reflected in his activism toward foreign affairs and the fact that he was trying to "practice a containment policy on black aspiration" (301) to the extent that he acquiesced to J. Edgar Hoover and the FBI's wire-tapping of Martin Luther King. Both the institutional nature of the presidency and Kennedy's bias toward the empire were not disguised. "In a brief post-mortem of the Bay of Pigs with Nixon (one of many meetings with Republican leaders he astutely arranged to emphasize the bipartisan responsibility for the defeat) he said, 'It really is true that foreign affairs is the only important issue for a President to handle, isn't it? I mean who gives a shit if the minimum wage is $1.15 or $1.35 in comparison to something like this?'" (274). Later presidents of the empire such as Ronald Reagan would appear to care a great deal, in the accelerating reversion to subsistence, especially that the wage be at the smallest possible end of the range.

But for a rich man like Kennedy, whose family's fortune was acquired through the insider trading of alcohol, and his advisors, the minimum wage was small potatoes indeed since they were to be asked to unravel 15 years of poorly executed policy in the Cuban missile crisis. "Since Pearl Harbor, however, Americans have lived under a conviction of international crisis, sustained, chronic and often intense" (Schlesinger 1986, 279). This crisis of intense and perpetual defense was the identifying signature of the Confederate States of America. Kennedy and his advisors would come to believe,

keeping everybody conscious of the basic Civil War metaphors at the heart
of the American darkness, that the Cuban missile crisis was the Gettysburg
of the Cold War. It undoubtedly depends which side someone is on to
deduce exactly what that might mean. Kennedy's assessment of the victory
"had three distinctive features: we enjoyed local superiority; Soviet national
security was not directly threatened; and the Russians lacked a case they
could justify before the world" (415). The first two were certainly militarily but the third seems to be a blatant projection. It was the United States
that was obsessed with justifying its case before the world. The Cuban
missile crisis was the one time the Russian Communists got as far out of
line as had been routine American policy everywhere else in the world, that
is arming small countries surrounding the Soviet Union. General Charles
De Gaulle, by then the President of France and trying to extricate the French
Empire from Algeria, observed that it wasn't the differences between the
United States and the Soviet Union that bothered him, but the similarities.

Buoyed by the victory, Kennedy contemplated withdrawal from
Vietnam in 1965, after a plausible re-election (414). De Gaulle, with the
wisdom of victory and defeat, understood the futile American position in
Southeast Asia and told Kennedy that France would have no part in further
military moves in Vietnam. Whether Kennedy would have made good on
the withdrawal became a moot question with his assassination in Dallas,
Texas, on November 23, 1963. Whether he was the victim of a coup d'etat
or a lone gunman, the effect was the same. Lyndon Baines Johnson was
boosted into the saddle and Texans were back in direct control of the White
House.

Dexter Perkins in *The Evolution of American Foreign Policy* asserts that
"The *tone* of our foreign policy is not set in the White House or in the State
Department, but in the great body of the citizenry" (1966, 152). What a
howler. This patronizing schmooze of democracy is not true now, nor was it
true when it was published. Perkins' remarks are perhaps true to the extent
that the White House and the State Department are not setting the tone
but the citizenry certainly aren't either. A very few minds in a handful of
bodies, many of them in secret armies like Eisenhower's CIA and the NSC,
(The National Security Advisor is beyond the reach of congress and is in
fact the defacto Secretary of State for the military government of the
Confederate Empire of America), concoct a policy which is then fed by a
complicit or originating media such as Luce's *Time* magazine or the LA

Times, like pabulum or manna to the disinterested, ignorant and largely powerless citizenry. This policy, much less its tone, cannot contradict, under penalty of death or revolution, the basic religious and reversionary impulse to empire spawned on the North American continent by speakers of English in South Carolina via slavery in Barbados.

For a century and a half the Americans cobbled together their own empire, displacing Cherokees, Lakotans, Comanches, Mexicans, Hawaiians, Filipinos, and Panamanians, to mention barely a few. It had a sufficiently large economic base, an entire continent with only the overhead of genocide and murder, that the Southerners calling the policy shots could respond to the English whimper to take the British Empire into receivership. Lacking the British talent for management of power, they bungled their way from crisis to quagmire. Southerners are skilled in the acquisition and maintenance of power, not its fruitful application. The decade of the fabulous 50s turned out to be a long one, from 1947 to 1975. The effects on the empire when Southerners clash for power is the subject matter for the next chapter in the Confederate election of 1964.

17

The Confederate Election of 1964

Lyndon Johnson got his first serious government job as the director of the National Youth Administration in Texas during the Depression as a direct result of Sam Rayburn's clout with Franklin Roosevelt. Only 26 years old and the youngest of all 48 state directors of the NYA (Caro 1982, 340), Johnson would come to owe a lifetime of political power, patronage and cooperation to Sam Rayburn. Sam Rayburn was "the son of a Confederate cavalryman who 'never stopped hating the Yankees. . .[and] will not in his long lifetime forget Appomattox'" (306). His office walls were covered with the pictures of a single man — Robert E. Lee. He objected when his district and the state of Texas were turning to Hoover in 1928 by saying "'As long as I honor the memory of the Confederate dead, and revere the gallant devotion of my Confederate father to the Southland. . .'" (306). Sam Rayburn was not just one more unreconstructed son of a Confederate cavalryman carrying the agenda of Robert E. Lee and Jefferson Davis. Rayburn was the most powerful Speaker the House of Representatives would ever have, the quintessential legislator of the 20th century. This anointer of presidents was living proof that the Civil War was not something that merely happened to strangers in the 19th century — it was something that happened to "my dad". Through his tenacity, devotion and hard work, he carried Confederate genes and their agenda for domination forward to the present.

His protégé Lyndon Johnson's rise to power is the subject of Robert A. Caro's meticulous work. To the charges of fraud brought against the questionable victory of Johnson over Coke Stevenson in the 1948 democratic senatorial primary in Texas, the rejoinder is made that "As in most close races in Texas, Johnson men had not *defrauded* Stevenson, but successfully *outfrauded* him" (Fehrenbach 1968 659). To "outfraud" is a Texas infinitive, the application of which may very well be infinite. Fehrenbach also recites the received wisdom that LBJ was "The most effective Senate majority leader in history" (664), in a book about Texas published in 1968 that manages to avoid using the word Vietnam. While other potential vice presidential candidates agonize about giving up their

241

power for the monkey seat of the VP, Johnson imagined himself as presiding over the Senate and remaining defacto majority leader. "He could now conceive of himself as virtually filling both high and important positions — and he was not far from wrong" (Haley 1964, 199).

Having things both ways is a Texas imperative, expressed in the 1960 election with a Texas law that enabled Johnson to run for re-election to his seat in the Senate as well as for vice president on the Democratic ticket. For a man of principle, this Texas insurance policy would have raised some dissonance at the level of the unreconciled differences between the state and the national platforms. Fortunately this was not a problem for Johnson, whose single guiding principle was the acquisition of power. Cheek by jowl comparisons of the platforms on the subjects of federal power, sit-ins, the depletion allowance, federal aid to education, desegregation, medical care, and the right to work, reveal diametric and direct contradictions. The Texas state platform "was essentially a State's Rights platform, while the national Democratic Party document was so radical that even the veteran socialist, Norman Thomas, branded it as 'Utopian, if not insincere'" (202-3).

Johnson's willingness to run on both platforms reveals a propensity to try to be all things to all people. The Democratic state convention in Texas in 1960 erupted in fist fights when the "vice-chairman of the Executive Committee, demanded that all Harris County delegates wearing miniature Confederate flags identify themselves. The giant delegation roared to its feet shouting 'dictators' and 'totalitarian' — drawing the retort from Mrs. Brooks that 'this is a Democratic convention, not a Confederate reunion'" (200). Without a map, uninformed or misinformed bystanders might not be able to tell the difference. Harris County (Houston) it will be remembered, was the only county in Texas that Strom Thurmond and the Dixiecrats carried in 1948.

Lyndon Johnson used to boast "that the Colorado River Authority and development — still the biggest and most expensive example of national socialism in Texas — is his 'proudest accomplishment'" (13). There was deep distrust of Lyndon Johnson backed up with considerable evidence for the general impression that "prior to the assassination of Kennedy, that despite Lyndon's alleged political magic, Texas would be swept from the Democratic ticket in 1964 if Goldwater were the nominee" (7). Two of the three Democratic power factions, the big city leaders and the Southerners, had agreed to Johnson's VP nomination in 1960, with only labor sitting out.

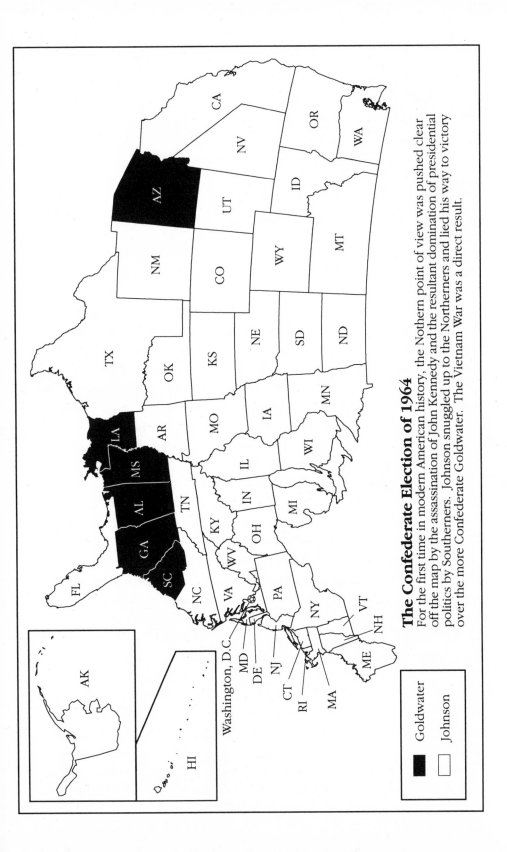

The Confederate Election of 1964

For the first time in modern American history, the Nothern point of view was pushed clear off the map by the assassination of John Kennedy and the resultant domination of presidential politics by Southerners. Johnson snuggled up to the Northerners and lied his way to victory over the more Confederate Goldwater. The Vietnam War was a direct result.

Goldwater

Johnson

Washington, D.C.
MD
DE
NJ
CT
RI
MA

AK

HI

Labor would have no place else to go in 1964 as Lyndon Johnson, after having sat for 15 years on a stack of progressive legislation as the "most effective majority leader in history" pushed it through Congress in the wake of the Kennedy assassination and, using a Fabian socialist term, called it the Great Society. His soon to be opponent in 1964, Senator Barry Goldwater of Arizona, (and Richard Nixon) had taken a chiding from Senator Kennedy during the 1960 campaign in Arizona when Kennedy noticed that Goldwater was absent from a Nixon photo op in the East and said "'If they can just get Barry out of that Confederate uniform that he has been using in the South'" (White 1988, 327). Getting Barry out of the Confederate uniform would be more than anyone could do.

Barry Goldwater, a conservative Republican from Arizona, moving in on the Republican nomination by the use of the "southern strategy," recognized his most intense support and political kin in South Carolina and the states of the old Confederacy. For the first time since the contest between Jefferson and Pinckney of South Carolina in 1804, the presidential election would pit two Southerners against one another in the "Confederate Election of 1964." Arthur Schlesinger Jr. identified 1964 as the time of one of the critical elections in American history in his collection of essays, *The Coming to Power*, and John Bartlow Martin's essay "The Election of 1964" recites some useful facts. Goldwater got his leg up in Arizona politics with his 1952 election to the Senate where "He rode in on Eisenhower's coattails — Eisenhower carried Arizona by 42,000 votes, Goldwater by 7,000)" (1971, 461). Even though he was "ineligible for combat in World War II, he ferried bombers to India and was discharged a lieutenant colonel. Later he became chief of staff of the Arizona Air National Guard, and as a major general in the USAF Reserve, commanding officer of the 999th Combined Air Force Reserve Squadron, made up of Members of Congress and congressional employees. He remained forever a friend of the military" (461).

This friend of the military, anti-labor and neo-Fascist according to labor, and staunch supporter of Senator Joseph McCarthy, wanted a total victory over communism (461-5). Considered by some to be a "dour authoritarian polemicist" (462), the need for a total victory over communism is the predictable effect of a weak mind chewing on the large bone of the Truman Doctrine. The Truman Doctrine only sought to contain communism; the Goldwater Doctrine demanded victory.

Goldwater's support in Texas and the Southeast was partly due to his consistent defense of the oil and gas depletion allowance. This tax in reverse, an extreme form of Calhoun's tax consuming principle, actually excuses the energy business from taxes on the grounds that they are using up a non-renewable resource and will need the protection of a huge cash reserve after they have finally "depleted" it entirely. Goldwater was a segregationist and told a Spartanburg, South Carolina Audience in 1960, "'I fear Washington and centralized government more than I do Moscow'" (464). Fear of Washington and centralized government is an old Confederate reaction, based on state rights and sounds as if the Civil War was still in progress. His operatives included Clifton White of the Young Republicans, John Grenier, Alabama state Republican chairman from Birmingham, and Peter O'Donnell, a young, rich, Dallas, Texan and chairman of the state Republican party (468). With the help of these Neo-Confederates, "Goldwater could do what no Republican had ever done: sweep the South" (470).

Henry Cabot Lodge Jr., son of the great imperialist, even while mouldering away in the Ambassador's tomb in South Vietnam, beat Goldwater and Rockefeller in the New Hampshire primary (472). The stop Goldwater movement by the somewhat less than right-wing whackos in the Republican party would founder in California where Goldwater got 51.4 percent of the vote and in Texas where he racked up 75.3 percent (474). The Republican platform had two planks: victory over communism and crime in the streets. Crime in the cities was the Republican code word for how to enforce their version of racial violence. It is no wonder that it resounded so strongly in South Carolina, where early in the 18th century the merging of the watch with the militia "Marks an important step in the shift of white priorities away from problems of external danger to questions of internal security" (Wood 1974, 274). What exactly was it that the Neo-Confederate Republicans had to feel so insecure about?

Goldwater's campaign theme, *A Choice Not an Echo*, was taken from the title of a book by Phyllis Schlafly. In *The Paranoid Style in American Politics* Richard Hofstadter identifies many of the critical elements in Goldwater's persona, campaign, and effect on the United States. Goldwater "saw with considerable clarity the distinction between interest politics and status politics, and went out of his way in his campaign to condemn the immorality of the first and to call for an intensification of the second"

(1965, 92). Interest politics, the art of looking out for your own economic interests as taken to an art form in Texas, can appear immoral. Status politics, or the fear of losing status, or losing out to Communists or Negroes, roosts in the reptilian archipallium where it nurses the reversionary impulse to simplify the future by making it indistinguishable from the barbaric past. This rigid and frigid system has been a blueprint for fascist authoritarian political systems at least as far back as Confucious.

In the United States, it is a reprise of the authoritarianism required to keep the slaveholding South together. Sympathy for Negroes, thin as it may be, goes back to the Federalists. It was continued by the Whigs, and literally infused the creators of the Republican party, Fremont and Lincoln. Goldwater departed from this Republican pattern and "By adopting 'the Southern strategy,' the Goldwater men abandoned this inheritance. They committed themselves not merely to a drive for a core of Southern states in the electoral college but to a strategic counterpart in the North which required a search for racist votes" (99). The search for racist votes did not pan out in the North in 1964 where they were drubbed by an even more duplicitous Southerner, but their victory consisted of having captured the Republican party. The modern Republican party was born in this racist repudiation of its moral past.

Moral turpitude in the exploitation of divisiveness was not entirely new in 1964, but it was made possible in large part because the right wing's economic interests were near their peak and at a saturation point. With their economic interests on ice, what better time to defend their mythical status as religious belief. Goldwater ". . . wanted, in short, to drive the politics out of politics" (121), and to replace it with religious and moral fervor, which is the only thing originally Republican about it. He reiterated many times during the campaign that he "did not *want* a general war" (124), preferring of course, to maintain status and his unilateral interpretation of external commitments by bluff.

Hofstadter suggests that both the campaigns of 1960 and 1964 "signify the deep perplexity of the American public over our foreign policies" (131). Much of the perplexity can be cleared up when we realize that broad interpretations of external commitments are in fact commitments to empire. The political struggle in the United States has always been between those factions seeking to operate it like a nation state or a country, and the competing factions that attempt to aggrandize its territory and influence by operating it as if it were an empire. The forces for empire almost always have the upper hand, because the empire is a reinforcement of the military religion. Hofstadter concludes by saying "They have demonstrated that the right wing is a formidable force in our politics and have given us reason to think that it is a permanent force" (137). Hofstadter died in 1970 and the permanent force of the Neo-Confederate right wing dominates American politics.

Its effect on the election of 1964 was to move the political center of gravity several degrees to the right. Lyndon Johnson acted presidential and looked smooth alongside the barbarian from the right. He repeatedly said that he sought no wider war and that he would never send American boys to do what Vietnamese boys should be doing for themselves. He successfully dispatched the Marines in and out of the Dominican Republic in the annual obligatory Confederate invasion of the Caribbean empire. Perhaps he misled himself into thinking that the situation in Vietnam could be handled as quickly. The Panamanian Flag Riots early in the Johnson administration set the tone for Johnson's incapacity at foreign affairs (Liss 1967, 144-7). This and subsequent Panamanian episodes demonstrated the empire's inheritance from the irascible Theodore Roosevelt.

The outcome of the election itself, where Goldwater did in fact only carry several of the states of the Old Confederacy, minus Texas and Florida, as well as his own Confederate territory of Arizona, was a Lyndon Johnson landslide. Fear of Goldwater was a stronger feeling than distrust of Johnson. What the American people and electorate failed to perceive, who felt the choice was between war and peace, was that Lyndon Johnson, capable of running in 1960 on two diametrically opposed platforms, also ran in 1964 on two diametrically opposed platforms, one public, one private. "In 1964, the population voted overwhelmingly against the policies which were put into effect immediately after the election, policies which, it appears, had been proposed unanimously by the president's advisers even prior to the election, though the electorate was never so informed" (Chomsky 1973, 289). The choice in the Confederate election of 1964 was soon revealed to have been a choice between two kinds of war. This was a direct consequence of having both candidates from "the South and southwest with its greater tradition of militarism" (Phillips 1975, 32). The imperial drive was masked in defensive terms (Chomsky 1973, 49), as the defense of South Vietnam was undertaken to save it from the Communist invasion from the North.

Students of history will recall that Adolph Hitler invaded Czechoslovakia in 1938 to save it from the Communists. Perhaps General Patton has been right all along that there was really no difference between the Nazis and the Democrats and Republicans. The motive was embedded in the "perceived significance of Southeast Asia for the integrated global system that was to be organized by American Power — and. . . dominated by American Power for the primary benefit of those who possess that power" (66).

It was not simply a matter of linguistic noise that the primary nominalization in South Vietnam, Vietnam, was typically dropped out of the phrase nominalizing the adjective so that it was the South that was being protected from an invasion from the North, the South that had to be defended, "we are fighting to save the South." This played well below the Mason-Dixon Line, however it might have played in Peoria, Illinois, and demonstrated the flipside of Johnson's use of Calhoun's Concurrent Majority, as whatever support he lost in the North was more than replenished by support from the war worshipping South. Chagrined voters in the North, who had responded to the peace loving public Lyndon Johnson, were dismayed that he used his landslide victory, which came with working majorities in both Houses of Congress, to enlarge the war. Johnson was elected on fear of Goldwater, fear being the most powerful emotion available for political manipulation. "The obvious conclusion to draw from this history is that peace-minded people should have voted for Goldwater, so that the 'mandate' would have been less overwhelming, since apparently it was only its scale and not its character that mattered" (110).

Articulate cynicism aside, the bombing of North Vietnam commenced in February of 1965 on an ominous and almost unanimous note. Ninety-seven percent of the United States Senate supported Lyndon Johnson's policy, but even this was not enough for Johnson's perceived need for consensus and Democratic centralism. He was never able to arm-twist and bully Senators Frank Church of Idaho, Ernest Gruening of Alaska, or Wayne Morse of Oregon. These three Democrats from the Pacific Northwest had nerve enough to oppose him, consistently, publicly, and intelligently, until 10 years later they were proved to be correct. Press coverage for people speaking at cross purposes with the imperial policies of the United States was no easier to obtain in 1965 than it had been for Henry Wallace in 1948 (MacDougall 1965, 129), or the Anti-Imperialists in the 1890s.

Lyndon Johnson mislead, lied to, and betrayed the American people as he created from his southern background and support, the paranoid, military and unnatural disaster of the war in Vietnam. "No one doubted, for example, that the South was the most hawkish part of the United States in supporting the war in Vietnam" (Phillips 1993, 239). The Vietnam War, the empire's war of aggression, divided the American people just as deeply as the defensive war against the Japanese in WWII united them. Volunteer infantry combat veteran Gregory D. Foster, in comments distributed by the Los Angeles *Times*-Washington *Post* News Service wrote "I am willing to concede that Bill Clinton and others of his persuasion may have acted more wisely — perhaps even more courageously — than I and others like me" (*UB* 1992, 32). The best and brightest young men of that generation who failed or refused to serve the bogus American policy of the Vietnam era provided the most public service of their time. They were and are loyal to the country, that is to say to the countryside, the mountains, rivers, trees, farms, beaches, and the people, even as they could care less about the fate of the policy of public liars, especially as it concerns the overseas empire.

Loyalty to an empire with its fluctuating indefensible policy and instable indefinite boundaries is nonsense. Governor Joe E. Brown of Georgia, during the Civil War, made the able bodied men of Georgia into petty officials, deputy sheriffs, constables, and put a postmaster at every crossroads, to keep them out of the Confederate Army. Loyalty, just as Robert E. Lee was loyal to northern Virginia, is confined to a locale. Half the eligible men in the Confederacy refused to respond to Jefferson Davis' conscription call in 1863, perhaps because he had just extended all enlistments for the duration except for granting furloughs to anybody who owned more than 20 slaves, as he made quite clear which class benefits from war. Or as Muhammad Ali, heavyweight boxing champion of the world and probably the most famous draft dodger put it, "I ain't got no quarrel with no Viet Cong." Muhammad Ali, a public man, suffered in public with the loss of his title and the outrageous hectoring of yellow journalists. His intelligence, courage and loyalty were never questioned by millions of others who suffered privately. Half the men of age in the Vietnam Era served the military policy of the liars and half did not. The election of Bill Clinton is a good time to acknowledge how poorly the talents of an entire generation were used.

Short wars sell better in the United States. Lyndon Johnson was the worst president of the 20th century. He squandered more opportunities to improve conditions both within the United States and without the United States than any president before or since. He personally poisoned and destroyed the idealism of an entire generation, perhaps wishing it could be as cynical and two-faced as he. He debased the currency and gave us the copper quarter and the Federal Reserve Note in place of the Silver Certificate, making Confederate money out of the American Dollar. He simultaneously began a war on poverty and neither the victims in Vietnam nor the poor have yet recovered. Virtually all of the veterans of the Vietnam War, those who volunteered and those who were drafted in violation of the Constitution, realize how callously they were used. Even those individuals and corporations who believe in the empire of the United States and who believe that it should be extended to all possible places and marginal markets for as long as possible, have come to realize that fighting the Vietnam War reduced the empire's resources, squandered its prestige, and hastened its demise, let alone what it did to the country. In other words the Vietnam War, which was made possible by and acquired its peculiar character in the Confederate election of 1964, was not good for anybody in the long run, and barely good even for a few defense contractors in the short run.

Opposition to the war in the short run, which of course included telling the truth about it, was not a simple task, for the facts cannot be brought to bear on religious disputation. David Halberstam, who reported it and lived to write about it, said "There were periodic Army and CIA investigations of reporters' sources. Not of whether the stories were accurate, but of who the sources were" (1979, 451). As might have been expected, as the war dragged on "The pentagon got rougher, it attacked not just the reporters' accuracy, but their manhood and their patriotism" (450). Not the least of the difficulties of getting to the truth were the facts that "Over fifteen years of Cold War competition with the Soviets, the American government had begun to take on some of the coloration of its adversary, in particular its preoccupation with secrecy. . . Functions that once belonged to the State Department were moved over to the CIA. . . The role of the advisor to the President on National Security. . . was *completely* the President's man and because he never had to testify before Congress" (493). Other people noticed the truth in De Gaulle's concern over the similarities between the Soviet Union and the United States where Eisenhower had turned the CIA into his secret army.

The best reporters had their stories neutralized while the published wire service dispatches, based on misleading military briefings, appeared on the front pages of what passes for newspapers in the United States. "In terms of news management, it was a great success. In terms of dealing with the Vietnamese Communists, it had no effect at all" (453). It was "No wonder the Vietnam War cut more sharply to the inner soul of America. . . than anything else in this century" (490). CBS had the temerity to broadcast Morely Safer's film on the burning of Cam Ne. The President's response was vintage Johnson, who called his friend Frank Stanton, the head of CBS: "'Frank, are you trying to fuck me? Frank this is your President, and yesterday your boys shat on the American flag'" (490). There is the soul of America all right. It boils down to who or which side is shitting on the American flag. Lyndon Johnson shat his lies on the American flag.

A principled Southerner and long time political ally of Johnson, Senator William Fulbright, the Chairman of the Senate Foreign Relations Committee, was disturbed by Johnson's reckless policy. "The Dulles years had been one thing, that had been Dulles and jingoistic right-wingers. Here were people he knew and vouched for following similar policies" (499). The size of Johnson's "interior doubt" (494) had every reason to be inflating. Wayne Worse and William Fulbright jumped Dean Rusk, the Secretary of State from Georgia, with Texan and Confederate ancestors, about the policies. "In Bill Fulbright's mind, Lyndon Johnson had broken a sacred promise dating back to 1964, when he had asked Fulbright to steer the Tonkin Gulf Resolution through the Senate. There would be no ground troops" (503). There was barely even an incident in the Tonkin Gulf, let alone one that posed even the slightest threat to American national security. There was no limit to the people Lyndon Johnson would mislead or lie to when it suited his purposes. Fulbright was to get one Congressional debate on essences before he was shut down by Democratic centralism "and so it was that never again were there televised hearings on the Vietnam War, though that was to threaten the spirit and the soul of America for another nine years" (506).

Robert McNamara, the best mind of Allen Ginsberg's generation and the Secretary of Defense, went to Vietnam to sort it out. "After nine months of research, the [his] group concluded that there was absolutely no way that they could win the war in Vietnam, and advised Secretary of Defense Robert McNamara accordingly" (Cousins 1987, 108). Before resigning in distaste, McNamara tried to convince Johnson of the results of the research, having discovered for himself the De Gaulle principle of imperial futility. Lyndon Johnson, however, was marching to the tune of the First Commandment of Texas, "I'll neither surrender or retreat," enunciated by Colonel Buck Travis at his defense of the Alamo. He was supported in this lunacy by the military apparatus of the empire for "At every stage in the descent into the quagmire [of Vietnam] the military played a dominant role" (Schlesinger 1986, 153).

Unlike John C. Calhoun, who as Louis Hartz says, "was caught in the classic agony of the brink-of-war philosopher. . . a man whose thought is cut in two by the tug of the liberal past and the pull of the reactionary present" (Thomas 1968, 170), Lyndon Johnson, whose thought was never troubled by conflicting tendencies, was trapped in the depth-of-war position of being unable to win, unable to stop fighting, and unable to stop lying about it. Former President Eisenhower, the Caesar who denied the Vietnamese the right to vote and another Texan who had memorized the tune to the First Commandment, is said to have made unprintable remarks when he learned about Johnson's cave-in when he stopped the bombing of Vietnam (Schlesinger 1986, 404). Many political leaders, including those in Vietnam, were assassinated during the Eisenhower, Kennedy and Johnson, terms in office and yet "There is no evidence that any of the three Presidents authorized or knew about the CIA's assassination policy" (413). Any spy outfit worth the money thrown at them would eat the evidence, if it ever existed. Richard Helms, former CIA director and ambassador to the Shah's Savak-ruled-Iran, wanted to ask Senator Frank Church how he could be so "God damned dumb" as to think there would be such evidence.

Evidence exists that Hubert Humphrey, who did not run in a single primary, did not deserve the Democratic presidential nomination in 1968. The popular choice of Eugene McCarthy was passed over in the Fascist circus in Chicago where Lyndon "the Liar" Johnson, afraid to attend the convention but still loaded with force and fraud power over the Democratic party, bulldozed the nomination to Humphrey. Humphrey had looked ridiculous enough, four years earlier in the government on horseback pictures from the Perdenales as Johnson's running mate. With his "balls" still in LBJ's pocket, the jig was up for Hubert Horatio Humphrey. It was said in the new cool medium of television that Humphrey was too hot for the living room where the audience reposes. "Humphrey vomited on the rug" (McGinnis 1969, 24). Humphrey vomited for four years on the only part of the American public who could have elected him. One two-faced Democratic cynic in a row was enough. His earlier observation that "free speech doesn't include the right to be taken seriously," as a putdown of the people trying to make sense to one another and get the government of the empire to stop the war, was all the proof required that his personal quest for power was going nowhere. Few could take this corrupted-by-power bumpkin seriously.

The election of Richard Nixon in 1968, his re-election in 1972 and his subsequent resignation are little more than white noise and a political interference pattern set up in waves as consequences of the election of 1964. Kevin Phillips' famous analysis of the election of 1968 as a watershed election, published as *The Emerging Republican Majority*, never once mentioned the Vietnam War as a factor in the Democratic defeat. Nixon was the political creation of the Los Angeles *Times*, capitol newspaper of the new southern state of California, and the gift of their boosterism to the nation. Even though Nixon had barely lost the election of 1960, "There, in the Old Confederacy, Richard M. Nixon made his greatest gains. . . Nixon managed to *increase* the Republican vote and *outrun* Eisenhower in no less than four states of the Deep South. . . Yet the sharpest bulge in the Nixon-Republican total was chalked up in the bustling, modern cities of the New South; in Dallas, in Houston, in Birmingham, in Atlanta, and in their suburbs" (White 1988, 359). Theodore White goes on to say that this was not an isolated episode but a trend, a trend that picked up speed with Goldwater's victories in the Old Confederacy.

Nixon had stumped the country for Goldwater in 1964, comfortable in the party chore boy role he had acquired as vice president. It permitted him to grow chummy with Republican leaders nationwide as he sewed the nomination up early with "Almost three hundred days of the grin" (McGinnis, 1969, 130). He was so composed, it was hard to tell the war was raging all around him, which war he said he had a plan to end. His election would move Gloria Steinem to remark "We're all niggers now" (130). Niggers or not, Nixon's plan to end the war turned out to be winning it by following the Curtis LeMay plan of bombing Vietnam into the stone age. General Curtis LeMay had run with Governor George Wallace of Alabama — remember there is always somebody to the Confederate right of any conceivable position — and in 1968, Nixon and Wallace together won 57 percent of the vote. The sectional nature of the campaign was made apparent by the selective venues where campaign material appeared. "The other southern commercials. . . had been provided by the Thurmond Speaks Committee of South Carolina" (McGinnis 1969, 124).

This trend toward the white power vote in the South received its quantum boost in the 1964 election when the choice was confined to white Southerners. According to Germond and Witcover, white Southern votes dribbled away from Democrats to Republicans, especially since 1968 (1989, 38). "In several of the larger states — Texas and Florida most obviously — the Republicans had been growing generally more competitive with every election" (153). Standing Lincoln on his head was one of the more obvious effects of the Confederate revolution at the presidential level. Bringing the war on Vietnam home, as many of its opponents suggested, had the boomerang effect years later in Los Angeles, Nixon's greater hometown where the police department is modeled on the Marine Corps, of the police "Jacking up thousands of local teenagers at random like so many surprised peasants" (Davis 1990, 268).

Nixon's power base hometown had become New York, as he took another page out of his mentor Eisenhower's book. The domestic section of the empire in the United States was growing numb from violence, televised and actual, while the National Guard shooting of several students at Kent State took the fun out of knocking on the doors of the powers that be. By 1972, few people were still wondering what had become of Nixon's plan to end the war. "Nixon was interested almost exclusively in politics, and mainly in foreign affairs. Domestic policy bored him; public works were especially deadly" (Reisner 1986, 408). Nixon's deadly grasp of the nuances of power were revealed in his decision to commence bombing Cambodia on Christmas Eve, a Christian surprise attack which went on for the 12 days of Christmas while the Quaker Nixon hunkered down at Camp David to take advantage of the strategic military element of surprise as well as of the fact that both college and Congress were in recess and organized opposition to his initiative would be smothered in tinsel, double crosses and colored lights.

Nixon and his foreign Secretary of State Henry Kissinger, a latter-day Hamilton to guide the collective American ignorance, engineered through the CIA, the assassination of Salvador Allende and removal of the democratically elected government of the South American republic of Chile. It was perfectly clear to Nixon that he was ruling an empire, even if other people remained confused and felt that the United States was in fact a country. Nixon's one line in history, other than the famous "I am not a crook" remark, will come from his initiative to China. Breaking the power and thralldom of the China Lobby in the United States was made possible in part by Barbara Tuchman's Pulitzer Prize winning book, *Stilwell and the American Experience in China, 1911-1945*, which prepared the intellectual and historical framework for this sea-change in policy. This initiative toward establishing mutually beneficial relationships between the United States and China was the only major non-reactionary foreign policy move the United States has yet made in the 20th century. It also demonstrates that Nixon realized he was operating an empire, based on the British Empire model of controlling the balance of power, and not the least of his intentions was to open up the Russian's eastern flank. A continuation of the U.S. alliance with Mao Zedong and his Chinese followers after the end of WWII would have made the subsequent wars for empire in Asia moot and unnecessary. This chink in the armor of the Truman Doctrine revealed some maturity in the southern dominated empire of the United States. Although Southerners are gifted in the acquisition of power, they lacked the British talent for dispensing it, such as having other people perform as cat's-paws to fight their battles for them, and were repeatedly clumsy in its use, for example the foreign policy disasters of Truman, Johnson and Nixon.

Nixon had also learned that old white people vote their pocket books, so in 1971 he started dumping money into the system. An unearned 20 percent increase in Social Security benefits, plus hooking them to a COLA, were important steps toward bankruptcy and inflation. Nixon stole the Post Office and gave sinecures to 15 of his staunch supporters as he "depoliticized" the postal service. Nixon took the dollar off the gold standard and let it float, with the cynical help of his treasury secretary, the Texan John Connally, ending the Bretton-Woods agreement to pay in gold that had guided international finance since the end of WWII. He floated to a victory over the Democratic candidate for peace, Senator George McGovern of South Dakota. After almost eight years of war, peace was still the minority position as the empire held fast to the Texas Commandment of no surrender, no retreat.

Nixon's unctuous fear of democracy led him to authorize the burglary of the Democratic party headquarters at the Watergate Hotel in Washington, although it could hardly be said he needed any of the information that might be contained there. The Democratic party, ripped apart by the unreliable cynicism of Lyndon Johnson, had all the self destruct mechanisms in place that it would ever need. "Invoking 'national security' as an all-purpose justification for presidential criminality, he set up a secret White House posse" (Schlesinger 1986, 281). Nixon is a textbook case of the application of the rule of empires over democratic nation states that whenever there is a conflict of interest between the empire and the democracy, the democracy inevitably looses. An imperial democracy is not possible so the American choice was to take the empire and let the democracy fend for itself.

In the American constitutional democracy, the Congress has three powers that were intended to be countervailing to the power of the executive branch: war making; purse; and oversight. Nixon chose to violate all three. He impounded money authorized by Congress, a type of free-lance line-item veto, found not so coincidentally in the Confederate Constitution. He bombed Cambodia on Christmas Eve. And he claimed executive privilege in withholding information, virtually cubing the 45 times Eisenhower, his presumable model, withheld information from Congress.

It is important that we comprehend American history and not be misled by Schlesinger's claim that both conservative and reform presidents, his representation of the two types of presidents operating their various shifts in the Klingberg foreign policy microcycles, are "Both Committed to individual liberty, the constitutional state and the rule of law" (47). Schlesinger is committed to wishful thinking, for after having made that assertion, the multiple citations of constitutional violations within his own text, Nixon's being simply among the most blatant, of Truman, Eisenhower, Kennedy, Johnson and Nixon, refute his own assessment. Ironing out the internal contradictions is precisely where the truth will lie.

Nixon was not impeached but merely hounded out of office, so unwilling are the American people to use the structure of their own Constitution. He was *threatened* with impeachment if he would not resign, and the final message of "hit the road Dick" was delivered by none other than the ultra-conservative Neo-Confederate Senator Barry Goldwater. As Nixon clung to power "He badly needed to hold as much of public opinion as he could, particularly in the South. . . . Nixon had to resign, the alternative was certain impeachment with only a tiny handful of Deep South senators and congressmen supporting him" (Halberstam 1979, 702). It is fundamental rather than incidental that Nixon's strongest bastion of support was in the imperial South.

The American people had come so far off the constitutional track that an amendment to the constitution had been rushed through permitting the president to appoint a vice president in the case of a vacancy, rather than test the original rules of succession leading from vice president to speaker of the House, leader of the Senate, and already appointed cabinet level officials. By such adhoc laws, Congressman Gerald Ford of Michigan, a southern state between the lakes where George Wallace won primary elections, was appointed vice president and became president upon Nixon's overdue resignation. The first words out of Ford's mouth were "Our long national nightmare is over," but it was clear he was referring to the Nixon problem and not the war, the oil embargo, and the other pressing situations that had intensified while Nixon was distracted as he attempted to distract the people from his pathetic case. The Congress had finally made it impossible for the president to continue the war on Vietnam and in 1975 most of the last remaining personnel and collaborators were helicoptered off the roof of the embassy in Saigon to the strains of Irving Berlin's *White Christmas*.

The decade of the 50s which began in 1947, was extended by the Calhoun-like effort of the Southern Democrat and conservative Republican coalition to force a static solution onto a dynamic situation, until 1975, making it the longest and most retrograde decade in the 20th century. In the process, the white South would lose most of its fear of being called Republican at the national level — having recognized their racism was welcome there — and the new majority was formed from the one that resurfaced in the Fraud of 1876. "That is why the dominoes fell in Southeast Asia; not because we failed to oppose communism but because we supported the kinds of corrupt, repressive, and incompetent 'leaders' who make the triumph of communism all but inevitable" (Walton 1976, 215). Lyndon Johnson, lacking even the rudiments of psychological insight, could threaten his opposition by saying "Armed hostility is futile" and not realize he was describing his own position more than the Viet Cong's and "by so clearly stating that America would never weaken or withdraw,

President Johnson also may have made it impossible for the Reds to negotiate" (Leckie 1968, II:453). The impossibility of the Americans negotiating, as can hardly be said too many times, was based on their religious belief in "I'll neither surrender or retreat," the gospel by Travis at the Alamo. Neither surrendering nor retreating was a dynamic strategy at the Alamo; it was an unworkable static solution in Vietnam. A military people with a single strategy are doomed. Manifest Destiny played well along the Nueces. Manifest Destiny along the Mekong was an unmitigated disaster. It was inappropriately exported by Texans to the Mekong's distributaries leading to Tonle Sap in Southeast Asia.

Telford Taylor, the chief counsel for the prosecution at Nuremberg where the Nazis were finally forced to face the music of their invasion of Czechoslovakia to save it from communism among many other crimes, "comes close to suggesting that the military and civilian leadership of the United States from 1965 to the present [1973] are liable to prosecution as war criminals under the standards of Nuremberg" (Chomsky 1973, 212). The Nuremberg standards, however closely they apply, will not be applied to the behavior of Americans until they lose harder than they have yet. While still in power, they are free to ignore civilized world opinion in favor of their preoccupation with war. "The military party denies neither the bestiality nor the horror, nor the expense; it only says that these things tell but half the story. It only says that war is *worth* them; that, taking human nature as a whole, its wars are its best protection against its weaker and more cowardly self, and that mankind cannot *afford* to adopt a peace-economy" (James 1967, 666).

Mankind can afford anything it chooses, for its success or failure is a matter of profound indifference to the planet it calls home. Wars, which are the metallic elaboration of the competition to control the economic future by force and fraud, propel them away from any greater understanding of the human predicament even as they hasten them toward a final day of reckoning. Their deadly nuisance value to each other is dwarfed by the unintended ramifications of their short term success. We've heard it said that "No more Koreas" came to mean that Americans would not fight again without going all out, meaning the use of the bomb and nuclear weapons. Technological fallout outstripped such a simplistic strategic bias. "No more Vietnams" means whatever the hearer thinks it means. To peace loving Americans, it meant no more foolish colonial wars of any kind. To George

Bush, it apparently meant no more wars where America gets bogged down and doesn't win, so he declared a victory over Iraq and brought the troops home, much as Senator George Aiken of Vermont suggested that Lyndon Johnson do in Vietnam in 1966. This will not stand, as Bush himself might say, since he left Saddam Hussein in power, a man he vilified as a Hitler, to continue his genocide of the Shi'ites and the Kurds, perhaps so that he or some other president needing a public relations boost could take him out at some more opportune time for their standing in or at the polls. Good enemies are indispensable. The pulse of American history throws slogans up like repetitive crests on an endlessly crashing wave. Remember the Alamo, Remember the Maine, Remember Pearl Harbor, but don't forget Saigon.

18

The Anomalous Administration of Jimmy Carter

Baker, Nevada, on the Utah-Nevada border, although not exactly in the middle of the Great American Sahara, is a few hundred miles in all directions from anything else resembling civilization. Two concrete workers stopped at the one man-one woman truckstop, gas station, bar, cafe and oasis to fillerup and have a beer. It was 1973 and Vice President Spiro Agnew from Maryland had just resigned, the first VP to do so since John C. Calhoun in 1832, in a plea bargaining intended for him to avoid the consequences of tax fraud. The talk turned to politics and the Rumplestiltskin-like proprietor launched into a tirade, reciting the names of all the presidents he'd lived under since Coolidge and saying something derogatory about each until he got to Nixon. He punctuated his Nixonian remarks by slamming his huge ham-handed fist down on the bar hard enough to rattle the glasses on his backbar as he shouted, "By God, I can take anything but a liar." When the grassroots speak with one voice, the empire finally listens.

Avery Craven, in *The Coming of the Civil War*, commented on the election of 1860: "Political campaigns in the United States incline to exaggeration and distortion. Opponents are vilified. . . only the fact that the people have come to understand that they are being lied to prevents dangerous reactions" (Craven 1957, 412). Wearing his questionable pardon of the criminal Nixon like a hairshirt, to which he had pinned a WIN (Whip Inflation Now) button, the appointed President Ford had to fend off a determined but unsuccessful onslaught from Reagan and the Neo-Confederate Republican right. Nixon had passed over his two chief Republican rivals, Nelson Rockefeller and Ronald Reagan, when he appointed Ford Vice President. And although Ford as president had then appointed Nelson Rockefeller vice president, he passed him over for the vice presidential nomination, which went to the cold and mouthy Senator Robert Dole of Kansas.

With the Republicans in deep disarray in 1976, Jimmy Carter of Georgia was elected president. Kevin Phillips had prognosticated wistfully that "A Republican loss in 1976 would indicate that post-industrialism has made 32-36 year cycles a thing of the past" (1975, 146). The 32 year cycles in the American presidency that obtained until 1932 were phenomenon attributable to the United States as a county. These cycles actually fell victim not to post-industrialism but to the "empire effect" in the institutional presidency. Obviously a Southerner, Carter was no Confederate, but rather a Georgian in the Joe E. Brown mould. At first, the northern Democrats welcomed Carter's candidacy, thinking at last here was somebody who could put out the political lights of their perennial problem in the South, George Wallace of Alabama. Carter was able to out maneuver late rallies by Governor Jerry Brown of California and Senator Frank Church of Idaho for the Democratic nomination. It is germane to notice that in the competition for political power in 1976, whether between liberals or conservatives and between Democrats and Republicans, the ultimate Carter victory for the nomination and the presidency is further proof of southern domination and the political power of the South.

Not being a Confederate however, Jimmy Carter's conception of the presidency put him at cross purposes with the empire and the miasma that had developed around the institutional presidency since 1947. "Carter's job as President, from the point of view of the Establishment, was to halt the rushing disappointment of the American people with the government, with the economic system, with disastrous military ventures abroad" (Zinn 1980, 551). This would be a tall order anywhere and Zinn is fairly cynical suggesting "Carter was continuing the old hypocrisy" (554) and "on close examination, these more liberal policies were designed to leave intact the power and influence of American military and American business in the world" (555). If that were fully and in fact the case, Carter would not have had such determined and vociferous opposition from Reagan, the military and the Republican southern right wing. What the correct conclusion depends upon is how the power and influence of the American military and American business is used in the world, not whether it is kept intact or allowed to deteriorate. While most of the discussion of the Carter anomalies will be focused on events outside the national boundaries, the consequences of the empire, there is one domestic empire policy problem that invites examination.

Zinn is careful to point out that although considered a liberal and member of the trilateral commission, Carter supported the Vietnam War virtually until the evacuation of Saigon. Running as an outsider, Carter walked up Pennsylvania Avenue in his inaugural parade and carried his own bags into the White House, establishing a folksy tone and human decency scale to his administration. He would be ridiculed later for those displays of common humanity by right to life types to whom long black limousines are a way of life and a focal point of power. That ridicule would be mild in tone compared to the barrage he received, virtually as he began his administration, for his efforts to make sense out of the pork barrel water projects which are the life blood of the conservative Republican South and West. "Carter was merely stunned by the reaction from the East; he was blown over backward by the reaction from the West. . . Carter's hit list had as much to do with his one-term presidency as Iran. . . Barry Goldwater, scourge of welfare and champion of free enterprise, has been a lifelong supporter of the Central Arizona Project, which comes as close to socialism as anything this country has ever done" (Reisner 1986, 11-12). Certainly Carter's broad and fractious disagreements with the western water policies and lobby contributed to his electoral defeat in 1980, not because of the relative value of the issues of water and his conduct vis-à-vis Iran, but rather because his handling of both issues offended almost exactly the same constituency.

Since none of these water projects have ever made economic sense, Carter can be forgiven for the naiveté that led him to think they would be easy to derail. Being a mere former governor of Georgia and Washington outsider, he was either unaware of the power or unaware of the fact that "The leadership of the appropriations and public-works committees that approve and fund water projects traditionally comes from the South and West, where water projects are sacrosanct" (321). The American economy has been described as state financed capitalism, where the Calhoun principle of redistributing the revenue in the direction of tax consumers is at the class basis of the division of power in the United States. These water subsidies are made to the largest corporations who pay $3.50 an acre foot for water that is purified by the taxpayers at a cost of $300 per acre foot (482). Carter got next to nowhere with his plans to clean up the waste, fraud and abuse, in the distribution of the political patronage that is disguised as the western water problem.

A typical example was the howl of protest sent up by Republican Senator Jake Garn of Utah, ranking Republican on the Banking Committee, at the prospect of losing the Central Utah Project or the CUP. This economic disaster in motion would have taken Colorado River water and pumped it into the Great Basin for industrial use in Provo and Salt Lake.

Utah has long been a special cog in the chain of Neo-Confederate and conservative control of American politics. The Mormons, under Brigham Young, moved to the Salt Lake Valley in 1847 to get out of the United States, only to have the results of the Mexican War put their new location back in. Not quite like Texas and yet racist until the President of the Mormon Church Kimball's "revelation" that it was okay with God to ordain black men as bishops, Utah and the Mormons radiate the conservatism of Texas, Arizona and LA throughout the Mormon kingdom. Hill Air Force Base near Ogden makes Utah part of the military chain of command and control for it represents Utah's largest payroll.

Keep in mind that more water is not created by moving it around, but water is actually lost through evaporation and spillage. The Wasatch Front in Utah was in a dry cycle during the Carter years of the late 1970s. By the mid 1980s, the weather cycle had changed and it was necessary to pump excess water out of the Great Salt Lake onto the desert in the hope that it would evaporate, as suddenly nature had given Utah more water than the people there could cope with. The Central Utah Project was an absurd, out of synch redundancy. Nature undoubtedly knows more about the efficient distribution of water than man can ever learn. According to Berkey, "'The United States has virtually set up an empire on impounded and redistributed water'" (Reisner 1986,488). The fate of hydraulic civilizations as recited in Wittfogel's *Oriental Despotism*, A Comparative Study of Total Power, is bearing down upon Los Angeles and the western United States. "The ruling class of hydraulic society is represented first by its active core, the men of the apparatus" (1957, 305). The conservative apparatachiks, Garn and Goldwater, were livid with Carter. His confrontation with the western water powers is not the behavior of a hypocrite trying to buttress the status quo, but rather the determined idealist confronting hypocrites and being sawed to pieces in the teeth of the reactionary economic reversion.

"Carter did initiate more sophisticated policies toward other countries in the world that oppressed their own people" (Zinn 1980, 553), Zinn reports begrudgingly as though he was expecting miracles from a man whose election was largely an accident of conservative and Republican excess. "Carter won 47 percent of the southern white vote. . ." (Black and Black 1992, 334), and only won a majority of it in Georgia, Arkansas, and Tennessee. Nevertheless, his support among black voters was strong enough for him to carry all the South except Virginia. His grasp of the true levers of power was neither strong nor anywhere near complete, yet even at that, it is said of Andrew Young, his Ambassador Extraordinary and Plenipotentiary, and the Representative of the USA in the Security Council of the United Nations, that he personally improved the relationships between the United States and 50 other countries. He was able to do that by recommending appointments sensitive to local and national cultural differences, rather than applying political patronage in the Republican style to let the campaign contributors with the biggest bucks man the embassies.

Evacuating the embassy in Saigon led directly to the Carter Presidency. "No More Vietnams" was the most resonant campaign theme in 1976. The war in Vietnam was an indefensible operation on any grounds. A handful of people and operations got rich from it such as President Eccles of First Security Bank and Utah Construction who built the deep water port at Cam Ranh Bay. Even those crass individuals who believe the United States should operate a maximal empire came to realize there is nothing even remotely strategic, geopolitically or otherwise, about Southeast Asia. An intelligently managed empire would have cut its losses early.

The "loss" of Vietnam, acting as a dead weight on the national consciousness, left the problem of what to do with the other colonies, client states, and satrapies the empire had picked up along the way. Caution has to be exercised when "regarding the United States as the happy empire of perfect wisdom and perfect virtue, commissioned to save humanity" (Schlesinger 1986, 54). Despite the presence in the canon of such tremendous and truthful books as William Appleman Williams' *Empire as a Way of Life,* there are people who dispute the fact that the United States is an empire, much as Harry Truman disputed the fact that there was a war going on in Korea that he had jumped the U.S. into, preferring to call it a "conflict," or as Theodore Roosevelt disputed the facts of his own imperialism.

The September/October 1991 issue of *Defense Almanac* has the nerve to refer, under its casualties section on page 47, to the Vietnam War as the "Vietnam Conflict" in a blatant effort to minimalize the dead and wounded and hyphenate the Vietnam War to the "Korean Conflict," the numbers of whose dead and wounded appear just prior to the numbers of dead and wounded in Vietnam in the chronology. The government lied about the war in Vietnam the entire time it was going on and they are still using tax money to lie about it now when they re-nominalize it as the Vietnam "Conflict." Where do Americans acquire the chutzpah to object when the Japanese pretend to be uncertain who started World War II? It is not possible to hide forever under language, because language only reflects meaning, it does not contain it. "Yet who can doubt that there is an American empire? . . . richly equipped with imperial paraphernalia: troops, ships, planes, bases, proconsuls, local collaborators [satraps] all spread around the luckless planet" (Schlesinger 1986, 141). Even after Vietnam "The United States still had over a thousand military bases throughout the world" (Zinn 1980, 557). Their own *Almanac* suggests 631 in 1991.

It is the activities of the empire, the Confederate Empire of North America to be exact, that summons up the blood of the right wing and the South, which are anathema to the impulse to liberty and self determination that are at the heart of the American experiment in democracy. The siege mentality, correctly induced by the bombing of Pearl Harbor, was inappropriately extended by the Truman Doctrine to every scrap of real estate not controlled by Communists in 1947. The 1976 bicentennial of the Declaration of Independence was a more than convenient marker to just how retrograde the American Revolution had become. We are dealing with "the political judgment that a great power has the right to impose a regime of its choice, by force, in some foreign land. The system of law, so interpreted, is merely a ratification of imperialist practice" (Chomsky 1973, 220).

It is possible that the United States lost the war in Vietnam because nobody any brighter than J. Danforth Quayle could be coerced into service. It is just as likely that the war in Vietnam was lost because it was democratized eventually along the lines suggested by Darlene Fife and Robert Head, the editors and publishers of the great resistance newspaper, *Nola Express*, from New Orleans in the enlightened South. They suggested that we "create an army that takes its orders from the bottom up" (1971). Everywhere it exists, government is a crippled parody of the possible. It is especially irksome when it yokes people of radically different ideals together. While the loss of the war in Vietnam brought the Confederate ideal of continuous defense to a close on the grand active scale, the universalizing tendency of exporting the American solution to every part and parcel of the still not Communist world barely died down. "In the mid-1970s there did flicker a moment when it was thought that perhaps the CIA should not be a law unto itself — I am thinking of the Church and Pike Committees' work — but that moment was quickly extinguished, thanks in no small part to the work of then CIA director George Herbert Walker Bush" (Hitchens 1991, 62).

To confine attention to three portions of the empire, Nicaragua, Panama and Iran, will reveal what is necessary to an understanding of Carter's presidency. Two of these are rather close to home in Central America, within the sweep of empire as imagined by Jefferson Davis and actualized by Theodore Roosevelt. The third one, Iran, was yanked by Truman under the American nuclear umbrella and had its government turned inside out by Eisenhower's CIA. Iran became the defacto eastern bulwark of NATO, inasmuch as Greece and Turkey were at loggerheads over their shared ethnic island of Cyprus, and not much use to NATO. These remnants of two empires had been turned by circumstances, (and their native peasants, who, short of genocide, never go away when empires crumble), back into countries. Cyprus, once a part of either empire and now itself a disputed remnant, probably reminds the countries contending for its domination of a time when they had more power.

Even though Zinn is good for noticing such things as, speaking of multinational corporations, "in Latin America they invested $3.8 billion and made $11.3 billion in profits" (1980, 557), it is disingenuous of him to remark that by the late 70s "there was growing evidence of U.S. impotence in the world arena" (579-80). He does not see beneath his imputation of impotence the deliberate hands of Jimmy Carter in the Iranian deposition of the Shah or "in the same year in Nicaragua, the very dynasty installed by U.S. Marines before World War II was toppled by a revolutionary army, and the U.S. government seemed unable to prevent this" (580). It was not unable, it was unwilling, and that is the no longer secret of the long range Carter success.

Carter could have found support on both sides of the issues. He chose to rely on the support which indicated the correct course of action was to stop interfering. Not a bad idea in the post-Woodrow Wilson world of self determination of peoples. Wilson was himself an idealist who owed his occupation of the White House, just as Carter did, to Republican disarray. The cryptic Somoza family dictatorship had been propped up in Nicaragua with American assistance for decades, not unlike the Batista dictatorship in pre-Castro Cuba. President Carter, with steely resolve, withdrew support sufficiently from the illegitimate (unelected) family government of Somoza,

that the Sandinistas were able to overthrow it. This took political courage in
a Confederate system still blinkered by the Truman Doctrine that rewards
cooperation with any right wing dictatorship in the mistaken belief that
they are closer to ultimate American goals simply because they aren't
Communist. Fascist dictatorships, whether of the left, right or Islamic
principalities, deserve no American support. What kind of government the
Sandinistas create for themselves is only part of our business if we think of
Nicaragua as a colony. If we think of Nicaragua as a country, then the
responsibility for their type and style of government belongs with them.
One of the key elements is to adroitly withdraw support to the point that
revolutionary leadership has a chance to gel as it succeeds, rather than
rushing in with guns and voting booths and installing a "democracy." Jimmy
Carter was beginning to imagine the United States as a country dedicated
to democracy and freedom once again and unwilling to impose its power to
prop up inappropriate dictatorships.

So too in the "Republic" of Panama, where the U.S. dollar is the
currency of choice, just as it was in Saigon and apparently will be again in
Ho Chi Minh City, did Carter strive to treat the Panamanians as a
sovereign people. Carter renegotiated the Panama Canal Treaty to give
control, ownership and operations of the canal back to the Panamanians
over right wing objections to abrogating the Roosevelt imposed perpetual
sovereignty. The renegotiated treaty hardly had a smooth sail through the
U.S. Senate. Zinn sniffed that it "called for a gradual removal of U.S. bases
(which could easily be relocated elsewhere in the area)" (Zinn 1980, 556).
The Calvinist streak in American politics is very deep: you're damned if you
do, you're damned when you do, and you're damned if you don't. The treaty
was a step in the right direction, and if George Bush backtracked on it
when he invaded Panama in December of 1989, marrying himself to Jefferson
Davis and Theodore Roosevelt in the process, it can hardly be said to have
been the fault or the intention of Jimmy Carter. Even though the statue of
Lenin has been yanked down in Moscow, his belief that "treaties are made
to be broken" is alive and well. It is traditional in the United States to break
treaties, such as those made with the Indians, when they no longer suit the
purposes of power.

The 99-year English lease on the Island of Hong Kong and the Kowloon
Peninsula will be running out soon. Ninety-eight percent of the people in
Hong Kong are Chinese. The half that speak English want to migrate to

England, (being British citizens and emblematic of yet another goofy aspect of empire, the conferring of citizenship on colonial residents then being upset when they try to exercise it), uncertain of the future under a Chinese Communist thumb. Cynics observe that although the sun once never set on the British Empire, now it never rises, not realizing that the Americans are handling the empire (British) and it is still quite intact. These same cynics may not realize that English is the language of freedom and it is not retreating. The speakers of English need not fear the loss of direct control, for it is possible to lead without ruling, to inspire without intimidating, to foster nationhood without force and to teach democracy by practicing it.

Democracy was not what was being practiced in the 1970s in Iran. The Shah of Iran displayed his power unmercifully through his secret police, the SAVAK. When we think of empires coming apart at the seams, think of the Ottoman Empire, principally Turkish, that was disassembled after 600 years under British direction at the end of WWI. The Turkish province of Azerbaijan was split in two, the northern half becoming part of the former Soviet Union, and the southern half, capitol at Tabriz, became part of Iran. The Azerbaijanees in Iran were not permitted to speak Turkish, to teach it in their schools, nor to publish or write in it. They were forced instead in their public discourse to use Farsi. Farsi is an Indo-European language, made to look foreign and Semitic because it is written with the Arabic alphabet.

Once again the issue came down to: does the U.S. continue to prop up a right wing dictatorship to protect its commercial and military interests in the Persian Gulf? Carter's correct decision was to let the Shah fend for himself. Jimmy Carter was not responsible for the fact that the Shi'ite religious fanatics who replaced the Shah were incapable of rational government, nor was he responsible for their livid hatred of "The Great Satan of America" for the CIA's decades of support for the Shah. The CIA found many ways to misuse the money and its mission in Iran, not the least of which was looking at political rallies for organized opposition to the Shah. They were unaware that belief systems defy taxonomy in fundamentalist cultures where the church and the state are indistinguishable and still one. The depth of the opposition to the Shah was obscured from the CIA's limited view because it was nurtured in the mosques at Qum. It would be like looking for the basis of American belief system and religion in its Christian churches rather than at Shaw or Lackland Air Force Base.

Before we go any further, it needs to be emphasized that Iran is an empire itself, masquerading as a nation. One third of the population of Iran is made up of the aforesaid Turkish Azerbaijanees. There are several million Kurds, several million Turkomans, and several million Baluchis inside the presently Shi'ite empire of Iran. The Baluchis in southeastern Iran are separated from the Baluchis across the border in western Pakistan, with whom their national and cultural sympathies lie. Baluchistan was once a separate place, a nation, now divided and shared by Iran and Pakistan. Iran is an empire, even if on a smaller scale than the United States. So is Mexico, which is fond of complaining of the loss of northern territory to the U.S. while at the same time feeling no compunctions to let the Mayans in the provinces of Chiapas, Campeche or the Yucatan, where Mayan languages are still spoken, take a vote on whether they'd care to continue as part of the Mexican empire. The armed highland Mayans of Chiapas forced the Mexicans and the world to pay attention to the effects of NAFTA on "fourth world" peoples, if only for a moment.

When the Iranian radicals invaded the embassy in Tehran with the support of the Shi'ite leadership, they were in fact invading the United States. While Carter is to be appreciated for recognizing the legitimate aspirations of some of the people inside the captive American colony of Iran for self government, he failed to comprehend the embassy situation, which involved the United States as a nation and not as an empire. One of the structures that makes nationhood a possibility on earth is the millennia old system of diplomatic contacts even between peoples who do not always agree. People cannot expect to always agree, yet mutually beneficial relationships can arise from initial disagreements. Civilized peoples who aspire to peace have agreed on the sanctity of the diplomatic mission, that the embassy of a nation located in the capitol of the host nation, is in fact part of the visiting nation and inviolable except as an act of war and invasion.

While it is laudable that President Carter did not want any American diplomatic personnel injured or killed, his failure to move quickly and decisively to resolve the situation put all diplomatic personnel, American and others, at enormous future risk to harm. His ratification of the invasion of the American homeland in the embassy in Tehran became his Achille's Heel. It set diplomatic standards back to the Neolithic. It helped to cost him the election and the respect of a significant element in American Life.

A single strategy does not work in all applications. Had he realized that the issue was not one of America imposing power on the Iranians right to think for themselves and establish a government of their choice, no matter how ridiculous, but as one of the right to defend legitimate "national" interests, he may have come to in time to not only have rescued the hostages, but to have rescued his presidency as well. A United States continuing to act more and more like a country again, had that behavior been permitted to carry on into the early 80s, might have served as a role model for other empires set to dissolve or mend their ways, such as the former Soviet Union did under Gorbachev. In addition, the United States might not be over the brink of bankruptcy brought on by a decade plus of Reagan-Bush military sprawl.

The Soviet Union's invasion of Afghanistan has often been referred to as their "Vietnam." It is significant to keep in mind that Carter was the first active president post Lyndon Johnson's war on Vietnam, just as Gorbachev was the first active leader of the Soviet Union post their war on Afghanistan. The sobering effect of pursuing colonial wars where there is literally nothing to win beyond psychological brownie points were underlying impellers in both Carter's courageous effort to remove support from right wing dictators and Gorbachev's similar effort to deny support to left wing dictators. This realistic facing up to the inevitable music is the source of the malaise that cushy conservatives in both systems try to palm off on the population trying to get the facts straight and their uninspired power out of their own and other people's hair. Dictatorship and empire are the activities out of synch with the human heart. Carter's presidency, far from being considered a failure, is highly thought of outside the Confederate Empire of North America, in Spain, China, and elsewhere. Carter was trying to get a Gorbachevian movement off the ground 10 years ahead of Gorbachev.

The Carter efforts to foster and instill the self determination of nations in Iran, Panama and Nicaragua, may have been misunderstood and unappreciated, even in the places they were intended most specifically to help, but it hits a big nerve in the American Dream. It is not however, the biggest nerve, and Carter's thin victory over Ford "helped clear the Republican landscape for Reagan and his growing conservative army" (Germond 1989, 24). While Carter was trying to disentangle the United States from the peripheries of its empire, the Breshnev Soviet Union was still trying to aggrandize theirs. The Soviets invaded Afghanistan on December 28, 1979, making Carter's work more difficult.

Carter's work was made yet more difficult by the inept challenge to his renomination by FRK, the "Fat Rich Kid" as Teddy Kennedy got tagged by a Carter aide (Collier and Horowitz 1984, 436). Carter had responded in undiplomatic fashion when asked what he would do if Kennedy ran against him by saying "I'll whip his ass." But whip his ass he did and Kennedy limped into the convention with perhaps a third of the delegates and "smashed Carter in a speech that became his only triumph, a moment he would preserve on a long-playing record and send out as a keepsake to his remaining supporters after Ronald Reagan's victory in November" (442). Carter, like many politicians in this increasingly public and unforgiving world, frequently had his foot in his mouth at the wrong time, as far back as 1976. His "famous confession that he sometimes had lust in his heart for women other than his wife was uttered to a *Playboy* magazine journalist as he was leaving Carter's home at the conclusion of the formal interview" (Ailes 1988, 163), making more than a few of his born-again Christian supporters uneasy. A great many liberal senators were made uneasy by the growing power of the conservative reactionary Reagan and would be taken out of office at the same time as Carter. These would include Church of Idaho, McGovern of South Dakota, the arrogant Magnusson of Washington who had never lost an election, and Bayh of Indiana. The fratricide in the Democratic party is structural since they try to span the FDR-LBJ bridge of trying to be all things to all people.

Carter had been trying to scale democratic expectations down when he suggested that the government can't solve everybody's problems. It got called "Jimmy Carter's eccentric effort to carry the Democratic party back to Grover Cleveland" (Schlesinger 1986, 241). There may be more to these hundred year swatches of reversionism than meets the eyes of historical apologists for the New Deal because "Social Security, as it had evolved, had come to rest on the myth that everybody earned his or her Social Security benefits and was entitled to them. Unearned benefits severed the exacting actuarial linkage between what you put into the fund and what you got out of it. . . by 1980 Social Security had become a giant Ponzi scheme [complete with indexing, disability, dependent and spousal support]. . . Who was going to pay for it?" (Stockman 1986, 182). Whatever else he might be, David Stockman was one of the very few Americans who have ever understood how the budget process of the United States affects its economy. His success at communicating that understanding resulted in his sponsor's failure of political nerve to implement the understanding and the U.S. had *The Triumph of Politics* once again.

Conventional wisdom attributes the growth of government to Democrats but "Between 1956 and 1977, Congress passed thirteen major acts expanding or liberalizing the social insurance programs. These included creation of the disability program in 1956, Medicare in 1965, big benefit increases in the 1970s, and automatic indexing of Social Security in 1972. Over two decades an average of *80 percent* of House Republicans and *90 percent* of Senate Republicans voted for these expansions" (409). The increases in the early 1970s were put in place by Nixon to "finance" his landslide re-election. "Table 6 makes clear that the preponderant share of the growth occurred during the Nixon-Ford era. . . [and] the fact remains that all the new and expanded programs were signed into law by Nixon or Ford" (409). Something else that grew during the Carter administration was planted during Nixon's sleepwalk: inflation. Preoccupied with his personal problems, Nixon barely noticed the middle eastern war of 1973 and the resulting OPEC and Arabian oil embargo, which allowed the cartel to quadruple the price of oil. The multiplier effect of the increased price of this commodity ratcheted through the world economy and reduced the value of all other commodities and services relative to oil. The value of currency required to obtain other goods and services was denominated in oil. Raising the price of oil reduced the value of the currency. It was inflated and made worth less if not entirely worthless.

Inflation had become the rage of 1980 at 13 percent with interest rates heading for 21 trying to keep pace. It seemed like a good time to warm up some Republican horseshit about balanced budgets. "It wasn't a bad idea, but only if you *balanced down*, and didn't leave the spending levels built in. . . The Carter Administration had gotten the balanced budget religion, too. But it was proposing to *balance up*" (52). It wasn't hard to find the source and get the religious message in the balanced budget religion. The prophet Reagan had rapped the rubber chicken circuit into a coma for the better part of two decades railing about the disastrous consequences of deficit spending. Then too, some people became fascinated "watching the grim footage of the charred remains of the U.S. servicemen being desecrated by the Iranian mullahs at the site known as Desert One" (107).

The 1980 election came close to being as interesting as 1860 or 1948, but it missed the four candidate requirement for a real train wreck by one. Congressman John Anderson of Illinois was unable to wrest the Republican nomination from Reagan and ran independently. It can never be known exactly which or how many of his several million votes were siphoned from Carter or Reagan. While some Carter administration officials were getting comfortable with the notion that Americans and the human race might have reached an age of limits, "when Ronald Reagan ran for the presidency, he made his shrillest attacks on the idea that we might be living in an 'age of limits'" (McKibbon 1989, 197). The Democratic party problem of trying to span too wide an arc of the political population is not shared by the narrowly focused Republicans. And while Carter was unable to convince the Democrats to revert to the days of Grover Cleveland, Reagan, as Schlesinger cynically suggests, had a much easier time of it returning the Republican party to the days of Calvin Coolidge. To begin with, it wasn't that far, temporally, nor has it ever been very far from the core of the modern Republican party. The Republican tax cuts by Harding in 1920 and those under Reagan in 1981-1986 were similar almost to the exact percentages and both designed to reward speculation. The white Republican party platform only has one plank with many splinters: how can we keep the money we have and expand it as fast as possible.

"Before and during the Civil War nonslaveholding whites had generally defended slavery — even with their lives — partly at least because the inferior status of slaves minimized the competition between whites and blacks and provided every white an unquestioned touchstone of superiority no matter how mean or abject his situation. After the war the similarity of their situations transformed the whites' proslavery sentiments into an open hostility toward the black population" (Ransom and Sutch 1977, 105). The Neo-Confederate triumph of the Republican party, as one by one southern conservatives, such as Strom Thurmond of South Carolina, Ronald Reagan of California, and John Connally of Texas, deserted the Democratic party, is based on organizing this racist hostility North and South and transforming it into votes.

They had thrown their weight to Eisenhower and Nixon in a process that had the gradual effect of making Republicanism respectable in the South. They would carry Texas in 1980 and, once again with two Southerners running, the "solid" South would be split up. "Carter's loss of the South to a California conservative illustrates the Democrats' difficulty in implementing their southern strategy" (Black and Black 1992, 337). It also illustrates the confining choice between two types of Southerners. It was Barry Goldwater's bold and temporarily unsuccessful stroke that kept the glue in the Neo-Confederate revolution hot for the thin but effective Reagan victory, 50.7 percent of the popular vote, that put an end to the anomalous administration of Jimmy Carter.

19

Ronald Reagan: Confederate Pony in Nicaragua

The administration of Ronald Reagan was the largest unmitigated financial disaster in American history, with many of the consequences tossed like time bombs into the children's future. Ronald Reagan began his political life in the United States in the Democratic party of Harry Truman, a staunch believer in the efficacy of the Truman Doctrine of containing communism. He retired from the presidency 40-some odd years later as a Republican without having moved so much as a single degree on the political compass. His administration was characterized by a reintensification of class warfare, extravagant military expenditures, and a plethora of tax and monetary mirages designed to shore up what he took to be the dwindling of the Confederate Empire of North America under Jimmy Carter. While many of his moves to save the empire occurred in the Caribbean in Grenada and especially Nicaragua, a pre-Civil War southern favorite where they spilled over into neighboring Honduras and El Salvador, they were by no means confined to the Western Hemisphere. He revived the holy war mentality of Eisenhower's Secretary of State John Foster Dulles, with his tilting at the windmills of the "evil" empire of the Soviet Union. Reagan's entire program was made possible through the use of sophisticated electronic demagoguery developed by the Mormon Richard Wirthlin. A perennial optimist, chapter 19 is a search for Ronald Reagan's lost Confederate pony, for as he used to say in one of his favorite jokes, with all this horseshit around there's got to be pony in here someplace.

The opportunities for and the temptation to sarcasm are enormous, for ironies abound in Ronald Reagan's administration and career. It would have been one thing if the computer demagoguery had been used merely to cinch up his election over Carter (and his subsequent re-election over Mondale), but "Now the strategist had a grand secret concept for a computer program to guide and help drive the Presidency" (Perry 1984, 164). War was hell in Hollywood during WWII on the sound stages at the backlot of Universal International Studios in Hollywood where Reagan became a veteran of the imaginary military experience. D. W. Griffith's 1915 racist movie, *The Birth of a Nation*, had helped turn Hollywood into the movie capitol of the world in service to the people of the picture, one more critical ingredient as the fulcrum tipped its balance of power away from San Francisco toward Los Angeles and California became a southern state. It was hardly a coincidence that "Louis B. Mayer, head of MGM, was Finance Chairman of the Republican Party's enormous campaign chest" (DeMarco 1988, 133). Filmmakers like Mayer fictionalized the American military experience and made religious icons out of actually decorated war heroes like Audie Murphy, a cotton farmer from Texas, as well as imaginary heroes of war like Ronald Reagan.

Dubious military resumes and the search for the proper image in American politics hardly commenced with Ronald Reagan. In Clifford Dowdy's work on *The Great Plantation*, we find William Henry Harrison "Not merely identifying himself with the people, [but] he made a presidential campaign issue of his presumed folksiness and, passing himself off as a denizen of log cabins, introduced into presidential elections the campaign carnival" (1957, 302). Old Tippecanoe (and Tyler Too) as the 1840 campaign theme emphasized, at least got his wings fighting actual Indians such as Tecumseh (Shooting Star) in the Battle of Fallen Timbers at the behest of Thomas Jefferson. American school children are taught to think of Lincoln as the first presidential inhabitant of a log cabin, but Harrison got there first. ". . . — Just as his campaign featured a log cabin, hard cider and the 'Same Old Coon' song in place of a platform. In all truth, his election was a triumph for the kind of campaigning that would change forever the use of the voting franchise in America. . . the sixty-eight-year-old front man of a political party" (305). It is easy to see how we could get the impression that American political history is rotating backwards like the visuals of wagon train wheels crossing the plains for the folksy Ronald Reagan, the host of *Death Valley Days*, had deliberately turned himself into the front man of the Republican party.

Reagan was a very congenial guy and he got a lot of help. Raymond K. Price, in 1968, describing the necessary emotional leap that has been basic to Republicanism since 1856-60 said: "'It's not the man we have to change, but rather the *received impression*'" (McGinnis 1969, 30-1). Price was speaking of Nixon of course, but the received impression (his italics) was precisely where Richard Wirthlin acquired the *Hidden Power* described in Roland Perry's book of the same name. When Reagan lost the 1976 Republican nomination to incumbent Gerald Ford, the fallout in the Reagan camp settled into two schools. One school, headed by his campaign director John Sears, bought into the Ford line that "Nobody any more conservative than me can ever be elected president." Therefore "Sears was challenged by the opportunity of directing Reagan more toward a centrist position" (Perry 1984, 70). Wirthlin, who was comfortable with Reagan's right wing ideology, had a better idea: he would change the way Reagan was perceived. "Under Sears, there would be a new Reagan. Under Wirthlin, true Reaganism would be given an acceptable face" (71). Knowing by the use of internal evidence that Reagan never changed from the 1940s to the 1990s, it is clear who won this argument in the Reagan camp, and what strategies prevailed in the electoral victory.

The conservative position in American and other politics is well known and was aptly described almost a hundred years earlier by Thorstein Veblen. "The office of the leisure class in social evolution is to retard the movement and to conserve what is obsolescent" (1931, 198). The social retards in the Republican party, just as their precursors in the capitalist slaveholding South before them, had access to tons of money. At almost the moment Veblen was first publishing *The Theory of the Leisure Class* in 1899, the 1900 election, a rerun of the 1896 election between William Jennings Bryan and William McKinley, showed that the Democrats had spent one cent per received vote and the Republicans had spent one dollar per Republican vote "including those that were virtually assured" (Wilson 1970, 228). It takes money to bend the political opinions of Americans and warp the outcome then and now if the sham is to be believable as the will of the people.

Except for Georgia, the least Confederate of all southern states and the home of Jimmy Carter, Reagan dominated the South as completely as Goldwater did plus adding to his totals the electoral votes of Florida and Texas. Appeal to racist sentiment in the South was only half the strategy however for the permanent Republican opportunity was and "can be organized generally out of racial fear, by a forthright Republican abandonment of all seeking of Negro votes in the North" (White 1988, 360). The Politician Information System or PINS, developed by Richard Wirthlin, was a two-faced Mormon Axe, sharp on both blades. The racial bias of the Reagan Republicans, *adios* Lincoln, was shared by the Mormons. "Not surprisingly, the two faiths — in the PINS technology and the Mormon Church — became inextricably bound in 1980, because Ronald Reagan, described by a senior Latter-Day Saint as a 'Mormon in heart and mind,' believed in the same political doctrines as they did. They wanted American to be right-wing and conservative in most matters, particularly military" (Perry 1984, 100).

Roland Perry's not well enough known but seminal classic *Hidden Power*, The Programming of the President, recites the basic PINS program, much condensed here. It has five main elements, survey data, fixed demographic adjustments of that data, historical voting information, assessment of Republican strengths almost to the precinct level, with the addition of the collective political judgment of recognized experts (100-102). This permits the PINS program, or whoever is operating it, to fine tune and adjust the throw weight of "received impressions" to precisely the right degree to get the issue or the candidate into majority territory wherever it is required and thus its characterization as electronic demagoguery. In a pious homily touting his autobiography *An American Life* in *Publisher's Weekly*, Reagan reassures us that Simon and Shuster's publication of his book "provides me with the opportunity to tell my story in a way that is as direct and honest as possible" (1990, 41). As direct and honest as Reagan could find possible is not very useful to discovering the real effect of his policies, reflected in the book's modest sales, for honest is not an analog word or a comparative adjective. It is digital; you are either honest or you aren't. And while it is wonderful that politicians take the trouble from time to time to try to explain themselves, Reagan was a practitioner of Truman's fine art of delib- erate misunderstanding with Eisenhower's gift for obfuscation. Having briefly noticed how he acquired power, what did he want it for and what did he do with it?

It is significant that Kevin Phillips in *Boiling Point* used the word "theology" when he argued "that capitalist-conservative theology eventually trespassed on middle-class psychology in several counterproductive ways" (1993, 50). It was apparent in Reagan's remarks at the dedication of the Reagan Presidential Library in Simi Valley, California, as broadcast on multiple TV channels, that his agenda was religious. Not that he was completely co-opted by the Mormons in his employ, but his language on that day was replete with admonitions to "keep the faith" with words like "prophet" and phrases like "sacred fire." This only refers in the most tangential way to the Christian religion, for the primary use even the Mormon's felt like they could put Reagan to was military. "Most mid-Victorians preferred, like Kingsley as he cried tears of pride during the Great Exhibition at the Crystal Palace in 1851, to believe that a cosmic destiny was at work" (Kennedy 1987, 158). It was the cosmic Manifest Destiny of America that was Reagan's true religion. "The Reagan adminis-tration represented a mighty comeback of messianism in foreign policy" (Schlesinger 1986, 55). While this messianism took several provocative turns, its overarching manifestation was that "In the age of Ronald Reagan, the official American version of the Cold War regressed. . . back to the holy war of John Foster Dulles" (193). This regression back to keeping the Cold War holy, the world free from Communism, the British Empire intact, and the Confederate empire in the Caribbean together, as befit the policies espoused by Confederate leaders like Jefferson Davis, demonstrated the Reagan difference. "The vital difference between the early republic and the Imperial Presidency resides not in what Presidents did but in what Presidents believed they had the inherent right to do. . . In the use of the war-making power, Reagan was a stout defender of the 'almost royal' prerogatives" (297).

The nearly royal nature of Reagan's conception of his military power puts him in the line of English kings and at cross purposes with the best intentions of at least some of the founders of American democracy. The notion of the president as commander in chief originated as we have seen with Charles Pinckney of South Carolina and may have been intended to apply most pertinently to defensive situations. It was South Carolinian style to "Trust those men with unusually wide powers" (Weir 1973, 326), and South Carolinian style was the royal British style, barely once removed. With the Cold War putting the southern dominated American government in a perpetually perceived defensive situation recapitulating their heyday as the Confederate States of America, Reagan had no compunctions about ordering the Marines into Lebanon, a la Eisenhower, strafing Quadaffi, and launching a war on Grenada, all without congressional approval. For Reagan and other politicians who behave like monarchs, "Law becomes, not a tool, but a burden, and actuality marches on, not with, but apart from legal history" (Spengler 1928, 82).

Law, national or international, was only a burden for the circumspect Jefferson Davis in the 1850s southern drive for Caribbean colonies. "Virtu-ally every year up to the Civil War, American adventurers would formulate schemes to invade, or would actually invade, some part of the Caribbean region" (May 1973, 29). While that may sound like ancient history, hardly a year went by in the 20th century when the United States did not invade some part of Latin America. Ronald Reagan would hector the Sandinista government of Nicaragua virtually every day he was in office. William Walker, who was supported more in the South than in the North, issued "calls for a slave 'empire' throughout tropical America and defends slavery as a 'positive good' with logic befitting John Calhoun" (113). Walker revved the South up on its need to project its problems and expand the slave empire to the degree that "The influential *De Bow's Review*, for instance, had predicted that Walker's activities would lead to the annexation of all Central America to the United States" (109). While Walker's activities may not have lead directly to control of the Caribbean Basin by the United States, by the time of Richard Olney, Cleveland's Secretary of State, practical American sovereignty was established and clearly demonstrated in the Spanish American War with Theodore Roosevelt's later "taking" of the Isthmus of Panama as icing on the imperial cake.

It was the interruption in American sovereignty that was motivating Reagan in Nicaragua, just as it had motivated the CIA and NSC under Eisenhower/Kennedy in Cuba. Nicaragua was apparently particularly irksome to the Reaganauts because it was where the anomalous work of Jimmy Carter at dismantling the empire and the typically American satrapy of the Somoza family had scored a genuine triumph. To return to the Walker history for a moment for only the insight that the right feedback loop can show us, "The New York *Evening Post* termed his achievements part of the 'irresistible law of modern colonization'" (78). It was modern colonization in 1854 and modern colonization in 1989. William Walker made Jefferson Davis uneasy, but it was a dispute over tactics rather than strategy for "Federal authorities in San Francisco, under instructions from Jefferson Davis, arrested Walker's agents" (83-4). This occurred after Walker had captured La Paz in *Baja* California, declared a republic of Lower California, and annexed Sonora. Davis was working diplomatically for the same goals and would undoubtedly have preferred, if it had to be a military operation, some actual military under his supervision as Secretary of War, rather than the free-lance colonizer Walker, referred to as a "filibusterer" in the 19th century.

That Walker was something of a loose screw or "loose cannon" can be seen in the fact that "In a little over a year Walker would be posing as a champion of the southern slave system and would describe his expedition as an instrument of the expansion of slavery" (90). Walker's original intention had been personal empowerment — everybody should have their own empire — for in "defying the flow of history, he reinstituted slavery in Nicaragua" (106). Walker's political expediency in dressing up his intention in clothes suitable to the South where he received the most intense response "all added up to a nineteenth century version of the banquet circuit" (126). This was the same banquet circuit that the latter-day Confederate Reagan would rap his gums numb on, inviting people to be afraid of Nicaragua because it is only a two days drive from southern Texas. The cowboy Marine Colonel Oliver North, used by Reagan as a cat's-paw and then cut loose to "twist slowly in the wind," hit the banquet trail himself. The comic opera aspects of both the Walker and Reagan capers in Nicaragua might best be summed up in the phrase "Mixed Pickles" (131) which is how Walker had the ammunition he had shipped to Nicaragua labeled.

The right label for Reagan's ultimate unmasking in the Iran-Contra affair is treason. His political operatives sold guns to the Ayatollah of Iran, "aid and comfort to the 'enemy,'" and used the money to circumvent congressional bans on military aid to the Reagan sponsored counter-revolutionaries in Nicaragua. "A renascent CIA launched a secret (or not so) secret war against Nicaragua" (Schlesinger 1986, 84). This war on Nicaragua, as well as the sneak attack on Grenada, violated the Neutrality Act, congressional prohibitions, OAS nonintervention pledges, the UN Charter, to name just a few of the treaties, laws, and agreements violated by this behavior. This is the same Arthur Schlesinger who maintains that the conservative as well as the democratic nationalist presidents adhere to the constitutional rule of law. "When the CIA set out to overthrow the government in Managua, Washington expressed indignation that this government dared seek arms to defend itself" (60). Colonies that stay in line are more in keeping with a seemly empire. Those who fight back for independence have to be resisted in the curious marriage of convenience the upshot of the Civil War saddled the American people with. From the northern point of view, everybody trying to get out of the empire must be brought back under force of arms if necessary. Since the South was now operating that empire and in virtual control of all the arms, why indeed not bring everybody back in who might want out. The Reagan corollary expressed itself in "Washington's present disposition in Central America. . . to globalize the stakes and to militarize the remedy" (60). This had to be religious war for Schlesinger can give the horselaugh to the economic interpretaion. "Foreign markets hardly seemed the object: the vast markets of Nicaragua?" (136).

While Ronald Reagan was raising money on the side for the clandestine financing of his war on Nicaragua, he was raising money out of the middle class with a tax cut for the wealthy. There are many aspects of Ronald Reagan that seem original, but in almost all cases he reverts to type. The Republican tax cut under Harding after World War I, for example, "provided for the repeal of the excess profits tax and the reduction of taxes on large incomes from a maximum of 65 per cent to a maximum of 40 per cent for 1921, and thereafter 33 percent. This was exactly the type of issue Bryan had been waiting for" (Levine 1965, 190). It is also a reduction to almost exactly the same percentages for the wealthy of the tax "reform" of 1986. Kevin Phillips is eloquent on both the timing and the typicality when he notes that "during these years, the top income tax rate on the richest Americans fell from 91 to 31 percent while the burden on the average household soared" (1993, 107). The predictable effect was that "the top 1 percent of Americans of the 1980s had reassumed the place they had held in the 1880s and 1920s in a restored conservative fiscal theology" (114). Whether or when the tax cuts for the wealthy in the 80s will lead to as prolonged and severe a depression as the tax cuts of the 20s did remains to be seen. The tax cuts in both decades led to rampant speculation reminiscent of the antebellum South. In Colonial Virginia, "There was a tacit agreement, however, that no faction would expose the peculations of another as long as the private gain was made at the expense of the public domain" (Dowdy 1957, 110). How both ancient and modern it is.

Making private gains at public expense is one of the Hamiltonian effects in the United States for "His tontine scheme, fashioned after the British tontine of 1789, involved a system of rights of annual payments to survivors, the annuities therefrom becoming the means of creating a permanent investment class" (Bourgin 1989, 83). The permanent investment class and the class warfare nature of the Reagan policies contradicts nothing in Calhoun's division of classes into tax payers and tax consumers (1931, 21). Calhoun noticed this aspect of class war in the relationship between the Patricians and the Plebeians in the Roman Empire. "They were impoverished, and forced, from necessity, to borrow from the patricians, at usurious and exorbitant interest, funds with which they had been enriched through their blood and toil; and to pledge their all for repayment at stipulated periods" (93). If the Roman example seems too remote for ready assimilation, Calhoun's description of the effect of kings and privilege on English finance and interests is most telling. "The most powerful interest, all things considered, under every form of government in all civilized communities, — *the tax-consuming interest*; or, more broadly, the great interest which necessarily grows out of the action of the government, be its form what it may; — the interest that *lives by the government*" (102). The italics here are all Calhoun's and the Reagan patronage of the class that lives by the government took two forms: lower taxes for the wealthy so they might speculate and consume more; and the direction of those taxes actually collected toward an aggrandizement of military activity. The short circuits in this feedback loop, properly invested in military stocks, could make the astute wealthy who used the same money twice, a double skim as contrasted with the double dip.

The cost benefit analysis of the empire, where literally everyone is encouraged in the belief that we are all in this together, is provided by Noam Chomsky. "The costs of empire are in general distributed over the society as a whole, while its profits revert to a few within. In this respect, the empire serves as a device for internal consolidation of power and privilege" (1973, 47). The empire is operated, in other words, for the rich; the poor merely stand and serve.

All the funny numbers aren't in the skewing of the tax code to benefit the rich however, and "The CIA's annual *Handbook of Economic Statistics* is a perfect example, and its 1989 edition makes for wonderful reading. My favorite number is the one putting the annual rate of growth in the U.S.S.R. during 1981-1985 at 1.9 percent, significantly above the rate for those years in Western Europe. The CIA also cooked up the idea that the per capita GNP of East Germany was greater in the 1980s than that of West Germany — the agency's numbers are right there in the 1989 edition of the *Statistical Abstract of the United States*. . . the target here was the American lawmaker and, through him, the American taxpayer" (Hitchens 1991, 62). You get what you pay for is a popular phrase in contemporary America and in this case it is apparent that Reagan was paying the CIA for numbers he could use to magnify the dangers in the putative security situation. Targeting the taxpayer, a good military metaphor, with phony numbers inflating Communist economic prowess was one handy way to keep the imaginary notion of the "evil" empire alive. "No aspect of this threat is more apparent than the way genuine national security requirements have been allowed to serve as the occasion for an assault on the wealth of the American People" (Cousins 1987, 24). The greater the imaginary threat can be made to appear, the greater the assault that can be made on all the people's wealth for the benefit of the absolutely rich. "What the American people were buying was not so much a program for the defense of the United States as a system for funneling massive public funds to private contractors. . . Grassley, Republican Senator from Iowa, was puzzled when the President failed to demonstrate equal outrage over far more consequential evidence of waste and fraud in military spending" (99). Grassley, in his naiveté, apparently failed to grasp that the primary purpose of empire is to make the powerful class more powerful at national expense.

The work of Kevin Phillips documents just how much the power of this class was augmented during the early 80s and is apparent in IRS statistics as reported by the Associated Press. "Americans with assets of at least $500,000 make up only 1.6 percent of the population but own nearly 28.5 percent of the nation's personal wealth. The 3.3 million richest Americans had holdings in 1986 of $4.3 trillion, with a net worth of 3.8 trillion — almost enough to finance the entire federal budget for four years." These are impressive numbers for 1986 but they acquire additional significance when contrasted with the numbers for 1982, four years earlier when there were only 2.2 million individuals with assets of at least $500,000 and their share of the wealth was 23 percent. The rich get richer and the poor get experience.

General Otis of the Los Angeles *Times* organized the class war in southern California, Ronald Reagan's home base, and "Political power in Southern California remains organized by great constellations of private capital, which, as elsewhere, act as the permanent government in local affairs" (Davis 1990, 102). This great money of the permanent investment class didn't pile up in Southern California and elsewhere by chance. "First, the inter-regional capital flows that had been the source of Southern California's prosperity were now institutionalized in national defense appropriations that shifted tax resources from the rest of the country to irrigate the Los Angeles area's aircraft plants and military bases: a huge regional subsidy that in later years was estimated to average $17-20 billion per annum" (120). These numbers are taken from the Committee on State

Finance and its published document "The Impact of Federal Expenditures on California, 1986." The practice of moving large blocks of money from the nation as a whole to selected military establishments such as those in South Carolina, Texas, and Southern California, provides the cash for the mill of peculation.

While Veblen could say "It is by no means here intended to depreciate the economic function of the propertied class or of the captains of industry," possibly because he was publishing in 1899 at an earlier peak of imperial expansion, he had already stated that "The relation of the leisure (that is, propertied non-industrial) class to the economic process is a pecuniary relation — a relation of acquisition, not of production; of exploitation, not of serviceability" (1931, 209). The relationship is utterly parasitic in a word, and it reached extreme proportions under the Reagan Doctrine of make the rich richer. The operation of the prosperity mirage of the 1980s also had precursors in the antebellum South of the 1850s and the speculation in the so-called "roaring" 20s that ushered in the Great Depression. The New Deal attempts by FDR to deal with the depression were like a nationwide Reconstruction period. The cotton South could never recover that "prosperity," just as it will slip away from post-Reagan America, and the distinguished economist Gavin Wright can say "And would the 'desert mirage' have been any nearer for American slaveholders in the 1860s had the war and the famine never occurred?" (1978, 97). While the North tried to adapt agriculture to mechanized implements to address the cost of labor, the South had no reason to adapt. Using the internal religious logic of Reagan, neither did the United States in the 1980s have any reason to adapt. They were going to irrigate the wealthy in a technological changeout of such proportions they would bankrupt the Soviet Union, which was falling apart on its own lack of steam and not doing anywhere near as well as the funny numbers from the CIA would have had us believe, and as a result bankrupted themselves. The real unraveling of the Soviet Union probably took place on lines of force first identified by Marshall McLuhan as he noticed that ". . . society begins to look like a linguistic echo or repeat of language norms, a fact that has disturbed the Russian Communist party very deeply. . . nothing could be more subversive of the Marxian dialectic than the idea that linguistic media shape social development, as much as do the means of production" (1964, 49). In other words, the Reagan money gusher was a redundant irrelevancy at the linguistic end of the Cold War. The

speculation at the heart of slaveholding (142) is the fiscal equal to the speculation at the heart of holding stock in the military-industrial complex and
benefits the same class of people.

The shifting of tax consumption toward the wealthy has its comic
aspects as with UDAG, the Urban Development Action Grant, essentially
an anti-poverty agency but where "Four years later the Reagan Administration would be able to tell the American taxpayers with pride that their hard
work had gone toward the construction of twelve new Hilton Hotels, six
Hyatts, five Marriotts, four Sheratons, two Ramadas, one Albert Pick, and
a Stouffers. . . in a pear tree" (Stockman 1986, 143). The Christmasy and
Santa Claus metaphor of the Reagan Administration carrying gifts toward
the rich was reaffirmed in the Defense Department where "Weinberger was
doggedly pushing up defense outlays from $133 billion in 1980 to $377
billion in 1988 — a one-quarter trillion dollar budget increase in just eight
years" (371). Casper Weinberger was known as Cap the Knife, God knows
why, a sobriquet he acquired working for Reagan when Reagan was Governor of California and increased spending tremendously. He will become
better known as Cap the Shovel.

Reagan's willful acts of misunderstanding included a belief that "He
thought the coming economic recovery would drastically shrink the deficit
numbers by 1987 or 1988. Never mind that the briefing book already showed
that these numbers were based on a booming recovery beginning in 1983
and lasting through the end of the decade" (359). Just how powerful this
economic boom would have to be to balance the budget, where doubters
were accused of "displaying inadequate faith [a word we find frequently in
discussions of Reaganomics] in economic growth. . . The eyeshades had
based their estimates on our new economic forecast, which projected *twenty
straight quarters* of 4 percent real growth" (364). That kind of growth could
only happen in the movies or at the secret CIA, but the wishful, its hard to
call it thinking, desire for the impossible to become true already showed
that "The 1983 deficit had now already come in at $208 billion. . . Not to
raise taxes when all other avenues were closed was a willful act of ignorance
and grotesque irresponsibility. In the entire twentieth-century fiscal history
of the nation there has been nothing to rival it" (373). It is a mistake to
dismiss the accurate evaluation of David Stockman, the former director of
Reagan's Office of Budget and Management, as simply sour grapes.
Stockman came as close as anybody ever will to understanding the budget

of the United States. His mistake, not unlike that of John Sears, was in imagining that he could take rigid simple Ronald Reagan in any direction Reagan didn't want to go.

Where the Confederate Empire of North America was headed under Reagan can be seen and sensed in congressional complicity to his "leadership." Congressional complicity did not come easy as "James Baker had directed a highpowered lobby which entailed a combination of personal cajoling, patriotic pleading, some old-fashioned horse trading and tough political pressure" (Perry 1984, 178). James Baker, an attorney from Houston, Reagan's chief of staff and later Secretary of the Treasury, was using his power in this instance to make Republican Senator Jepsen from Iowa cry and vote for an $8 billion dollar AWACS sale to Saudi Arabia. Baker, the rich Texan, ultimately became the most powerful person in Reagan's administration, even though he was not a California insider, and kept that power as George Bush's Secretary of State. "Controversy over any tax measure in the British Parliament was invariably accompanied by the presentation of accounts, reports and papers to the lower house. . . — all of this information was available to the legislature. Many MPs, of course, paid little attention to the figures and fine print and even fewer probably knew how to interpret them. But such papers were accepted as reasonably accurate and as the basis on which policy should be made" (Brewer 1989, 130). Although Brewer was describing the British Parliament during the 18th century rise of the English speaking empire, it fits as a working description of the houses of the American Congress. Such sloppy legislating where representatives routinely vote for and against bills they've never even read, much less understood, does not bode well for the long-term vitality of the English speaking civilization. Even Reagan's admiration and insistence on the line item veto and the balanced budget amendment, two bedrock items in the Constitution of the Confederate States of America, would not help.

The fiscal irresponsibility of the Reagan Administration really got off the ground with the passage of the Garn-St. Germain bill to deregulate the banks when he said "It looks like we've finally hit the jackpot." Truer words of a speculator, through the gambler's panache, have never been spoken. They had already early on shot through the Tax Reform Act of 1981, which gave real estate developers nationwide the ACRS (Accelerated Cost Recovery System) where the former double declining depreciation allowances were made even more lucrative and extended to all developed real estate. The ultimate result of ACRS was the utter and complete uneconomic over building of commercial real estate throughout the United States, to the benefit of a few rich developers and bankers, a picture window on the Savings and Loan debacle.

But it is in its similarities to the rise and fall of the British Empire that the Confederate Empire of North America bears its closest resemblances. There too, "The science of political arithmetic promised much more than it could deliver" (224), just as the imaginary chickens in the Laffer Curve of Reagan growth never came home to roost. Relying on the chimera of economic growth to bail them out was futile practice. "Indeed, O'Brien argues that economic growth comes a poor third to the imposition of new taxes and the introduction of higher rates on existing taxes as an explana-tion for greater aggregate revenues" (100). Realistic men raise taxes and rates when they need more revenue; unrealistic men raise the debt. "The solution to this problem, one that was adopted by almost all administra-tions towards the end of a war or shortly after the declaration of peace, was to convert the short-term liability into a long-term funded debt" (116), where not so incidentally, it would benefit the investing class. This process has been with the speakers of English for a long time as "By the 1670s, goldsmith bankers like Blackwell and Vyner — who together were owed 645,000 pounds by Charles II — were assigning the interest on the royal debt to their creditors, thereby involving their depositors in what we might call the precursor of the national debt" (207). Indeed it was the precursor of the national debt and it wasn't the only thing Charles II lent his good name to, for the Lord's Proprietors he chartered to South Carolina in the Indies named their capitol after him as Charles Town.

The similarities hardly end there and included the fact that "The single most important task of this bureaucracy was to raise money. . . no matter how sophisticated the mechanism or means, the state's ability to borrow was contingent upon the belief among its creditors that it had the capacity and determination to meet its payments" (88). While the Reagan bureau-cracy raised a lot of money, it was never enough to pay for all the legislation he signed, and although "Britain was able to shoulder an ever-more ponderous burden of military commitments thanks to a radical increase in taxation, the development of public deficit finance (a national debt) on an unprecedented scale, and the growth of a sizable public administration devoted to organizing the fiscal and military activities of the state" (xvii), the Reagan Administration inherited the sizable public administration but deleted any significant increase in taxes, preferring to reduce them.

In a section called "War, Money, and the Nation-State," Paul Kennedy points out that "Above all it was war — and especially the new techniques which favored the growth of infantry armies and expensive fortifications and fleets — which impelled belligerent states to spend more money than every before, and to seek out a corresponding amount in revenues" (1987, 70-1). The accelerated technological changeout in the Reagan United States certainly caused his administration to spend more money than ever before, even as it chose to funnel potential revenue to pay for it directly to the rich in the form of tax cuts. Neither was it getting all that many bangs for its bucks as "the fact that the Reagan administration in its first term spent over 75 percent more on new aircraft than the Carter regime but acquired only 9 percent more planes points to *the* appalling military-procurement problem of the late twentieth century" (522). It also is heavily suggestive of the fact that the primary Republican intention was irrigating the military complex rather than providing for the common defense, in their imaginary and rhetorical war with the Soviet Union, for except for the postage stamp sized war on Grenada and an occasional strafing of Quadaffi, the Air Force was barely used in Reagan's Administration. "Historically, the only other example which comes to mind of a Great Power so increasing its indebtedness in *peacetime* is France in the 1780s, where the fiscal crisis contributed to the domestic political crisis" (527). It also contributed to the rise of Napoleon and the subsequent British victories over him which ushered in English speaking hegemony over much of the world and put Western European Civilization on the slope of Spenglarian decline. You don't have to take the word of a heavy German fatalist for it if you find the more modern Cassandra of Kevin Phillips more appealing: "And since 1815, when the duke of Wellington disposed of Napoleon at Waterloo, essentially the same ideological combination has dominated world affairs, under the successive flags of Britain and the United States" (1994, 139).

The ultimate consequences for the United States, who made the basket catch of the British Empire in 1947, will be severe. "In the first place, given the worldwide array of military liabilities which the United States has assumed since 1945, its capacity to carry those burdens is obviously less than it was several decades ago, when its share of global manufacturing and GNP was much larger, its agriculture not in crisis, its balance of payments was far healthier, the government budget was also in balance, and it was not so heavily in debt to the rest of the world" (Kennedy 1987, 529). All of these tendencies were acutely exacerbated by the bankrupting policies of Ronald Reagan.

Much before the self-induced collapse of the Soviet Union, in the "Conclusions and Recommendations" section of a publication called *Deterring through the Turn of the Century*, the results of the Discussion Group on Strategic Policy initially co-chaired by Brent Scowcroft, who would become the National Security advisor to President Bush, and published jointly by the Johns Hopkins Foreign Policy Institute and the Center for Strategic and International Studies in Washington, D.C., we discover the rationale for these policies. In a ponderous discussion of ICBM modernization, Midgetman and MX missiles, Trident submarines and B-1 bombers, their conclusion is: "For the foreseeable future U.S. security must continue to rest on deterrence and offensive forces; there is no near-term alternative" (Brown 1989, 19). When you imagine there is no alternative, then there is no alternative. The American defense establishment is an imaginary, self-fulfilling prophecy and is as worthless as the Maginot Line.

The capital requirements of war, to say nothing of the fact that war destroys capital, it does not make it grow, are easy to underestimate if war is your religion. Nothing is too good for what we believe. "The total fixed capital required to form a large navy was therefore enormous" (Brewer 1989, 34-5). Exactly how enormous can be seen in the facts that Brewer goes on to recite that the other largest capital intensive activity in England during the rise of the empire, the woolen industry and mills, required "a mere 18 per cent of the fixed capital required to launch the British Navy" (35). In England from 1688 until the end of the American Revolutionary War, a period also known as the Second Hundred Years War, "In less than a century the unredeemed debt had increased fifteenfold in current prices" (114). Reagan accelerated this aspect of the crippling paralysis of empire also as in his mere eight years in office, the national debt, we should say "empirational" debt, of the United States tripled to the point where interest on the debt is the largest item in the budget as well as a continuous source of comfort to the idle rich.

During one lull in the Second Hundred Years War, in 1763 after the French and Indian War in North America, some reality set in. "After 1763 it was feared that the cost of servicing the debt had outstripped the nation's capacity to raise taxes and that a national bankruptcy might ensue" (124). Such fears are common shoptalk in the post-Reagan United States. Brewer's conclusion to his study of the fiscal basis of the rise of the British Empire, to say nothing of the entire book *The Sinews of Power,* could be read with benefit by anyone concerned over the fate of the United States, for he could nearly as easily be describing the Reagan effect on the United States. "These interests struggled to understand, subjugate or exploit the fiscal-military juggernaut that emerged, through the collision of conflicting forces, after 1688. They tried to do so by one of two, somewhat contradictory, processes: on the one hand, by circumscribing the state's power; on the other, by colonizing the state in order to gain control of its resources" (251). Ronald Reagan did both and cheerfully passed the White House and the accumulating unsolved problems (which will wind up in the hands of the disenfranchised youth who have been successfully colonized by this geriatric theocracy) along to his successor, who was equally disinclined and ill-equipped to cope with them. "The sinews of War are infinite money" according to the epigraph from Cicero's Orationes Philippicae. The Confederate Empire of North America no longer has access to infinite money, having lost the economic consequences of World War II to Germany and Japan respectively. The consequences for the practice of this religion will be with us shortly. The children of North America deserve to be told the truth that there is no pony in this pile of horseshit; Ronald Reagan is a thief.

20

George Bush: Voodoo Economic Transparency

George Bush colonized Texas politics for the Republicans based on his magnetic instincts for power. A Confederate Yankee from Massachusetts and Yale, it didn't take long for Bush to shed his Ivy League trappings. The imperial tradition of going south and becoming one of them did not originate with Bush. "John Quitman was one of the more prominent Americans who quickly discarded loyalty to his original state and section" (May 1973, 46). General Quitman was the man with tons of Texas help who would have invaded Cuba in the 1850s if he had just been able to get Franklin Pierce, Jefferson Davis and the rest of the government off his back. Bush became a Texas Southerner and acquired political control of the Republican party. Texas lacks an income tax, and Bush used to maintain his permanent address in a Houston hotel suite to take a $25,000 annual advantage of this loophole, even though until his loss in the 1992 election he was only in Texas approximately two weeks per year. His victory in the 1988 presidential election gave him the power to set the financial course of the empire. The solutions that occurred to him, having once been the director of the Central Intelligence Agency, were for war and more of the same but worse. A transparent weakling, George Bush was the reflection of the last strong personality he was with. He steered the Confederate Empire of North America directly toward the precipice its regressionary policies continue to back it up to.

Having acquired the Texas disease of love of power for its own sake, Bush had received a respectable "43.6 percent of the vote, the best Republican showing for major office in Texas history" (McGinnis 1969, 38), in an unsuccessful bid to upset Senator Ralph Yarborough in 1964. The reference to major office here means statewide, for Eisenhower as a native son had carried Texas handily, where the road had already been paved in 1928, much to the chagrin of that son of a Confederate Sam Rayburn, by the first conservative Republican presidential victory in Texas of Herbert Hoover. Bush was picked up and put into Congress by Harry Treleaven, on leave from the J. Walter Thompson advertising agency. To Treleaven, politics is a product and represents a marketing opportunity. The opportunity he found in Bush was a likable guy who "knew that the red light meant the television camera was on" (38). It was perfect that nobody knew what he stood for and that he was behind in the polls. They would concoct a fighting underdog image and put Bush out on the street with "his coat slung over a shoulder; his sleeves rolled up; walking the streets of his district; grinning, gripping, sweating, letting the voter know he cared. About what, was never made clear" (40).

Bush's victory at least made him a believer in the power of media politics, but he would lose a Senate bid to Lloyd Bentsen and spend the next 10 years accumulating resume fodder, such as the chairmanship of the Republican party, the directorship of the CIA and the ambassadorship to China. Republican John Connally, a native Texan and former Democrat, Secretary of the Treasury as well as governor (he was wounded during the Kennedy assassination, possibly ruling himself out as a co-conspirator), and rival for the 1980 Republican nomination claimed that "George Bush sat on his butt in all those jobs." Bush got off his duff and jogged himself into the short end of a microphone flap with Ronald Reagan in the New Hampshire primary. Bush had already won a small victory in the Iowa caucuses and showed up at the debate imagining a one-on-one with Reagan. John Sears, however, had padded the also ran account by inviting four additional Republican wannabes, irritating Bush and the main sponsor, the *Nashua Telegraph*. When they tried to cut Reagan's microphone off, Ronald angrily "leaned forward and said, 'I'm paying for this microphone'" (Perry 1984, 90). Bush acted churlish, lost his nerve and the nomination eventually went to Reagan in the male dominance pattern of American politics that probably originated with baboons. Media politics had come a long way in a short time in the wrong direction since as recently as 1920 "For the first time in convention history a loudspeaker system was used. . . Now even Carter Glass's thin wispy voice penetrated to all corners of the auditorium" (Levine 1965, 166). The loudspeaker had put an end to the rich baritone control William Jennings Bryan had exerted over the Democratic party by the use of his superior pipes. Ronald Reagan brought his own microphone to the campaign, there is no political substitute for money, and went home with the victory.

What better place to warehouse a blank former spook for eight years than in the no-power do-nothing transparency of the vice presidency, where

Bush was ensconced and pretended to be either in or out of the loop as political expediency dictated. Reagan and Bush were the perfect candidates for TV political advertising. McLuhan wrote "'the party system has folded like the organization chart. Policies and issues are useless for election purposes, since they are too specialized and hot. The shaping of a candidate's integral image has taken the place of discussing conflicting points of view'" (McGinnis 1969, 21). The shape of the Reagan-Bush image beat Carter in 1980 and Carter's pollster Pat Caddell claimed "'We [political consultants, strategist, pollsters] have pre-empted the political system. We decide who are the best and more likely people to be successful" (Perry 1984, 175). When asked what kind of people they were looking for he replied: "'We look for people who give quick and often facile answers. People who look good on TV and who can project the kinds of messages we want to project. Whether or not they understand them is a different question. Because of TV, we don't look for people who have deep, thoughtful, complex and complicated approaches to life, because we wouldn't be able to put them on TV'" (176).

TV, where the truth is too hot to broadcast, had found its perfect candidates in the cool facile transparent Republicans. And the perfect media consultant for these matters turned out to be Roger Ailes, whose 1988 book *You Are the Message*, "The Secrets of the Master Communicators," ought to be required reading, if for no other reason than it is based on more than 20 years of successful experience. At 28 years of age, Ailes was hired to produce the TV programs that elected Richard Nixon in 1968. His critique (McGinnis 1969, 69-73) of the first program is detailed and flawless. Never mind that he wanted to keep the farmers off TV, or that he wanted somebody to play "hide the Greek [Spiro Agnew]," (97) or that he put Nixon in the "arena" (64). The man knew what he was doing and nowhere is it more apparent than when he suggested to Nixon "to 'come in under' the questioners in tone. . . Several people, Ailes included, thought it had been his best TV appearance of the campaign" (152). Ailes is the man who gave the befuddled Ronald Reagan the requisite confidence and support to make a joke of Mondale's "youth and inexperience," which permitted Reagan to laugh his way back into the White House. Roger Ailes is the single consistent variable factor in the elections of Nixon, Reagan and Bush. It is the transparency of Roger Ailes that will grace the electronic Mt. Rushmore of the future, not the politicians he has cantilevered into office over their considerable and documented shortcomings. William Gavin, summing up the Ailes produced Nixon victory and reflecting the influence of McLuhan, suggests "It's not in the words, but the silences, where the votes lie. . . It's got to appear non-calculated, incomplete — *incomplete*, that's it, the circle never squared, the random gobs of attitude" (197-8). It is not possible to be much more politically correct and perfect in the United States than to have a few "random gobs of attitude" stashed in the arsenal, since it is the attitude that determines the tone.

The conservative capture of the Republican party commencing in 1964, the first big gob of attitude hinted into being by Goldwater's victory, was by now an accomplished fact. "Simply put, the idea was to join the South and West in a conservative coalition" (Phillips 1969, 204). This was said of the Nixon imperative and the coming Republican hegemony at the presidential level. The controlling ideas of John Calhoun are frequently cited, although their authorship is often forgotten or ignored. Bush's 1988 racist appeal in South Carolina was a reprise of Goldwater's victory there. As John Gunther once observed "Politics in South Carolina need not concern us greatly. This is a 'white supremacy' state par excellence" (1947, 726). It is possible Gunther meant we need not kill much time identifying the obvious, but the power of the white supremacists in South Carolina, transparent as it is, should be a matter of serious concern. The Democrats had chosen to ignore the fact that Georgian Jimmy Carter failed to capture the majority of white southern voters (Germond and Witcover 1989, 37), and as a result engineered Super-Tuesday. "Tom Murphy. . . declared 'The southern primary is going to elect the next president of the United States'" (42). The Democrats exhibit the symptoms of more than a single problem here, because they put Super-Tuesday together to restore southern influence in presidential politics, apparently oblivious to the fact that it hadn't waned in the previous 40 years, it had only turned Republican. The American people might be right not to trust anybody that blind with high office. We see again "The deft Ailes" (125) throughout the Bush campaign. Bush had found his allies in South Carolina where "Atwater had recognized the potential importance of the South early in the game" (148). A brilliant but hateful political tactician who died in 1991 of a brain tumor, Super-Tuesday wasn't early enough for Atwater who managed to deliver all 37 South Carolina delegates and 48 percent of the popular vote to Bush a week before Super-Tuesday. This was possible because "South Carolina was Lee

Atwater's home ground, and the Republican governor, Carroll Campbell, was a friend and client of Atwater's" (151).

It will be fatal to ignore the transparent influence of South Carolina, the colony and state that gave the South its slaveholding style trying to recreate London, England, exactly, the home of the preeminent American political philosopher John C. Calhoun, the state that led the secession from the Union and now leads in the selection of victorious Republican presidential candidates. It was apparent to Kevin Phillips as early as 1968 that "South Carolina has been the most Republican of the Cotton States in presidential elections since 1952" (1969, 229). "When the votes were counted March 8, Bush had a landslide" (Germond & Witcover 1989, 152). Bush carried 14 states in the South as well as Massachusetts and Rhode Island. His random gob of attitude was catapulted by the pre-Super-Tuesday victory in South Carolina into a dense cloud of momentum. The military metaphor, so prominent in South Carolina, transposed itself nicely into the general campaign. "In the hands of Bush's hired guns, the concept of campaign as educational exercise crumbled before the concept of campaign as warfare, and Dukakis was gunned down in the process" (466). Who would have thought that when Nixon visited Mao Zedong that the Republicans would eventually reveal themselves as Maoists all along as Mao said "Politics is war without guns."

The politically naive can be confused by the discrepancies between the Bush campaign and his inaugural plea for a "kinder, gentler, nation." "But if a campaign for the presidency is supposed to provide the voters with the material with which to make an informed decision on the individual they want to lead their country, they should see the same one on the campaign trail as the one who eventually is sworn in and addresses them on Inauguration Day. That did not happen, and it is not likely to happen, as long as 'Anything Goes' continues to be the marching song of the political mercenaries who, in Roger Ailes' phrase, 'war-gamed' the presidential campaign of George Bush in 1988 — and stand ready to do the same in the campaigns of the future" (467). Actually, the Bush sworn in would soon reveal himself to be the same Bush who campaigned.

Through the random gobs of attitude and dense clouds of momentum, clues to the intentionality of behavior continually radiate. One such clue was the launch of the campaign from Fulton, Missouri, scene of Sir Winston Churchill's famous "Iron Curtain" speech where "peace through strength" could be stated as a campaign theme. This reiteration of the British Empire's, now the Confederate Empire of North America's, intention to keep the empire together and the Communists at bay, illustrated one of the most serious consequences of being an empty suit. With no life or ideas to call his own, the chameleon Bush was compelled to settle for acting like whatever power source he is closest to at the moment. In Fulton, Missouri, it was a combination of Churchill and Truman in his reification of the by now 40-plus year old rigid Truman Doctrine. Virgil Jordan, the president of the National Industrial Conference Board's prediction in "Capital needs of Industry for National Defense," that "At best, England will become a junior partner in a new Anglo-Saxon imperialism, in which the economic resources and the military and naval strength of the United States will be the center of gravity" (MacDougall 1965, 34), had long since come true. One clue to the state of the empire George Bush would find himself at the helm of was contained in Henry Wallace's description of it in the late 40s. "'We have come to this world crisis because willful men with private interests are dictating our foreign policy. Their interest is profits, not people. They seek to protect and extend their foreign investments against the democratic actions of peoples abroad'" (338).

Expanding a colonial empire in the search for private profits for private interests, the English had learned some exquisitely painful lessons. "The first was the way in which the country was contributing to the long-term expansion of other nations. . . The second potential strategical weakness lay in the increasing dependence of the British economy upon international trade, and more important, international finance" (Kennedy 1987, 157). After 1945, the United States began to deliberately recapitulate these two processes. "Like mid-Victorian Britons, Americans after 1945 favored free trade and open competition, not just because they held that global commerce and prosperity would be boosted in the process, but also because they knew that they were most likely to benefit from the abandonment of protectionism. Forty years later with that confidence ebbing. . ." (526). Not only were the United States arriving at the financial condition of Victorian England, they were arriving at this state by the use of the same ineluctable processes. "All of these [financial] crises were attributable to military hostilities and the conditions of war [except two]. . . Nearly all of the slumps in foreign trade before the end of the American War [1783] were connected to the conduct of war" (Brewer 1989, 191).

The relationship between putative economic prosperity and war in the United States is well known, as it was World War II that finally broke the grip of the great depression. The perpetual Cold War had provided an economic pump where "Government borrowing both contracted the amount of existing private credit and made new loans harder to obtain" (202). This process of financial contraction in the direction of government debt for military purposes was apparent throughout the period following WWII and became most pronounced after the war in Vietnam. "Perhaps the single most frequently made complaint about the expansion of the eighteenth-century fiscal-military state was that it had created a 'financial interest,' a consortium of bankers, 'monied men,' investors, speculators and stock-jobbers, who lived parasitically off the state's need to borrow money to fund its wars" (206). While it may not have been the most frequent complaint in the United States in the second half of the 20th century, it certainly had its innings and it had the same effects. "The most lucrative contracts were for the supply and remittance of money either to garrisons such as Gibraltar or to pay troops. . . Not surprisingly, many members of the 'financial interest' became very rich" (208). Not much was or could be done in the early stages of the growth of this debt in England as "Support for the debt paralleled its gradual penetration into the society at large" (210). Once into the society at large, "The options of eighteenth-century fiscal legislators were severely limited as long as they refused to countenance a properly policed tax on wealth" (217). George Bush is not about to police the rich with anything like a fair tax and preferred the campaign sorcery of "Read my lips — no new taxes."

Reading George's lips is at least as productive as reading his mind. The flow of capital to military purposes and the contraction of capital for other purposes resulting in high interest rates produced an effect not unlike Reconstruction in the South after the Civil War. "The significance of the high southern interest rate is difficult to exaggerate. . . [there was] little incentive to invest time or money in practices without an immediate payoff" (Ransom and Sutch 1977, 187). The immediate payoff, the 90 day or quarterly return on investment, almost defines the limited view on the transparent American financial horizon of the 1990s. Peace through strength works, but only for a short while and especially for the privileged few. How were we surprised that "Among the surprises of 1991-92 were the revelations of how George Bush's sons and brothers were enriching themselves in the investment business — and in several cases having scrapes with the law" (Phillips 1994, 100)? George Bush was the perfect representative of the leisure class and "National leaders do not rush to say so, but the bailout of the early 1990s was the biggest in America's history" (94).

"Unlimited military spending probably posed even more of a threat to our own economy and our social and political institutions than it did to those of the Soviet Union" (Cousins 1987, 81). Norman Cousins' *The Pathology of Power* was published prior to the collapse of the Soviet Union, former "evil" empire, and also prior to the collapse of the Confederate Empire of North America. A consequence of all the spending on weapons was "Salesmen representing the Pentagon travel the world, pressing the merits of American weapons in competition with salesmen from other governments" (95). These salesmen are familiar figures in European history, such as Sir Basil Zaharoff who was "Knighted by the British, even though he lived in France" (84). Superintending the salesmen are CEOs like "General Dynamics Chairman David S. Lewis, who received a yearly salary of $1,000,000, charged the government $320,000 for his frequent company plane trips. . . to his country home in Georgia" (120).

This apparently baffles optimistic idealists like Cousins who can write with an apparently straight face "How could a firm as important as General Dynamics ever allow itself to perform practices that would expose it as a predator on the public treasury?" (153). The last man to try to make the United States budget make sense, David Stockman, Reagan's OMB director, was told by James S. Baker III, Bush's Secretary of State but then Reagan's Secretary of the Treasury, "'You've made as many mistakes as the rest of us around here. So stick that unwarranted pride of yours right up your ass, and get back in the trenches with the rest of us'" (Stockman 1986, 375). The power of diplomacy is never lost on Baker. The politicians and the military-industrialists are like Roman politicians (Spengler 1928, 487), simply plundering the provinces of their money and other removable assets.

Clueless George steered the ship of state directly toward the waterfall. "In consequence, the United States now runs the risk, so familiar to historians of the rise and fall of previous Great Powers, of what might roughly be called 'imperial overstretch': that is to say, decision-makers in Washington must face the awkward and enduring fact that the sum total of the United States' global interests and obligations is nowadays far larger than the country's power to defend them all simultaneously" (Kennedy 1987, 515).

The hope had always been before, where the budget was targeted to a maximum of two and one-half wars, was for the wars to be fought one at a time. The transparent overlay of the United States onto the British Empire is apparent in the following citation: "Interestingly, such warnings about the American armed forces being 'at full stretch' are attended by maps of 'Major U.S. Military Deployment Around the World' which, to historians, look extraordinarily similar to the chain of fleet bases and garrisons possessed by that former world power, Great Britain, at the height of its strategic overstretch" (519). This was hardly coincidental as FDR and others had negotiated for the use of some of the exact same bases. Even before the collapse of the Soviet Union, "It is instructive to note the uncanny similarities between the growing mood of anxiety among thoughtful circles in the United States today and that which pervaded all political parties in Edwardian Britain and led to what has been termed the 'national efficiency' movement" (529).

Regrettably, the movement toward efficiency in the United States is not tempered with much realism as many would prefer others to be realistic while they remained extravagant. There is little appreciation in the United States for the news that "In the same way, it may be argued that the geographical extent, population, and natural resources of the United States suggest that it ought to possess perhaps 16 or 18 percent of the world's wealth and power, but because of historical and technical circumstances favorable to it, that share rose to 40 percent or more by 1945; and what we are witnessing at the moment is the early decades of the ebbing away from that extraordinarily high figure to a more 'natural' share" (533). Just as the British Empire peaked at around 25 percent of world production in the decades following the establishment of their hegemony over Napoleon and declined to its present level, so too will the United States' peak of 40 percent, revert to a more defensible level. The problem with the southern, military, religious domination of the American government is that these people believe they arrived at that peak as a result of a cosmic Manifest Destiny and they are not predisposed to believe that God will let them down, whether gently or abruptly. The real American competition now is decidedly economic from Germany and Japan and is compounded by the barely veiled threats and unspoken promises from the military to make downsizing the United States military establishment more expensive than keeping it at full strength.

Examples abound of what can be done. "Since modern war is so costly and is usually counterproductive, the Japanese feel that there is a lot of merit in their *zenhoi heiwa gaiko* ('omnidirectional peaceful diplomacy'")" (469). This does not resemble the Bush solution. "I know of no concrete and substantive programs for bringing about badly needed and technically feasible social change. . . The demand for redistribution of wealth and power, if it passes beyond rhetoric, will not be tolerated by the privileged" (Chomsky 1973, xxviii). There were no programs in 1973, nor are there any in the 1990s. "David O. Maxwell, who received retirement benefits totaling $27.6 million when he stepped down as chairman of Fannie Mae last year, stood to collect $5.5 million more but turned down the additional payment" (AP January 22, 1992). National socialism real estate is a demanding profession, given that the history of the United States can be read as one grand real estate swindle, but it hardly should command or require a $27 million dollar pension. The exact width of the financial integrity of the American privileged class is the moral gulf between a $27 million dollar pension and a $33 million dollar pension. "The result feels very much like the actual moral texture of the Reagan-Bush era: a supersaturation of corruption that fails any longer to outrage or even interest" (Davis 1990, 45). The people have grown numb to the conclusions where instead of intelligent constructive competition with the Japanese, "First is the bizarre fact that the region's [LA] leading foreign export by volume is simply empty space; more than half the containers which arrive in San Pedro filled with computers, cars and televisions return with nothing in them" (135). How long can empty suits thrive exporting space. The Neo-Confederate policy has two planks. The rich corporate base of the economy has to be free to aggrandize itself while the masses are expected to seek the high moral tone in economic subsistence. The class bias, akin to Calhoun's, in this business as usual — no solution, where the rich continue to lift themselves by the bootstraps of the poor, reveals a bankrupt imagination on the part of the speakers of English.

Dead spirits exporting space can only revert to type and accelerate the regression. "Like most of the pilfered documents from the White House, it had been passed on to Baker by one of the tight band of about six ex-CIA men working for the Reagan campaign. Several of them had come with Baker from the campaign of ex-CIA Director George Bush, and they were employed to use their dubious talents of 'intelligence gathering'" (Perry 1984, 145). The acorn is unlikely to fall far from the oak and the Baker-Bush team had much to "benefit from a natural tendency on the part of the privileged in any society to suppress — for themselves as well as others — knowledge and understanding of the nature of their privilege and its manifestations" (Chomsky 1973, 65). Suppression of the knowledge of the nature of privilege is a necessary ingredient in government as imagined by John C. Calhoun where security dominates liberty (Calhoun 1931, 53). As the United States fulfills the pattern of its models, England and Rome, "The might Roman Republic, which, after attaining the highest point of power, passed, seemingly under the operation of irresistible causes, into a military despotism" (85). The despotism was not to be resisted by Bush and the Texans as he said at his confirmation hearing to be CIA director: "I think we should tread very carefully on governments that are constitutionally elected" (Hitchens 1991, 64). Perhaps he threw out that sop to mollify the critics of the then recent Nixon-Kissinger overthrow of the elected government of Salvador Allende in Chile. In the life of the barbarian, "Prowess manifests itself in two main directions, — force and fraud" (Veblen 1931, 273). The history of the CIA is replete with force and fraud. The comic relief can be located in the mirror image of the class act of Baker-Bush as the millionaire Texans, looking down their tony noses at the masses, in the fact that "The only class which could at all dispute with the hereditary leisure class the honor of an habitual bellicose frame of mind is that of the lower-class delinquents" (247).

Government is filled with lower class delinquents who've made good in one way or another, and Bush came to power in the United States with one of his old associates from the CIA playing a lead role as the dictator of Panama. The photographs of General Manuel Noriega and George Bush on the same couch together, not exactly in deep rapport, but nevertheless working out details of CIA activity in the Caribbean wing of the Confederate Empire of North America, eventually became too much to bear. Bush invaded Panama in December of 1989, while Congress was not in session, as a Christmas present for the right wing, recapitulating the autocratic Theodore Roosevelt who had given flesh, blood and soil to Jefferson Davis' demand for an empire as least as far south as the Isthmus of Panama. Back in the empire again, the military forced Noriega out of hiding with hard rock music and brought him to trial in the United States. Where and from what pool of persons, might it be asked parenthetically, could a jury of

General Noriega's peers be assembled. He is doing big time in the empire's prison.

There was a lot of Theodore Roosevelt displayed by Bush in the belli-cose frame of mind he approached the election with. Being an empty issue-less suit, he wrapped himself in the Pledge of Allegiance to the flag, as well as the literal flag itself. Bush ordered American troops to Saudi Arabia, almost immediately upon learning of the Iraq invasion, and apparently after consulting only with Brent Scowcroft, the National Security Advisor. The mirror-like surface of George Bush will reflect the influence of the last strong man, or woman in the case of his wife Barbara, he is closest to or has last been seen with. He takes advice from Ailes, Baker, Scowcroft and Darman, a bright young man who had earned his wings reading for Ronald Reagan. "Yet Darman was not simply in control of the 'in-out' basket. Like a young Stalin in Lenin's Russia, he learned fast that guarding the informa-tion flow meant power" (Perry 1984, 180). The information flow coming out of the Middle East meant that Iraq, on the receiving end of American aid for nearly 10 years and up to a few months prior as Baker bent the rules to ship them arms, presented the United States with a unique opportunity to occupy Saudi Arabia, a dream held in abeyance for 40 years, as well as a chance to rescue the dwindling military budget in the face of the Commu-nist collapse, and a chance to try out some of the sophisticated new weaponry that trillions of research and development dollars had provided. Here could be all the "horror and thrill" (James 1967, 666) of war that the militarists had been forever preparing for. The Cold War and the Truman Doctrine itself had sprouted wings just as Henry Wallace "demanded that there be an ultimatum to the Arab feudal lords, 'who are truly puppets of Anglo-American oil,' to lay down their arms" (MacDougall 1965, 373). For all the erratic stabs at rhetorical window dressing condemning naked aggression and trying to locate the previously held liberty of the Kuwaiti people, the war was about the control of the supply of oil. It was finally revealed that what George Bush really cared about was whose hands were on the gas pump in Kuwait.

"In the debate I argued that the United States was using Iraq's invasion of Kuwait as a convenient opportunity for asserting its military power in a strategically-vital area of the world. The United States is an empire in decline" (Kaufman-Osborn 1991, 8). Professor of political science Kaufman-Osborn's opinion is widely held and grounded in a realistic assessment of the facts. It is worth noting that the initial impulse to deploy troops to Saudi Arabia was defensive and referred to as Operation Desert Shield. Then, not unlike conditions in 1916 and 1964, virtually the day after the 1990 elections, when Bush announced he was ordering an additional quarter of a million troops to Saudi Arabia, he changed the debate from peace or a defensive war to a choice between defensive war and offensive war. In 1916, because Wilson had kept the U.S. out of war, "The President was re-elected by the votes of the South and West in 1916. . . meanwhile the country began to prepare itself" (Perkins 1966, 69). In 1964, LBJ was elected because he took a peace position in public, as Bush did, while he and his advisors prepared for war without informing the electorate (Chomsky 1973, 289).

Kuwait, it needs to be emphasized, was the creation of the British foreign office in 1920 as it dismantled the Ottoman Empire, which had ruled the area from 1300 until the end of WWI. Defending the dotted lines of the British Empire, especially when they were drawn around such a lucrative pool of oil, was a kneejerk reaction of the Confederate Empire of North America. In an unintended irony and blatant projection, the London *Daily Telegraph* noted that "The attempts to reduce a sovereign nation to the status of a provincial oil field. . . increases the pressure on the United States and its allies not to delay military action a moment longer than necessary." It was the British who had made a provincial oil field out of Kuwait in 1920; Saddam Hussein wanted its resources under his control in 1990 with two intentions: to force an increase in the price of oil and redistribute the proceeds. There was plenty of jingoism to go around. If the economic transactions between nations and cultures are mutually beneficial, there will be no need to police trade routes, or reflag Kuwaiti tankers. If the transactions are not mutually beneficial, police are required to defend them. The sanctions imposed by the United Nations, dominated by the United States, were only slightly more representative of world opinion than the sanctions Truman used as a justification to start the Korean War. "Furthermore, the UN sanction of a military response to the North Korean attack was not an entirely satisfactory justification, since the UN was at the time totally dominated by the United States and the United States was using that domination to give an international flavor to a decision in fact made unilaterally" (Walton 1976, 351). While a few intelligent southern senators, including Nunn and Fowler of Georgia, Sanford of North

Carolina, and Hollings of South Carolina, voted against the Senate resolution to use force to enforce the sanctions against Iraq (it passed 52-48), the preponderance of support for this measure in both the House and the Senate was recorded in the South. (See chapter 21 on the gunbelt for DOD demographic details).

Even though the United States itself had hardly been attacked, discounting the habit it had picked up of "reflagging" Kuwaiti oil tankers during the 10 year war between Iran and Iraq, which ought to provide some clue as to just whose oil they think it is, the forces of democratic centralism popped out of the Speaker of the House, Congressman Tom S. Foley of the 5th district of Washington's mouth the moment the vote was recorded. The precedent for this occurred during World War I. "'When the country is at peace,' the judge declared, 'it is a legal right of free speech to oppose going to war and to oppose even preparation for war. But when once war is declared this right ceases'" (Johnson 1963, 101). Prior to the Senate's irrelevant confirmation of the Bush war on Iraq, the movement for peace in the United States was widespread and respectable. Once the blitzkrieg began, opposition to it was snuffed like the flame on a candle. News of the war itself was distorted. Bill Sternberg of the Washington Bureau of the Associated Press said "A report accompanying the letter details instances of how military officials censored interviews, limited press access and delayed transmission of stories for reasons that had nothing to do with operating security and everything to do with sanitizing the nature of war and polishing the image of the military. . . After the ceasefire, Frank Bruni of the Detroit Free Press was told it would be 'inappropriate' to write about a young soldier who was killed when he picked up an unexploded American cluster bomblet" (AP July, 1991). The *image* of the military *is their security*. The number of soldiers who died as a result of accidents or who were killed by friendly fire was greater than the number of deaths attributed to enemy fire. At Hollywood High School in California on Memorial Day 1991, the high school celebrated this religious holiday by recalling everybody who had ever graduated there and subsequently died in war. This marriage of the religious, the military and the filmic, would only be possible to reproduce in the movie capitol of the people of the picture. Before, during and after the war, the deadly feedforward loop of all previous and potential wars was boosted wholesale into the collective consciousness from the TV pulpit. An almost endless stream of former generals and admirals, most of whom retire to live in the South and many employed as consultants to the defense industry, explained the war with wall charts and called the shots that pass for the liturgy.

Declaring there would be no more Vietnams, Bush "Arranged to finance the Gulf War by turning American troops into mercenaries and hiring them out to a coalition of wealthy nations. . . Bush learned Aiken's lesson well, because that's exactly what he did — declared victory and brought the troops home" (Quillen 1991). The millionaire mendicant, James S. Baker III, was seen all over the globe rattling the empty tin cup of Texas, raising money to pay for this designer war. "The quick victories won by American arms strengthened the psychological position of the imperialists [in 1898 where]. . . success, as in a Calvinist scheme, is taken as an outward sign of an inward state of grace" (Hofstadter 1965, 175). George Bush had taken the United States back to its roots and the result was reflected in his meteorous rise to a 91 percent approval rating in the polls. For several months after the war, a sizable number of the men and politicians in the United States were too giddy with testosterone to make sense. The electorate came down to earth long enough in 1992 that 62 percent of them preferred any-body but Bush. Meanwhile though, Bush was so flush with the heat of victory that he proposed and got forgivance of an $8 billion dollar debt the Egyptians owed the U.S. in honor of their support during the blitzkrieg. It was   hardly coincidental that this act of largesse was acquiesced to by congressional "leaders" in an out of control economy racking up over a billion dollars a day in deficit spending. Iraq's timely invasion of Kuwait came just as the collapse of the empire recession in the United States began in August of 1990, trailing the Soviet Union, but following its lead.

While millions turned out for war parades in the United States, where even Ron Kovic, the mutilated hero of the Vietnam War, was shut up in his opposition to the war on Iraq, the war parades in England, where this empire got its first bearings, were mercifully short. According to Larry Eichel with the Knight-Ridder News Service, whose headlined "British War Parade Dull — and Short:" article said, "This was how Britain officially welcomed home those who served in the Persian Gulf war yesterday — with a modest rain-soaked parade that took precisely 7 1/2 minutes to pass any given point. The parade ended with two minutes of total silence. It was not an expression of respect for the 42 British soldiers who died in the gulf.

Rather, it was an expression of confusion over whether the parade was truly over, which it was" (June, 1991). Some of the English may finally have been coming to the conclusions expressed by the great Victorian novelist Ford Madox Ford, whose tetralogy *Parade's End* includes the shorter novel *No More Parades*. For the rest of the English, including former Prime Minister Margaret Thatcher who was awarded an honorary doctorate degree in 1991 by the University of Kuwait, presumably in colonial economics, the enlightenment may be a long time coming. It is as though "The punitive expeditions of 1983-91, which at first had reassured Americans, were starting to look like the punitive expeditions of Rome: pleasing and usually triumphant in the short run, irrelevant in the long run" (Phillips 1994, 59).

The English thrill at having the Americans play their role so grandly was not confined to statesmanship but passed into the realm of the truly divine. Queen Elizabeth II traveled to Tampa, Florida, to knight General Schwarzkopf on the "front steps of MacDill Air Force Base, headquarters of the U.S. Central Command. . . Schwarzkopf displayed the two-cross medallion [no relation to the double cross] of knighthood, the highest honor Britain can bestow on a foreigner" (Associated Press, May 1991). The 9-day royal entourage then flew via Concorde to Texas. "The queen's visit to Texas marks the first time a British monarch has stepped foot on Texas soil, even though Great Britain was one of the first European nations to recognize the fledgling Republic of Texas 151 years ago" (AP). The queen visited four Texas cities, Austin, San Antonio, Dallas and Houston. She had begun her visit in Washington D.C. and ended it in Louisville, Kentucky. Some people refer to this as a visit to the United States, but all of her stops were conveniently and strategically below the Mason-Dixon Line. The English knew what they were transporting from Barbados to South Carolina and they had come back to claim it. In restoring the Emir of Kuwait to his throne, responding so quickly to defend the royal Saudi Arabian family oligarchy, and keeping the royal British Empire together one more time, the reversion of power to the defense of monarchies was complete. Sam Houston's imaginary and potential Texas was fairly effectively covering, for the time being, most of the globe. Not merely dominating the South clear back to Richmond, it was dominating the South clear back to London. The shock of recognition between British royalty and Texas is much deeper than the historical record or news of royal family members playing footsie with cowboys can convey.

If the London observation of the end of the war was short and dull, the reception George Bush attended at Shaw Air Force Base in Sumter, South Carolina, was especially revealing. He had flown there from Bermuda, another spot in the perennial British Empire, to hold a homecoming for USAF Airmen home from Desert Storm. At Rebel Field in Harlingen, Texas, there is a museum of flight filled with WWII vintage airplanes and known by its curators as the Confederate Air Force. They refer to themselves as "colonels" and "the business of saving these historic aircraft was conducted with good old Southern humor, which percolated through the colonels' outrage at the mass destruction under way by the military" (Moll 1987, 14). The Confederate Air Force air show conducts daily WWII air power demonstrations, referred to as "An orgy in the glorification of war" (30). The atavistic motivation for this air force and these celebrations is basic to Texans such as Sam Rayburn and George Bush. "The Texan rebels had a cause, the same noble motive that unites the 6,000 members of the Confederate Air Force today" (30).

Bush told a cheering crowd in Sumter, South Carolina, that as a result of the war, "No one, no one in the whole world, doubts us any more," (AP March 18, 1991). The "us" in this sentence can only refer to the southern and military dominated United States. They operate the real Confederate Air Force and having lost the cause in 1865, had convincingly relocated it in 1991 in Bush's final transparent impersonation of Robert E. Lee.

Part V

Consequences of Confederate Victory

"I'm on my way from 'Frisco, going back to Dixie land"

Jimmie Rodgers

21

The Gunbelt: Defense Department Demographics

Twenty-one seats in the U.S. House of Representatives changed hands as a result of the 1990 census. Twenty of them went to five states of the old Confederacy plus California and Washington. These seven states were the top recipients of Defense Department spending in Fiscal Years (FY) 1989 and 1990. Fifty-four percent of all Defense Department (DOD) spending in FY 1989 took place in these seven states plus Maryland, a border slaveholding state that did not secede, and South Carolina. These nine states received Defense Department per capita spending in all classes—contracts, civilian and military payrolls—at a rate over four times greater than the average of the states, primarily in the Northeast and Midwest, that gave up those seats and that power. The other seat moved to Arizona, a special southern geriatric case and former Confederate territory. The center of population in the United States has always been south of the Mason-Dixon Line. This shift of nearly five percent of the voting power in the House of Representatives to the Confederate military South, and those parts of the West that it has added to its domestic empire, is the result of deliberate DOD policy and governmental action and not the grace of God. It reflects and measures the political anemia of the North.

The easternmost tent peg on the gunbelt is shrouded in the Neolithic with the smelting of six percent tin alloyed with copper to create bronze. The military control of the supply of metal (and more recently oil) has passed through Rome to England and Spain, to South Carolina and on across Texas from which it takes its directives to Los Angeles, California. The "Gunbelt" will make a vivid tracing through the numbers of this migration of power to the South and West as it identifies the consequences. The migration follows the military religion of the siege formally adopted at Appomattox. Power follows the sun to the romantic imagery of Hollywood in *Gone With the Wind*, *The Birth of a Nation*, and Gaston Melies' 1911 version of *The Immortal Alamo*. Power leads the civilization westward in the spending power of the gun.

For the sake of simplicity, the numbers crunched on the official 1990 census are taken from the June 15, 1991, issue of *Congressional Quarterly*, and the DOD numbers are taken from *Sea Power/Congress/Defense*, and the *Statistical Abstract of the United States*. It felt most appropriate to use FY 89 DOD numbers and even though total DOD spending is down slightly for FY 90, the ratios of DOD dispensations to various states were holding steady. The 1990 census was used rather than the 1980 census figures. Using 1980 numbers would make the per capita ratios of money sent to the receiving states even larger and more gross.

No attempt was made to finesse the potential of a 1990 census undercount since "The states that gained most in the census — such as California, Texas, Florida and Arizona — would generally be even better off under an adjustment. Many of the states that sued to force an adjustment — such as New York, Pennsylvania, Illinois and Michigan — would do worse if one were ordered" (CQ, 1607). These four states are among the big losers of population. Much of the undercount and a noticeable though hardly majority proportion of the total increase in the border states can be traced to Hispanic immigration, which has historical reasons for being attracted there, in addition to the general fiscal well being of the area due to large influxes of DOD and other federal money. This is not simply the best section of the empire in which to get a tan. Until the collapse of the Soviet Union, it was also the best place in the empire to get a job. DOD money has made the southern United States the most dynamic section of the empire, attracting attention from all quarters.

More than half, or 459 out of 889 major military installations in the United States are in 12 states, eight of which are former slaveholding states plus California, Washington, Arizona and Hawaii. Hawaii, a special southern imperialist acquisition for its pineapple plantations and strategic Pacific position, has been discussed previously.

The state of Washington, outside of the geographic South, is the northern linchpin of the gunbelt with major military installations such as the Hanford Reservation where the Manhattan Project was developed, Fairchild Air Force Base near Spokane, Ft. Lewis Army Depot and McCord Air Force Base near Tacoma, the Whidbey Island Naval Air Station, the Navy yards and Trident submarine base at Bremerton, and the Boeing Corporation, always one of the top 10 and frequently among the top five defense contractors in the DOD system. Washington was referred to as the "Soviet of Washington" as recently as 1980 when Democratic Senators "Scoop" Jackson and chairman of the Senate Appropriations Committee Warren G. "Cro"-Magnusson were still putting the finishing touches on the 150 hydroelectric systems on the Columbia River — a close cousin to the Tennessee Valley Authority — that killed the salmon. The Bonneville Power Administration distributes electricity from this system, making it the cheap energy in the Northwest with federal money, much as the effect of the depletion allowance provides that service for the oil patch that is primarily centered in Texas.

The Washingtonians learned Texas economics well where "Texas during the 1850s was financed publicly almost entirely by federal money" (Fehrenbach 1968, 278), and "Texans, in office and out, had a long habit of accepting any Yankee dollar they could get. . . One study showed that this, over a period of thirty years beginning in the 1930s, topped the national average by 27 percent" (652). This is the report of a serious Texas partisan and should make clear why the federal budget will never be balanced and the national debt will continue to grow. Among the Texas projects during that period would be included the Houston Ship Canal by Jesse H. Jones, the Colorado River Authority by Lyndon B. Johnson, plus the curious news that at the time he was deposed as Speaker of the House of Representatives, James Wright's Dallas district was receiving more federal money per capita than any other of the 435 congressional districts, including the Super-Conductor Super-Collider project at Waxahatchie. It certainly takes the mystery out of the notion that "If there was a single trend in the entire period following World War II, it was that Texas, despite drought and oil gluts, grew increasingly more prosperous" (660). So too has the state of Washington, which like Texas does not have an income tax. Succeeding Wright of Texas as the Speaker of the House of Representatives was Tom S. Foley from Washington's fifth district centered at Spokane.

Fifty-six percent of all DOD spending for FY 89 took place in 10 states, seven of which were former slaveholding states. In order of gross expenditures they are California, Texas, Virginia, Florida, North Carolina, Georgia, Washington, Maryland, Hawaii and South Carolina. Twenty of the 21 seats that changed hands in the House of Representatives went to the top seven recipients of DOD money and the other one splashed over into Arizona. There are no compelling reasons to regard this as coincidence. We need only recall Thorstein Veblen's observation that the southern leisure class cultivates three non-economic employments: politics, theology, the military. The seven former slaveholding states plus California and Washington received an average of $1,577 DOD dollars per capita. Due to its relatively small population and strategic position, the huge DOD numbers for Hawaii are anomalous and would distort the results. Hawaii is not included in this per capita rate. South Carolina and Maryland, while not increasing their number of House seats, have population growth that is keeping pace with the national average and while not gaining seats aren't losing them either.

The five states which lost the most seats, New York three, and two each for Illinois, Ohio, Pennsylvania, and Michigan, received an average of $386.40 DOD spending per capita. More than four times as much DOD money per capita in the states which gained the seats can explain the draw of population out of the rust belt, especially in an economy where a $500 tax cut for middle class taxpayers is considered to be significant. Even the states that lost the other 10 seats, one apiece from Iowa, Kansas, Kentucky, Louisiana, Massachusetts, Montana, New Jersey, Oklahoma, Wisconsin and West Virginia, received an average of $810.88 of DOD money, $115 less than the national average per capita DOD spending in the entire U.S. and only slightly more than half the percentage bestowed on the South. Except for Hawaii, the small state in an intensely strategic location, and Virginia, also a somewhat special case where the statistics are distorted by the location of the Pentagon within its borders, South Carolina gets more Department of Defense spending money per capita than any other state. Not a bad legacy for South Carolina's militant character, the home of John C. Calhoun and L. Mendel Rivers, Congressman from the first district of South Carolina centered on Charleston and for 30 years the chairman of the House Armed Services Committee. Organically speaking, South Carolina is the pituitary gland, minuscule in size but crucial in effect, that stimulates the archipallium that distributes the adrenaline in the endocrinology of war and fighting as the first choice and universal solution to problem solving. This unequal movement of federal money taking power with it to the gunbelt is a paean to Calhoun's principle of how the power to tax distorts the effects of government and rewards the tax consumers, of which the Texans, the South Carolinians, and the southern Californians are the acknowledged masters, with the Washingtonians as serious understudies. "He was the South incarnate" (Coit 1950, 517), said John C. Calhoun's

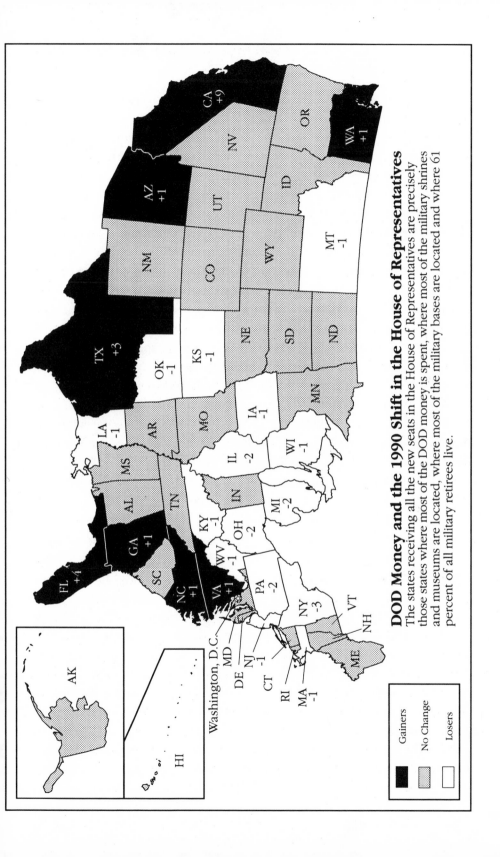

DOD Money and the 1990 Shift in the House of Representatives

The states receiving all the new seats in the House of Representatives are precisely those states where most of the DOD money is spent, where most of the military shrines and museums are located, where most of the military bases are located and where 61 percent of all military retirees live.

Gainers

No Change

Losers

biographer. He was and is the South incarnate, for this new evidence does not disturb Coit's 40-year-old summation.

To keep the religious bloom on this sage of South Carolina, 26 of 38 or more than two-thirds of the U.S. Army museums open for viewing by the public are located in the 11 states of the former Confederacy. Many of these museums are on or near the shrines made holy by the Confederate religion where the Civil War battles raged. Along these same lines, it may not surprise anyone to learn that 42 percent of all military retirees live in the 11 former Confederate states, and of equal pertinence, that 815,611 or more than half of all military retirees live in the eight states of Texas, Florida, California, Virginia, Washington, Georgia, Arizona and North Carolina. These are, it is germane to remind ourselves, precisely the same eight states that reaped the 21 seat harvest of the shift of power in the U.S. House of Representatives. When the number of total retirees there is added to the totals from the smaller states of the former Confederacy, 61 percent of all retirees live in Washington, Arizona, California and the old Confederacy.

With such an attractive military climate, it will further come as no surprise to learn that of the 15 states providing the largest reserve callups for the war on Iraq, nine were Confederate, one was California, and the other five were simply the most populous states outside the South, namely New York, Pennsylvania, Illinois, Ohio and Michigan. The South is home to most of the military museums, most of the military money, most of the retirees, most of the military history and most of the political power.

How this old time religion and southern power works in practical terms can be seen in an examination of the vote patterns in the United States Congress on the issue of whether or not to resort to the use of military force to enforce the U.S. directed United Nation sanctions against Iraq for its impolitic invasion of the oil fiefdom and colony of Kuwait. The Senate and House vote totals are recited in the *Congressional Record*, January 12, 1991: S403 and H485. To consider the Senate first where the vote was 48 against and 52 in favor of the use of force, a defacto declaration of war, the close-ness of the vote reveals the deeply divided mood of the country and the slightness of the victory for the use of force. Both senators from 13 states voted against the use of force, three of which represented the former slaveholding states of Georgia, Arkansas and Maryland with only Georgia and Arkansas actual participants in the Confederacy. The other 10 states where both senators were opposed were north or north central including

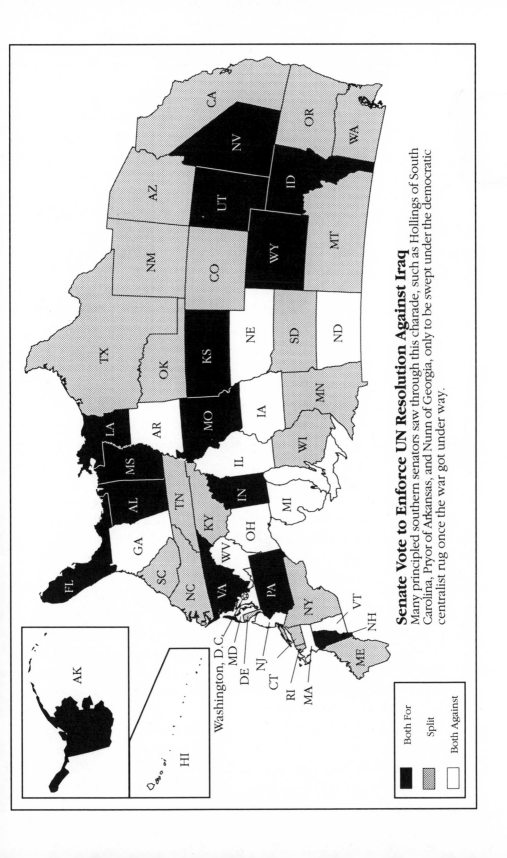

Senate Vote to Enforce UN Resolution Against Iraq
Many principled southern senators saw through this charade, such as Hollings of South Carolina, Pryor of Arkansas, and Nunn of Georgia, only to be swept under the democratic centralist rug once the war got under way.

Both For

Split

Both Against

Nebraska and Iowa, homes to several significant democratic nationalists with only the senators from one western state, Hawaii, both voting no. Hawaii's international vulnerability could be making it cautious and diplomatic. Other states voting no were West Virginia, North Dakota, Ohio, Illinois, Michigan, Massachusetts and New Jersey.

On the other hand, both senators from 15 states supported the use of force to begin the war. These states included: five former Confederate states, Alabama, Virginia, Florida, Louisiana and Mississippi; five conservative western states, Wyoming, Utah, Idaho, Alaska and Nevada; one slaveholding border state, Missouri; and four others, New Hampshire, Pennsylvania, Indiana and Kansas (on the Texas highway to the north). The Senate vote was split in 22 states, especially many of the larger ones where the diversity of the population and opinions found expression in their senatorial representation. Those states splitting their vote include: four former Confederate states, Texas, Tennessee, North Carolina and South Carolina; two former slaveholding border states, Kentucky and Delaware; nine western states, Washington, Colorado, Montana, Oklahoma, South Dakota, Oregon, New Mexico, Arizona and California; and seven midwestern and northeastern states, Minnesota, New York, Rhode Island, Connecticut, Wisconsin, Maine and Vermont.

To notice the effect of the literal states of the old Confederacy on this vote, if we factor those 22 Senate votes out, the remaining 78 votes were split 40 against the use of military force and 38 in favor. In other words, without the votes of the old Confederacy there would have been no U.S. Senate support for the last 20 feet of George Bush's hitherto undeclared war on Iraq. Never mind that this charade was conducted in public as a parody of democracy, for President Bush had said he intended to use force regardless of the outcome of the vote. The vote in favor continues to fail when we factor out the other eight senators from the slaveholding border states at the commencement of the Civil War, which leaves 36 opposed and 34 in favor.

In the House of Representatives, a similar pattern reveals itself upon examination. The House vote of 250 YEAS to 183 NAYS, a 67 yes-vote majority in favor of the use of force, is sorted out in terms of how it reveals and affects southern domination of American politics in this manner. The 116 House votes from the 11 states of the old Confederacy, barely more than one-quarter of the total, were cast 93 YEAS and 23 NAYS, a 70 yes-vote majority. Without the votes of the former Confederacy, the

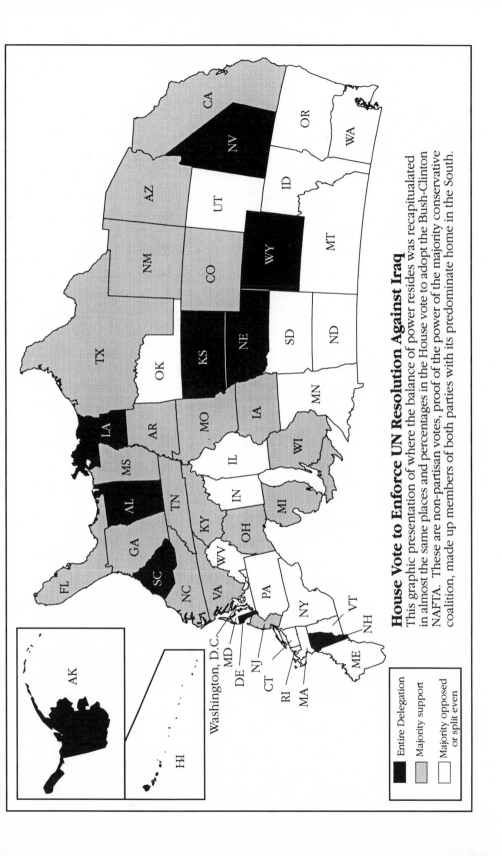

House Vote to Enforce UN Resolution Against Iraq

This graphic presentation of where the balance of power resides was recapitualated in almost the same places and percentages in the House vote to adopt the Bush-Clinton NAFTA. These are non-partisan votes, proof of the power of the majority conservative coalition, made up members of both parties with its predominate home in the South.

Legend:
- ■ Entire Delegation
- ▨ Majority support
- □ Majority opposed or split even

resolution, in effect to start war on Iraq, would have failed by three votes with 160 NAY votes to 157 YEAS. If the House votes of the border states are also subtracted the vote against the use of force reduces to 151 NAY votes to 141 YEAS, where it would fail by the wider majority of 10 votes. When the 45 House votes from California, a state subducted by slavery, geography, right wing anti-labor boosterism and military spending into the southern orbit are factored out, the margin of defeat for the use of force increases by 21 to 134 NAYS to 113 YEAS. The rest of the country, without its Confederate, former slaveholding, and California political steering committee voted against the use of force by a 21 vote margin.

To take a lateral test of this information's validity, the victory in the House of Representatives three years later to ratify the Bush-Clinton NAFTA treaty was also dependent on the margin of victory in the states of the former Confederacy. The Confederacy had picked up nine more seats in the 1990 reapportionment and so were casting 125 votes instead of 116. The vote for the entire House was 234 YEAS and 200 NAYS. The representatives from the old Confederacy voted 82-43 in support of NAFTA. Minus the Confederate portion, the NAFTA vote would have failed 152 YEAS to 157 NAYS, or from a 34 vote margin of victory to a five vote margin of defeat. The relationship between the empire's economic and military future is as simple as the fact that the functional purpose of the economy is to raise money for the military, hence the close relationship between these two votes.

It is not coincidental that the states voting the United States into war and NAFTA are almost exactly the same states benefiting from the Department of Defense spending. Without the yes votes from the states of the former Confederacy, the resolutions to, in effect declare war on Iraq, failed in both the Senate and the House of Representatives. The United States is dominated by southern military mentality. The United States is the church of the loaded gun.

Since 1860 the South has institutionalized its preference for being under siege. It began much earlier in white South Carolina, under siege from the Yemassee Indians or the Black slaves, the British during the Revolutionary War, the Jackson administration during the Nullification Crisis of 1832, and the Republicans during the Civil War of 1861-65 on through Reconstruction until the Fraud of 1876. The contemporary siege began in earnest with the bombing of Pearl Harbor and the imaginary Communist menace made the siege perpetual with the southern ratified

Truman Doctrine of 1947. They use this psychological state of siege to arm themselves, to the great detriment of the national budget, to the degree that even former Senator Tower of Texas' invitation to "his colleagues to suggest cuts — from their own states" (Cousins 1987, 158) was greeted with sly silence.

Former soldiers, such as the admirals and generals who explained the designer war on Iraq in the nation's televised mass, play a revolving door strategy. "In one three-year period, 3,200 Pentagon officers with the rank of major or higher left their jobs in order to jump to defense firms" (157). It would be nice work if the country could afford it. What it created in southern California was "The urban equivalent of the Spanish Main for corporate buccaneers" (Davis 1990, 144). As long ago as when World War II revolutionized California's economy, "As might be expected, most of California's wartime gain in population has been recorded in Southern California" (McWilliams 1946, 372). A complete mapping across America from 1940 to 1990 would show DOD money and the attendant population piling up principally in the greater LA basin as it followed the federal military money South.

Dexter Perkins and Paul Kennedy have written books that are replete with references to how the American Empire resembles and was nurtured by the British Empire. Democratic nationalists objected to the formation of an empire. As Henry Wallace said: "I am interested in peace because I want our American system to demonstrate the enormous vitality of which it is capable. That vitality is being wasted in preparations for war" (MacDougall 1965, 423). The Cold War with the Soviets was a nearly perfect war, not the less so for its being largely imaginary, for "It may even reasonably be said that the intensely sharp competitive *preparation* for war by the nations *is the real war*, permanent, unceasing; and that the battles are only a sort of public verification of the mastery gained during the 'peace' interval" (James 1967, 663). That the preparations for the Cold War were an economic disaster of the first magnitude goes all but unacknowledged by public officials. "These actions brought the deficit down to $200 billion [per annum]. That's where it festers now, threatening one day to shatter the financial integrity of the American economy" (Stockman 1986, 398). Stockman was exiled to the wilderness for his realism, to become just another voice crying there. His assessment was of the good old days of $200 billion annual deficits in the mid-1980s. For the remainder of the

Reagan-Bush era, the current accounts deficit was double these numbers and ran more than $1 billion a day as the United States staggered toward its fiscal precipice. The Clinton administration seems to have cut those numbers in half, or back to $200 Billion, but the American people have still walked off this military cliff holding hands. The fall so far has been relatively peaceful; the crash landing is not apt to be so.

The rationale for keeping many generals on the payroll can be astounding. "So the truth of the matter probably is that in the infinite, complicated economy, of the Civil War it was better to keep Ben Butler a major general, even though soldiers were needlessly killed because of it, than it was to inject him back into the political whirlpool" (Catton 1958, 237). Who exactly gets killed through this application of ineptitude is also revealing. "Though Blacks compose 14 percent of the population from the ages of 18 to 24, they accounted for 22 percent of recruits. Moreover, Blacks made up 26.7 percent of the Army's infantry and 19.9 percent of the Marine Corps' infantry, two job specialties that would face the greatest risk in war. . . most socioeconomic groups are represented in the services, except for children from relatively high-income families" (*Congressional Quarterly*, special report, January 5, 1991 30). It is especially bad form in the highly stratified class society of the United States to place the children of the relatively high-income white families, such as J. Danforth Quayle, in positions where they can be shot at. Race and privilege has its rank. "An Act for Raising and Enlisting such Slaves as shall be thought serviceable to this Province in Time of Alarms" (Wood 1974, 125) was passed in Colonial South Carolina in 1704 and revised in 1708. American Blacks have a long tradition of disproportionate (relative to what they receive from the society) military service. They are joined in this disproportionate treatment by the Hispanics.

As germane as the warnings against militarism are, they go unheeded. "Parenthetically, let every nation beware of gathering possessions solely on the advice of its military or naval high command" (Roosevelt 1970, 166). Not everything stated parenthetically should be ignored, but Bush ordered the first military contingents to Saudi Arabia in August of 1990 after consulting solely with Brent Scowcroft, his "National" Security Advisor who is independent of congressional oversight. The war on Iraq provided a momentary distraction from the structural and psychological recession that also began in August of 1990, virtually at the same moment of the orders to occupy Saudi Arabia. The war on Iraq contributed greatly to the recession because uncertain consumers held anxiously on to their money.

Even such a superficially benign idea as the one floated by Senator Sam Nunn of Georgia (before the war on Iraq) that his Senate Armed Forces Appropriations Committee could rescue some of its turf by making protection of the environment a military activity, has long antecedents. John Quincy Adams was a pioneer (1818) in reforestation and preservation of the live oak stands in the Southeast. "He understood better than any American of his day how indispensable live oak was to any nation that aspired to naval and sea power." (Bourgin 1989, 172). John C. Calhoun, criticized for his ambitious plans to develop the West, said "'I concurred entirely in the opinion that no projects absolutely impracticable ought to be recommended. But I would look to a practicability of a longer range than a simple session of Congress'" (174). Regrettably, a single session of Congress now passes for the long view where with no enemy fit to prepare to destroy 20 times over, "It is much more difficult to recede from a scale of expenditure once adopted than it is to extend the accustomed scale in response to an accession of wealth" (Veblen 1931, 102). It was just such a recision in scale that prompted Nunn to suggest that the good earth be primed to catch the disintegrating battalions. Efforts to scale the defense expenditure back to realistic levels, we could be twice as safe for half as much, are resisted by military apologists such as Defense Secretary, William Perry, with oblique references to other imaginary threats as well as their public promises to make closing bases more expensive than keeping them open.

The death threat or the threat of death is making the most serious challenge to the military for available funds. Most Americans, whatever they might give by way of lip service to the contrary, are not impressed with the Christian notion of going to heaven when they die, either that or they are all sinners of such magnitude they cannot be forgiven and may be on their way to hell. In any case, most would prefer to go to the hospital and to postpone death forever. The medical industry's capitalization of the fear of death is giving the military a run for its money. It is a form of proof, should any idle peasants care to examine it, that whatever vitality English speaking culture may have had is rapidly being sucked out of it by the reversionary military and the uncalled for fear of death. They are the two biggest blood suckers on American vitality. Death is the door to the future where everybody's personal plans deserve to disintegrate.

One of the disintegrating plans in the Texas military matrix, to locate the Super-Conductor Super-Collider research facility at Waxahatchie, Texas, was once held up by reluctant Japanese Yen. The House of Representatives finally got wise to the Texan wish to reduce taxes while simultaneously increasing federal spending in Texas and momentarily killed this extravagance. The Texans looked to Japanese money to pay for their war on Iraq because the federal treasury, which James S. Baker III once led, is bare. Baker was Reagan's Secretary of the Treasury during the largest looting of a public treasury in world history. "The State of Texas stands as a historic reminder that Americans, on these shores, did not create something entirely new, nor emerge entirely innocent" (Fehrenbach 1968, 448). Fehrenbach compares the Texas success of expropriating land (and labor) to that of the Normans or the modern Israelis. He is deadly accurate when he reports that "His national myths were more influenced by the Alamo and the burden of a century of a wild frontier than concepts conceived at Philadelphia" (257). It is the Texas version of American history, not the one floating out of Philadelphia suspended by the frequently violated Bill of Rights, that is calling the shots of North American Destiny. The Texan version of history has taken Americans a long way in the wrong direction.

Every culture has its own civilization and the western future has been greatly circumscribed and pointed in the other direction by its reversionary dependence on the military, of which the numbers recited for the gunbelt are barely the tip of the iceberg audit. The great problems of the 20th century, rather than being solved, were disguised as frenetic military maneuvers, so much so that it appears that World War I had never taken place and may need to be fought over, once again commencing in the Balkans. It is as if that old joke about the arch bishop being found alive, to which the punch line is that World War I was a mistake, finally came true. The difference between culture and civilization is the difference between "the living body of a soul and the mummy of it. . . Culture is the self-evident. . . the fatal imposition of thought upon the inscrutable quality of creativeness [is a symptom] of a soul that is beginning to tire" (Spengler 1926, 353). Despite all the rampant unemployment, "In the last terrible stages of evolution it will culminate in the *Duty to Work*" (362). No fun for anybody in other words as entropy gradually paralyzes the bankrupt American political imagination.

Spengler projected that the western paralysis would set in around the year 2000 but the Americans have actually been rushing the process, for with the coming of television and its illiterate impatience, we have imagined the future and brought it toward us. The American civilization has mummies to burn and having published and broadcast its "secrets," including the irreversibility of asymmetrical time, impatiently awaits its fate. "Time gives birth to Space, but Space gives death to Time" (173). The discoveries of Columbus gave birth to space, creating the whole other half of the now spherical world. And the rush to fill the space killed the sidelong plunge of the culture and its experiment in democracy, for the peasants of the present and future, are as free of history as they are of time. Their challenge is to avoid mummification in the fatal imposition of Confederate thought on their practical creativity.

Except that people get cold and create buildings to warm themselves and reflect their collective souls, the rest of the evidence is largely transitory. "The Doric column, the Egyptian pyramid, the Gothic cathedral, *grow out* of the ground, earnest, big with destiny, Being without waking-consciousness. The Ionic column, the buildings of the Middle Kingdom and those of the Baroque, calmly aware and conscious of themselves, free and sure, *stand on* the ground" (Spengler 1928, 92) The architecture of the soul would not be so interesting except "so complete is the congruence, in the Western and every other Culture whose art we know at all, that is has never occurred to anyone to be astonished at the fact that strict architecture (which is simply the highest form of pure ornament) is entirely confined to religious building" (123). The Pentagon, thrown up in religious ecstasy at the prospect of Communist siege expressed by the Truman Doctrine, meets the test of theological adornment. The Great Hall of the People in Beijing, imagined into being in a mere eight months after the 1949 Maoist triumph of ridding China of foreign domination, borders Tian An Men on the west along with the Forbidden City on the north at the religious and ceremonial center of the Middle Kingdom. This is the same Middle Kingdom, whose boats in the fleet of Cheng Ho, one of which would have been large enough to contain the *Nina*, the *Pinta*, and the *Santa Maria*, beat the American Salvation Army to Mogadishu in Somalia by 600 years.

"The ceremonial center at Teotihuacan was laid out along the axis that pointed north toward the Pyramid of the Moon. This great street, which the Aztecs named the Micaotli, or 'Avenue of the Dead,' is about two miles long. . . To the east rises the overwhelming mass of the Pyramid of the Sun. . . All of this produces a feeling of eternity, as if everything had been constructed in order to elevate the spirit of the spectator" (Forbes 1973, 42). At a distance, the Temple of the Sun at Teotihuacan often appears to "float" above the landscape, so completely is it merged with the natural environment and appears to be so effortlessly supported by it.

Contemporary North American religious architecture is more closely related to those buildings which "grow" up out of the land, for the new banks which superintend the distribution of imaginary money in a city like Seattle, have their piles driven deep into the soil so that their glass and steel artifice can more easily withstand the earthquakes the area is prone to. While the new religious banks may stand for centuries, the people limp sideways out from under their towering insignificance and usurious burden of debt, for no provisions are being made for the overdue fiscal earthquake on the Confederate fault line. Just as it took blood to "liberate" the slaves and the capital they represented, so too will it take blood to liberate the funny money the rich in this contemporary Confederate system have so lavishly feathered their nests with. "For the first time in modern U.S. History, stock prices decoupled from the real economy, enabling the Dow-Jones industrial average to keep setting records, even as employees' real wages kept declining" (Phillips 1994, 86), with the ". . . volume of trading thirty or forty times greater than the dollar turnover of the 'real economy'. . ." (80). Imaginary money will fail to attract sufficient depositors or cushion the fall. The mummies will walk from the house of the dead. The bankrupt government of the United States, creator of an artificial military prosperity in the southern regions of the country, is looking for a soft place to land.

22

One Big Plantation:
King Cotton, Prince Albert, Sacred Cows

The prevailing economic model in the United States is the plantation. Formerly expressed in such specific realms and activities as King Cotton, Prince Albert and the sacred cows, the plantation model expanded vertically to include microchips and fiberoptics. It should come as no surprise in a southern dominated culture where "The classic works of Phillips and Gray viewed the slave plantation as the pre-eminent institution of Southern agriculture, stressing the tendency for wealth to concentrate in the hands of a relatively small planter class" (Wright 1978, 25), that this should be so. Plantation economics concentrates wealth in the fewest possible hands while the rest of the population will receive subsistence.

At its maximum angle of extension, the experiment in democracy undertaken in 1776 offered the American people the model of "One Big Union," where everybody's labor was treated with respect. On the "One Big Plantation," labor is treated with contempt. The colonial slaveholding plantation model established by the English in South Carolina is too pervasive. As it modified over time into transnational corporation economics, with wealth continuing to concentrate in fewer and fewer hands, "The American race problem is simply a special version of the world colonial problem which, in the last analysis, is a problem involving the exploitation of labor" (McWilliams 1951, 339).

The plantation model is not confined to agriculture, although "Capitalistic farming, in the form of the plantation, is not the product of this century, but has been an American phenomenon wherever large scale operations and investments were necessary, as in the West Indies, in South Carolina, or in California. It is not, moreover, necessarily a phenomenon involving slave labor but appears in certain areas with white native, Mexican, or other immigrant labor. Inherent in the plantation regime are many of the characteristics of capitalistic enterprise, especially the large unit of production which makes the farm colonist a losing competitor and calls either for his absorption or his expulsion. This phenomenon, it should be

pointed out, is the effect of the spread of the plantation, and not the intention of the persons within the system" (Klingberg 1975, ix).

In other words, a plantation system does not require slaves but a slave-
like exploitation of labor, and there is little or no room for a small operator,
just as on Barbados circa 1670. "*Economic exploitation* is the expropriation
of the product of labor without compensation. The *rate of exploitation* is the
fraction of that total product of labor which is exploited" (Ransom and
Sutch 1977, 3). Peasant labor was expropriated in the medieval and feudal
models prevalent in Europe at the beginning of the European incursion
into the Western Hemisphere. The rate of expropriation of slave labor by
the English was sufficiently large to create the British Empire and the pool
of capital required to finance the industrial revolution. While certain
colonies, such as those centered at Boston and Philadelphia, may have been
founded in the search for religious and economic freedom, the expropriation of labor was never far behind.

"During the predatory culture labour comes to be associated in men's
habits of thought with weakness and subject to a master. It is therefore a
mark of inferiority, and therefore comes to be accounted unworthy of man
in his best estate. By virtue of this tradition labour is felt to be debasing, and
this tradition has never died out" (Veblen 1931, 36). The dignity of labor is
an oxymoron dispensed with contempt from the ruling class. "There is no
need of pointing out how prone the men of to-day are to revert to the
spiritual attitude of mastery and of personal subservience which characterizes that stage" (196). The debasement of labor by the master class and its
need for servants establishes the economic style. "Their office is of a
parasitic character, and their interest is to divert what substance they may to
their own use, and to retain whatever is under their hand. . . They are
conventions of ownership; derivatives, more or less remote, of the ancient
predatory culture" (209). The predatory nature of the American economy,
where 15 percent of the population currently victimizes the rest, is apparent
to all who work in it with their eyes open.

Ralph Lerner, in his essay "Calhoun's New Science of Politics," cuts to
the heart of the Calhoun effect on the ruling coalition of conservative
Republicans and southern Democrats (of both parties) who hold power.
"Some interpreters have had no difficulty in seeing in all this a more or less
open appeal for the planters and capitalist manufacturers to collaborate
against the lower classes" (Thomas 1968, 218). The difficulty would be not

so much in seeing it as missing it if people bother to look. When the South and the rest of the United States came out of the Reconstruction doldrums, "Hawaii was also the laboratory in which the formula for American expansionism — the outward expression of our domestic racial imperialism — was first worked out. Nations that practice imperialism must also practice racism" (McWilliams 1951, 171).

This was the same imperial expansionism that displaced the Creek and the Choctaw Indians for cotton plantations in the South and the Commanche for cattle ranches in Texas. In California, according to Dr. Cook: "'One is tempted to follow through the persistence of the forced-labor idea in subsequent years. It would be possible to show how the cheap labor market passed from the Indian to the Chinese and how the same rationale of peonage and compulsion was applied to the latter. One might then pass on to new groups, each of which gradually replaced the other — ... down to the 'Okies' of our time'" (McWilliams 1946, 47). It is hard to miss how this economic exploitation directly contradicts the best impulses of democracy, as expressed by Lincoln in his second inaugural address as he spoke of "malice toward none, with charity for all" as a way of achieving "a just and a lasting peace among ourselves and with all nations."

If slave, peon, coolie and Okie exploited labor can make a success out of plantation agriculture, the challenge to the master class was to discover where else it would work. "The corporation, in fact, became the striking feature of American business life, one of the most marvelous institutions of all time, comparable in wealth and power and the number of its servants with king-doms and states of old" (Beard and Beard 1925, 409). The corporation, as a marvelous institution, got one of its biggest boosts in southern California. "Another was the Southern Pacific — not a mere railroad, but the largest private landowner in California" (Reisner 1986, 349). Plantation, railroad, corporation, and epitome of the huge success with size that accumulates in the United States with the exploitation of labor, the Southern Pacific Railroad was aptly characterized by Frank Norris in his novel *The Octopus*. Its indelible contribution to corporate culture came in *Santa Clara County v The Southern Pacific Railroad Company* (1886) when Chief Justice Waite of the United States Supreme Court extended the due process clause of the 14th Amendment to corporations, literally giving them legal "bodies." This exceptionally creative reading of the constitution enabled a law passed to protect the rights of former slaves to become the bulwark of corporate irresponsibility. This efficient management tool was the narrow waist of the hour glass the sands of the plantation system funneled through to its present transnational corporate (TNC) splendor.

"One of the points made and discussed at length in the brief of counsel for defendants in error was that 'Corporations are persons within the meaning of the Fourteenth Amendment to the Constitution of the United States.' Before argument, Mr. CHIEF JUSTICE WAITE said: The court does not wish to hear arguments on the question whether the provision in the Fourteenth Amendment to the Constitution, which forbids a State to deny to any person within its jurisdiction the equal protection of the laws, applies to these corporations. We are all of opinion that it does" (118 U.S. 396). Chief Justice Waite was not only legislating here, he was legislating unanimously and did not even wish to hear the arguments. It was a *fait accompli.*

Language is innocent of meaning. In spite of the superficial innocence of the unanimous Supreme Court decision acquiring the force of law in *Santa Clara County v The Southern Pacific Railroad Company*, after all corporations must be only groups of people associating voluntarily and what we extend to one person we should extend to groups, we are entitled to and we must keep in mind the truly significant and immense differences between a former slave and a corporation the size of the SPRR. A corporation is a person within the meaning of the law. We will return again and again to the startling consequences of this marriage between plantations and corporations where "in California industry and agriculture are one" (McWilliams 1949, 163). By this one act of judicial fiat, the SPRR and other corporations by extension of precedent, became entities with both government and personal power, while acquiring virtually no responsibilities to society.

The ruling in *SCC v. SPRR*, having been with us for over a hundred years, has acquired the force of natural law. There was nothing "natural" about the way the land in California was parceled out, as former Governor Haight said: "'The acquisition of large blocks of land by capitalists or corporations either as donations or at nominal prices'" (McWilliams 1969, 21), was the rule. The Lords' Proprietors in South Carolina acquired title in much the same facile fashion. Ultimately, the shared characteristics of California agriculture and corporations are crucial. "California agriculture is monopolistic in character; it is highly organized; it utilizes familiar price-fixing schemes; it is corporately owned; management and ownership are sharply differentiated; it is enormously profitable to the large owners" (266). It is precisely profitable to the degree, suggested earlier by Ransom and Sutch, of the rate of expropriation of the labor (and of the environment, which we will get to shortly). To focus for a moment on one of its salient features, the differentiation between management and ownership, "If the overseer somehow managed to please the master *and* the slaves, he was guaranteed a long tenure on the plantation" (Blassingame 1972, 176). The overseer, as middle manager, was the visible symbol of authority on the plantation and within the corporation.

Corporations and plantations display a four-tiered structure. At the top is ownership, sometimes royal, virtually always absentee, and in the modern corporation, either family held or spread among the owners of public stock offerings. The second level of management, the officers and boards of directors of the corporations, has its counterpart in giant agribusiness, just as there was a level of control between the plantation owner and the overseer. The third level is composed of middle management and overseers, actually accountable for production goals on their shifts and divisionals. At the base of the economic pyramid where the actual work takes place, we find the slaves, the peons, the coolies, the Okies, the workers, and the "servants" of the corporations, as Charles and Mary Beard referred to them. In the contemporary scene we find the "temps" (temporary workers), the modern migrant workers who go from job to job without benefits or security.

Management is a ticklish business and courses in it predominate in the continuous learning environment of regressionary capitalism. Some of the subtleties are expressed when "The slaveholder also kept up the pretense of absolute control by refusing to take note of every deviation from the rules. . . In effect, each planter had to learn to be selectively inattentive to rules infractions. . . The same obsequious behavior was not demanded of ordinary slaves and those in positions of trust" (182). When the plantation slave system broke into open revolt, such as the Stono Rebellion, the Nat Turner Rebellion, or that of Denmark Vesey, it was both a symptom of oppression and a stimulus for more oppression. "There was so little identification with the master's interest in the quarters that he frequently had to resort to coercion and to more and more oppressive laws" (183). It will come as no surprise that slaves had a hard time identifying with the master's interests, just as corporate loyalty among the servants they employ is a manufactured response, yet still some daydreams are a long time dying. "But the enchantment born of the old dream at Jamestown reaches across the ages, and to the Virginia plantation owners today, as to the planters of the great ages, the plantation represents more than a way of earning a living: it is beauty, expansiveness and dignity, and a perpetuation of that graciousness which America has discovered can exist in a democracy" (Dowdy 1957, 320).   Tune out the violins and unquestionably the psychedelic virtues of plantation or corporate life all revert to the master class merely feigning democracy. The distress among the workers is continuous and profound, where even their inventions, much less their labor, belong to the corporation. "Except for the skillful aspirants to power, the bulk of the population was blocked off from advancement, and this caused a shifting and unsettledness as families and individuals groped to discover their own level" (107). The English speaking civilization, emphasizing competition and independence over cooperation and belonging, stimulates high levels of anxiety. After the Civil War, this anxiety expressed itself in the "crop-sharing labor system with the displaced and starving Negroes. By this grim expedient for survival, the paternalism of the plantation was extended into the present" (316).

The slavery system in the United States survived in 1784 against a Jefferson-introduced draft of the territorial ordinance where "The tragedy lies in the fact that Congress failed by a single vote to adopt a total prohibition of slavery in the territories" (Bourgin 1989, 119). By such razor thin margins are cultures directed and Senator Robert W. Barnwell could say in 1845: "Our institutions are doomed and the Southern civilization must go out in blood" (Rosen 1982, 88). The South went out in blood and came back stronger for it with Calhoun still calling the shots. "Northern business interests ought to join the Southern aristocracy in keeping working people (white or black) in their place" (91). The reversionary wish to impose static solutions on dynamic situations blinds people to the fact that "There was a disaster even for the South in the premise that every civilized society must be built upon a submerged and exploited labor force" (Hofstadter 1959, 90).

The disaster was hardly confined to the South for "The many ways in which farmers were victimized by tariffs, railroads, middlemen, speculators, warehousers, and monopolistic producers of farm equipment were all but forgotten" (188). The ripoff of farmers, farm (slave) labor, and the vitiating of the fertility of the soil, is the basis of the superficial and tempo-rary wealth of the rest of the empire, and is the ultimate source of funding for the American religion of militarism.

This process is not confined to European civilizations either, for the exploitation of the rice farmers in Japan was exactly the financial margin necessary to fund the rise of their "Co-Prosperity Sphere" as they colonized Asia following an English/American model. "This huge requisition upon the cultivator in Japan was what ultimately made possible the financing of the national war machine. The ratio of 60 percent to cultivator and 40 percent for taxes and rent needs to be contrasted with the normal ratios in Burma and Siam of 90 to 10" (Benedict 1974, 313). In California "'The rapid transition from field to orchard crops. . . was certainly accelerated by the use of a labor supply [Chinese] that was cheap even by comparison with Negro slave labor in the South'" (DeMarco 1988, 102). The 1992 peach pickers in Edgefield County, South Carolina, are barely one half-step from slavery (NBC). The Catholics, who started slavery in California, were not favorably disposed to the organization of labor. "Mahoney rejected the vote's legitimacy in a tantrum more becoming of a Valley lettuce grower or South-ern textile magnate than the supposed pastor of Los Angeles's Latino poor" (Davis 1990, 358). And as if that were not enough, "having deliberately alienated the Los Angeles labor movement, the archbishop chose to high-light his relations with Riordan and other millionaire Catholic patrons" (361). Riordan was later elected mayor of Los Angeles.

Anyone who thought the results of the Civil War would put an end to the exploitation of labor was mistaken for all that was accomplished was "the exchange of one set of masters for another. . . The real meaning of the Bargain of 1876 was revealed the following year when the railroad workers precipitated the first acute labor crisis in American history" (McWilliams 1951, 266). Labor crises would abound in the United States for "When it succeeded in thoroughly organizing a craft, it often found its purposes defeated by an influx of foreigners ready to work for lower wages and thus undermine the foundations of the union" (Beard and Beard 1925, 582). The open nature of the empire is still providing a haven for nearly a million displaced foreigners a year, willing to work for lower wages, keeping the position of workers steadily undermined.

This is not a recent phenomenon as H.P. Stabler's report at the State Fruit-Growers Convention for 1902 said: "'We have so degraded a certain class of labor, that there is not a man who lives in any agricultural locality who wants to get in and do this work'" (McWilliams 1969, 97). So the owners continuously turned to an imported supply of labor designed for "Keeping wages at the lowest possible point. . . The bookkeeper at the Hotchkiss Ranch had to be a trained linguist" (118). Just as Charleston became the most linguistically diverse location in the Colonial United States based on the importation of labor, so has California replaced it in contemporary times. Enforcing the status of the workers at the lowest economic level was reinforced during WWII because "To appreciate what a bonanza this program was to the large farm-factories, it should be pointed out that the *braceros* were limited to agricultural employment" (McWilliams 1968, 267).

Labor exploitation in the WWII era was not confined to agriculture, however, as Truman's tantrum when he seized the coal mines in 1946 during a strike demonstrates. His solution was characterized as a "slave labor bill" (MacDougall 1965, 42). Truman was also accused, due to his own anti-labor stand, of not opposing the Taft-Hartley bill strong enough (173). The veto couldn't be sustained because it ran straight up against the ruling coalition of northern reactionaries and southern conservatives. "The Taft-Hartley slave labor bill became law. . . [in Truman's] failure to command the votes of more than half of the members of his own party in Congress" (177). The ruling "more than half" of the members of his own party were from farther south than Missouri. Philip Murray of the CIO's promise is still out there dangling in the wind. "'I made FDR a promise which, under God, I hope to keep, that the CIO will not stop until it has organized the South, 'til we have removed the chains from the victims, colored and white'" (174).

"The Western Labor Union was founded at Salt Lake City on May 10, 1898, because the AFL had not organized unskilled workers" (Zinn 1980, 301). The real test of labor, as of culture in general, is how well does it treat the disadvantaged. If the Taft-Hartly Act after WWII put labor on the road to being out of business, WWI was no prize in labor relations. Striking miners in Arizona were railroaded out of the state on cattle cars (Johnson 1973, 89), and "In the first year of the war the NCLB [National Civil Liberties Board, forerunner of the ACLU] recorded over a hundred instances of mob violence" (64). They hanged Frank Little, an IWW organizer in Butte, Montana. The IWW or Industrial Workers of the World is the source of the ideal, one big union. Many unions in the United States have a history of cooperation with management, such as in the steel industry. For 20 years after WWII the profits from the steel business were parceled out as dividends on one hand and as wages and benefits on the other while the physical plant was allowed to deteriorate, eventually putting both the owners and the workers into other occupations. "But the sad truth is that the labor movement. . . has settled for being a junior partner, often a well-paid one, in American capitalism" (Walton 1976, 274).

How this came to be was through the application of typical divide and conquer strategies of the owners. In a review of *Poverty and Compassion* by Gertrude Himmelfarb entitled "Down and Out in Victorian England," we discover that "The traditional interpretation of the dock strike of 1889 held it to be an impressive victory for a particularly impoverished group of workers. This simplistic view is marred, however, by the fact that some 80 percent of the employers in fact favored the workers' aims. Though the strike benefited the more skilled dockers, their victory militated against casual laborers, who were reduced to an outcast class. The strike, therefore, can be presented as a triumph for middle-class or capitalist interests" (Zeigler 1991). Only a continuous unbiased audit of results such as this one can reveal where the heart of the system pumps its blood. The master class benefits "by the more disturbing fact that the poorest *one-third* of American society has not been 'mobilized' to become regular voters" (Kennedy 1987, 531). Ronald Reagan, who signaled the final death knell of the American labor movement in 1982 when he broke the PATCO Strike, was a firm believer in the beginning or "nigger" minimum wage. The victory of the master class over the outcasts, and the failure of labor to organize everybody into a share of both the rewards and responsibilities of the economic system, characterize the ongoing victory of the plantation.

The colonial system of exploitation is difficult to escape, based as it is on cultural norms. "The strategy of dominance used by colonial powers is the same as that used by the white majority in the United States in its relations with colored minorities" (McWilliams 1951, 338). It worked so well within the United States, where "The federal government ruled New Mexico for sixty-three years as a dependent province" (McWilliams 1968, 121), how would it play overseas? We have already seen how Hawaii was the laboratory for the extension of the plantation system onto an already existing coolie system. The Republican platform of 1896 stated: "The Hawaiian Islands should be controlled by the United States and no foreign power should be permitted to interfere with them" (Beard and Beard 1925, 485).

It is Republican doubletalk from the United States that imagines its presence in Hawaii as domestic rather than foreign. "The United Fruit plantations [in the banana republics of Central America] are reminiscent of the South during the pre-Civil War era" (Liss 1967, 106). Eisenhower's CIA put Guatemala's banana plantations back into the Confederate Empire of North America in 1954. In 1908, the Democratic party platform said: "We reaffirm the position thrice announced by the Democrats in national convention assembled against a policy of imperialism and colonial exploitation in the Philippines or elsewhere" (Johnson 1973, 174). The Democrats could announce against the policy all they wished; the Republicans were setting policy with Confederate impetus.

Looking a little deeper into the banana plantation agriculture of United Fruit, we find on their board of directors in 1959, General Walter Bedell Smith, who had been Eisenhower's commanding officer in 1941 and later served as Eisenhower's Director of the CIA (McCann 1976, 61-2). The chummy lines of force in this oligarchy in the banana republics demonstrate the relationships in the military, political, corporate plantation with predictable results. "At its peak, United Fruit Company served as the sole economic support for a total population of almost half a million workers and their dependents" (123).

It is instructive to notice that the company struck the phrase "culture of poverty" from its report even though it did not deny creating and perpetuating it. What they left in was perhaps even more of an indictment regarding the workers' "desire for freedom," which was ". . . not just an abstract longing but was an attitude based on the fact that they were not free at all, that they were completely at the company's mercy for everything they needed simply to stay alive" (95). There is nothing in McCann's description that contradicts the Liss assessment that these arrangements were typical of slave plantations in the antebellum South. At this time, United Fruit was managed from Boston and "Where once the company had shaped the social history of its tropical realm, it now lagged decades behind, denying the existence of injustices which lay at the heart of how we did business" (98).

It is not surprising that management would deny the existences of injustices at the heart of how they did business. These injustices are at the heart of the "One Big Plantation" system of business. We can, if we choose, deny that this is plantation agriculture, deny that it is colonialism, deny that it is imperialism, deny that it is racism and deny the profits bankrolled by this expropriation, not only of the labor of the workers but of the lives of their entire families. The facts speak otherwise and are available for examination.

John Calhoun, the principal rationalist for the plantation system and the expropriation of labor, once he had formulated the notion that slavery was a "positive good" (a curious double affirmation), set about extolling it as a positive benefit for northern capitalists as well. "Not only American Capitalists but also the British ruling classes had a stake in the preservation of Southern slavery. . . [for it was not unlike] the subjection of one nation to another, as in the British Empire" (Thomas 1968, 159). Whether the exploitation of colonies is a sound idea or not is open to discussion, as Theodore Roosevelt Jr., in *American Imperialism*, cited figures for Italy, Germany, France and Japan as he claimed that "in many instances colonies have been a continuous loss" (1970, 73). He is joined in that opinion by Strabo, especially when the colony requires garrisoning to keep it in line.

Roosevelt could observe, in his tenure as governor of Puerto Rico, that "The rich coastal plain was largely in the hands of big sugar companies" (108). This should not make the relative poverty of ordinary Puerto Ricans a mystery "As the rich coastal lands were most valuable for sugar production, the growing of vegetables, etc., was greatly circumscribed" (108). This is precisely how indigenous people are impoverished: the imposition of single crop plantation agriculture typically displaces a diverse peasant stable economy that provides a balanced diet. Perkins (1966, 51), notices the instinct to domination in the American colonial character, but he goes on to rationalize how benign the single crop agriculture is. It is benign only for the bottom lines of the typically foreign master class.

Any remotely objective assessment of the evidence reinforces the conclusion that "In a sense the southern dream of a tropical slave empire survived even after the Confederate defeat" (May 1973, 255). Slavery jumped the 98th Meridian to California where it had already been thriving under

Catholic masters, it jumped halfway across the Pacific Ocean to the coolie plantations of Hawaii, and the rest of the way across to the plantations in the Philippine Islands. During the war in Vietnam "The SEADAG symposiasts see a bright future for Vietnam as the Imperial Valley of East Asia. The farm workers in the Imperial Valley might tell them what that implies for the mass of the population" (Chomsky 1973, 280). Chomsky goes on to suggest that conditions in Asia would be even worse, without the obsequious nods to ineffective rules of law and lettuce boycotts. The colonial exploitation of labor takes place both within and without the putative boundary confines of The Confederate Empire of North America, for "Like a miniature Mexico or Bolivia, Fontana is a debtor nation held in thrall to its Orange County and West L.A. creditor-developers" (Davis 1990, 425).

While these arrangements may make sense temporarily for the master class where the planters lived in town (Rosen 1982, 25), as they did in Charleston, and the owners may live now on the other side of the planet, the long term prognosis is unfavorable. "In areas where the nominal price counted — as in contracts, instruments of debt, and other legal documents — someone took a beating and someone made a killing" (Weir 1983, 96). The beatings and the killings, curious predatory economic holdover terms from the actual slaving past, continue. One result is an "obsession with physical security systems, and, collaterally, with the architectural policing of social boundaries, [which] has become a zeitgeist of urban restructuring, a master narrative in the emerging built environment of the 1990s" (Davis 1990, 223). This is yet another of the consequences of having an urban plantation and the colony right in the backyard of the "mother" country.

As the modern corporate system continues its global search for high profit levels, "The 1978-82 wave of factory closings in the wake of Japanese import penetration and recession, which shuttered ten of the twelve largest non-aerospace plants in Southern California and displaced 75,000 blue-collar workers, erased the ephemeral gains won by blue-collar Blacks between 1965 and 1975" (304). The reversionary effects on the workers are obvious and include having their medical coverage and pension programs canceled (420). That is particularly unfortunate, because just as in the rise of the British Empire where landlords passed on the consequences of the land tax, "The true burden of the land tax may have been borne not by landlords but by farmers and their labourers" (Brewer 1989, 203). In all economic systems, whether they literally pay them or not, the burden of finance and the actual taxes are all paid by the poor. How this affects the rich and the master class was neatly summed up by President Kennedy adumbrating Ronald Reagan as he rationalized his preoccupation with Cuba, "Who gives a shit if the minimum wage is $1.15 or $1.35?" (Collier and Horowitz 1984, 274).

We see the power of the rich working overtime at present in California as they seek to eliminate the anti-smoking campaign from California television because it is cutting into tobacco corporate profits. If tobacco was the product of Vermont, Oregon or Minnesota, are we expected to believe that its production, distribution, and prominent role in 400,000 premature local deaths annually would be subsidized and sanctified with the force of law? The former Surgeon General of the United States, C. Everett Koop, has stated that the smoking of tobacco is the most documented cause of disease in history. When greater restrictions are put on tobacco use domestically, the southern dominated government provides subsidies to export the poison drug to American colonies overseas. Tobacco is one form of the revenge of the Indians. More money has been made with less expenditure of effort in the abuse of the nicotine drug base of this product than any other, which may be why the Clinton Administration would like to tap its income stream with higher taxes to fund what it persists in calling "health care reform." As the product of a mere handful of southern states, it is deathly proof of the southern domination of the drugged American political system.

The manufacturers of Marlboro cigarets were able to tattoo their product onto the backs of the hands and into the drug habits of the American cowboy. The cowboys, 19th century hippies according to the cowboy poet Vess Quinlan of Alamosa, Colorado, who says "There hasn't been a real cowboy born/In almost a hundred years" (1990, 9), are a special type of indentured servant, suspended in tobacco smoke, whiskey and three chord country music, halfway between slavery and peonage, behind the wheels of their partially paid for pickup trucks. The spread of the cowboy culture from Texas north to 12 western states gave Texas mythical and political title to Marlboro Country, as they were "bankrolled by English lords and lawyers, financiers, and businessmen" (Rifkin 1992, 89) in a financial invasion reminiscent of the Lord's Proprietors colonization of South Carolina. The Knights of the Golden Circle, primarily a Texas organization, whose name "symbolized its purpose — the creation of a great slave empire" (May 1983, 149), would have its intentions ultimately realized in Houston's actualized fantasy of the extension of Texas power, which came north out of Texas with the cowboys on horseback. The black "cow boys" who wrangled colonial South Carolina (Weir 1983, 174) were the prototype for the exploited labor of the American cowboy.

Sacred cows, as they stampeded down the prairie dog streets of Abilene connecting the North and the South back together on the railroading chance to make a buck, were far indeed from the moist green of England where the British breeds were developed. It was farther still to India where the Brahmans came from that the Texans on the King Ranch crossed with the Shorthorns for their heat and drought resistant qualities to create the new breed of Santa Gertrudis. If cowboy labor is exploited, cf "Take This Job and Shove It," so too is the land, for sacred cows in the West are an economic nuisance, a psycho-social pacifier, and an environmental catastrophe. "According to a 1989 report by the National Wildlife Federation and the Natural Resources Defense Council, 68 percent of the 138 million Bureau of Land Management acres recently inventoried were, by the agency's own definition, in 'unsatisfactory condition. Poor grazing practices continue to be endemic to the vast majority of those lands,' according to the report" (Wuerther 1989, 39). Wuerther is a former BLM botanist. Three-fourths of the water pumped into California to make the "Cadillac Desert" bloom is used unnecessarily to grow fodder for livestock. T.R. Fehrenbach, as he was extolling the virtues of Stephen F. Austin as "the greatest colonial proprietor in North American history," also noted that "Destroying nature and creating civilization as they knew it was already a fetish in North American minds" (1968, 145). In other words, the environmental degradation of the West as practiced by the livestock industry reached new heights there, but it did not begin there and environmental degradation itself was old hat by the time it reached Texas.

Some South Carolinian colonists kept plans to return to England after they had "made their killing" and that contributed to the notion of the land as a commodity to be exploited. When the southern states made cotton king of their new economy, they reduced the hardwood forests of the Mississippi Valley to ashes and turned the soil into dirt. "Bernard DeVoto. . . is responsible. . . for directing my attention to the significance of the soil depletion in the Southern states and the interrelationship of the consequent

Western expansionist and abolitionist movements" (Coit 1950, vii). The capitalist slaving pressure was for not only more land but new land, "new soils, for instance, offered an escape from lands depleted by one-crop agriculture" (May 1973, 12). May also cites this depletion of the vitality of the soil as one reason for the Southern interest in the sugar plantations of Cuba in the 1850s (24). After the Civil War, "Commercial fertilizers only allowed farmers working this exhausted land to hold their own" (Ransom and Sutch 1977, 188). This was one beginning of the high tech solutions to soil depletion problems by learning to rely on petrochemical farming to keep single-crop plantation agriculture profitable.

With the labor exploited, the land exhausted, "The opportunity for economic stability offered by the world's largest aquifer, however was squandered for immediate gain. . . The Ogallala region supports not so much a farming industry as a mining industry" (Reisner 1986, 455). They mined the land, they mined the water, and even before the land's productive capacity is exhausted, it is frequently paved over or smogged out for industry. "Ranchers across from the mill picked grapefruit from their trees for the last time in the fall of 1942" (Davis 1990, 389).

The last grapefruit in Fontana is an example of how the welcome mat is withdrawn from small operators in the predatory reversionary economy, even though "What the evidence points to, in other words, is not that larger slave farms were more efficient, but that there was an upper bound on the possibility of efficient expansion" (Wright 1978, 85). Just as the putative limits on the economy of scale/profit ratio put the middle class out of business in Barbados, so too in the United States since the Great Depression have 50 million people, small farmers and ranching families, been driven by social policy off their land to the cities to work at such employments as they can find. This urbanization of America recapitulated the rise of London during the enclosure movement when English country peasants were deprived of their land. The contemporary expression of the limits on size relative to efficiency are leveraged buyouts, or in the case of Fontana, it was invited to put itself back together with LA money once the Kaiser steel mill had run its economic course.

Whether on the plains of Texas and Kansas, or the California suburbs, the pattern of exploitation of labor, land and the environment is the same. The forests of the Pacific Northwest are also "mined" at the ridiculous price of $1 per tree and the logs exported, just as they might be from any other colony. Louisiana Pacific and Georgia Pacific beat a strategic retreat from the Pacific Northwest back to the South to cut second and third growth hardwood after they reduced the old growth coniferous forests of the Pacific Northwest to an unprofitable and barely remaining 10 percent of their original profusion. This left Plum Creek Corporation, a publicly held limited partnership (it's the liability that is being limited), the second largest timberland owner in the Pacific Northwest with 1,800 employees, a spur off the Burlington Northern Railroad, to plunder the rest of the old growth forests and suck up any remaining profit. The railroad beginnings of the Plum Creek Corporation are reminiscent of the plantation origin of the Southern Pacific RR. After having clear cut Cabin Creek and earned the sobriquet of "'Darth Vader of the state of Washington,'" they claim to be cleaning up their act. "'It's just plain unfair to taint us with accusations that date back to 1987 or earlier,' Plum Creek President Dave Leland said" (Larsen 1990, 31). Unfair to whom would be a fair question. "Neither we, nor any other, will take the wood of any man for castles, or for anything else which we are doing, except by the permission of him to whom the wood belongs" (Swindler 1965, 306), so says the *Magna Carta*. The national forests belong to the people. Their exploitation by corporate and government chicanery is headed for a showdown with the rightful owners, in the courts, in the forests and on the streets, thanks largely to Earth First!

The predictable result of class exploitation is class warfare. It is important to keep in mind that the populist impulse of an unsuccessful leader like William Jennings Bryan, who "resented predatory wealth, not wealth itself" (Glad 1968, 33), is distorted by the beneficiaries of predatory wealth. Henry Wallace, who to some degree, picked up where Bryan left off, said "that most of the statistics showing how the lot of the Negro had improved left him 'cold' and ashamed, because the life span of Negroes was still ten years less than that of whites, and discrimination continued in too many places and ways" (MacDougall 1965, 326). What was true of the relative economic and social position of Negroes in 1948, although somewhat changed by the 1990s, is largely still true, especially in the size of the gap separating the Black and White races. "In 1948, the Di Giorgio Fruit Corporation reported sales and commissions of $11,837,545.55, and net earnings for the year after taxes, of $247,701. Yet by masquerading as a 'farm'. . ." (McWilliams 1949, 166). That profit ratio may not seem unreasonable, except the true profit is concealed by the masquerade, as the corporations and the plantations are one and the same economic model. Nowhere is this made more apparent than in the colonial Idaho, where the J.R. Simplot Corporation, a potato and sugar beet plantation with myriad locations and products including fertilizer, largely sponsored the development of Micron, a high tech computer chip manufacturer in Boise. Micron management suggests that Micron employees live in the southeast quadrant of Boise where Simplot, through tie-ins to the Boise-Cascade Corporation, controls the development of housing.

While the tantalizing study of the complete connections between plantations and corporations is yet to be made, keep in mind that plantation economics is no longer just concerned with stoop labor. "One angry journalist quoted a former investment strategist for Goldman Sachs acknowledging that white-collar workers were 'in the kill zone. The target of the 1990s is middle-management'" (Phillips 1994, 87). Meanwhile, "Permanent class warfare also reinforced bourgeois political discipline" (Davis 1990, 113).

The class warfare has its ironic moments for the master class has "begun to wage war against the very immigrant labor upon which their master-race lifestyles depend" (208) It would be hard to make bourgeois political discipline or class warfare any more alarmingly apparent than in the recent passage in California in the 1994 election of Proposition 187 by a 60 percent margin. This proposition doesn't restrict immigration — lets keep the supply of low cost labor coming — it just restricts the services such exploited individuals are entitled to. The bourgeois lifestyle being protected here, the "Lifestyles of the Rich and Famous" as the TV program extols them, is strictly plantational, with perhaps a summer home in Rhode Island. "Charles Loring Brace describes a visit to the home of one of these squires. . . such opulence. . . galleries and verandahs. . . the easy indolence of manner and the atmosphere of wealth and leisure" (McWilliams 1969, 52-3). It is not like that on the street, where "Celebrity architects are rushing to design jails, prisons, and police stations" (Davis 1990, 256). Designer jails are designed for designer criminals and "One result is that Black males from Southcentral [LA] are now three times more likely to end up in prison than at the University of California" (307).

The Texas-Anglo alliance currently operating the one big plantation, also known as the English speaking empire or in the former public relations documents as the "free world," has only been able to muster a barbaric reversion in response to demands for genuine economic democracy. The predatory nature of the world economy is not a natural occurrence but a cultural manifestation where the avenues of genuine reform are blocked by hermetic seals. The heavy weight of the earth is moved around and continues to rest on the shoulders of billions of peasants on six continents, within and without the empire. The individual impulse to live and create is stifled by exploitation. The impulse to democracy suggests a nearly astronomical range of peasant possibilities, once the scar of empire from the wounds of colonialism is permitted by God's grace to heal.

While we are holding our breath waiting for that to happen, remember that what was once "Good for General Motors is good for America." GM paid a $5,000 fine in 1947 for conspiring, with George Firestone and other corporate leaders destined to benefit, to put the Los Angeles public transportation system out of business. A result was the LA freeway mess and the automobile, rubber, oil and gas basis for the American consumer economy after WWII. Not realizing that one current American dilemma is the transportation problem, the multi-millionaire CEOs of Chrysler, Ford, and GM were tagging along at the people's expense when President Bush threw up on Prime Minister Miyazawa of Japan, as if they were the answer and not the problem. What GM might have realized in a global economy, where sight is possible all the way around the earth, is that someone would notice that while they were announcing plans to eliminate 75,000 jobs in North America, they had created 75,000 jobs in Europe, where profit margins are higher and labor costs are lower. The owners of GM are like other transnational corporations which occupy countries and are licensed by them but not beholden to them since they believe land is a commodity to be exploited rather than an inheritance to be cherished and passed on. The corporations have an irresponsible political force and power, acquired in SCC v. SPRR, currently beyond the reach of government law. General Motors is a portable plantation.

23

Mexico: So Far From God,
So Close to the United States

Few places of equal size on earth can exceed or even match the diversity of Mexico. From the Guatemalan-Belize border on the south to the Rio Grande and the dotted lines through the American Southwest, Mexico comprises a cultural treasury. That treasury was looted by the Spanish empire almost beyond civilized comprehension as the Catholic Spaniards enslaved the Indians, plundered the portable treasures, and attempted to destroy the literature, religion and belief system of the people. For three centuries before imperial fatigue set in, the Spanish ruled over the vitality of the Mexicans, only to abandon them to their own devices early in the 19th century, leaving behind their colonial residue, the Catholic priests, their Moorish cathedrals and plazas, and the Spanish language. Chapter 23 examines the ongoing Mexican contribution to the Confederate Empire of North America, made doubly relevant by its close proximity to the U.S. and the fact that "There is simply no equivalent in the world for the present state of Mexican-United States relations" (Kennedy 1987, 517).

Mexican diversity has absorbed many lifetimes of ethnographic inquiry and its diversity is hardly limited to its geography, climate or human populations. The botanist Edgar Anderson reported that he found more varieties of maize (corn) in a small suburb of Guadalajara than were to be found in all of the United States (1971, 212). What is true of the maize is also true of the people who domesticated the maize. A simple list of the cultural groupings from the Pima Bajo, Tepehuan, and Tarahumari in the north, through the Aztecs in central Mexico, to Zapotecs and Mixtecs in Oaxaca, Olmecs along the Gulf Coast, and Mayans farther south in Chiapas and the Yucatan, (of which these are the merest sketch), would absorb several pages.

At the time of the Spanish Incursion under Cortez in 1519, the Aztecs at *Tenochtitlan* (now Mexico City) ruled over most of Mexico. It was a significant benefit to Cortez that he was mistaken for the bearded white God Quetzalcoatl, whose accumulating deity had been inherited by the

Aztecs from the Toltecs and of whom it had been predicted that he would return across the water. The initial Spanish victory in Mexico is a prime example of a culture literally getting carried away by its own fantasies. In his conclusion to *Aztec Thought and Culture*, Miguel Leon-Portilla says "Their culture of metaphors and numbers was overthrown by weapons of steel and fire" (1963, 182). Centuries, perhaps even a millennia before, *Teotihuacan*, the largest city of pre-Columbian Mexico, was not simply a ceremonial center, but was the largest of a type that "were industrial focuses with all the structural facets of a formal state" (Forbes 1973, 42).

Deeply religious and speaking *Nahuatl*, a language with a prepossessing capacity for abstraction, "We can summarize the Mexican concept of the Ultimate Realty by saying that it is a great, creative, active force or power possessing the quality of self-creation" (56). This capacity for creation, often in the face of formidable odds, is still at the root of Mexican vitality. *Nezahualcoyotl* or the Starving Coyote, the philosopher king of Texcoco a generation prior to Cortez, is considered to be the greatest of all Indians and "was not only an able administrator and statesman, but like the Hebrew Sage he was a poet of distinction. . . He was such a wise law maker that many nearby principalities adopted his codes. Eighty of his laws exist on manuscripts today" (303). What happened to the rest of them is what happens whenever Catholics are faced with vitality out of synch with St. Paul, which they cannot comprehend, and "the great library in Texcoco perished in the destructive flames by the order of Father Zumarraga" (303). It ranks among the worst Catholic crimes against humanity.

It is hardly surprising then that while the Catholics raped and burned and the Spanish soldiers pillaged, once rid of their dominating influence, the Mexicans made conscious moves toward their Indian past (Roosevelt 1970, 9). While Spanish remains the link language uniting *La Raza Unida*, or the cosmic race, Spanish genes which make up barely 10 percent of the Mexican pool, while not vanishing without a trace, are so distributed that "The Spanish strain. . . is perhaps the least significant element in the heritage of the people" (McWilliams 1968, 8). With less European and African influx than any other locale in the Western Hemisphere, Mexico is the most populous "Indian" nation in the world. Due to the English speaking habit of displacing Indians by genocide and removal, the most cohesive indigenous cultural survivals in the United States occur in Arizona and New Mexico, "saved" by European contact with the Spaniards. The surviving vitality of Mexico, essentially indigene, should cause the speakers of English to reflect on their history and intentions toward the Indian nation of Mexico.

The Spanish had colonized California, Arizona, New Mexico and Texas, all of which places they thought of as belonging to New Spain or Mexico, and "While a dozen or more settlements were founded in Florida, largely as a protective flank for the silver of Mexico, the fate of these settlements was sealed when the British occupied Charleston in 1670" (26). The text of *How the South Finally Won the Civil War* is making clear that the fate of a great many more places than the Spanish outposts in Florida was sealed by the launch of the English speaking slave empire at Charleston. The quasi lateral movement of European peoples into the Western Hemisphere followed some lines of force. Colin Renfrew in *Archeology and Language* makes a convincing argument for the gradual settlement of Europe from Asia Minor by speakers of the Indo-European languages beginning nearly 10,000 years ago in a process of "wave of advance" he describes using Christopher Hawkes' concept of "Cumulative Celticity" (1989, 244-8). This process leaped the Atlantic to Boston and Charleston, then aided by the Revolutionary War in America and the Industrial Revolution, accelerated across the North American continent, taking the northern half of Mexico in the process.

It was not an accident but cultural determinism that led the war-like Charlestonians of South Carolina into southern Mexico where "The first flag to fly over Chapultepec when Mexico City was captured belonged to the Palmetto Regiment" (Rosen 1982, 87). Few people dispute the fact that "The South had fostered the Mexican War" (Kazin 1991, 63) because of its proximity and the relative size of the gain. John C. Calhoun of South Carolina had not met with much success initially when he circulated the postulate that "'the interests of the *Gentlemen* of the North and of the South are identical'" (Hofstadter 1959, 84), and the Southerners had grown progressively more defensive about slavery and their position after 1832. The southern slavocracy saw Texas and the half of Mexico obtained by the war as their salvation, provided they could keep northern and free labor interests at bay. Charles Sumner in the Massachusetts state legislature, an opponent of southern expansionism, saw fit to quote the *Charleston Courier* in 1847 which avowed that "Every battle fought in Mexico, and every dollar spent there, but insures the acquisition of territory which must widen the field of Southern enterprise and power in the future. And the final result will be to readjust the balance of power in the confederacy (sic), so as to give us control over the operations of government in all time to come." The prophetic aggression of the *Courier*, whatever lapses of political nicety it reveals, has been right on the money.

Octavio Paz, the Nobel Prize winning Mexican poet, professes to see some naturalism in modern bourgeois democracy. "Their political, economic and technical transformations seemed to be inspired and guided by some superior coherency. History has its own logic, and if we can discover the secret of its functionings, we can control the future" (1961, 176). Paz permits himself the luxury of considering this Spenglarian notion false, and falls back on a topsy-like evaluation that white slave owning capitalistic power just grew to its present hegemony. It is Paz who is mistaken, and if the logic of the secret function of history is lost on him and others unwilling or unable to deduce its structure, until perhaps any given history is "over" and can be looked back through with 20-20 hindsight, it is not lost on the people guiding it, even if they are doing so unconsciously. The initial military victories of the Americans over the Mexicans were due to superior fire power and military discipline and as it became part of the initial Manifest Destiny of both sides, one to dominate, the other to submit, it is now part of the common tendentious history. It was willed into being by the compelling religious power of the militarized South.

The acquisition of half of Mexico so destabilized the United States that its ramifications were the major constellation of causes leading to the Civil War. Whoever controls the West, controls the future. Not so facetious cartoons showing the United States-Mexican border being drawn across the Isthmus of Tehuantepec reveal the depth of resentment among some American military men like Jefferson Davis who felt that they had conquered Mexico only to see the government give half of it back. Agitation for more of Mexico did not cease during the 1850s right up to the eve of the Civil War, when Democratic President Buchanan whose sympathies were with the South was urging the Senate to assume control of Chihuahua and Sonora in 1860 (May 1973, 159).

Civil War in the United States was such a painful possibility in Sam Houston's eyes, and we have already seen how accurate his eyes were at sighting in the geography which would one day be dominated by Texas, that "It was common knowledge throughout the state that the hero of the Texas Revolution was planning to invade Mexico" (146). Houston's intentions were clear. "Houston briefly dreamed of a great, patriotic campaign to conquer all Mexico, which might make him President of the United States and allow him to save the Union short of civil war" (Fehrenbach 1968, 342). Two observations about such a dream need to be kept in mind: Houston, who was reviled by fellow Texans for opposing secession from the Union, had already completed the map of North America that would one day fall under Texas' thumb; remember the function of war as a domestic pressure relief valve. "It is a matter of record that in 1876 (sic) President Hayes toyed with the idea of provoking a war with Mexico to divert attention from the shady deal by which he had robbed Tilden of the presidency" (McWilliams 1968, 109).

If Houston dreamed of conquering all of Mexico (again) to save the Union, and Jefferson Davis never lost faith in his belief that Mexico would be better off as part of the United States, John C. Calhoun was wrathful in his indignation at the "all of Mexico" school of thought. "'What can be gained, if success would finally crown our efforts, by subduing the country? What could we do with it? Shall we annex the States of Mexico to our Union? Can we incorporate a people so dissimilar in every respect — so little qualified for free and popular government — without certain destruction to our political institutions?'" (Niven 1988, 309). There is no need to dwell on the delicious irony of Calhoun as a sudden champion of free and popular government, any longer than to notice that "Ritchie [editor of the *Union* newspaper in Richmond] virtually accused Calhoun and his followers of treason during wartime" (309). Calhoun was not an easy man to shut up and it was not the first time he had been accused of treason, the fall back position of disputants in the American military theocracy. The better question is which, there can be more than one, of the American political institutions would the acquisition of all of Mexico be most likely to insure the destruction of.

Calhoun's position prevailed temporarily, although not supported by Jefferson Davis. When the Confederacy had seceded itself into existence, Davis' attitude toward acquisition of Mexico, he had coveted it in public for two decades, became more charitable. No longer in need of senators from slaving states to control the Congress, they were all slaveholders now, he dispatched Ambassador Pickett to Mexico in an attempt to secure Mexican diplomatic recognition for the Confederacy. Pickett began this attempt at rapport building diplomacy, and a thinly disguised effort to secure the

Confederate southern flank, by asserting that the Mexicans could relax for "There is really no difference between slavery and peonage," hardly an observation that served to calm the Mexicans.

The fine points of distinction between the two systems for expropriating labor as forms of economic basal metabolism can be left to proponents of either or both. Many of the medieval similarities between plantations, haciendas and rancherias, in South Carolina, California and Texas, have already been pointed out. The feudal system of peonage was imported by the Spanish, and General Porfirio Diaz, the putative author of the lamentation "Pity the poor Mexican, so far from God and so close to the United States," as well as the regressive dictator of Mexico from 1876 until 1911, was ousted from power as "The peons, or serfs, demanded the break-up of the great estates, some of which had come down from the days of Cortez" (Beard and Beard 1925, 594). It was on these gigantic land trusts, great estates, or *encomiendas* as they were referred to in Spanish Mexico, so similar to the land grants in South Carolina and California, that Spanish Longhorn cattle were first introduced and thrived in the area from Vera Cruz to Mexico City. "Cortes claimed 23,000 Indians for his own *encomienda*" (Rifkin 1992, 46). Whether these Indians are referred to as slaves or peons, Jefferson Davis chose to emphasize the similarities, and the effects are clear to the historians, the people and the surviving children of the oppression under General Diaz.

The turn of the century provided little relief from the nearly continuous penetration of the "border" and Mexican national integrity. President Wilson occupied Vera Cruz in 1914 and General Pershing invaded Mexico chasing Pancho Villa in 1916 (Beard and Beard 1925, 595). The greater war with Germany (who would offer the Mexicans the possibility of territory lost to the United States in return for Mexican support in WWI) distracted American attention from the Mexican "problem." With so little respect for the border from the American military, it is hardly surprising that Mexican maps of this period showed the states of the border area that had formerly belonged to them as "territory temporarily in the hands of the United States." It is essential that the opinion of the oppressed become part of the feedforward loop. "The latest invaders of Aztlan, in their racist onslaughts on the Chicano, managed to dispossess the Chicano. Chicano lands became gringolandia. Under the force of gun and whip. Chicano labor built up the huge agricultural combines of the Southwest for the foreign invader with the blue eyes and quick, silvery tongues that promised much and delivered neo-colonism and slavery" (Sanchez, 1973, 33). WWI stimulated a labor shortage on Texas and California plantations that was partially filled by an influx of Mexican workers. The influx picked up speed after 1924 with the passage of the Immigration Act of 1924, which excluded the Japanese because they were too successful. It is difficult to exaggerate "The miserable condition of Mexican labor in California" (McWilliams 1969, 128), where they were recruited as strike breakers to boot (223-4) in this American colonization of Mexican labor.

"Three facts should be noted about the great wave of Mexican immigration which brought to the Southwest after 1900 nearly ten percent of the total population of Mexico: it was overwhelmingly concentrated in the old Spanish borderlands; in point of time it coincided with the birth of the Southwest as an economic empire; and, in each instance, Mexican immigrants labored in the building of industries in which there had been an earlier Spanish-Mexican cultural contribution" (McWilliams 1968, 163). This astute evaluation of the tremendous number of immigrants, their timing, and their contribution in conservative or traditional roles, suggests a pattern that has grown stronger in numbers even as their willingness to remain in the same exploited preoccupations has diminished. "But when the Spanish-speaking people re-invaded the borderlands three hundred years later, their leaders were landless peons who forded across the Rio Grande in the dead of night" (162). In popular terminology, the "wetbacks" demonstrated no more respect for the "border" than the southern dominated American military. What was different is that earlier in "The failure of Spain to consolidate the borderland outposts. . . [where] No effective liaison existed between these groups; their experiences have run parallel but have never merged" (81), we see the reflection of the general Spanish failure to consolidate in North America. Now the Mexicans are providing that consolidation and from their common humanity and oppressed condition are creating a vital political force. As of 1948, "Not one Mexican serves in the California state legislature" (18), even though during WWII, Americans of Mexican heritage served in disproportionate numbers relative to their distribution in the total population, especially in Bataan (259).

Mexican peons might not have been so landless and attracted to the United States if certain American entrepreneurs like Harry Chandler, the publisher of the Los Angeles *Times*, who owned 833,000 acres of land in

Mexico, just south of the "border" (McWilliams 1949, 360), hadn't stimulated their economic distress. Formerly escaped Black American slaves occasionally fled from Texas to Mexico, even as peons fled in the other direction. "Governor [Coke] Stevenson proclaimed the Good neighbor Policy in Texas merely called upon the citizens of the state to adopt a non-discriminatory policy as to 'all persons of the Caucasian race,' thereby attempting to deny long-resident Negro citizens a status sought to be conferred on Mexican nationals" (McWilliams 1968, 270). The exacerbation of differentiated status levels awarded to Black Americans and Mexican Americans is one other way the general fiction of white supremacy and the functional consequences of the application of power through the supremacy of some white men is maintained. Mexican Americans have displaced Black Americans as the largest, most cohesive and functional minority within the United States.

This was no simple task as these were the foot people who represented a Trojan Horse type of trick upon the American military. If they insist upon all of Mexico, they will get it through this process of "The revenge of the cradle" (Davis 1990, 326). While this was taking place and before Americans of Mexican heritage, Pena and Cisneros, were elected to the mayor's offices in Denver and San Antonio and subsequently appointed to cabinet secretariats in the Clinton administration, "thousands of our rural citizens live in dire misery, and other thousands have no recourse but to emigrate to the United States" (Paz 1961, 178). As Paz points out, "Capital, after all, is simply accumulated human labor" (185). Mexican capital is presently strungout on both sides of the former border where its potential awaits organization. "History demonstrates that no class has ever voluntarily surrendered its gains and privileges" (185). The class struggle on the North American continent where it was envisioned in detail by John C. Calhoun, "The Marx of the Master Class," has some distance to go before it is finally worked out. Peonage in its contemporary form as migrant labor may itself fall victim to the fusion between Mexico and the United States.

This fusion is occurring in part because of Mexican family cohesion. "Families in Tepoztlan are strong and cohesive, held together by traditional bonds of loyalty, common economic strivings, mutual dependence, the prospect of inheritance, and finally, the absence of any other social group to which the individual can turn. . . without a family the individual stands unprotected and isolated, a prey to every form of aggression, exploitation, and humiliation" (Forbes 1973, 43). With parts of large extended families on both sides of the rapidly disappearing border, cultural identity is stronger than national identity.

Besides their family cohesion and warmth, the Mexicans are bringing and sharing their immense vitality, their basic good health, their native intelligence (which flowers when given the opportunity of education), and their survival skills. The Mexican capacity for creation may be just what the bankrupt Confederate Empire of North America needs at this point since "The verb *yucoya* means 'to invent' or 'to create mentally,'" (55) and they personify the adhoc vitality the less robust empire is missing in its imperial fatigue. There is a certain amount of role reversal taking place as the migrants dominate the movement north and the Empire, at least until 1994 especially in California, has pretended to be powerless to do anything except submit. Those remarks are not intended to discount the ferocious hassle between the INS and the migrants, only to observe that the ultimate results seem to be constantly increasing numbers of migrants who make it to stay, whether part of amnesty programs or independently.

The disappearing border is another indication of the correctness of the appellation "empire" to describe the English speaking activity in North America, because a country actually has a border that can be identified and defended, an empire does not. Unable to acquire the perspective in Mexico that would enable them to put a halt to the panic breeding that doubles and redoubles their population, the Mexicans come north seeking their salvation at K-Mart, where their exploited labor is welcomed. It has been possible for a long time for the Confederate Empire of North America to postpone its fiscal responsibility, ignore the bridges that are falling down and schools that are falling apart, focus on foreign affairs (the proper activity of an empire), and wrap themselves in an oil drenched flag. It is not possible to abjure geography and the forces that are fusing Mexico and the United States together.

This fusion takes the form of a pulse, now encouraged, now discouraged. The contact between peoples on opposite sides of a "border" has been usefully described by Arnold Toynbee: "To use the appropriate and expressive Latin terms, which brings out both the kinship and the contrast between the two kinds of contact, the *limen* or threshold, which was a zone, is replaced by the *limes* or military frontier, which is a line that has length without breadth" (1972, 234). The understanding of the border as a zone enables it to be mutually beneficial, as in much of the empire past of the United States. On the other hand, the current backlash in California which is attempting to seal the border, as if the United States were a country, and increase the negative consequences of trying to cross it as if it were a military frontier, is one extreme of the pulse. NAFTA will exacerbate conditions in Mexico, increasing the pressure to migrate, even as the slight contraction in military spending in California has sent politicians there searching for scapegoats for their economic problems. In fact, the Mexican incursion into California is a net economic gain.

President Clinton successfully bribed sufficient members of Congress who opposed NAFTA with porkbarrel promises (the late 20 century equivalence of beads and trinkets) and the fast track negotiations that Bush put in motion to ram this so-called free trade agreement down the people's throats concluded. Just as the votes of the senators and representatives of the old Confederacy were the margin of victory for approval of Bush's war on Iraq, so too were the votes from the members of the old Confederacy in the House of Representatives the margin of victory for Clinton-Bush's NAFTA. With 125 votes after 1992 (as opposed to 116 before as the power of the South continues to grow), representatives from the Confederacy voted 82-43 in support of NAFTA. The vote for the entire House was 234 yeas and 200 nays. Subtracting the Confederate portion, the vote on NAFTA would have been 152 yeas and 157 nays. When it is a question of empire, military intervention, or exploitation of labor, it is the support of the South that gives American policy its basic Confederate character.

NAFTA will enable transnational corporations (portable plantations) to produce goods in Mexico at wages one-tenth of the prevailing rate in the formerly unionized North in a reaffirmation of the slave labor and peonage relationship of labor to capital on this continent. On January 1, 1994, when NAFTA went into effect, the first world got a wake up call from the fourth world Mayan Indians of Chiapas, who with guns, organization, and their future on the line, took control of San Cristobal and other Chiapan cities, towns, and their native villages. The theory of Mexico as a safe haven for capitalist investment deserves to be rattled. The accelerated industrialization of Mexico under NAFTA will force 20 million more peasants and Indians off their ancestral land, as surely as the enclosure movement in England forced its peasants off the land and the accelerated industrialization of the United States forced its peasants off the land.

Landless Mexicans can choose to fight, to immigrate to Mexican cities, or to the United States. The weepy left in the United States, presenting their case in the pages of *The Nation,* even as they correctly identify some of the upshots and ramifications, fall back on the idiotic notion that if they just work harder they can make an international success out of these changes yet. There is nothing in the history of the American labor movement which would suggest they have even a ghost of a chance. NAFTA is an agreement among the oligarchies of Canada, the United States and Mexico to continue exploiting the labor and the environment of the entire continent, relatively more free from some of the middle class considerations of economic democracy.

Mexican President Salinas de Gortari used to insist that Mexicans were eager to work for $1.57 an hour, with the only other viable alternative even more massive migration to the United States proper. On the one hand, the close cooperation between the Clinton-Bush administrations and the PRI with Salinas de Gortari deserves to be welcomed, even as it should alert us to being wary of whether or not the "identical interests of the gentlemen of the North and South," in Calhoun's political system, would in fact benefit all the people. Close economic and democratic cooperation between the United States and Mexico is a laudable goal; NAFTA was not it. All of Mexico, and immigration virtually otherwise unlimited, certainly had a hand in the destruction of the institution of a fair price for fair labor. The concomitant destruction of the natural environment that low-cost productivity reflects is typical of southern capitalism's belief in land and the earth as just one more commodity, rather than the home we all live on. This migration of workers to the United States and of factories to Mexico is drawn by the magnets of capital. The withdrawal of the availability of family planning information from the "third world" was permitted and encouraged by the rich white men such as Reagan and Bush when they operated the empire, precisely because it helps to insure an uninterrupted supply of cheap exploitable labor. Catholic complicity in this denial of family planning freedom is well documented.

These immigrants north are passed on the Alcan highway by old white people in Winnebagos on their retired way to Puerto Vallarta, Lake Chapala and Acapulco. Bismarck pegged the retirement age at 65, since very few people lived that long in 19th century Germany. With the wonders of modern medicine and the political impulse rooted in the fear of death driving it, the decrepit geriatric theocracy annually throws a larger percentage of disposable income at the medical industry's increasingly expensive postponement of death than it does at the failing system of education or even lately the military establishment. This capitalization of the fear of death is so plainly the final stage of the empire's ramification that there will be grim fun at the grim reaper's ultimate triumph. It has created a Social Security system funded by tax raids (FICA at 16 percent) on the labor of the young and the other than white. This two- way traffic on the road to *Cibola* will one day grind to a more equitable halt.

Many Chicanos aren't anywhere near as bitter as their experiences entitle them to be. "Build cabron, build, and lift up La Raza and all Humanity, and create out of your hurt and bitterness, forge out of your hope and love, develop out of moot history a salient universe that is multi-hued and loving. . . it is understanding, not vicious backlash, that shall triumph" (Sanchez 1973, 159). The triumph of multi-cultural understanding, being rushed into the future by a dynamic new Mexican majority in North America, within and without the empire, will be resisted by the centripetal pressure to reversion. Having acquired all of Mexico, it is clear the United States has only the old exploitative model to try to cope with it. The Aztec roots in metaphor will meet their mirror images in the urge to being coming up out from under the English speaking unconscious mind. The creation of new models will be the business of the currently impoverished children of both (all) races and languages as they walk out from under the collapsing roof of the empire.

The Mexicans arriving in the United States and their prominent position in electoral politics in the Southwest, indicate an interest in the institution of democracy that would startle and perhaps melt the cold, cold heart of Calhoun. The political system they leave behind in Mexico, the PRI or *Partido Revolutionario Institutio* that came into power early in the 20th century has been compared in form and single party intent to the communist party of the former Soviet Union. With discouraged competition from the PAN, the opposition party, the PRI routinely elects its choice for president. Oligarchy is traditional in Mexico as "The Spaniards arrived in Mexico they found complete and refined civilizations. . . [that] made it possible for them to accomplish the extraordinary task of founding what Arnold Toynbee calls a Universal Empire, based on the remains of older societies" (Paz 1961, 89). The universalizing tendency of the Anglo-Texan

Empire of North America is also based on the remains of the older English Empire system. It is not surprising then, that the tyranny of the Aztecs over the people they ruled made the arrival of the Spaniards seem "a liberation to the people under Aztec rule" (93). A change of tyrants to the Spanish military and the literal rape of the countryside by Catholic priests constructing cathedrals, "(Spanish Catholicism has always expressed the same will; hence, perhaps, its belligerent, authoritarian, inquisitorial tone)" (99), hardly improved the lot of the people. With two kinds of mutually antagonistic oppressors, the PRI and the Catholic church, even the remote possibility of economic democracy in the United States has its appeal.

Aside from anarchy, where everybody is responsible for all of their behavior all the time, democracy is the most difficult form of government. The unity of principles in the Confederate Empire of North America and the Aztec hegemony in pre-Columbian Mexico are striking. "The Aztec state was both military and theocratic" (92), where the worship of gods who became more and more alike was not unlike the modern American worship of their flag as the symbol of their religious-military belief system. Aspirants to democratic control of their political life on both sides of the border will have to deal with the fact that deals constructed between Clinton-Bush and Gortari and their stand-ins and replacements will have the best interests of the ruling classes in mind, if they follow historical precedents, and only secondarily the interests of the binational peons of all races and cultures.

The Mexican people's challenge to the American theocracy (not the PRI) is outside the mold. As they imitate American models, they are shedding their traditional reliance on submission. Nearly 40 percent of the total population of North America is Hispanic and the demographic trends indicate that they will one day soon be the majority. The opportunity for an expanding democracy is heavily weighted on the downside by the present prospect of a largely bilingual continent, half Spanish, half English, and half educated in either language, resolutely under the thumbs of theocracies whose best interests only peripherally include the over-populated and continuously expanding work force.

The superior economic competition being waged by Asia dominated by Japan and Europe dominated by Germany is driving the Mexican and American empires into a North American marriage of convenience and necessity. Whether the results can be made beneficial to substantial segments of the total population depends on the strength of the people. The geriatric, reversionary institutions of power presently in place are exhausted and bereft of ideas.

Houston and Davis wanted all of Mexico, while Calhoun the conservative would have settled for half. Clinton is pushing the merger now with Gortari's assistance, as the gentlemen recognize their identical interests, interests grossly similar to those Jefferson Davis was extolling the benefits of in 1861. Calhoun's desire for just enough Mexico to maintain slaveholding control of the U.S. Senate is a demonstration of his perpetual wish for static solutions to contain dynamic situations. Through all of the static resounds the irrepressible cry for freedom. The marriage of Mexico and the United States, truly a shotgun wedding, will have all the dynamism that speakers of both Spanish and English will be able to handle.

24

Twenty Nations in One

What is a nation has the ring of a question resonating at the heart of the matter. The United States, once a nation of 13 self-liberated colonies, has become an empire superimposed on many nations. Since both the nation and the empire use the same name, The United States of America, confusion abounds at where the nation ends and the empire begins. Like all words, nation reflects meaning, it does not contain it. This is anything but a semantic problem for nations and empires have different things to do in their relationships with their own and other people. Those who most stridently insist on the U.S. acting like an empire, make believing in it a loyalty oath, a test of beliefs as in "The Pledge of Allegiance," a religious incantation if one was ever promulgated. "We pledge allegiance, to the flag, of the United States of America, and to the republic, for which it stands, one *nation*, under God, indivisible, with liberty and justice for all." Note that allegiance is not being pledged to one "empire." It is time to ravel and unravel the confusion surrounding the differences between loyalty or allegiance to the nation and obeisance to an empire.

The word nation apparently came into the English language as a past participle of the Latin infinitive verb form *nasci*, to be born. Being born someplace has a lot to do with what we think of as a nation, nativity, and the nation as a homeland. In general, the people who inhabit a nation profess common interests with supposed ties of blood, further manifested by ties of language, religion, customs and like institutions with a sense of social homogeneity and mutual trust. This general description does not seem to be quite adequately describing the entire United States of America in the late 20th century.

A nation could be an agglomeration of tribes or peoples of common ethnic stock or perhaps of different stocks fused by long intercourse. A nation could also perhaps have a single language or closely related dialects, a common religion, history, traditions, a sense of right and wrong and a more or less *compact* territory. More loosely, a nation could be the body of inhabitants of a country united under a single independent government, the one definition in the lexicon that comes closest to fitting the U.S., if we think it is united. The template is enlarged to answer the questions: what is a nation; is the United States of America a nation now or an empire; if it is a nation, has it always been or will it always be, as the loyalty test requires, indivisible?

The United States of America were once divisible by two during the bloody epoch known as the War Between the States, which President Lincoln saw as a test of whether "that nation nor any nation so conceived and so dedicated" could long endure. The Confederate States of America began a divisional of short temporal duration but of infinite political effect. The nation was reunited as a result of the Civil War and ultimately regained its political bearings under a Southern Compass Steering Coalition. The U.S. is more accurately described as the Confederate Empire of North America.

When the principles of "nationism" are matched up with examples outside of North America, perspective is increased. The prevalence of wars for national liberation, where individuals and groups try to forge a national identity, make this significantly more than an academic discourse. The so-called nation of Nigeria, once the location of an empire known as Benin, was formed as many have been, out of a one-time English colony. During the 1960s, Nigeria was divided by a bitter civil war, as the Ibos in the east sought to separate themselves from the dominant Yorubans in the west and call their country Biafra. Here is a nation put together as an "agglomeration of tribes," but which did not share ethnicity, common traditions and language, or the same sense of right and wrong.

Nigeria is a simple example of yoking a nation together out of multiple parts, because it met an imperialist need, and like most former British colonies where English became the link or the dominant language, attempts to form democracies prevail. India, as diverse a "nation" and democracy as exists on earth, is an unmanageable example, stunning subcontinent, and gross remnant of the British Empire, with seven or eight major languages, hundreds of dialects, several distinct and mutually unappreciative religions, three or four races, etc. Little besides English, geographical contiguity, the thirst for democracy where only a few hundred people are killed each election, and the guns of the ruling Hindus keep India together.

India, like the Hindu religion, is an ancient accumulation of diverse elements. Since WWII, when Hitler and Gandhi liberated India from the

English, the world witnessed civil war in India which separated the Moslem areas in the Indus Valley and the Brahmaputra lowlands from the rest of India. The nation of Pakistan, based on religion and created in two parts, failed some tests for national integrity. The tests of "compact" territory and common ethnicity were settled by another civil war conducted on non-continuous territory resulting in the creation of the Bengali nation of Bangladesh.

It would seem within reason that the smaller a national entity is, the more apt it would be to meet all the indigenous requirements of nationhood and without ambitious and aggressive neighbors, might even retain independence. If a nation as large as India were separated into parts that would individually meet a significant portion of the test of nationhood, there would be as many nations there as there are in all of Africa. The Kashmir would like to be independent, so would the Sikhs, not to mention the speakers of Tamil around Madras and the Tamilian separatist movement on Sri Lanka.

On the western edge of Pakistan and in the eastern portion of Iran, live the lovely Baluchis. Baluchistan passes the tests of blood, custom, mutual interest, history, traditions, and compactness, but is not a nation now, being parts of two others, and any attempt by anyone outside of Iran and Pakistan to create the nation of Baluchistan would be labeled meddling in the internal affairs of the aforementioned "nations," which are in fact mini-empires.

Geopolitical examples abound, as the Commonwealth of Independent States made up of former republics of the Soviet Union, are fractious testimony to what can happen when empires unravel. Russia, the largest "nation" in the former Soviet Union, is composed of numerous enclaves such as Tatarstan which would all vote themselves independent if they could. The Soviet Union was an empire riding herd on 20 other nations, including parts of eastern Germany and Poland. The Confederate Empire of North America is an empire riding neo-colonial herd on at least 20 nations within and without its more obvious borders. Who rules whom and for what purposes? As recently as the 19th century the peninsula we call the nation of Italy consisted of Lombardy, Bologna, Sicily and the Papal States, until they were united by Garibaldi. On the modern stage, political independence has superseded the other elements composing the fabric of a nation. Wars for national liberation along ethnic, linguistic and religious lines are waged against the political powers that be on all continents, in the centers as well as on the peripheries of both old and new colonial powers and constantly disintegrating empires. North America is not alone even as it consists of only 15 percent of the earth's land mass.

For 150 years, a series of more or less English speaking colonies existed on the Atlantic coast of North America. They declared their independence of England in 1776 and made it stick by 1783. They formed a nation voluntarily and shared language, some mutual interests, history, and a compact territory. They did not share the same traditions, customs, nor the sense of right and wrong, for the predominant economic model of the southern half of the new country was based on slavery, and constitutionalized as "slaves, and other property," where each slave was counted as three-fifths of a person for the purposes of apportioning representatives to Congress in the remarkable scheme suggested by Pinckney of South Carolina.

As the English speaking Americans swept across the continent, destroying the cultures, languages, customs and lifestyles of the native America nations, they rationalized it as God driven Manifest Destiny. The Indians learned quickly that the word nation has more magic than tribe, so they became nations, such as the Iroquois, the Cherokee, the Creeks and the Choctaws of the South. In 1994, the Nez Perce in northern Idaho are insisting on their sovereignty. In the Southwest, the largest of the Indian nations, the Navaho, still surrounds the much smaller Hopi nation. Everywhere they were betrayed. Is it military sagacity that prevents the United States from getting any more deeply involved in helping to stop the "ethnic cleansing" by the Serbs in the former "empire" of Yugoslavia, or is it moral maturity since the English speaking empire of North America is a monument to ethnic cleansing and lacks the moral legs to preach to anybody on the subject?

As the English language dominates commercial discourse and has established itself as the world language, it is fitting to recall its humble origin. Even though it has been a long time, English speaking people have reason to understand what occupation by foreign armies means. There, on the plains of Kent during the time of Christ, the language that was to become English was being born. Other people were also being born, the offspring of Roman Soldiers and English women, "stock fused by long (400 year) intercourse." In England, by the 13th century, the *Magna Carta* established that "No scutage or aid shall be imposed in our kingdom except by the common council of our kingdom" (Swindler 1965, 306). This principle was reduced to the political slogan, no taxation without representation, by the American revolutionists. The power to tax is the power, and as we have learned from Calhoun, the government's unequal dispensation of that power creates classes that benefit and classes that suffer. The many people of the nations underneath the umbrella of power of the Confederate Empire of North America suffer the abuse of the empire's taxing power.

The United States is a commercial tradition that works. It masquerades as a nation out of convenience. While purporting to defend religious freedom, it practices military religion typified by flag worship. The diversity of actual beliefs in North America defies taxonomization. The shared language of English is under assault by millions of immigrant speakers of principally, Tagalog, Korean, and Mexican Spanish. "Bring me your tired, your poor, your huddled masses, yearning to be free," is incised deeply into the American psyche. Never mind that many of the masses remain poor and exploited, turn criminal for revenge, and mug the mouth that invited them.

North America will continue to be ravaged by immigrants uninvited by the pre-Columbian natives until the United States actually becomes a nation and discovers and defends a national boundary rather than and instead of the circumscribed limits of risk of the transnational corporations and portable plantations that occupy it. "As the growing population surpasses our resources, living conditions will worsen and the United States will become more and more like the poverty-stricken countries the recent wave of immigrants are fleeing. One of the great liberal propaganda feats of the 20th century has been to convince many Americans that massive immigration is an essential part of the American way of life" (Stacy and Lutton 1985, 46). Except that the real propaganda in this citation is hiding the fact that the immigration laws are written and enforced by conservatives seeking cheap labor, the effects of this description are accurate. Half of the population of the Philippine Islands would move to Los Angeles if it were permitted. A million of them already have. A nation has identifiable and defensible borders. An empire makes the restless elements of the conquered and subject people welcome as stoop and slave labor.

The empire could easily become too diverse to cope without turning into a police state. E.M. Forster's look through the layers of conflicting belief in *A Passage to India* could tell Americans something about the consequences of becoming a cultural backwater speaking a multitude of tongues, a lateral and horizontal Tower of Babel. The U.S. has adopted the India Indian model and this "passage to India," will not likely resemble Walt Whitman's quest for mystical enlightenment. Just as "No one lost except the nation at large" (Reisner 1986, 503) in the hydraulic socialism of the western water projects, the nation at large lost out to the empire. It is as easy to predict the past as it is the future, since both ends of the continuum are circumscribed by the blinders politicians wear to conceal their limited imaginations. The future will be indistinguishable from the past, the past of other empires dissolving. Yesterday's version of tomorrow, so popular in the CIA driven 1950s, inevitably evaporated under perpetual assault from the real world. The nation at large is a holding action; the natives of the nations within are restless. Where are these nations within? How did the U.S. turn into an empire? What does this futureless future hold?

We've already looked at Mexico, the largest nation both within and without the U.S. borders of the Confederate Empire of North America, for it will one day be driving the bus, chowing down on the whole enchilada. People who suggest that the "border" with Mexico be sealed should realize "That the definitive imposition of slow growth would require the construction of a California Reich" (Davis 1990, 209). There are undoubtedly Mexicans who feel they have already been mishandled by a California Reich and trendy California politicians will be shooting their ads with a get-tough face in front of the border as a backdrop. There will be more changes here than can be imagined for "what the Aztecs of A.D. 1500 were organizing lies for us well in the future" (Spengler 1928, 46). And even if "It requires no special insight to foresee that a point will soon be reached when a serious struggle will develop between Anglos and Hispanos" (McWilliams 1968, 221), the forms that struggle will take and reveal will astound even an observer of McWilliams' exactitude. Mexicans intermarry more readily with the existing population than the African American minority and in a couple generations, half of the people north of the Rio Grande will be at least part Mexican. "Turn everybody inside out and make them honorary Mexicans," is how the Belgian born American poet Andy Clausen described the process of the Mexicanization of the United States as long ago as 1968 in his work *Extreme Unction.*

The U.S. has witnessed many ethnically inspired riots in the form of the black power rebellion of the 1960s. Even with, and right in the teeth of, the passage of the Civil Rights Act of 1964, young black men, impoverished and unempowered, took it upon themselves to set fire to Watts in Los Angeles, Detroit, Newark and other American cities. The black separatist movement is part of the haunting legacy of slavery where the efforts to extend the benefits of the other two-fifths of full citizenship still lag behind the results. Are the Black ghettos likely nations within an empire, requiring informal passports and visas, or are they simply neighborhoods where nearly everybody is Black? Few white people go there except on business in the daytime as even the Reverend Jesse Jackson has reported relief when he realized that the person walking behind him was white.

Both Martin Luther King Jr. and Malcolm X. were snuffed, King curiously enough after many years of surveillance by the FBI, just when he began to make his campaign a poor people's campaign, thereby tripling his constituency and the potential threat to the established white southern power. The poor whites in the mountainous areas of the South had refused to provide much help in the war against the North.

Most European immigrants of the last 200 years were successfully hectored out of their native tongues and their offspring speak variations of Standard American English. There was more intermarriage between these Europeans also, and it is from this base that the melting pot analogy arose. The metallic metaphor of the melting pot has given way to Ishmael Reed's promulgation of the notion of a bouillabaisse, a stew in which all the parts continue to simmer, sharing some elements of taste and imagination but keeping most of any original integrity they have had (1989, 5-6). Look for instance at the surnames of the young people getting married this week in any American Newspaper and the linguistic alphabet soup will astound you.

It will also astound you if you visit Los Angeles, putative "Capitol of the Third World," as a new book describes it. LA has always been that way. The 22 founders of Los Angeles included "2 Spaniards, 1 Mestizo, 2 Negroes, 8 Mulattoes, 9 Indians, and 1 Chino" (McWilliams 1968, 36). More than 100 languages are spoken in the LA school system, still dominated by speakers of English, who superimposed the largest Confederate military base on the Los Angeles Basin from its humble support of the Confederacy in 1860. "The dynamiting of the *Times*, more particularly, the plea of guilty entered by the McNamaras, aborted the labor movement in Los Angeles. . . The serious consequences of this abortion largely account for the subsequent political pathology of Los Angeles" (McWilliams 1946, 283). LA's labor was over-ruled in favor of the open shop. It was made into a military base by white racists and opened to the rest of the world, where "The sense of detachment from the rest of the continent gives way to a feeling of its integral relation to the rest of the Pacific World" (374).

The alphabetic script of Korean and the ideographic scripts of Chinese and Japanese keep their respective communities together within their ghettos in the empire. The immigration process "Transformed Monterey Park into North America's first Chinese-majority suburb by 1985" (Davis 1990, 207). Chinese labor was among the first oriental labor to be exploited in California, for the building of railroads and on plantations where the Chinese were the vital factor for 1860-70 (McWilliams 1969, 67) and taught the other Californians how to plant, cultivate and harvest orchard and garden crops (71).

Japanese were rapidly included in the plantation system's need for cheap and effective labor (90), and their homogeneity made labor organization difficult (102). It is crucial to note that the Japanese were so successful in California agriculture, even at slave wage rates, that their exclusion by the Immigration Act of 1924, was a result of resistance to them stemming from their ability to marshall their resources sufficiently to begin buying land (116). Their continued success, in California and elsewhere, is predicated on such minute attention and by "Japanese Yuppies" with $1-2 million in home equity (Davis 1990, 137). "Los Angeles's leaders were rudely awoken for the first time to the real nature of colonial subservience upon the inscru-table workings of a Japanese economy bloated with fictional capital" (138). The contention for colonial control of Los Angles between the Japanese and the Confederate Empire of North America shows no signs of abating and can only accelerate. California and Los Angeles are truly west of the West and their disintegrating influences reverberate around the Pacific Rim.

Bilingual education was initially an effort to assist the Mexican and Chicano minority. The language of instruction is a multi-lingual program now. The reactionary attempt to pass "English Only" laws is simply symptomatic of the attempt to retain power and the botched effort to teach the slaves to talk the talk. The million Tagalog speakers from the Philip-pines came to the U.S. as upshots of American colonialism. The objections to empire on moral and economic grounds include ". . . not merely on account of such Filipinos as might come to the United States but also because it forces competition with manufactories in the Philippines, where a much lower standard of living prevailed" (Roosevelt 1970, 171). Only when a portable plantation or corporation could control factories in both locations could that objection be overcome. For nearly 100 years, the various presidents of the United States "definitely contemplated the ultimate independence of the islands" (150). Contemplate is not exactly the most active verb in English and only the vile excesses of Ferdinand Marcos were sufficient to spring the Philippines on a wobbly road to independence. "We have had the best of intentions. . . but we as a nation have not profited from them and we are not, because of our type of government, fitted to carry out any far-range colonial objectives" (198). The results are a matter of record; so too are the intentions which were everything but the best—paternal, predatory, criminal.

The Filipinos, hundreds of thousands of Koreans, the unhappy refuges from Johnson's war on Vietnam, all help to make California one of the most diverse and violent places on earth. The U.S. Army used to send its doctors to the emergency rooms of LA hospitals so they could experience battlefield trauma and gunshot wounds first hand. More or less hiding out in the pine covered hills of northern Idaho, are a groups of white supremacists who imagine they are hoarding weapons to create an "Aryan Nation." This is only a pretty picture if you're selling guns or drugs, something the white supremacists who are actually in charge, are routinely accused of doing.

The U.S. is the world's largest supplier of weapons and in the Camp David accords that ended the day to day fighting between Israel and Egypt were multi-billion dollar annual arms deals for both sides. Egypt's $7 billion colonial arms debt to the U.S. was sanctimoniously forgiven by George Bush in honor of its support for his blitzkrieg of Iraq to bring Kuwait back into the empire. Israel is one of the 20-plus nations making up the empire, significantly removed geographically, but center and right, theologically and militarily. As Mexican President Salinas de Gortari put it, more or less answering the question of do you think "we" have a problem, what about the Jews, "so close to God and so far from the United States."

When the Catholics during the Dark Ages they smothered Europe with, grew weary of putting people to death for translating the Bible into English, they were capitulating to the fact that once able to read, the protestants would prefer the Old Testament. The U.S. protects Judaism

because it has a warrior spirit and history to match its own. Fehrenbach's
history of Texas is replete with references to the similarities between the Old
Testament Texans and the modern Israelis. The United States Department
of Justice, under Janet Reno, brought the Apocalypse about as close to home
as you can get it when they set fire to and destroyed the mini-nation of the
Branch Davidians in Waco, killing most of the inhabitants. No one shall
leave this empire, much less on theological terms. Many think they are in
the Old Testament when they are really in downtown Dallas or Lubbock.
The prevalence of these internal and external proletariats, in Toynbee's terms,
indicates the ripeness of the empire's hours.

There is a powerful, well organized, hyper educated, Jewish nation in
the United States, predominantly in the Northeast, New York, LA and
Miami. It shares Miami, the capitol of Cuba, with a lot of angry bypassed
Blacks and the Cuban mayor. Miami is either a paradise lost, it began barely
a hundred years ago as a lemonade stand, or an advance guard testing ground
of whether or not an empire so strungout and diffused can long endure. A
hotbed of racial, ethnic, linguistic and pharmaceutical violence, it has
replaced Charleston as the American point of penetration from the
Caribbean Indies. Many chapters in the horror story of Haiti have to be
played out in Miami.

There are many other recent migrants from the tropics. Nicaraguans,
Guatemalans and El Salvadorenos abound in southern cities. "Community
workers in this poor and overcrowded neighborhood, the home of tens of
thousands of refugees from US-financed state terrorism in Central America,
tell bitter tales of police brutality" (Davis 1990, 286). The continuous
Caribbean Confederate empire of the South ran into some more static
during Bush's 1989 invasion of Panama, a "vest pocket Republic" (Liss 1967,
20). Haitian refugees piled up and the task, worthy of Solomon, of
deciding whether they were political or economic refugees preoccupied the
judges. President Clinton, with the pacifist aggressive help of former President Carter, talked himself into making the annual obligatory invasion of
the Caribbean in Haiti in 1994. More than a million immigrants from
Puerto Rico, one of the United States' other colonial islands in the sun, give
New York and New Jersey a healthy dose of their particular ethnic flavor.

The restless differences between and among these various ethnic,
cultural and linguistic factions are not being smoothed out in the political
process. Sixty percent of New Yorkers polled recently would leave if they

had any where to go. Richard Reeves in an editorial headlined "New York slips further down the drain," is a native whose opinion deserves to be heeded. "The criminal drug of choice used to heroin, a sedative; now it is crack cocaine, a violent stimulant. . . the rich buy protection from the poor in ignorant imitation of Marxist cartoons. . . New York is like living in modern Calcutta or medieval London" (1991). Reeves recently moved to Los Angeles, perhaps to get closer to the action. At least New York and LA are "Unlike Chicago in 1986, where economic devastation in the ghetto could be laid neatly at the door of white political supremacy" (Davis 1990, 309).

LA is more diverse than that, where "A chilling February 1988 study from the Southern California Association of Governments warned that. . . $110 billion in new freeway construction would be needed just to stabilize existing congestion" (200). Part of the need to stabilize the automobile congestion is apparent in the "Anti-pedestrian bias of the new corporate citadel, with its fascist obliteration of street frontage" (229). Walking in the large cities of North America is an open invitation to be the victim of a crime. LA of course is where the government finally tracked down the Symbionese Liberation Army and burned their last stand house to the ground (252).

Events are even catching up with Texas, as reported in the *Portland Oregonian* on December 25, 1990, "After decades of reveling in wild, unfettered growth, Houston — the only major U.S. city that has no zoning laws — is now, gingerly and grudgingly, contemplating a change." The wildness of Texas is reflected in death. "Meanwhile in Texas, where the report predicted an increase of about 300 murders — more than the United States as a whole is expected to see. . 'We're all pretty mystified as to why it has become so violent,' said Ruth Post of the Houston Police Department" (AP 8-5-91). Violence is everywhere presented as a solution; why should that mystify anybody. The violence represents the failure of mutual trust, required for a nation at peace with itself, and the lack of belief in achieving goals through peaceful means.

Except for the War of 1812, the border with Canada was established by peaceful means, even if "Canadians feel like a colony of the U.S." (Reisner 1986, 507). Canada was always the 90 degree right turn in the Frederick Jackson Turner *Frontier Thesis*, where British loyalists could go to escape Yankee independence, or the 90 degree left turn for American refugees from the war in Vietnam who chose not to hang around and have their constitutional rights to avoid involuntary servitude violated. The peacefully established border in the west, as reported by Frederick Merk in *The Oregon Question,* and the profound difference of opinion between British (Canadian) and American attitudes toward the fur trade and the use of natural resources, reported by Merk in *Fur Trade and Empire, George Simpson's Journal,* all belie the current situation. The British imagined a steady state economy that would tap the resources as benignly as possible for as long as possible.

The American model of ruthless competition and exploitation prevailed and the border was closed to Farley Mowat, author of *Sea of Slaughter* and other great works on the collision of cultural and natural history in North America, when he wanted to come to the United States in person to expose the desecration of the natural world. Quebec, a French speaking nation surrounded by a country that is in economic fact a colony, is several steps removed from the "*Liberty, Equality, and Fraternity*" the French Revolution was based upon. Quebec had another revival of interest in independence in 1994. The NAFTA and other free trade agreements have continued to make Canada one of the larger and more compliant economic colonies of the Confederate Empire of North America. The Chinese contingent from Hong Kong, the yacht people, are piling up their millions in Toronto and Vancouver's banks and real estate. They are curiously disinvited from the U.S. proper but welcomed in Canada for a half million dollars a pop.

The Mormons in Utah and surrounding states, hardly compliant themselves in the 19th century and longing for independence, have become an integral part of the empire. A more recent example of a religious nation within sprang up in the deserts of eastern Oregon in the form of a more direct passage to India, the Baghwan Shree Rajneesh, and his ill-fated commune, country or cackle factory of Rajneeshpuram. This misplaced Indian prophet Baghwan from Poona bilked his band of believers from one country to another until expiring in 1989 from terminal Rolls Royce, a frequently fatal disease of the wealthy. Some of his nearly 100 Rolls Royces wound up as collateral and plunder in the hands of recalcitrant Texans in the S & L debacle.

This catalog of countries within a country or nations within the empire doesn't begin to exhaust the many colonies, client states, and allies by fiat that the empire keeps itself propped up on. Parts of the old nation of the

Confederacy itself, namely Georgia, Virginia, Arkansas and Tennessee, re-elected senators without opposition in 1990, a testament to the vital nature of democracy in the southern region. While Nunn, Warner, Pryor and Gore were shoo-ins with sinecures, opposition in senatorial elections in the South took the forms of the former Black mayor of Charlotte, Harvey Gant, and his unsuccessful run against the racist Jesse Helms in North Carolina, and the neo-Nazi David Duke's also unsuccessful run at Bennett Johnston's senate seat in Louisiana. The consequences of senatorial sinecures in the states of the former Confederacy for the children of all races, the most defenseless and disenfranchised of all nations within, are stated in the second annual *Kids Count* Data Book which rates and measures children's well being for each state. The 10 worst states for children to live in are Georgia, Louisiana, South Carolina, Mississippi, New Mexico, Florida, Arizona, Tennessee, Alabama and North Carolina (*ZPG* 1991, 7).

The consequences of following Calhoun's two-class track on the railroad of reversion will be the "ultimate impoverishment of the masses to a bare subsistence level" (Thomas 1968, 154), as Richard N. Current put it. Half of the children in the United States are already there, especially considering the condition of their schools. The geriatric nation on the other hand, especially since the Republican largesse of Nixon, is doing quite well. The expanded debt of the military extravagance has not curbed their consumption and there is no willingness to pay the debt now, since the process of enlarging it benefited the rich. There will be no interest by the disenfranchised young in paying it either, even though they are being expected to pay it in the form of higher taxes, lower wages, inflating currency and the monstrous (16 percent) FICA (Leonard 1988, 2), which keeps the wheels of the idle rich old folks in the Social Security system driving themselves to the polls. The financial war between the generations over priority funding for schools or hospitals, where the medical industry has capitalized the fear of death, is already with us. "The medical men of the West seek to obtain for their knowledge the *force of civil law*, as in the matter of vaccination or the inspection of pork for trichina" (Spengler 1926, 344). The fear of death and its capitalization (no one's dying to get into heaven anymore) has a greater claim on resources than education or the celebration of life, proof should anyone be seeking it, of the pathetic failure of Christianity.

"Almost everyone is either on a corporate payroll or waiting hopefully at the studio gate" (Davis 1990, 18), but there isn't room for everybody in this picture as the movies of the people of the picture and the corporate plantations move off shore. The crimes currently being perpetrated against the natural world by the corporate culture cannot be sustained, at home or abroad, even in the short run, much less in the long run, by simplifying the rules of GATT to make them easier to commit (Shaeffer 1990, 16), in the sacred name of free trade. Where "'Corruption dominates the ballot box, the legislatures, and touches even the ermine of the bench'" (Wilson 1970, 175), to what branch of the government might the people turn for redress? At maximum Calhoun reversion, we find that "In practice, pluralism tends to resolve sectional and class conflicts at the expense of the national interest which is represented by nobody in particular, by no section and no organization" (Thomas 1968, 142), as Philip Drucker describes it. The president manages the military and rules the empire outside the borders, the legislators bring home the bacon to their separate fiefdoms, and the nation of the United States disappears. "Clandestine activity would become an economic way of life" (Wood 1974, 217), for Black slaves in colonial South Carolina, just as the underground economy in the United States, that which thrives outside the taxing scrutiny of the empire, is clandestine and vital for survival.

At the level of the culture's collapse forward into civilization, "It ended by transforming the entire surface of the globe into a single colonial and economic system" (Spengler 1926, 335). The consequences for the people are impoverishment, for even in Japan as Professor Hisao Yamada, the Director of the National Centre for Science and Information Systems at the University of Tokyo put it in conversation, "Japanese companies are rich; the Japanese people aren't rich."

A claim on attention almost hitherto unmade is required to emerge still able to see. In separating the differences between what one does and what one says about what one does as well as the differences between the effect one is having and the effect one thinks one is having, is precisely where an objective perspective becomes most valuable. An objective perspective steeled in an incorruptible psychology is one not seduced by romantic entanglements, such as Hector hallucinating a spear bearer, when he was in fact upon the field alone. The tragic gulf between the United States and the rest of the world is the size of the distance between people who want only to be and people who feel they have to win. The United States is a winner's tragedy, a nightmare of having nothing to fight for except the battle, of destroying freedom in a pitiful exercise to save it.

Nations come into being when their people acquire style, when they surrender their villages to a greater good. In the American instance, that moment was the late 18th century and the codification of the Enlightenment in the Bill of Rights. The struggle for maintenance and enhancement was yanked sideways into the commercial abyss of empire. Nations are based on ideas. The American people came not exactly out of nowhere but from everywhere to forge a nation too idealistic to withstand the commercial terror at the heart of expropriated labor and passed with southern domination from nationhood to empire. From the Dutch village of New Amsterdam to the rise of the world city of New York on the ashes of its foundation during the Civil War, is the classic case of the corrupting influence of armaments on commerce. In the world cities of New York, LA, Miami, Seattle and Houston, the nation of the U.S. is dissolving into new ethnic crypto-villages and a top-down uncivilized struggle for existence. The competition for resources, plantations, income, is ceaseless.

Unable to face the music of the crumbling cities, the politicians and their followers retreat to suburbia and beg the question. The answers to unasked questions have to be so comprehensively restructured that they cannot even be formulated in the native tongue. The unutterable questions and solutions that would save English speaking civilization from its petering out into police trivialities cannot even be concocted in English. "It follows, however — and this is the most essential point of any — that we cannot comprehend political and economic history at all unless we realize that the city, with its gradual detachment from and final bankrupting of the country, is the determinative form to which the course and sense of higher history generally conforms. *World history is city history.*" (Spengler 1928, 95).

From the final bankrupting, we come to a final solution. "But the final solution will come only when the present wasteful, vicious, undemocratic and thoroughly antisocial system of agricultural ownership in California is abolished. The abolition of this system involves at most merely a change in ownership" (McWilliams 1969, 325). The system of ownership described in California is the system of ownership of the privileged world wide, the same one fobbed off by the English onto South Carolina. It is disingenuous to suggest that the final solution involves "merely" a change in ownership. Underneath the "merely" lies global land reform and total revolution. The size of the opportunity is equal to the difficulty. That the people are too diverse and more difficult to organize than money, suggests the revolution will be a long time coming.

The most recent world revolution was Luther's Reformation, also a revolt against religious autocracy, where "Luther placed practical activity. . . at the very center of morale" (Spengler 1926, 316). While thought itself can be practicably applied, it cannot function independently. ". . .understanding divorced from sensation is only one, and not the decisive side of life. . . In the history of actuality Archimedes, for all his scientific discoveries, was possibly less effective than that soldier who killed him at the storming of Syracuse. . . Men of theory commit a huge mistake in believing that their place is at the head and not in the train of great events" (Spengler 1928, 17). Comprehending the collapse of one civilization and even creating a model that complies with the major attributes of the collapse of others, as Spengler's work does, is as useless in bringing a new one to fruition as Alexander's toting of Homer along on his decadent rampage in Asia. Put another way, the history and effect of English speaking peoples would not be a warped syllable of garbled time different if Shakespeare had been strangled at birth.

The actual work to be done by actual people will receive little glory. "Yet we have observed already that the barbarian invaders of the derelict domain of a crumbling universal state are heroes without a future. . . but for the retrospective glamour of romance and tragedy that their literature has succeeded in casting over their escapades" (Toynbee 1956, 287). Peasants are too busy and organic to get greatly concerned with their history. The Japanese theory that history had ended with the collapse of the Soviet Union implied a grasp of the future as peopled primarily by peasants. In today's urban villages, even as LA is a massive assemblage of villages stacked side by side, the peasants are doing their work. The struggle with peasants, to keep them in school, to keep them out of or into prisons, to keep them from forming political parties for self protection, (gangs in the vernacular, Symbionese Liberation Armies or Branch Davidians in the particular), will be an endless behavioral and employment sink for the collapsing civilization.

Much of it will take the form of a police state and that the LA police department is modeled on the Marine Corps will not matter. The strongest will survive because nature abhors weakness. "Our ancestors have bred pugnacity into our bone and marrow, and thousand of years of peace won't breed it out of us. If there were any tribes of other type than this they have left no survivors" (James 1967, 662). Only approximately half of the eligible voters, the few who feel they still have a major stake in the outcome, bother to ratify the rhetoric of the empire in their quadrennial elections, but the peasants will still be around when the empire is only an academic memory. "The word 'pagan' (man of the heath or country-side) survives to this day to tell us who it was that this propaganda affected last" (Spengler 1926, 360). The field of the future in the nations within belongs to the last to be taken in by the empire's party line and the first to get cracking on practical personal solutions.

25

The Democratic Nationalists

Only six times since the Civil War have reasonably liberal Democrats been able to achieve a presidential victory. The victories of Grover Cleveland and John Kennedy turned out to be inconsequential. The three significant victories, Wilson in 1912, Franklin Roosevelt in 1932, and Jimmy Carter in 1976, all followed and were a direct result of Republican excess and disarray. Clinton's victory in 1992 was certainly a result of Republican disarray. It most closely resembles the Wilson victory of 1912 when the Republican right wing also ran two candidates and split their vote. George Bush only got a majority of the vote in one district of 380 that are outside the boundaries of the old Confederacy. As for Perot, "His most important effect on the 1992 political outcome was to damage Bush and divert a large chunk of the Republican coalition" (Phillips 1993, 244). Since the liar Lyndon Johnson's lopsided victory in 1964, only Jimmy Carter in 1976 was able to garner more than the 43 percent of the vote that went to Clinton. That's all Clinton can plan on in 1996 and his re-election, should he even be re-nominated, could be in the hands of Ross Perot, or some other self-appointed right wing demagogue, sabotaging the equally pathetic and vulnerable Republicans.

Democratic victories are, in other words, aberrations and erratic exceptions to the prevailing political power in North America. That power returns to office immediately following the impulses to democracy, where it continues to exacerbate conditions on the looping pulse of American history. Both Wilson and Roosevelt were dragged into European war by the regression to the right demanding "save the English." The minority democratic position achieved its most forceful exposition in the careers of William Jennings Bryan, thrice nominated, thrice beaten, and in Henry Wallace, dumped from FDR's ticket at southern insistence and who later mounted his own Progressive party campaign.

The first serious Republican candidate for president in 1856 was the liberal John C. Fremont from northern California. Old liberal Republicans from the original Fremont-Lincoln school threw in the towel to McKinley and Theodore Roosevelt. More contemporary liberals, Warren, Stevenson, Humphrey, Rockefeller, Romney, McCarthy, McGovern, Church, Brown, Mondale, Hart, Jackson and Dukakis, were unable to articulate a winning strategy because the liberal position is at cross purposes with the empire and the military religious force power of the civilization.

There is a democratic black hole in the Texan domination of North America in the northern great plains, from which many of these liberals hail, extended westward from the upper Midwest and the lake country. Nebraska, Iowa, Minnesota, South Dakota, and Illinois are home to Bryan, Wallace, Humphrey, McCarthy, Mondale, McGovern, and Stevenson. Let's examine the unsuccessful flings at power of the democratic nationalists and locate the structural impotence of the nationalist position vis a vis the empire, where, as Henry Ebel once put it, the American electorate intuitively eliminates the weaker of the two candidates (1973).

The expression of democratic nationalism that Americans associate with Jefferson and Jackson (themselves empire builders) in the formative years of the republic, disappeared into the sectional quests for empire of Jackson's political progeny, Polk, Pierce and Buchanan. The next Democratic president in the Jackson line was Jefferson Davis of the Confederacy. The Civil War put the quest for empire temporarily to rest, except for the subjugation of the remaining independent Indians, and by the turn of the 20th century, the quest for empire was firmly in imperialist Republican hands when both Cabot Lodge and Beveridge of Indiana vilified Jefferson (Josephson 1940, 68). Sympathy for the Negro position in American politics, originally a Federalist-Whig-Republican preoccupation, was abandoned to northern democratic nationalists when northern Republicans began their fusion with Bourbon Democrats from the South in the Fraud of 1876. Exactly when democracy in the United States disappeared depends for its date on what type of Americans are under discussion. It disappeared at different times for different groups and in the 19th century had yet even to make an appearance for the female half of the population. For democratic presidential aspirants, such as the defrauded Samuel J. Tilden of New York, the date was 1876 when the democrats were served notice that they would forever be on the defensive. Grover Cleveland eked out a couple of narrow victories in the Republican hegemony after the Civil War and resisted strident demands to imperialize Hawaii while he was president. The Republican platform of 1896 advocated the annexation of Hawaii, to save it from "foreign" influence and domination. William Jennings Bryan made his first run at the presidency in 1896 and it began with his famous "Cross of Gold" speech.

Like Calhoun, Bryan believed that "There are two ideas of government." The similarities end there. "'There are those who believe that, if you will only legislate to make the well-to-do prosperous, their prosperity will leak through on those below. The Democratic idea, however, has been that if you legislate to make the masses prosperous, their prosperity will find its way up through every class that rests upon them'" (Wilson 1970, 451). The differences between the leak through (trickle down) and the wick up theories of economic well being are at the heart of the democratic challenge. Bryan advocated the free coinage of silver at the rate in value of 16-1 relative to gold. The gold standard was the favorite of the English and their American imperialist sympathizers because it operates to the advantage of creditors. "'You shall not press down upon the brow of labor the crown of thorns, you shall not crucify mankind upon a cross of gold'" (452). The aristocratic English attitude toward labor was solidified with the British Empire's successful foundation based on the expropriation of slave labor in Barbados and South Carolina. Bryan's frequent use of religious metaphor should not distract us from his understanding, springing from the soil of Nebraska, of the prophetic value of fertile land. "'Burn down your cities and leave our farms, and your cities will spring up again as if by magic; but destroy our farms, and the grass will grow in the streets of every city in the country'" (451).

Bryan lost the election of 1896, although his popular vote total of 6,511,073 was more than any Democratic nominee had ever received. "The electoral votes would go 271 for McKinley and 176 for Bryan, but the score by states was so narrow than an additional 15,000 votes strategically distributed might have given Bryan the Presidency" (Wilson 1970, 230). McKinley's election, the annexation of Hawaii, and the Spanish American War [how awkward to get a war going in a democracy that hasn't been attacked! (May 1961, 145)], set up a 1900 rerun of the election of 1896, in effect a referendum on the empire and imperialism. Walter Lippmann, commenting in the introduction to *American Imperialism,* says "'For this book, as I read it, is a confession that the imperialistic dream of 1898 had proved to be unrealistic, that the management of an empire by a democracy like the American democracy is impossible'" (Roosevelt 1970, xiii). Despite the principled opposition to American participation in the establishment of an empire by Andrew Carnegie (Harrington 1935, 216), and others, including old-line Lincoln Republicans (218), who held out until the last dog was hung in Boston in the 1920s (220), what the Spanish American War really re-established was that whenever there was an issue that would pit the empire against the democracy, the empire would prevail and the democracy would succumb.

William Appleman Williams, after a lifetime of study said: "Our idiom has been empire, and so the primary division was and remains between the soft and the hard" (1980, 30). It is possible to see the differences as digital, soft or hard, but it is also possible to reconstruct the behavior along an analog continuum. "But the history of the United States is not the story of triumphant anti-imperial heretics. It is the account of the power of empire as a way of life, as a way of avoiding the fundamental challenge of creating a humane and equitable community or culture" (96). Note Williams' choice of the religious term "heretics" to describe the opposition to this theocracy and its perpetual holy war. Thomas Bailey Aldrich announced that he could not vote for McKinley for "'I would sooner vote for Bryan. To be ruined financially is not so bad as to be ruined morally'" (Harrington 1937, 666). His concern was that the United States had "bought the Filipinos, just as if they were so many slaves" (666).

Bryan himself, inveterate optimist as most democratic nationalists either are or are forced by circumstances to pretend to be, still described the U.S. in 1900 as "'a republic standing erect while empires all around are bowed beneath the weight of their own armaments'" (Levine 1965, 5). Bryan's loss by a wider margin in 1900 is evidence of the strength of the empire's grip and its consolidation of power. Expressed in campaign dollars, the Republicans spent $2.5 million to the Democratic $100,000 (Wilson 1970, 275). "Walter Hines Page, the American Ambassador to Great Britain, regarded Bryan as little more than an untutored frontiersman with no understanding of the great issues of Anglo-American relations" (Glad 1968, 167). The great issue, as everybody is aware by now, was how to keep the English speaking empire in power, not one of Bryan's agendas. If Bryan's partisans can say "In the long run, history upholds Bryan rather than McKinley" (76), part of such an assessment has to be ascribed to the American economic, moral, and strategic blunders in the Philippine Islands. In the short run, of course, he was vilified to the point of treason by Theodore

Roosevelt (84), who was McKinley and the empire's choice for vice president (Pringle 1955, 113).

The Republican dismissal of Bryan as country hick had its counterparts in the formation of the British Empire. "A country platform was virtually the only larger ideological context in which ministerial opponents could place their hostility to government policy [with Whig and Tory variants]. . . But, when it came to discussing war, foreign policy, money and the state, it was the *lingua franca*" (Brewer 1989, 157). It was the power of money, concentrating in cities such as London, Charleston and New York, which expropriated the land and labor of the countryside that defines the empire's victory over the nation. Richard Hofstadter, who did not comprehend the essence of Free Silver as a political idea, felt that Bryan embodied the average man and provided expression for his situation rather than leadership out of it. Nevertheless, he could admit "The many ways in which farmers were victimized by tariffs [shades of Calhoun], railroads, middlemen, speculators, warehousers, and monopolistic producers of farm equipment were all but forgotten" (Hofstadter 1959, 188). Bryan had an eloquent grasp of democratic particulars as in his understanding that equality means to be equal before the law. That ordinary people were not is patently obvious.

If Bryan felt he was issuing a second Declaration of Independence, and his populist supporters "saw themselves as patriots assembled to save the nation from the greedy and otherwise evil forces and interests that would destroy it" (Wilson 1970, 173), we can take it as evidence of how far backwards the regression had carried the United States since the issuance of the first Declaration of Independence. Bryan's incapacity to remember names, imputed to his continual rehearsing of speeches to the "silent, subterranean hosts in Arlington" (161), is due to the neurological process where internal audio and external audio reception occupy the same neuronal channels. Bryan was his own microphone and speech writer. Philip Drucker, discussing Calhoun's pluralism as a key to American political thought, suggests that "An industrial society cannot function without an organ [Bryan's larynx was not up to the task] able to superimpose the national interest on economic or class interests" (Thomas 1968, 146). In the case of the establishment of the American empire, this necessitated "Collusion against the national interest" (146). While it might be ultimately ascribed to the Calhoun principle that security always overrides liberty, no American national security was even slightly at risk in the acquisition or non-acquisition of the Philippine Islands and "From Plato to Rousseau, political thought has ended up by demanding that factions be suppressed, that is, that freedom, to be preserved, be abolished" (148). The interests of the empire were superimposed on the nation. The only freedom to survive was the freedom of the privileged class to make and set policy in the direction of empire.

Having lost twice, Bryan was out of favor with the Democrats and "Judge Alton B. Parker, the Democratic Presidential candidate in 1904, publicly called him and his followers aspiring Benedict Arnolds and held him responsible for the dangers the country now faced" (Levine 1965, 87). Treason is the first retort of the imperialists, uttered apparently to keep themselves from being tagged with it, where it more properly fits, if *loyalty to the country* is the issue and not loyalty to the empire. New York City, commercial seat of the empire and its house organ, the New York *Times*, treated Bryan with disdain: "'The Capitol was cold to him. . . Nobody cared a rap about his views. He Came. He Failed. He went'" (47). Bryan kept his grip on the real issues. "'The real question is not what the President THINKS the people want, but WHAT THE PEOPLE ACTUALLY WANT'" (55). Bryan lost to Taft in 1908, racking up three defeats for three nominations, not because he was a loser, but because the forces that conceived of the United States as a country were in the minority and the forces for empire were triumphant.

Bryan was still considered a serious candidate for a Fourth nomination in 1920 (153-4). "He exuded the confidence of a man who expected to control the convention, shape the platform, and select the candidate. In an editorial addressed to all prospective presidential candidates he demanded that they publicly announce their platforms" (160). He had served as Wilson's Secretary of State and tried by the observance of a strict neutrality to keep the United States out of England's war with Germany. His deep thought, candor and convictions are commodities in short supply in the 1990s, but he knew "a liberal in one area may be a conservative in another, not only at the same time but for the same reasons" (363). The abbreviated attention span of contemporary American political discourse would insist on making nonsense of such a cleanly delineated distinction. That Bryan wound up on the wrong side of the so called "Monkey Trial," opposite Clarence Darrow, is no excuse to ignore his fundamental support for ordinary people. The man had a sense of humor and even if he could not keep the U.S. out of the European war, he could advocate the cancellation of European war debts in exchange for a European disarmament, not because he was such a nice guy, but since the debts would never be repaid anyway, why not "'buy a PRICELESS peace with a WORTHLESS debt?'" (202).

Even though Roosevelt and Bryan wound up on the same side of some issues, Roosevelt never forgave him for the $25 million indemnity to Columbia for the loss of Panama. "'The payment can only be justified upon the ground that this nation played the part of a thief'" (Pringle 1955, 234). Roosevelt objected to the payment, the notion of thievery which he orchestrated, and to the appellation "imperialist." He torpedoed William Howard Taft out of the presidency by running against him and Woodrow Wilson in 1912. Together they received 1.5 million more votes than Wilson as Republican disarray let the minority Democrats take one of their widely separated and periodic flings at power.

While Wilson let his administration be sandbagged into war, he led the nation in a ruthless suppression of human rights. "Although the Espionage Act of 1917 has been roundly condemned by nearly every historian as one of the most dangerous pieces of legislation ever written, Woodrow Wilson thought of it originally as a very mild measure" (Johnson 1963, 55). Mild or not, opposition to WWI provided a reprise of sorts to the activities of the Anti-Imperialist League of the 1890s, with vicious new twists in the way opposition would be dealt with. "Few people have ever been so intolerant of their fellow men as Americans in the First World War" (63). Freedom for serious political dissension was virtually suspended as "Eugene V. Debs, the Socialist leader, went to jail [a 10 year sentence] for a speech in Canton, Ohio, that was vaguely antagonistic to the war" (72). Senator Hiram Johnson was of the opinion that "free speech still existed in America only in the United States Senate" (79).

What brought such reactionary lizards from the American political closet was their antipathy to peace expressed in an innate southern love of war supported by the suppressed media. "For four and a half years these two men [Burleson and Lamar] held life or death power over many a newspaper and almost every magazine in the country. That they used this power unwisely and with no consideration for traditional freedoms of speech and press is indisputable" (82-3). What we are witness to is that even with an elected Democrat in the presidency, the American empire joined a war to make the world safe for the British Empire, even as the rights that supposedly distinguish the United States as a nation were buried in reactionary rhetoric and jail at home. A. Mitchell Palmer, the Attorney General of the United States who had asked Congress for a peacetime sedition law so he could imprison radicals "must have been aware of the fact that Hoover had specifically directed his men not to use search warrants" (144). Felix Frankfurter, later to be a justice of the Supreme Court and the other 11 lawyers trying to sort out the Palmer raid mess "accused the Justice Department of violating at least four constitutional amendments" (159). With such illegal power in the hands of the Attorney General, how much farther can democracy fall, other than the other six amendments in the Bill of Rights. "Palmerism was defeated, however, only in the most limited sense. . . Despite two full scale investigations, Congress never censured him" (164).

The imperial duplicity of his aide, J. Edgar Hoover who carried out the raids, is a great scar on the American landscape. "Even to the present day — and despite overwhelming evidence to the contrary — Hoover insisted that 'I deplore the manner in which the raids were executed then, and my position has remained unchanged'" (174). Even James Kilpatrick, the conservative and principled columnist, who by 1992 had found his natural home in Charleston, South Carolina, can write "He professed to loath communism, yet he practiced the worst aspects of communism every day. . . we are beginning to see J. Edgar Hoover for what he was: the ultimate un-American" (*UB* 1992, 4). Many of the people thrown in jail during WWI and after had to wait until the administration of Calvin Coolidge to be freed while Woodrow Wilson felt "No one had been convicted for expressing his opinions and that there were no political prisoners" (Johnson 1963, 177).

Faced with such out of touch and deliberate misunderstanding on the part of the president, there was "A bitter five-year struggle — a struggle for an amnesty that in Senator Borah's opinion 'ought to have been granted the next day after the war closed'" (193). Most European prisoners of war were released within a year after the war's end. The question of a pardon or an amnesty is interesting. "In Baldwin's opinion, a general amnesty would be a confession of guilt on the part of the government and a recognition of the principle of free speech, while an individual pardon meant nothing except that the government was exercising its right to be generous" (186). The government of Woodrow Wilson, paternally anxious to apply the principles of self-determination globally by universalizing an American solution to every problem, was unable or unwilling to permit their application at home.

Before he left the Wilson administration, Bryan had tried to keep the United States out of WWI with its strident negative consequences for civil liberties. His was a genuine interest in neutrality and the usefulness in arbitration that only such genuine neutrality can offer. He did not see the British with the popular blinders of Henry Cabot Lodge. As the waves of advance rise and fall on the pulsing microcycles of American opinion and American foreign policy fell into disrepute, "There was, to be sure, a brief period in the 1930s when Bryan was held in higher regard. In a decade when Americans rejected all world responsibility and regarded their partici- pation in World War I as the greatest aberration in the nation's history. . ." (Glad 1968, 161). It is clear that Bryan's interests were the interests of the United States as a country, rather than as an empire, and if this is a romantic view, it is one shared by George McClellan, who "fundamentally wanted to preserve a union at the expense of no region and with all the best character- istics of all regions preserved in it" (Dowdy 1957, 314). The romance of the nation gave way to the realism of a Civil War to preserve the union and imperial wars to aggrandize it into a global empire.

There is a tendency to confuse isolationism with a desire not to be militarily involved. This confusion surrounded Senator Borah of Idaho in the 1930s. "Senator Borah submitted to the Foreign Relations Committee a gloss on the [Monroe] Doctrine, which. . . dissociated interventionist principles from the principles of 1823" (Perkins 1966, 83). Politicians espousing skepticism of the wisdom of rushing to save the British Empire at its many weak points are accused of wanting to isolate themselves. Repub- lican speculative excesses of the 1920s led to the election of Franklin Roosevelt in 1932. To avoid being accused of doing nothing, as Hoover was, Roosevelt tried to do everything, whether it was right or not, and the major ramifica- tion of the New Deal legacy was massive consolidation of power in the federal government in Washington D.C. That consolidation of power would become extremely useful to the militarists who succeeded FDR, and for a time there was a strong American intention to not get sucked in once again to a European war to save the English, especially if it meant an alliance with the dreaded Communists under Joseph Stalin in Russia. "Why not let the two Titans destroy each other?" (92), ultimately gave way to a war to help Stalin crush Hitler, a profound waste of time. Would the map of Europe be drawn significantly different in the 1990s if the United States had stayed the hell out of the wars against Germany? Only democratic congresswoman

Jeanette Rankin of Montana had the presence of mind to vote against the entry of the United States into both World War I and World War II.

"Bereft of a coherent and plausible body of belief. . . Americans have become more receptive than ever to dynamic personal leadership as a substitute. This is part of the secret of Roosevelt's popularity, and, since his death, of the rudderless and demoralized state of American Liberalism" (Hofstadter 1959, VII). Roosevelt's dynamic personal leadership, also known as the cult of his personality, permitted him to cave in to pressure from the South as he pulled the rug out from under vice president Henry Wallace, giving the 1944 VP nomination to Harry Truman, the most grievous political blunder of the 20th century, doing more than perhaps even Hofstadter could imagine to demoralize American liberalism as he took the one liberal who would have made a difference out of the path of power. FDR's personality was not a fit substitute for a coherent belief system. The limited number and usefulness of the ideas driving the empire are at least coherent. Roosevelt rode the last ridge of transition between the United States as a country and the Confederate Empire of North America.

Even in the empire, Wallace had a role to play as FDR offered him the sop of Secretary of Commerce which he carried over into the early days of Truman's administration, until his independent views of foreign policy ran him up against the prevailing militarist tone and he resigned. Bryan's role as Wilson's Secretary of State was a similar demonstration of the incompatibility of the nation with the empire. Five southern senators opposed Wallace until the end, Byrd, McCarran, McKellar, Stewart, and O'Daniel (MacDougall 1965, 14). He received support from New Deal senators such as Kilgore of West Virginia, Claude Pepper of Florida, and Glen Taylor of Idaho, who would become his Progressive party running mate when Pepper demurred out of loyalty to the Democratic party. Among the speeches contributing to his disfavor in the Democratic party, one at Madison Square Garden stands out. "Only the United Nations should have atomic bombs and its military establishment should give special emphasis to air power. It should have control of the strategically located air bases with which the United States and Britain have encircled the world" (63).

The English speaking empire is only prepared to submit to world opinion when it directs it. Wallace "specifically rejected the American Century, that term of Henry Luce, publisher of *Time, Life,* and *Fortune,* who saw America as a sort of latter-day Britain presiding wisely over the world and remaking it in the American image" (Walton 1976, 14). As has been observed, it was the Luce position that prevailed, and Henry Wallace was on his long way from being the most efficient cabinet member in the Roosevelt administration (4), to being a pariah. No one ever accused him of lacking nerve. "Even in Norfolk, Virginia, where Wallace and Clark Foreman on November 23rd successfully held an integrated meeting in defiance of the police, he attacked the Truman Doctrine, Truman's plan for Universal Military Training, and the House Un-American Activities Committee" (170). In the wonderful switch of nomenclature that made the War Department into the Department of Defense, almost at the same time George Orwell published *1984* and made doublespeak a household word, Wallace offered his own suggestion in "I say we should be relying on a Department of Peace" (349).

What you say is what you get. What you do is what you believe. What Henry Wallace did was go everywhere he could in the service of his belief in democracy and the United States as a nation. L. Mendel Rivers of South Carolina called his speeches a "Grave Disservice." The Southern right wing wanted his passport yanked. Churchill, knowing where the knife is concealed, called him a crypto-Communist, while Senator Vandenberg of Michigan settled for saboteur (MacDougall 1965, 137). Wallace was attracting overflow crowds (154) and "His greatest thrill on the present trip was the temporary breakdown of racial segregation that occurred during his visit in Austin, Texas" (161). While he could speak at the University of Texas, with both student support and opposition, Johns Hopkins University in Baltimore wouldn't ask him to speak. "'Considering the nature of their financial foundations, I never blame the president of a great educational institution. He's got to be true to his bread'" (208). There is unintended educational service provided in the denial of an invitation or the right to speak. Not all of the Wallace-Taylor inroads to the South were as peaceful as even the events in Austin. In Birmingham, Alabama, Glen Taylor was arrested by Bull Conner, the commissioner of police for entering a church through the door reserved for "colored folk." Taylor was convicted of breach of the peace, assault and battery, and resisting an officer in the performance of his duty. "'I'm a United States Senator, you can't arrest me'" (390) Taylor protested as police hauled him away.

The Progressive party's work in the South, where they got next to no votes in the 1948 election, adumbrated the freedom rides of the 1960s.

"They did so by means of a head-on attack against both the theory and practice of white supremacy. With the objective of mass support for an end to all forms of racial segregation, the Progressives loudly refused to obey the Jim Crow laws governing meeting, eating and sleeping places" (707). That is always risky business in the South, where they held "At Houston and El Paso, the largest unsegregated political meetings in Texas, perhaps in the South, since Reconstruction" (739). Can it be made any clearer that the impulse to democratic nationalism is at cross purposes and radically perpendicular in purpose to the southern dominated empire of the United States. "To list the cities in which New Party leaders found it difficult or impossible to find adequate meeting places would mean to virtually compile a Postal Guide" (403). Albert Einstein, one of hundreds of prominent entertainers, scholars and geniuses to support Wallace, felt it necessary to protest an action permitted by Newark safety commissioner Keenan to drown out a Wallace rally (406). With weight like Einstein's on board, what difference can it make that some Neo-Confederate pipsqueak senator with a sinecure like James O. Eastland of Mississippi would try to red-bait Wallace as a Communist (412).

Among the interesting upshots of the four party election of 1948 for a practicing democracy, two stand out. The biggest impediment to third or even fourth party candidates are the state election laws. Never particularly uniform, an expression of state rights, they were actually tightened in turn after Roosevelt's Bull Moose party run in 1912. They were further byzantined after Robert M. La Follette's run in 1924 to make it even more difficult for third party candidates to get on the ballot. Preservation of the two party system benefits the two parties, period. It is not a benefit to democracy. The aristocrats dismiss independent complaints about the arbitrary and capricious nature of state election laws by saying, much as the following study reported in the *Yale Law Journal*: "The suspicion becomes all to strong, therefore, that complaints about legal requirements are either attempted shields for inadequacy or evidence of unwillingness to think realistically" (293). To think realistically, in "Yalese" (for instance Bush, Brown, and Clinton in 1992) and American politics, means to think in established channels with lots of money. Ross Perot in 1992, not exactly a third party but certainly outside the two party system, had significant difficulty with the legal jungle even with virtually unlimited personal funds at his disposal. It is not likely that a serious democratic challenge will have access to much money. It is much more likely to be completely broke.

The other interesting upshot of 1948 was that "Whereas the Dixiecrats of 1948 were welcomed back into the Democratic fold with everything forgiven, no such generous attitude prevailed toward the Progressives" (865). The progressive element was read out of the party in this example of the power of regression and obeisance toward the South and to empire at the expense of democratic nationalism. By 1952, the Dixiecrat's first choice of Eisenhower for the Democrats, had feathered his nest in the Republican party, squeezing out the liberal Earl Warren of California and the conservative Taft of Ohio. Taft fit right in with the right wing persistence in thinking that politicians who opposed them were guilty of treason rather than poor judgment. For two elections in a row, Eisenhower, the native son, carried Texas and the nation against the liberal Adlai Stevenson of Illinois. Stevenson's strongest opposition for the democratic nomination and his eventual running mate was the Southerner who convinced Truman in the New Hampshire primary of 1952 that he shouldn't try to run again, Senator Estes Kefauver of Tennessee. The South is all over the map and dominates American political power.

Sympathy for Stevenson had diminished by 1960, when the Democratic nomination went to John Kennedy of Massachusetts, as JFK was accused of buying the primary elections from Hubert Humphrey, especially in West Virginia. There is no place for a poor man in American presidential politics (White 1988, 108-114). Lyndon Johnson's appeal was strictly confined to the South. Stevenson became the U.S. Ambassador to the U.N. and an advisor to Kennedy. Among his advice was the suggestion to withdraw the air support from the NSC/CIA invasion of Cuba, the critical element in its failure. The last thing anyone needs on a military expedition is poor diplomatic advice. Southern outrage may have contributed to Kennedy's unsolved assassination. Within 72 hours of being sworn in as president, Lyndon Johnson countermanded Kennedy's plans for a phased withdrawal from Vietnam. Johnson put Humphrey on the 1964 ticket to mollify the traditional northern Democrats and put Humphrey's "balls" in his pocket.

The absurd conduct of Johnson's war on Vietnam flipped the United States out of the frying pan of discontent into the fire of 1968. Senator Eugene McCarthy of Minnesota challenged Johnson and his mouthpiece

Humphrey in New Hampshire, receiving approximately 40 percent of the vote and claiming a moral victory. The exhausted cowardly Johnson withdrew as a candidate, on or about April fool's Day, rather than face the wrath of the lied to electorate in a referendum on his presidency. Robert Kennedy joined the fray and was killed immediately upon winning the California Democratic primary, or as soon as he became a serious contender for power. Martin Luther King Jr. had already been assassinated in Memphis, not long after he had broadened his appeal from its NAACP base to include all poor people. Johnson's absentee iron grip on the Democratic party delivered the nomination to Humphrey over the peoples' choice of McCarthy in the Fascist city of Chicago. Nixon boxed the more liberal Rockefeller out on the Republican side. The yellow journalists had ripped the Mormon Governor of Michigan, Republican George Romney, to shreds for having the courage to say the Johnson administration had brainwashed him by withholding evidence when he went to Vietnam to find out for himself what was happening there. These cowardly choices by the impotent and so-called "free" press demonstrate their complicity to the Vietnam War crimes; it was the Johnson administration that deserved to be shredded for its many lies. When the two party system is working right, that is to say to its own benefit, addressing the needs of the power elite as it did in 1968, it keeps democratic nationalists from even getting a nomination. Native son of the Yahoo Belt, George Wallace of Alabama and his American Independent party, anchored the southern right. Together he and Nixon got 57 percent of the vote.

In *The Selling of the President 1968*, a popular classic and required reading, it is stated that in the era of cool TV politics when the tube brings the action right into the living room, the hot "Humphrey vomited on the rug" (McGinnis 1969, 24). Which was not much compared to the vomit he had been strewing as vice president for four years. The closest he came to victory resulted from a spot called "The Mind Changer. . . It showed Hubert Humphrey as a person" (141). The Nixon victory, in Murray Kempton's immortal summation, made him "the President of every place in this country which does not have a bookstore" (169).

The United States had already moved far beyond the notion of a debate over political judgment with the cancellation of the Fulbright hearings into the conduct of the war (Halberstam 1979, 506). Senators Church, Morse and Gruening gradually converted people to their side, where they behaved as Borah did during WWI, providing a modicum of comfort to the government silenced opposition. "Borah was one of the few senators who usually adopted a civil libertarian position during the war" (Johnson 1963, 208). The truth was no more provided by newspapers than it had been shared with George Romney. This is traditional in American wars such as the one in Cuba in 1898 where "The U.S. press was simply not reporting the story comprehensively" (Wilson 1970, 232). Democracy depends on information, and if it can be controlled, distorted, or turned into disinformation, democracy doesn't function. Democracy did not function during the war in Vietnam.

By 1972 people had cause to wonder what had become of Nixon's plan to end the war, other than trying to bomb North Vietnam into the Stone Age and launching a Christian surprise attack on Cambodia on Christmas Eve, little had changed. Senator George McGovern, a decorated WWII pilot and soft spoken liberal from South Dakota who wanted to end the war, won the Democratic nomination. His personal choice for vice president, Senator Thomas Eagleton of Missouri, was hooted off the ticket for having taken the rational step of seeking advice for depression, much as George Romney was hooted off the national stage for reintroducing the loaded verb "brainwash" back into the national vocabulary. The Eagleton affair points up the weakness of the embrace of the Confederate principle of first ballot victory, no controversy, as established in Montgomery in 1861. Nixon's idiotic choice of Agnew is another case in point. Surely if a convention is going to decide, as Adlai Stevenson permitted the 1956 Democratic convention to select Kefauver over Kennedy, it won't be as tidy for television but it will get candidates acceptable to a larger cross section of the people. It is a significant whiff of southern power to note that the walk to Kefauver away from Kennedy for VP in 1956 began with Senator Albert Gore Sr. of Tennessee.

"In every Presidential election except that of 1932 in which the Democrats staked their case on hard times, something happened about August to raise prices" (Glad 1968, 27). Actually, Nixon got a running start on his 1972 landslide re-election in the fall of 1971 by dumping money on the geriatric class via an otherwise unwarranted 20 percent increase in Social Security. His own political and social security was what was really at stake. Nixon had learned the first law of American presidential politics; when times are good, incumbents are re-elected. Nixon, the third big Republican fiasco of the century up to that point, the other two being Theodore Roosevelt in 1912 and Hoover in 1932 as the empty bag man, turned the White House temporarily over to the Democrats again, this time led by Jimmy Carter in 1976. When a democratic nationalist finally won, even he was a Southerner. Distinguished members of Carter's cabinet, Congressman Brock Adams of Washington as Commerce Secretary, Governor Cecil Andrus of Idaho at Interior, and Portland, Oregon, Mayor Neil Goldschmidt at Transportation, could return to elected public life. Adams was elected to the Senate from Washington, Goldschmidt to the governorship of Oregon, and Andrus once again was governor of Idaho. This is testimony to the integrity of democratic nationalist administration. That Brock Adams' career was later unraveled on sexual abuse and rape charges, does not alter his progressive voting record.

Carter's policies so irritated the empire mongers that the Reagan revolution swept him and enough liberal senators out of office to let Reagan stamp the decade of the 1980s as his own. Reagan had little trouble dispensing with the dishrag Mondale in 1984, although Mondale's choice of Geraldine Ferraro for vice president, rather than letting the convention decide, was another example of fatal distress at the top. Gary Hart, who had actually worked for the presidential nomination and who would have been a better candidate for either position, was frozen out by this empty gesture toward the feminist vote. Mondale's endorsement by the AFL-CIO and the National Organization of Women illustrated the central democratic nationalist problem, other than money. They attempt to appeal to everyone, men and women, all factions, minorities, intellectuals, blue collar workers and "organized" labor. The process of American individualism leaves them stranded at the polls. Lyndon Johnson was the last person to pretend to be all things to all people and we know how that turned out. The organizing principle of the empire, money and power, is simpler to grasp and execute. Republicans are the party of rich white men. Democrats are the party of everybody else, and although the simple organizing principle of education and learning is available to them, their boat continually sinks on the shoals of factionalism.

Gary Hart was defeated by his libido in 1988 and the Bush-Dukakis contest illustrated several crucial things about the political situation in North America. The states Dukakis carried, Washington, Oregon, Iowa, Minnesota, Wisconsin, New York, Massachusetts, Rhode Island, West Virginia

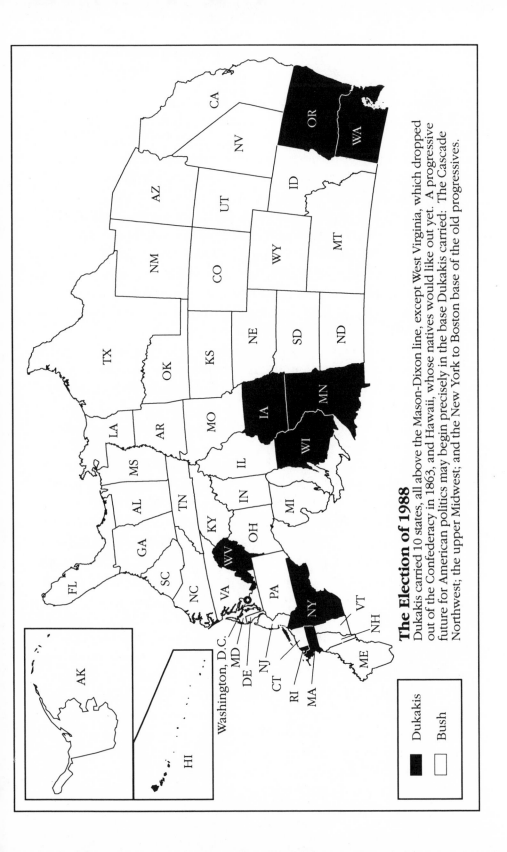

The Election of 1988

Dukakis carried 10 states, all above the Mason-Dixon line, except West Virginia, which dropped out of the Confederacy in 1863, and Hawaii, whose natives would like out yet. A progressive future for American politics may begin precisely in the base Dukakis carried: The Cascade Northwest; the upper Midwest; and the New York to Boston base of the old progressives.

■ Dukakis

□ Bush

Washington, D.C.
MD
DE
NJ
CT
RI
MA

AK

HI

and Hawaii, are all above the Mason-Dixon Line except West Virginia and Hawaii. Hawaii is a special case in the process of being bought outright and otherwise co-opted into the empire of Japan, while West Virginia dropped out of the Confederacy in 1863. The 1988 election indicates that there are still strong pockets of democratic nationalism in the Cascade Coast of the Pacific Northwest, in the New York-Boston-Providence Northeast where it started, and in the upper Midwest where many of the serious democratic nationalist contenders come from. The rest of the barely United States was a pure Confederate sweep, from Virginia to California including Florida and of course the place where Yankees with any tax avoiding ingenuity like Bush call home, Texas. Just like in the days after the Civil War, "The United States was far from a unitary nation. . . For some years however, Texas and its Southern Allies maintained an acceptable stabilization and compromise" (Fehrenbach 1968, 633). With the exception of the four years of Carter, having the run of the place from the Truman Doctrine until the end of the Bush presidency for 45 years under the guidance of Texans like Eisenhower, Rayburn, Johnson, and Bush, with the "Loony Tunes" from Confederate California, Nixon and Reagan thrown in for good measure, still qualifies as acceptable compromise.

"The individual in today's world, therefore, can no longer look to the nation as the main source of his security" (Cousins 1987, 191). This is so because the nation has disappeared. It has been swallowed by the empire. Inside every empire are many nations trying to get out. The empire "is not only incapable of protecting the lives, values, and property of its citizens; it has actually become inimical to life and creative freedom" (192). The enabling act for the Central Intelligence Agency in 1947 prohibits the U.S. government from lying to the American people (207). Laws march alongside power. When they enhance it they are obeyed. When they restrict it they are ignored. In addition to a prohibition on lying, the CIA was explicitly forbidden involvement in "'police, subpoena, or law enforcement powers or internal security functions'" (Hitchens 1991, 60). The Confederate Empire of North America is in fact a police state where crucial decisions are made outside public scrutiny. Democratic nationalist demands, such as "No candidate for the highest office in 1992 can be counted as genuine unless he or she announces that the elected government will be the only one" (64), are likely to go unheeded.

Characterizing the current American system of government as Confederate should not be confused with the issue of sectional solidarity for many democratic nationalists have thrived in the South, such as Jimmy Carter. They are simply in the minority almost everywhere now except in the pockets of victory evidenced by the states Dukakis carried. In the old days, it was "surely an exaggeration to describe the rural North as a homogeneous, egalitarian society of freeholding farmers, but that region was much closer to such an ideal than was the South. So much for 'economic democracy'" (Wright 1978, 39). Democracy, economic or otherwise, is not possible in an empire. North America could just as easily break into political pieces as it could keep its present confused shape of an empire dictating to nations, within and without its disappearing borders. A large measure of the democratic nationalist failure is its inability to keep the distinctions between the country and the empire separated long enough to articulate a convincing vision of the United States as a nation.

Considering the congressional complicity with the imperial presidencies, as in the votes on NAFTA or the war on Iraq, it is likely already too late. ". . .so now peoples' rights are paraded for the multitude, and all the more punctiliously the less they really signify. . . Through money, democracy becomes its own destroyer, after money has destroyed the intellect" (Spengler 1928, 464). The Congress and Senate of the United States are peopled by ombudsmen and deliverers of constituent services, rather than senators and representatives, who focus on their states and districts. The president concentrates on the empire because he has military power and little else except pressure from the transnational corporations to work with. With no elected official or officials to look out for it, the nation disappeared. And on the presidential side, where it takes so much money to buy TV time, righteous democratic nationalists, such as former California governor Jerry Brown, cannot survive the Hollywood Primary, "The money-grubbing pilgrimages of Democratic hopefuls to Malibu" (Davis 190, 141). Money rules the empire. The peasants will be revolting.

26

The Inescapable Conclusion

Anyone doubting the thesis of *How the South Finally Won the Civil War* and how completely the rest of the United States is compromised by the southern domination of American politics should take another look at the results of the 1992 presidential election and the southern conservative triumphs in the mid-term elections of 1994. Earl and Merle Black in *The Vital South, How Presidents Are Elected,* claim "The modern South is the largest, the most cohesive, and, arguably, the most important region in the United States in terms of establishing the partisan direction of presidential politics. In every one of the nine presidential elections between 1932 and 1988 in which a single party captured all or nearly all of the South's electoral votes, the South has been on the winning side" (1992, 344). In 1964 and 1980 the South was on the losing side as well and in 1992 the South was on the side of the winner, the loser, and the also ran.

The Black brothers sometimes understate their case and refer to Barry Goldwater as "one of the few northern senators who opposed the Civil Rights Act [of 1964]" (150). You won't find Goldwater referred to as a "northern" senator in many places and his organic opposition to civil rights represents unadulterated southern values. In fact, Neo-Confederate Goldwater was the unifying force between conservative California and the states of the Old Confederacy that helped lead the modern South to their current domination of American political power.

All of the final three white men on the ballot in 1992 were southerners, two from Texas and Clinton, who claimed in Houston with a straight political face to be more of a Texan than George Bush could ever be. Clinton's most persistent opposition for the democratic nomination, the former two term governor of California, Edmund G. Brown Jr., aka Jerry, was tarred with every liberal brush available by the Democratic Leadership Council (the southern white boy party, this DLC, according to the Reverend Jesse Jackson) and the media. In the ever-escalating war of American politics, it is no longer necessary to red-bait an opponent by calling them Communist. The simple term "liberal" will do, or the "L" word in hand grenade shorthand. It won't be that long before a majority of Americans are sneering at moderates. But Brown and his candidacy were also referred to and described as a drive-by shooting, an out of control toboggan, 1-800-guerrilla, scorched earth, and as the Viet Cong candidate. The name calling was offered instead of a debate. Jerry Brown represents precisely that part of California and the rest of the United States not subducted into the Confederate Empire of North America.

Clinton is the fourth white Southerner the Democratic party has elected since World War II. In a profound way, he is a parliamentarian president, having parlayed his leadership of the DLC into the nomination over Brown and the other casualties of Tsongas, Kerry, and Harkins, men who hail respectively from the democratic nationalist black holes of Massachusetts, Nebraska, and Iowa. The DLC and southern faction of the party is its controlling element. In its simplest sense, the 1992 general election was over before it began since Americans do not re-elect incumbents during hard times. Idealess in a culture where ideas are scorned, the Texan Bush was sailing the ship of state across a flat earth. When the 12 year leap of the Republicans toward speculation, bankruptcy and recession was coupled with its upshot, the additional candidacy of the billionaire populist Ross Perot, the farther right wing had to share votes, much as it did in 1912 between Roosevelt and Taft, and Clinton was elected with 43 percent of the vote.

Ross Perot, with his paid volunteers (no oxymoron here), bought his way in to the stud poker game of presidential politics and upped the ante on the political parties, which are themselves remnants of the collapsing structure. Absent his billions, Perot's pedestrian ideas would attract no attention at all. There are literally thousands of people with more to say politically but they get no coverage because they can't afford it. Free speech has become the private property right of millionaires and billionaires. However Perot is not simply another loud Southerner fatally attracted to the limelight as the George Wallace of the 1990s.

Perot is the present personification of a special type of political hacker in the English speaking system of which a recent prototype is Oliver Cromwell. Perot is a cool post-McLuhan candidate, an arm chair TV daddy making the pointed stick and the talking head respectable video. With his beady eyes focused on the debt, which is only a symptom and not the disease, he appeals to Americans who are much too comfortable nattering about symptoms because the cure for the disease will disrupt the comfort

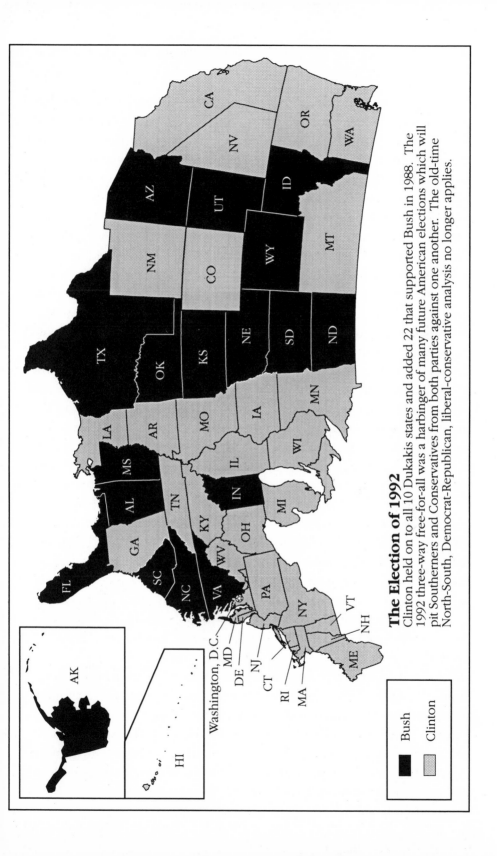

The Election of 1992
Clinton held on to all 10 Dukakis states and added 22 that supported Bush in 1988. The 1992 three-way free-for-all was a harbinger of many future American elections which will pit Southerners and Conservatives from both parties against one another. The old-time North-South, Democrat-Republican, liberal-conservative analysis no longer applies.

Bush

Clinton

level of them all. Deviations from southern domination are unlikely. The gridlock, which is only a symptom for the institutional rigidity it masks, cannot be massaged away through policy, personality, nor persuasion. It is structural and the truth will eventually become obvious to everyone: change the structure or perish. When English speaking institutions become too fossilized and debt ridden to reform themselves, the meat cleavers of simplistic solutions will cleave to the roof of mouths like Ross Perot's, leading to a convulsion on the Civil War scale of intensity that produced Oliver Cromwell and the Protectorate. Heads, such as that formerly attached to the body of King Charles I, undoubtedly will roll.

Underneath the debt is the political and geographical pauperization of North America. Reagan's raising of the debt through the roof was simply the path of least resistance to poverty. We would be equally as poor, one way or the other, whether we had spent the imaginary money, which we did, or denied it to ourselves, which we apparently cannot bear. Clinton and Perot both reveal themselves as unrealistic charlatans when they speak of restoring the American Dream, which they choose to define as keeping the inflated economic expectations alive in the American breast that each generation can be materially richer and have more than the preceding generation. According to Toynbee, once "The masses become estranged from their leaders, who then try to cling to their position by using force as a substitute for their lost power of attraction" (1972, 211), the jig is up. Each empire unravels on organic lines. For Egypt, "The price of her preservation was petrifaction" (212). The Americans, as rigid and brittle as the United States is, would probably be only too happy to settle for petrifaction. The problem for the United States is, that unlike Egypt, the US has serious Asian and Middle Eastern competition for power. The US is apt to unravel more quickly and consistent with its endemic violence.

The relative economic prowess of the United States is being cut in half from its overweening 40 percent of world productive capacity at the conclusion of World War II. That temporary and unrepeatable phenomenon is still being misunderstood as the outward manifestation of an inner state of Grace, the perpetual fruit of Manifest Destiny, and God's way of granting Americans the religious right to be richer than all others. The gas is going out of this balloon. Clinton's laudable effort to tax the rich into a share of the pauperization backfired as the rich, on their own sayso, don't have enough to go around and can be expected to continue spending whatever they have left to have him and his few surviving allies thrown out of office. As for the disappearing middle class and the poor, they have already received more than will be available in the future, regardless of who is in office. A middle class is a nuisance in a banana republic. America spent its way through its golden age. The rising tide of expectations that once lifted all of John Kennedy's boats has become the ebbing tide of polluted beaches where a few yachts with no other place to sail to remained moored.

The election of 1992 only postponed the convulsion coming to the English speaking civilization of North America, for the Democrats have a knack for making the Apocalypse last longer, but the essentially Republican victories in 1994 put it back on track. Once again a controlling majority of voters in the vanishing middle class was tricked, as they had been in 1980, into believing that a future designed by the reactionary rich would include a place for their aspirations. If hot air was a suitable substitute for rational government, the Republicans would have solved every problem long ago. The Democratic right wing still has its temporary presidential upperhand on the Republican right wing but with only two right wings flapping in the breeze for power, it is small wonder that the system is traveling in tighter and tighter circles. Clinton never got anymore than minimalist cooperation short of bribery from the Congress, superficially in the hands of a majority of Democrats, actually controlled as usual by the coalition of conservative Democrats and Republicans whose grip on the levers of power was hardly loosened by the 1992 election despite some gains by racial minorities and the satisfying election of several brilliant women to the Senate. The fatal attraction of the right in the 1994 election put both the Senate and the House in Republican hands, but the power will never stray from the conservative coalition.

Clinton's share of the 1992 votes was about what McGovern, Mondale, Humphrey, and Carter in 1980 got, not more than 43 percent, and all a democratic candidate for president has any historical reason to expect. His single hope for re-election, presuming the Democrats are suicidal enough to re-nominate him, will ride on the "righter" wing once again fielding two candidates. Clinton acts much more like his boyhood hero Kennedy, whose policies were barely distinguishable from those of the Republicans he replaced, in the passage of the Bush designed NAFTA and the "get tough on crime" bill, rather than a democratic nationalist. He also shares many similarities with Lyndon the Liar. With much of the rest of the world in equally severe disarray, the opportunity presents itself to set a broad course that might last, such as the Truman Doctrine. It is not the kind of world picture that invites a "one policy fits all" response however. Absent a brilliant grasp of events not yet displayed, Clinton is fated to adhoc himself into a coma as a caretaker, and if he's lucky enough to be re-nominated, receive the respectable 43 percent of the votes that a Democrat, even a Southerner, can count on. Clinton owes his term in office to one of the cyclical aberrations of conservative excess and unless the major empire builders once again run two candidates, he will find himself the youngest of several former presidential librarians.

Much will be incorrectly made of the partisan nature of the Republican takeover of the House and the Senate in 1994 but it will make no practical policy difference whatever that dozens of conservative Democrats in the South lost elections to somewhat more conservative Republicans. Newt Gingrich mobilized his crusade against Washington DC, with more zealotry than Goldwater in 1964 and as desperately as Jefferson Davis in 1861. Even moderate Republicans have few expectations that such an anti-government crackpot could even begin to govern, and correctly fear that he will merely make matters worse in the 104th Congress. The celebrated defection from the Democratic party of Senator Shelby of Alabama — only the latest in the Reagan-Thurmond-Connally-Gramm series of overdue defections — would have been worth a lot more if the Senate had been split 50-50.

Outside of the Old Confederacy, in a geography dear to the hearts of Neo-Confederates, the former Soviet of Washington (state), the results were more conclusive. In this landscape where the military expenditures of the Confederate Empire of North America are still increasing, despite their feigned concern about unproductive "pork," six of eight principled Democratic representatives to Congress were replaced by right wing Republicans, several of whom such as Hastings in the 4th district, Metcalf in the 2nd, and Linda Smith in the 3rd, have bona fide anti-government public records. Linda Smith for example is the author of stealth Initiative 601 which barely passed in 1993, largely because it was on the ballot with the even worse Initiative 602. The intention of 601 is to hobble the state legislature's ability to meet its legitimate responsibilities to the public school system. It is the Washington equivalent of California's Proposition 13.

The fickle voters of Washington, a majority of whom identify themselves as independent, are especially susceptible to Fascist radio and TV because their independence frequently does not extend to any useful ability to think for themselves and consequently they are unable to separate religious propaganda from factual persuasion. In addition to the poisoned atmosphere of talk radio, Washington citizens were subjected for several months to a nearly ceaseless stream of carpetbaggers for single issues such as Americans for Term Limits, DC Statehood, and the irrepressible National Rifle Association whose supporters nationally made up one-third of the electorate that bothered to vote. The political action committees for these single issue interest groups openly flout the intention if not the letter of the law in their brazen work directly for identified candidates as they feign no authorization or connection with the candidates or their committees.

The deadly combination of discredited political consultant Ed Rollins and the NRA was able to defeat Tom S. Foley, the Speaker of the House of Representatives by the same one percent margin they gunned Governor Florio of New Jersey down with the year before and for the same reasons. Ed Rollins and some of his fellow hatchet men, masters of the attack ad, as well as a hatchet woman representative of the NRA, under the non-toxic label of "political consultants," were able two days later to speak of these matters in a post-mortem on C-SPAN with less visible emotion than a group of pathologists fixated on a petri dish.

The use of Charlatan Heston — aka Moses — posing as a friend of eastern Washington as he preached to the soon to be shorn sheep on the benefits of AK-47s, was only the latest Hollywood manipulation of politics that began in 1934. Louis B. Mayer of Metro-Goldwyn-Mayer and also the chairman of the California Republican party, exploited movie stars in fake newsreels to discredit and defeat Upton Sinclair's EPIC (End Poverty In California) campaign for governor of California, along with the predictable help of the Los Angeles *Times* until ". . . nothing could withstand the MGM offensive" (Manchester 1973, 121.) Once again many Americans, the people of the picture, succumbed to a Hollywood offensive and the glitter of the TV tube's silvery screen. Money and media manipulation are Fascist substitutes for political thought.

Coincidentally, 1934 was the year of the first election of Warren Magnusson to public office in Washington state. With the defeat of Tom Foley for opposing the manufacture of AK-47s, the first sitting Speaker of the House to be defeated since Pennington of pro-slavery New Jersey lost his re-election bid in 1860 for opposing slavery, the Magnusson Era in Washington politics is over. Basing control of Congress on conservatives in office from Washington state, as beholden as they are to the fickle voters in the manipulated middle class, is a very flimsy strategy.

All politics are local, Tip O'Neil is supposed to have said, and the NRA, as the citizen auxiliary of the military worship of war, fear, and hate, has claimed all of North America as its locale. The NRA didn't do as well with Charlatan Heston in the Democratic nationalist black hole of Nebraska against Senator Bob Kerry who was re-elected against their well-funded wishes. Kerry, one of the principled survivors of the Vietnam War, has been shot at with real guns too many times to be intimidated by the money, makeup and pursed lips of right wing actors. He walks with his healed wounds without fear on the real rather than the celluloid earth. The voters in Washington are capable of comprehending how.

Meanwhile, in the cabanas of the religious right, down their pipeline to the heart of Congress, Americans are going to discover the actual sources of their power and greatness and get back to their roots. These roots include, but are not limited to territorial aggression, genocide, ruthless exploitation of resources, expropriation of labor, and reliance on the British concept of balance of power, all balled up with a Christian God's Manifest Destiny. Lurking in the future of an American Mussolini, the temptation to invade some additional latter day Ethiopias to restore the greatness of the American Empire will overpower what good sense the resistance to such behavior can make and accelerate the decline. The alternative to relative poverty is an acceleration of poverty. The world class nature of English speaking civilization was launched, to use the Hispanic interpretation for balance, with the pirate Sir Francis Drake. Before Paoli's double entry bookkeeping can make any sense, there has to be something of sufficient mass to account for. There is nothing and nowhere left to plunder that will not ultimately represent a net loss.

The preponderance of evidence supports the following description of the political power structure in the United States. It is a fiscally irresponsible, geriatrically subservient, naturally ignorant, white supremacist, male dominated, southern controlled, military empire, with suzerainty far beyond the oceans that wave its edges and way over its quasi borders with Canada and Mexico. The domination of the United States by older white southern males of means (property) is not far from the ideals set up in the voting franchise they granted themselves in the 1780s that ushered in the Virginia Dynasty.

The Confederate States of America under the leadership of Jefferson Davis were fighting for their independence and several other things the South either had or wanted prior to the War Between the States: slavery, state rights, control of the West, honor, white supremacy, an expansive foreign policy and control of the federal government. Before the Civil War, the South controlled the presidency, the Army, the Supreme Court and half of the Senate. Today the South controls the presidency, the military, the Supreme Court, and both houses of Congress. The only issue they failed on was outright slavery, having eventually achieved a form of independence in the redomination of the Union that Lincoln and the North fought to keep together and freed the slaves in. The evidence supports the conclusion that by continuing to religiously pursue its agenda, the unreconstructed South finally won the Civil War.

The pertinent struggles were not on the battlefields, which were left behind to be enshrined, where the least interesting aspects of war take place. The South regained state rights and white supremacy commencing with the Fraud of 1876. It won political control of the West through the domination of Texas and the conversion of California to southern right wing, open shop, racist, conservative military ideals, connected to the South by the conservative link and landbridge of Goldwater's Arizona. The South's honor was restored by the passage of time and the religious enshrinement of war as a solution to imperialist problems by the time of and as a result of, the Spanish American War, which also restored an expansive foreign policy and put legs under the "Southern Dreams of a Caribbean Empire." The South regained domination of the US federal government and made a basket catch of the British Empire at the close of World War II with the adoption of the Truman Doctrine, the beginning of the Cold War with its perpetual state of siege, and the election of General Eisenhower, who was born in Texas.

Texas is the fulcrum of political power in North America, and the territory it dominates is almost uncannily the same as that imagined in 1844 by President Sam Houston of the Republic of Texas. Houston's vision may actually have been modest for certainly the Texans attempt to dominate the South not only "clear back to Richmond," but clear back to London as well. For only five of the 50 years since the end of WWII, during the administrations of Kennedy and Ford, were the presidents Northerners. The rest were Southerners and US policy is in fact made by or made acceptable to a ruling coalition of conservative Republicans and southern Democrats and Republicans that constitutes an absolute majority in both Houses of Congress. There will be no serious contention for power that doesn't originate in the South, where as a result of militarily dictated population shifts, a majority of the population now resides. None of this contradicts the class divisions and political theory and guidance of John C. Calhoun, the "Marx of the Master Class" and the most influential political philosopher in American history.

The Boston-Philadelphia-Chicago-San Francisco happy story of the American economic democracy, the one taught in most of the school systems of the North where the Civil War supposedly freed the slaves and gave the South its political comeuppance, needs to be tempered with a more realistic look at where the power now actually resides and where policy originates. The received wisdom of the traditional American version of history has been ignored here, partly because it is widely available, largely mistaken, patently useless except as a tool to pump the beleaguered masses up with, and most significantly, because it goes against the grain of the history of the people who have been setting policy for the past 50 years. "History is the framing of questions by a particular human being in a particular space-time context. . ." (Toynbee 1972, 485), and *How the South Finally Won the Civil War* is no exception.

The Southern preoccupation with militarism, grounded in the Alamo and the tears of Robert E. Lee in the Legend of the Lost Cause, provides the religious and psychological basis for this chill from Appomattox. With Lee's the only picture on Sam Rayburn's wall, its been over 130 years since he offered his sword to General Grant. It is time to declare a Confederate victory.

Unfinished Business:

Some other fruitful areas of research were turned up by the writing of *How The South Finally Won The Civil War*. The relationship between total DOD spending and total federal spending presence in the various states relative to the population shifts in the 50 years from 1940 to 1990 needs to be examined and placed on actuarial tables for easy reference. The phenomenal population shift to California will be shown to be directly proportional to DOD and other federal expenditure. The complete explication of "How California Became a Southern State" is a fit subject for several volumes and a decade of hard work.

A study of the complete relationship, emphasizing similarities and differences between plantation capitalism and corporate capitalism, especially as regards the exploitation of the natural environment (land) and the work environment (labor) would enlighten us all. It could logically begin with the Southern Pacific Railroad, plantation and corporation without peer, and move toward the contemporary transnationals and such present arrangements as those of the Simplot Corporation with Micron. Tony Schwartz suggested that "McLuhan said that scientists of the past organized knowledge for convenience of retrieval, but he found that for himself discovery came from organizing things that he did not know, and then studying them" (1983, 24). The science of the future will originate in organizing things we do not know and making sense of the patterns since we will be judged not only by the conclusions we come to but on the questions we raise as well.

The language traps in English need to be exposed by a study of syntax and morphology since the deglaciation with emphasis on the syntactical and pragmatic determinants of cultural behavior. English, with its subject-verb-object (SVO) syntax, and its concept of civilization as an endless conquering of frontiers and accumulation of objects has left us surrounded with maximum mini-storage: the accumulation and consumption of the patently worthless. When the syntactical limitations are backed up with the cultural proclivity for free speech and individualism over community cooperation, the recipe for disaster is nearly complete.

If it is possible to compose a political construct in American English that would lead to peace and free the speakers of English from their predestined internal contradictions, it has not been published yet. It is not, to put it mildly, the 1994 Republican contract on America. The ideas that could save English speaking civilization cannot even be put in English. Problems cannot be solved at the same level they are created, according to Einstein. The American civilization is a linguistic echo of the English language. Understanding the relationship of languages to macro social behavior and unique political thought is crucial for human survival.

A study of the comparative morphology and syntax of the grammars of English, Maya, Nahuatl, Japanese, Chinese, Spanish, Lakota, Linear A & B, German, Hebrew, Arabic andor other languages would reveal what can and cannot be originally thought of expressed and done in a particular language. The *Magna Carta* for instance did not spring up in Zaire or Hunan or Dalmatia or Tenochtitlan or Honshu, but only in England.

With Marxism in the dustbin of history, economic and linguistic alternatives to capitalism, with some salubrious worker-owner relationships where the means of production are controlled by the labor that operates it and not by the national socialist state, to eliminate featherbedding, exploitation, and a focus on short term gains, need to be formulated. An economy where all economic transactions are mutually beneficial is the only type that will lead to peace. A related issue would be to create an organizing principle for the democratic nationalist agenda sufficiently appealing on its own merits and not cobbled together out of reactionary dissatisfaction with the ruling coalition.

Continuous, realtime learning and education is the organizing principle of human life where the cultures that survive are precisely those which pay the most attention to their children and what they learn. Education is the organizing principle of human life and the organizing principle of state government in the United States. State rights could reassert themselves once again out from under the unworkable bureaucracy of the empire. Human life will survive to the degree that it is able to make its organic organizing principle its political organizing principle.

A good history of the peace movements in the warfare state of America would be an indispensable addition to knowledge. It could commence with Thoreau's opposition to the Mexican War, or earlier with Tory resistance to the Revolution, and move through the anti-draft riots in New York and resistance to conscription on both sides in the Civil War, the Anti-Imperialist League, the IWW and others during WWI, the Vietnam peace movement, all the way up to Ross Perot, Sam Nunn and Ernest Hollings and other principled objections to the war on Iraq. Some principles and potential strategic and tactical approaches could be elucidated by a thorough study of the perpetual failure of peace.

There is a literary corollary to *How the South Finally Won the Civil War*, where much of 20th century American literature has been dominated by Southerners. These would include the Fugitives under the leadership of Allan Tate from Vanderbilt University in Nashville, the canonization of the Mississippian Nobel Prize winning author William Faulkner, and the contemporary novelist and poet James Dickey of the University of South Carolina. Kenneth Rexroth got the first good licks in on the numbing effect of the Fugitives.

Part VI

References

"Only tools with pedigrees were used"

Stephen Thomas

Works Cited

The author acknowledges the fair use of brief selected passages from the following authors and their works while heartily recommending them for reading, for various reasons made clear within the text.

Adams, B. [1903] 1967. *The New Empire*. Cleveland: Frontier.

Ailes, R. 1988. *You Are the Message*, Secrets of the Master Communicators. Homewood, IL: Dow Jones-Irwin.

Anderson, E. 1971. *Plants, Man & Life*. Berkeley & Los Angeles: University of California Press.

Andrus, C. H. Winter 1989. A Crisis of Will. *Oh! Idaho*. pp. 9-10.

Arizona, a State Guide. 1940. WPA. New York: Hastings.

Arrington, L. J. 1958. *Great Basin Kingdom*, Economic History of the Latter-Day Saints, 1830-1900. Lincoln: University of Nebraska Press.

Bailey, L. R. [1966] 1972. *Indian Slave Trade in the Southwest*. Los Angeles: Westernlore Press.

Beard, C. A., & M. R. 1925. *History of the United States*. New York: Macmillan.

Beringause, A. F. 1955. *Brooks Adams*, A Biography. New York: Knopf.

Beringer, R. E.; Hattaway, H.; Jones, A.; & Still, W. N. Jr. 1986. *Why the South Lost the Civil War*. Athens & London: University of Georgia Press.

Black, E., & Black, M. 1992. *The Vital South*, How Presidents Are Elected. Cambridge & London: Harvard.

Blassingame, J. W. 1972. *The Slave Community*, Plantation Life in the Ante-Bellum South. New York: Oxford.

Blumenthal, S. 1990, August 13. A Woman of Independent Means. *The New Republic*. pp. 23-26.

Bonner, T. D. [1856] 1965. *The Life and Adventures of James P. Beckwourth*, Mountaineer, Scout, Pioneer, and Chief of the Crow Nation. Minneapolis: Ross & Haines.

Bourgin, F. 1989. *The Great Challenge*, The Myth of Laissez-Faire in the Early Republic. New York: Braziller.

Brewer, J. 1989. *The Sinews of Power*, War, Money and the English State 1688-1783. New York: Knopf.

Brown, D. 1970. *Bury My Heart At Wounded Knee*. New York, Chicago,San Francisco: Holt, Rinehart & Winston.

Brown, H. 1989. *Deterring Through the Turn of the Century*, the Discussion Group on Strategic Policy. Washington, DC.: the Johns Hopkins Foreign Policy Institute and the Center for Strategic and International Studies.

Burns, R. 1990. *The Civil War*. PBS.

Calhoun, J. C. [1850] 1948. *A Disquisition on Government*. New York: Poli Sci Classics.

Caro, R. A. 1982. *The Years of Lyndon Johnson, The Path to Power*. New York: Alfred A. Knopf, Inc.

Catton, B. 1958. *A Stillness at Appomattox*. Pocket Books, S & S division of G & W. New York: Doubleday.

—1981. *Reflections on the Civil War*. Edited by John Leekley. New York: Doubleday.

Chasan, D. J. 1989, November. Professor Hyman's Proposal. *Washington*. 6:3. pp. 23-27.

Chomsky, N. 1973. *For Reasons of State*. New York: Pantheon.

Clausen, A. 1974. *Extreme Unction*. Salt Lake City: Litmus.

Coit, M. L. 1950. *John Calhoun*, American Portrait. Boston: Houghton Mifflin.

Collier, P., & Horowitz, D. 1984. *The Kennedys: An American Drama*. New York: Summit Books.

Colton, R. C. [1959] 1985. *The Civil War in the Western Territories*. Norman: Oklahoma.

Cook, R. 1991. *1992 * Race to the Nomination*. Washington D.C.: *Congressional Quarterly*.

Congressional Quarterly. 1991, January, 5. Volunteer Forces: Into the Breach. p. 30.

—1991, January, 12. H 485. S 403.

—1991, June, 15. Bureau Releases New Estimates, Remains Wary of Adjustments. pp. 1606-1608.

Cousins, N. 1987. *The Pathology of Power*. New York: Norton.

Cox, J. 1992. "Turbulent 'Times' in L.A." *USA Today*. 3:13. p 2B.

Craven, A. 1957 *The Coming of the Civil War*. Chicago:
University of Chicago Press.

daCosta, R. 1990, May. How to Recapture the Technological Lead.
Aerospace & Defense Science. p. 5.

Daily Telegraph. 1991, September, 24. London.

Dana, R. H. Jr. [1840] 1937. *Two Years Before the Mast*. New York:
P. F. Collier & Son Corporation.

Davis, B. 1957. *The Long Surrender*. New York: Random House.

Davis, J. [1881] 1958. *The Rise and Fall of the Confederate Government*.
Two Vols. New York: Yoseloff.

Davis, J. 1855. *Reports of Explorations and Surveys, to Ascertain the Most
Practical and Economical Route for a Railroad From the Mississippi
River to the Pacific Ocean*. Made under the Direction of the Secretary
of War, in 1853-4. Vol II. Washington: House of Representatives.

Davis, L. J. 1990, September. Chronicle of a Debacle Foretold, How
Deregulation Begat the S & L Scandal. *Harper's*. pp. 50-66.

Davis, M. 1990. *City of Quartz*, Excavating the Future in Los Angeles.
London & New York: Verso.

Davis, W. C. 1991. *Jefferson Davis*, the Man and His Hour. New York:
Harper Collins.

Defense 91 Almanac. 1991 September/October. Superintendent of
Documents. Washington, D.C.: U.S. Government Printing Office.
—1990. *Sea Power/Congress/Defense*. pp. 90-107.

DeMarco, G. 1988. *A Short History of Los Angeles*. San Francisco: Lexikos.

DeRosier, A. H. Jr. [1970] 1972. *The Removal of the Choctaw Indians*.
New York: Harper & Row.

DeVoto, B. 1943. *The Year of Decision: 1846*. Boston: Little & Brown.

Dorn, E. 1974. *Recollections of Gran Apacheria*. San Francisco:
Turtle Island.

Dowdy, C. 1957. *The Great Plantation*. A Profile of Berkeley Hundred
and Plantation Virginia from Jamestown to Appomattox. New York:
Rinehart.

Drew, D. [1870] 1969. *The Book of Daniel Drew*. New York:
Frontier Press.

Drucker, P. [1955] 1963. *Indians of the Northwest Coast*. New York:
American Museum of Natural History Press.

Ebel, H. 1973 *The First Part of the Revelations of Moses the Son of Jehoshar*. Ft. Lee, New Jersey: Argonaut.

Eichel, L. 1991, June, 22. British War Parade Dull – and Short. *The Denver Post*: Knight-Ridder News Service.

Eisenhower, D. D. 1967 *At Ease*, Stories I tell to Friends. New York: Doubleday.

Fain, J. 1990. "Richard Nixon Has This Uncanny Ability to Cheapen Everything He Touches." Cox News.

Faulk, O. B. 1969. *The Geronimo Campaign*. New York: Oxford.

Fehrenbach, T. R. 1968. *Lone Star*, A History of Texas and the Texans. New York: Macmillan.

Foner, E. 1988. *Reconstruction*, America's Unfinished Revolution 1863*1877. New York: Harper & Row.

Forbes, J. D. 1964. *The Indian in America's Past*. New Jersey: Prentice-Hall.

—1973. *Aztecas Del Norte*. Greenwich, Conn: Fawcett.

Foster, G. D. 1992. "Clinton Shouldn't be Judged Harshly for Vietnam Decision." *Walla Walla Union-Bulletin*. *LA Times—Washington Post*. p 32.

Glad, P. W. 1968. *William Jennings Bryan*, a Profile. New York: Hill & Wang.

Germond, J. W., & Witcover, J. 1989. *Whose Broad Stripes and Bright Stars?* The Trivial Pursuit of the Presidency 1988. New York: Warner.

Gregg, J. [1854] 1974. *Commerce of the Prairies*. Edited by Max L. Moorhead. Norman: Oklahoma.

Halberstam, D. 1979. *The Powers That Be*. New York: Knopf.

Haley, J. E. 1964. *A Texan Looks at Lyndon*, a Study in Illegitimate Power. Canyon, Texas: Palo Duro Press.

Harrington, F. H. 1935. The Anti-Imperialist Movement in the US 1898-1900. *Mississippi Valley Historical Review*, XXII, vol 9. pp. 211-230.

—1937. Literary Aspects of American Anti-Imperialism, 1898-1902. *New England Quarterly* X, Dec. pp. 650-667.

Hawk, B. 1964 *Black Hawk*. An Autobiography. Edited by D. Jackson. Urbana, IL: University of Illinois.

Head, R., & Fife, D. 1971. *Nola Express*. New Orleans, LA.

Hendricks, B. 1939. *Statesmen of the Lost Cause*. Boston: Little & Brown.

Hitchens, C. 1991, October. Unlawful, Unelected, and Unchecked,
     How the CIA Subverts the Government at Home. *Harper's*.
Hernton, C. 1965. *Sex and Racism in America*. New York: Grove.
Hofstadter, R. 1958. *Great Issues in American History*, Vol I, 1765-1865.
     New York: Vintage.
—[1948] 1959. *American Political Tradition*. New York: Vintage.
—1965. *The Paranoid Style in American Politics*, and Other Essays.
     New York: Knopf.
IRS. 1990, August. "Only 1.6% own 28.5% of Nation's Wealth." AP:
     Walla Walla Union Bulletin.
Ivers, L. E. 1974. *British Drums on the Southern Frontier*, the Military
     Colonization of Georgia, 1733-1749. Chapel Hill: University of
     North Carolina.
James, W. [1910] 1967. *The Writings of William James*, a Comprehensive
     Edition. Edited by John J. McDermott. New York: Random House.
Johnson, D. 1963. *The Challenge to American Freedoms*, World War I and
     the Rise of the American Civil Liberties Union. Mississippi Valley
     Historical Association: University of Kentucky Press.
Johnson, D. B. & Porter, K. H. 1973. *National Party Platforms*,
     1840-1972. Urbana: University of Illinois.
Josephson, M. 1940. *The President Makers*, the Culture of Politics and
     Leadership in an Age of Enlightenment. New York:
     Harcourt & Brace.
Kaufman-Osborn, T. 1991, March, 7. *The Pioneer*. Walla Walla:
     Whitman College.
Kazin, A. 1991, February. The Generals in the Labyrinth.
     The New Republic.
Kennedy, P. 1987. *The Rise and Fall of the Great Powers*, Economic
     Change and Military Conflict from 1500 to 2000. New York:
     Random House.
Kilpatrick, J. 1992. "FBI's Hoover Was Ultimate Un-American.
     Walla Walla Union-Bulletin. p 4.
Klawans, S. 1994, September 5/12. "Films." *The Nation*.
Klingberg, F. J. 1975. *An Appraisal of the Negro in Colonial South
     Carolina*, a Study in Americanization. Philadelphia: Porcupine Press.

Lamm, R. D.; Caldwell, R. A.; & Mehlman, I. H. 1989. *Hard Choices.* The Center for Public Policy and Contemporary Issues. Denver: University of Denver.

Lapham, L. H. 1990, September. The Visible Hand. *Harper's.*

Larsen, R. 1990, September. Reformed Sinner Preaches Environmental Sensitivity. *Walla Walla Union Bulletin.*

Leckie, R. 1968. *The Wars of America.* Vol I. Quebec to Appomattox & Vol II San Juan Hill to Tonkin. New York: Harper & Row.

Leonard, H. B. 1988, April. Shadows in Time: The Perils of Intergenerational Transfers. *The Generational Journal.*

Leon-Portilla, M. 1963. *Aztec Thought and Culture.* Translated by Jack Emory Davis. Norman: Oklahoma.

—1969. *Pre-Columbian Literatures of Mexico.* Translated by Grace Lobanov and the author. Norman: Oklahoma.

Levine, L. W. 1965. *Defender of the Faith,* William Jennings Bryan: The Last Decade 1915-1925. New York: Oxford.

Lincoln, A. 1953. *The Collected Works of Abraham Lincoln.* Vol V. 1861-1862. New Brunswick, NJ: Rutgers University Press.

Liss, S. 1967. *The Canal,* Aspects of United States-Panamanian Relations. London: Notre Dame University.

Lowie, R. H. [1954] 1963. *Indians of the Plains.* Garden City, New York: Natural History Press.

Magdoff, H. 1969. *The Age of Imperialism,* The Economics of U.S. Foreign Policy. New York: Monthly Review Press.

Manchester, W. 1973. *The Glory and the Dream,* A Narrative History of America 1932-1972. Boston-Toronto: Little, Brown and Company.

May, E. R. 1961. *Imperial Democracy,* the Emergence of America as a Great Power. New York: Harcourt.

May, R. E. 1973. *The Southern Dream of a Caribbean Empire,* 1854-1861. Baton Rouge: Louisiana State University.

MacDougall, C. D. 1965. *Gideon's Army.* 3 Vols. New York: Marzani & Munsell.

McCann, T. P. 1976. *An American Company,* The Tragedy of United Fruit. New York: Crown.

McCullough, D. 1977. *The Path Between the Seas,* the Creation of the Panama Canal: 1870-1914. New York: Simon & Shuster.

McGinnis, J. 1969. *The Selling of the President 1968*. New York: Pocketbooks.

McKibben, B. 1989. *The End of Nature*. New York: Random House.

McLuhan, M. 1964. *Understanding Media*: The Extensions of Man. New York: McGraw-Hill.

—1968. *War and Peace in the Global Village*. New York: McGraw-Hill.

McWilliams, C. 1946. *Southern California Country*, An Island on the Land. New York: Sloan & Pearce.

—1949. *California: The Great Exception*. New York: Current Books, Inc.

—1951. *Brothers Under the Skin*. Boston, Toronto: Little & Brown.

—1968. *North From Mexico*, The Spanish-Speaking People of the United States. New York: Greenwood.

—1969. *Factories in the Field*, The Story of Migratory Farm Labor in California. New York: Archon.

McPherson, J. M. 1991, November, 7. How Noble Was Robert E. Lee? New York: *The New York Review of Books*.

Meriwether, R. L. 1974. *The Expansion of South Carolina*, 1729-1765. Philadelphia: Porcupine Press.

Merk, F. 1963. *Manifest Destiny and Mission in American History*. New York: Knopf.

—1967. *The Oregon Question*. Essays in Anglo-American Diplomacy and Politics. Cambridge: Belknap & Harvard.

—[1931] 1968. *Fur Trade and Empire*. George Simpson's Journal 1824-25. Cambridge: Belknap & Harvard.

Michener, J. A. 1985. *Texas*. New York: Ballantine.

Moll, N. 1987. *Confederate Air Force*, Past Perfect, Ready for Action! Osceola, WI: Motorbooks.

Morrison, S. E. 1971. *The European Discovery of America*, The Northern Voyages. New York: Oxford.

Mowat, F. 1984. *Sea of Slaughter*. Boston & New York: The Atlantic Monthly Press.

NBC 1991. *Expose*. Peach Orchards in Edgefield County, South Carolina.

Nevin, D. 1978. *The Mexican War*. Alexandria, Virginia: Time-Life Books.

Niven, J. 1988. *John C. Calhoun and the Price of Union*, a Biography. Baton Rouge & London: LSU Press.

Nolan, A. T. 1991. *Lee Considered: General Robert E. Lee and Civil War History*. Chapel Hill: University of North Carolina.

Norris, F. 1935. *The Octopus*. New York: Doubleday.

Oswalt, W. H. [1966] 1973. *This Land Was Theirs*, A Study of the North American Indian. New York: Wiley.

Pastor, R. A. 1990, September. Salinas Takes a Gamble. *The New Republic*. pp. 27-32.

Paz, O. [1950] 1961. *The Labyrinth of Solitude*, Life and Thought in Mexico. New York: Grove Press.

Penrose, R. 1989. *The Emperor's New Mind*. New York: Oxford.

Perkins, D. 1966. *The Evolution of America Foreign Policy*. New York: Oxford.

Perry, R. 1984. *Hidden Power*, The Programming of the President. New York: Beaufort.

Phillips, K. 1969. *The Emerging Republican Majority*. New Rochelle, New York: Arlington House.

—1990. *The Politics of Rich and Poor*. New York: Harper.

—1993. *Boiling Point*, Democrats, Republicans and the Decline of Middle-Class Prosperity. New York: Random House.

—1994. *Arrogant Capital*. Boston: Little, Brown & Co.

Pollard, E. A. [1866] 1990. *Southern History of the War*. Facsimile Edition. New York: Fairfax.

Pringle, H. F. 1955. *Theodore Roosevelt*. New York: Harcourt.

Prucha, F. P. 1962. *American Indian Policy in the Formative Years*. Lincoln: Nebraska.

Quillen, E. 1991, June, 16. The Mother of all Victories. Denver: *The Denver Post*.

Ransom, L., & Sutch, R. 1977. *One Kind of Freedom*, The Economic Consequences of Emancipation. London: Cambridge.

Reagan, R. 1990, September. *An American Life. Publisher's Weekly*. p. 41.

Reed, I. 1989, Fall-Winter. Beyond Columbus. *Before Columbus Review*. A Quarterly Review of Multi-Cultural Literature. 1:2-3. pp. 5-6.

Reisner, M. 1986. *Cadillac Desert*, The American West and its Disappearing Water. New York: Penguin.

Renfrew, C. 1989. *Archeology & Language*, The Puzzle of Indo-European Origins. New York: Cambridge.

Reeves, R. 1991, May, 21. New York Slips Further Down the Drain. AP. Walla Walla, WA: *Union Bulletin*.

Rhodes, R. 1986. *The Making of the Atomic Bomb*. New York: Simon & Shuster.

Riegel, R. E. [1926] 1964. *The Story of the Western Railroads*, From 1832 Through the Reign of the Giants. Lincoln: Nebraska.

Rifkin, J. 1992. *Beyond Beef*, the Rise and Fall of the Cattle Culture. New York: Dutton.

Roche, T. W. E. 1973. *The Golden Hind*. New York: Praeger.

Roland, C. P. 1960. *The Confederacy*. Chicago: University of Chicago Press.

Roosevelt, T. 1899. *The Winning of the West*. New York: Putnam's.

Roosevelt, T. Jr. [1937] 1970. *American Imperialism*, Colonial Policies of the United States. New York: Arno-New York Times.

Rosen, R. 1982. *A Short History of Charleston*. San Francisco: Lexikos.

Sahm, D. ND. At The Crossroads. *Together After Five*. The Sir Douglas Quintet. San Francisco: Mercury.

Sanchez, R. [1971] 1973. *Canto Y Grito Mi Liberacion*. New York: Doubleday/Anchor.

Santa Clara County v. The Southern Pacific Railroad Company. 1886. (118 US 394-417).

Sauer, C. O. 1967. *Land and Life*. Berkeley & Los Angeles: University of California Press.

—[1966] 1969. *The Early Spanish Main*. Berkeley & Los Angeles: University of California Press.

—1971. *Sixteenth Century North America*. Berkeley & Los Angeles: University of California Press.

Schaeffer, R. 1990, September-October. Trading Away the Planet. *Greenpeace*. 15:5. pp. 13-16.

Schlesinger, A. M. Jr. 1971. *The Coming to Power*, Critical Presidential Elections in American History. Editor. New York: McGraw-Hill.

—1986. *The Cycles of American History*. Boston: Houghton Mifflin.

Schwartz, T. 1983. *Media the Second God*. New York: Anchor.

Scullard, H. H. 1979. *Roman Britain*, Outpost of the Empire. London: Thames and Hudson, Ltd.

Seward, J. 1994. *Seward's Follies*. Tokyo-Houston: Yugen.

Simon, J. O. 1968. *The Grass Prophet Review #3*. Berkeley: Noh Directions.

Soustelle, J. [1955] 1962. *The Daily Life of the Aztecs*, on the Eve of the Spanish Conquest. Translated by Patrick O'Brian. New York: Macmillan.

Spengler, O. 1926. *The Decline of the West*. Vol I: Form and Actuality. Translated by Charles Francis Atkinson. New York: Alfred A. Knopf, Inc.

—1928. *The Decline of the West*. Vol II: Perspectives of World History. New York: Alfred A. Knopf, Inc.

Stacy, P., & Lutton, W. 1988. *The Immigration Time Bomb*. Monterey, Virginia: The American Immigration Control Foundation.

Statistical Abstract of the United States, 1990. U.S. Bureau of the Census. 110th Edition. Washington, D.C.

Sternberg, B. 1991, July, 5. Washington Bureau of the Associated Press. Mitchell, SD: *The Daily Republic*.

Stockman, D. 1986. *The Triumph of Politics*, Why the Reagan Revolution Failed. New York: Harper & Row.

Stoecklein, D. R. 1991. *The Idaho Cowboy*, a Photographic Portrayal. Ketchum, Idaho: Stoecklein Publishing.

Strode, H. 1955. *Jefferson Davis, American Patriot*, 1808-1861. New York: Harcourt, Brace and Company.

—1959. *Jefferson Davis: Confederate President*. New York: Harcourt, Brace and Company.

—1964. *Jefferson Davis, Tragic Hero*, 1864-1889. New York: Harcourt, Brace & World, Inc.

Swindler, W. F. 1965. *Magna Carta*. New York: Bobbs-Merrill.

Temple, R. 1986. *The Genius of China*. New York: Simon & Shuster.

Terrell, J. U. 1972. *Apache Chronicle*, The Story of the People. New York: World.

Texas State Travel Guide, It's Like a Whole Other Country. 1991. Austin: State Department of Highways and Public Transportation.

Theroux, P. 1988. *Riding the Iron Rooster*, By Train Through China. New York: G.P. Putnam's Sons.

Thomas, J. L., Ed. 1968. *John C. Calhoun*, A Profile. New York: Hill and Wang.

Tibbles, T. H. 1972. *The Ponca Chiefs*, An Account of the Trial of Standing Bear. Lincoln: Nebraska.

Toner, Robin. 1992. New York: the *New York Times*.

Toynbee, A. 1966. *Change and Habit*, The Challenge of Our Time. New York & London: Oxford University Press.

—1972. *A Study of History*. New York & London: Oxford University Press.

Trenholm, V. C., & Carley, M. [1964] 1972. *The Shoshonis*, Sentinels of the Rockies. Norman: Oklahoma.

Trimble, M. 1977. *Arizona*, A Panoramic History of a Frontier State. Garden City, NY: Doubleday & Company.

Tuchman, B. 1988. *Stilwell and the American Experience in China, 1911-1945*. New York: Macmillan.

Veblen, T. [1899] 1931. *The Theory of the Leisure Class*. New York: Random House.

Vestal, S. 1963. *Joe Meek*, The Merry Mountain Man. Lincoln: Nebraska.

Vidal, G. 1973. *Burr*. New York: Bantam.

Waite. 1886. 118 U.S. Documents. pp. 394-417.

Wallace, E. & Hoebel, E. A. 1952. *The Commanches*, Lords of the South Plains. Norman: Oklahoma.

Walton, R. J. 1976. *Henry Wallace, Harry Truman, and the Cold War*. New York: The Viking Press.

Webb, W. P. 1931. *The Great Plains*. New York: Grosset & Dunlop.

Weigley, R. F. 1973. *The American Way of War*, A History of United States Military Strategy and Policy. New York: Macmillan.

Weir, R. M. 1983. *Colonial South Carolina*, A History. Millwood, New York: Kto Press.

White, T. H. [1961] 1988. *The Making of the President 1960*. New York: Atheneum / Book of the Month.

Williams, W. A. 1961. *The Contours of American History*. Chicago: Quadrangle. [Cleveland: World].

—1980. *Empire as a Way of Life*. New York: Oxford University Press.

—1988. *The Tragedy of American Diplomacy*. New York: W. W. Norton.

Wilson, C. M. 1970. *The Commoner*, William Jennings Bryan. New York: Doubleday.

Wissler, C. [1940] 1966. *Indians of the United States*. New York:
    Doubleday.

Wittfogel, K. A. 1957. *Oriental Despotism*, a Comparative Study of
    Total Power. New Haven: Yale.

Wood, A. 1990, September, 24. China is Running Out of Water.
    Walla Walla Union Bulletin. p. 4.

Wood, P. H. 1974. *Black Majority*, Negroes in Colonial South Carolina,
    from 1670 Through the Stono Rebellion. New York: Knopf.

Wuerther, G. 1990, September-October. The Price is Wrong.
    Sierra. pp. 38-43.

Wright, G. 1978. *The Political Economy of the Cotton South*. New York:
    Norton.

Zbick, J. 1992. "Coalfield's Perfect Hell." Leesburg, Virginia:
    America's Civil War. p 22-28.

Zeigler, P. 1991. "Down and Out in Victorian England." Review of
    Poverty and Compassion by Gertrude Himmelfarb.
    The New York Times Book Review, 9-8-91.

Zinn, H. 1980. *A People's History of the United States*. New York:
    Harper & Row.

ZPG Reporter. 1991, April. A State by State Report Card on the Nation's
    Environment from Durham, North Carolina and the Institute for
    Southern Studies. Washington D.C.

Index